Peter Cresswell studied Social Anthropology at Cambridge University and went on to do a B.Phil. in Sociology at York University. In recent years, he has researched the origins of Christianity and its textual transmission. He is the author of *Censored Messiah* and *Jesus the Terrorist*.

Thanks are due to Dr Alan Bale for checking my Greek translations and transcriptions, to Jon and Eloise for turning charts and sketches into artwork, to Bill for critical guidance, to my publisher Michael Mann for taking on the project and to my wife Julia for providing unwavering support.

the Invention of Jesus

How the Church Rewrote the New Testament

PETER CRESSWELL

WATKINS PUBLISHING

LONDON

This edition first published in the UK and USA 2013 by
Watkins Publishing Limited, Sixth Floor,
75 Wells Street, London W1T 3QH

A member of Osprey Group

1 3 5 7 9 10 8 6 4 2

Typeset by Bookcraft Ltd, Stroud, Gloucestershire

Printed and bound in Italy by L.E.G.O. S.p.A.

A CIP record for this book is available from the British Library

ISBN: 978-1-78028-546-7

www.watkinspublishing.co.uk

Distributed in the USA and Canada by Sterling Publishing Co., Inc.
387 Park Avenue South, New York, NY 10016-8810

For information about custom editions, special sales, premium and
corporate purchases, please contact Sterling Special Sales
Department at 800-805-5489 or specialsales@sterlingpub.com

Contents

Preface

This is unashamedly a serious book, the product of much analysis and some original research. But it has also been deliberately written so as to be accessible to readers with a general interest in the formation of the New Testament. To follow the argument, there is no need to have specialist knowledge or even expertise in biblical Greek.

The issues are important and that is why I have written and presented this book in what I hope is a readable form. I do not believe that unnecessary jargon helps.

It is not assumed that the reader will be familiar with ancient Greek, though that is the language of most of the texts. The analysis has necessarily to be of and with this language. Translations and explanations are however given for every example and at every stage.

After an introduction, which provides the context, I provide a brief outline of the history of biblical writing. In Chapter 2, I offer some exercises in English, mimicking types of scribal error that can be used to analyse the text. This prepares the way for investigating the early Greek manuscripts of the New Testament.

Where I have arrived at firm conclusions, these are given in bold towards the end of each chapter. Sometimes, I offer explanations that I believe best fit the information available, though without being proven to the same level of confidence. These are included as part of the discussion and analysis but not as findings or conclusions.

What I regard as my most groundbreaking and exciting discoveries centre on the two earliest Greek bibles, with complete or almost complete copies of the New Testament, Codex Sinaiticus and Codex Vaticanus. I have been able to throw more light on their purpose and relationship with each other, partly through the deployment of some new techniques of textual analysis (Chapters 3–6).

I have also, I believe, found the solution to an unresolved issue concerning the working relationship and division of labour between the scribes in Codex Sinaiticus (Chapters 11–13). This has implications in any consideration of the function of the Church, in the early fourth century, in disseminating its message under the auspices of Rome.

It has also been possible to trace, by studying the texts, how doctrines have evolved and how inconvenient facts have been masked or covered up. So, for example, I have been able to show, not only how the author of the gospel of Matthew used the gospel of Mark to fashion his text, but how his version of Mark must have differed from the one that we now have in a crucial respect (Chapter 8). I have analysed the earliest texts of the women who were present at the cross, including calculated 'correction' and subsequent mistranslation, to uncover who these women really were (Chapter 10). The answer is, unsurprisingly, not what the Christian agenda now claims, but what would have been in an original Jewish story and for that matter what might have been historically correct.

I have made clear in this book what texts I have studied and how these have been used. This is so that readers can, if they so desire, check for themselves. It is also because the texts do not always agree.

Faced with the large number of different versions of the same text in early manuscripts, Christians have over the centuries sought to reconcile these, in the past through the strenuous efforts of individuals and more lately via the work of committees. This is not a way that an original and definite version of the biblical 'truth' can ever be arrived at. One reason is that experts can and do differ, and will continue to disagree – and as a result the compilations by committees will continue to vary over time.

Another reason is, as will be seen, that the texts were changed over time to suit the purposes of the Church, as these evolved, and those of the individuals using them. For large parts of the gospels, there is no surviving manuscript evidence for a period of about 300 years after the events to which they relate. It is possible to deduce some of the changes that were made during this long intermission. It is certain that a number of changes were made and that the text evolved before it even reached the point of being written down in the forms that have survived and are available now.

The text that used to be standard, arrived at by comparison, was called the received text or 'textus receptus'. But this was based on some manuscripts now accepted as being later in origin than others, either now taken more seriously or more recently discovered. The term currently applied to the reappraised consensus is the critical text. It is heavily based on Codex Sinaiticus and Codex Vaticanus, the two very early and related manuscripts that form the main focus of this study.

It should be emphasised that my concern is with these and other early manuscripts; how they relate to each other and how they were changed over time. Where I make a general reference to the bible as it is now in use, it will be to the 'received text' or more specifically to the 'critical text'.

It is incidentally extraordinary how much can be learned from the careful analysis of even a single piece of source text (see, for example, the analysis of John 17, 15 in Codex Vaticanus, pp 103–105).

I make my own judgements over the use of English either in direct translations of specific manuscripts or of the critical text. If I quote passages from the New Testament, without reference to a specific source, then I will in general follow the latest version of the critical text at the time of writing, Nestle-Aland 27th edition. It should be remembered that a consensus view on an interpretation is just that and not infallible (see Chapter 8).

While I have checked my copy many times, it is inevitable that some mistakes will have slipped through. I welcome, through my publisher, both comment on my analysis and ideas and notification of any errors, so that these can be rectified in future editions.

References to my data, analysis and conclusions, as well as direct and indirect quotes, are permitted but must in all cases be acknowledged. For the rest of this book, I have adopted the convention of using the first person plural.

Introduction

I could only meet with promises and delays – promises which came to nothing and delays of a most wearying kind ...

And thus after five months of weary waiting, I left Rome without accomplishing my object. It is true that I often saw the manuscript, but they would not allow me to use it; and they would not let me open it without searching my pockets, and depriving me of pen, ink and paper; and at the same time two prelati kept me in constant conversation in Latin, and if I looked at a passage too long, they would snatch the book out of my hand. So foolishly and meaninglessly did the papal authorities seek to keep this precious manuscript to themselves.

Samuel Prideaux Tregelles on his attempt in 1845 to study a very early copy of the bible, Codex Vaticanus, held in the Vatican library

When accounts containing the Christian message were first put down in writing, it was in the context of a split between messianic, fundamentalist Jews and a sect that wanted to take the message and modify it for a wider audience. In protecting Judaism, in repelling what it saw as alien, the messianic movement had become the popular heart of resistance to occupation by pagan Rome. It harboured claimants to the throne of David and thus to rule in place of the Romans as legitimate kings of Israel. It provided focus and inspiration for those willing to engage in active resistance, in rebellions that were put down, one by one, over the years.

Shortly after one of these unsuccessful uprisings, a character described variously as Saul and Paul in the New Testament, made a serious effort to ingratiate himself with the movement. Saul saw the uncompromising messianists as a powerful group, a means of furthering his ambitions. They regarded him as a threat, not least because he may have been a member of the Herodian family,[1] and initially rejected him.

Saul, it appears, clung on to generate for himself a role in gaining converts among gentiles. He saw the need to adapt, to abandon the requirement for circumcision and a variety of dietary rules, to make the religion more appealing. This led to more conflict with Jewish leaders back in Jerusalem.

The final rift came and Saul's communities of gentile converts became the adherents of a new sect. This combined the Jewish concept of one God with a different type of messianic message, no longer freedom from Rome (which the new sect had to live with) but spiritual liberation through sacrifice. Translated to Greek, messiah became 'Christ' and its adherents 'Christians'. The story of the latest messianic contender, who had failed to regain the throne of David, was gathered in and adapted. In so doing, an Aramaic 'Yeshua' was transformed into a Greek 'Jesus'.

In Palestine, meanwhile, resistance continued and culminated in a war with Rome in which the zealots were crushed and their religious leadership diminished. The centre had vanished. There was nothing and no one left to counter an alternative, Christian message.

This, when it was first put in writing, altered the role of the adopted messianic leader, Jesus, described in the gospels as a 'Son of David' and thus as a claimant to the throne of Israel. The message put out by some of his Jewish supporters initially was that he had survived crucifixion by the Romans.[2]

Saul's followers, in a religion that was to coexist with Empire, could not have Jesus as a rebel against Rome. So he was converted, in their original story, into a self-sacrifice, appeasing God for the sins of mankind. Increasingly, as the gospel was copied, fellow Jews rather than the Romans were blamed for the death of Jesus. Whatever Jesus' message may have been, it was made into one of accommodation and conflict avoidance: turning the other cheek, rendering to Caesar, 'going the extra mile'.

That first template, which provided the narrative for the gospel of Mark and arguably that of Peter, no longer survives (see Chapter 7 and Appendix X). The first gospels were revised and other versions were created, including possibly some that have since entirely disappeared. There is also no surviving record for this crucial period of around 80 years, until the mid second century. But the texts that are available now, though much altered over time, can be examined for evidence of earlier and even original themes. Though it has been disguised, there is within the text an original story of resistance against Rome.

There is striking evidence from the names of key characters, crudely scrambled or mistranslated, that better fit a Jewish zealot framework. There are relict references that clearly come from another narrative. There are some huge inconsistencies in the text.[3] We can carefully dissect all this to discover something of what has survived the attentions, over the centuries, of editors and censors. We can also sometimes see how later gospels, in attempting to improve on previous texts, modified the message.

To take the analysis further, to see how some key Christian concepts came to be incorporated into the story, requires more detailed study. It is this process that will be the focus of our efforts. Only incidentally, and as it relates to our prime objective, will we be commenting on the intricacies, flaws and inconsistencies of religious doctrine. The investigation here is primarily of the Greek manuscripts, bibles dating from the early fourth century and, where available and relevant, earlier papyrus fragments.

We propose in this book to examine how some of these manuscripts came to be written, the source material they used and how they relate to each other. We will examine the texts to see what this can tell us about changes that were made over time and also during the course of their production.

Though the methodology may at times be exacting, the results are enlightening and sometimes surprising. Our aim has been to produce an account that is both rigorous and accessible.

We start our journey among dry debris from the Egyptian desert and end it in the pressured atmosphere of a Roman scriptorium, most probably in Palestine.

CHAPTER 1

Papyrus to parchment

Fragments of the books of the New Testament, written on papyrus, survive from very early times. They were tipped out on rubbish heaps in ancient Egypt, along with other documents that had become worn out. Or they were reused as materials for binding new books. Sometimes, during periods of persecution, forbidden religious books were hidden in crevices in walls or in pottery jars in the desert.

Although papyrus is fairly durable, little or nothing would have survived to the present day but for the continuing dry climate in the places where manuscripts were hidden or left. The desiccating desert air has helped to preserve texts from decay.

For as much as three thousand years, the reed beds of the Nile delta had provided writing materials for the ancient world. The tall papyrus reeds were gathered and stripped of their bark to expose the white pith. This was then cut in strips and laid on a flat wet surface in two layers, at right angles. The strips were pounded between cloths to crush the fibres into a flat sheet, with the starch so released binding the two layers together.

After being dried in the sun, the sheets were polished smooth and trimmed to be ready for writing. Pens were made from smaller reeds, their ends crushed to create tiny brushes. These were dipped in ink made with gum and carbon, often from fine soot, to which water was added when needed. Colours were created using natural vegetable and mineral products.

In the first century of the Common Era (CE), the favoured form for a long document or literary work was a scroll made by overlapping papyrus sheets and pasting them together. A wooden roller would be added at either end, enabling the reader to find a particular text by holding a roller in one hand and rolling out the scroll with the other.

For transient texts, such as drafts, notes and letters, the Romans used a tabula consisting of a few wooden leaves containing wax which would be written on, smoothed over and used again. Later this was adapted to form a notebook, with parchment made from animal skins replacing the reusable wax leaves, held between wooden covers. This became known as a codex, from the Latin for a tree trunk or wooden block.

From the examples that have survived, it is clear that Christians used papyrus in the form of a codex, rather than a scroll, from the outset for their sacred texts. The leaves were sewn and bound together rather than pasted into one long sheet. It may be, as has been suggested, that this was to differentiate these from the books of Jewish scripture. Alternatively, it is possible that the Roman notebook was first used as the common form for letters written to the early churches. These would have been the first Christian documents. When the need was felt to write an account of the life of Jesus and his claimed miraculous rising from death, the medium that was already in use was retained. The codex was certainly a more convenient medium to use later for long books, such as the four officially recognised accounts of the life of Jesus (gospels) and other books incorporated into a new Christian testament.

In the first few centuries, parchment was also occasionally used for codices instead of papyrus. It had the advantage of being available for writing on both sides of the page. With the codex, it was only possible to write easily in lines on the side that had horizontal strips. So in most cases half the space was wasted.

On the other hand, parchment involved the use of animal skins, costly to produce and to process. With each skin generating perhaps four pages, it can be seen that a long book such as a bible needing hundreds of pages would entail considerable expense. There were many stages in the production process including repeated soaking in lime, scraping, stretching, drying, cutting and stitching.

It may be that variations in the size of the papyrus crop, excessive demand or restrictions placed by the Egyptians on exports helped encourage a switch towards parchment for books. It was increasingly used as a substitute from the beginning of the fourth century, when the first known complete books of the bible were produced. There are two surviving examples from this time, a codex until recently stored in a monastery on Mount Sinai, Codex Sinaiticus, and another that has for centuries been kept in the Vatican, known as Codex Vaticanus. Some parts of the Old Testament are missing in both of these documents, but the four canonical gospels survive in both. While in Codex Sinaiticus, the New Testament as a whole is almost complete, Codex Vaticanus breaks off in the middle of the Epistle to the Hebrews.

The surviving papyrus codices offer, by contrast, for the most part portions of individual gospels, letters attributed to Paul and others and Acts. The majority of the papyri have been dated to the third and fourth centuries, but there are some small fragments that may have been written as early as the mid second century. It was at about this time, towards the end of the second century, that a move began to create an accepted canon of four gospels, excluding a multitude of works deemed heretical by orthodox Christians.

A major sect, the Gnostics, promoted the idea of spiritual attainment through self-knowledge and belief in a dual divinity consisting of a perfect, higher being and a 'demiurge' who had created an imperfect, material world. Over a period of years, the sect was persecuted out of existence and its books banned and destroyed. Some were concealed to avoid destruction, including a whole library of texts, discovered centuries later buried in a large pottery jar at Nag Hammadi in Egypt.

The discarded fragments of papyri, found on the ancient rubbish tips, encompass a wide range of canonical and non-canonical writings. Taken together with manuscripts deliberately concealed, as at Nag Hammadi, these demonstrate a much greater diversity of views than there is within Christianity today.

The relative scarcity even of fragments of early copies of the canonical gospels suggests, however, an additional possibility. Copyists sometimes made improvements or restored what they believed, however erroneously, to have been original. When a change was made for doctrinal reasons, there would have a motivation not merely to discard, but to destroy the original and any other copies like it.

We know, from later records, that manuscripts were sometimes replaced, ostensibly because of wear and tear. The early bible translator Jerome reports that in the mid fourth century papyrus documents in the library at Caesarea were replaced, because they had become worn, with copies made on parchment. While this might indeed have been a good reason, it could also have provided an opportunity to change the text.

Establishing what suppressive acts may have taken place, as much as nineteen hundred years ago, is not an easy task. Such censorship would have been secretive and it involved the elimination of evidence. But a lot can be deduced, as will be seen in later chapters, from circumstantial, inferential and in some cases direct evidence that such motivated editing did take place.

It is the case that, when all the fragments of gospel papyri prior to Codex Sinaiticus and Codex Vaticanus are taken together, there is only enough to fill a book about the size of a modern bible. We do not mean a master copy. We mean everything, all the manuscripts, all the copies that there are.

Not only this but, given that many of the fragments replicate each other, there are also huge gaps. Around a third of the text of the New Testament is simply missing; there are no witnesses to these portions prior to the early fourth century, prior in fact to Codex Sinaiticus and Codex Vaticanus. The missing portions are very often in vital parts of the text, for example at the beginning or end of a gospel where there may be a version of Jesus' origins or his death at the hands of the Romans.

The outer parts of a codex are certainly most vulnerable, once the wooden or leather cover (assuming that there ever was one) is damaged or missing.

So, accidental and coincidental loss is likely in most cases. But the possibility remains that there may be radically different earlier versions for some of these missing sections that have subsequently been suppressed.

There is a powerful case and a strong consensus among scholars that Mark was the earliest of the four canonical gospels on which the later gospels of Matthew and Luke depended for the passion narrative (see Chapter 7). The evidence is that the gospel of John was also later than Mark. Its author, though evidently drawing on an additional source for the story of the crucifixion, will also have been aware of and reliant on Mark and the other synoptic gospels.

It is therefore a matter of more than passing interest that, among the surviving pieces of ancient papyrus, there is *only one* (from around the early third century) that relates to the gospel of Mark. This fragment (**P**45) is missing the whole of the gospel's first three chapters, most of chapter 4, part of chapter 13 and all of chapters 14–16, as well as many bits within the core of the text. So, in respect of this vital first source, there is no early information on John the Baptist, the claim to Jesus' divinity, the recruitment of his followers, the betrayal by Judas, the arrest of Jesus, the trial, crucifixion, claimed resurrection and ascension into heaven. Indeed, as will be seen, there are some crucial gaps in later texts that form the basis of the New Testament as it is now.

There is also no papyrus witness for the last two and a half chapters of Matthew. So there is no early information for this gospel either on the trial, crucifixion and claimed resurrection. Other parts, lacking in the body of the text of Matthew, include the naming of the apostles, the claim made by the sons of Zebedee and Peter's 'great confession'. In Jesus' long denunciation (Matthew, chapter 23), 'Scribes and Pharisees' are singled out by name no less than seven times, as a continuing refrain. But the surviving papyrus text picks up precisely after the last of these, so that there is actually no mention of just who Jesus was condemning in what has survived from the earliest manuscripts.

As with many other omissions, this is likely to be the product of chance. It is, however, frustrating to have no early texts for crucial passages. The collaborating Sadducees, as well as doubtless the Romans, would have been much more likely targets for Jesus' invective, as reported in Matthew, chapter 23. Indeed, there are many contrary passages in the gospels indicating that Jesus was on friendly terms with the Pharisees. Prominent Pharisees may indeed have been among his close kin.[1]

If, as we suggest, an anti-Pharisee bias *was* introduced, it would have helped in discovering *when* it was introduced, if the record had been more complete. The relevant papyrus text, **P77**, is mid second to third century and the only witness at this point, lacking not merely most of Matthew chapter 23 but the whole of chapter 22. This is significant in that chapter 22 has a description of an exchange with Pharisees, borrowed from Mark's gospel but stripped of its element of friendliness. Was this 'improvement' created when Matthew's gospel was first written, or later on? There is no early record. So, we just do not know.

It may be with this, as with other missing elements, that later complete texts on which the gospels are now based would be reflected in the early texts, were they also complete. We will however point to instances (see, for example, Chapters 8 and 9) where we believe this not to be the case. Some changes were undoubtedly made, as doctrine evolved, in the first two centuries. But the most substantial editing was of the Nazarene/Nazorean record at the very outset, when the gospel of Mark was first compiled. This is estimated to have happened around 75–80 CE, from which period we have no surviving written record.

Early papyri do nevertheless provide a more complete picture for the gospels of Luke and John. One papyrus codex (**P66**), with a possible mid second century date, gives in full John's version of the crucifixion. It could have been produced around thirty years after a Christian source, possibly John of Ephesus, first wrote the gospel using some original material. In the text of the gospel, this material is claimed to be the witness of the 'disciple whom Jesus loved'.

But, whatever the Jewish original source may have written, it is clear that this gospel has been heavily edited to have the most strongly anti-Jewish slant of all the four canonical gospels. This could not, of course, have come from the supposed Jewish witness that the Christian source claims to have used. It is certainly early testimony. But it still dates from a century or more after the events to which it relates.

The picture is patchy and incomplete for another century and a half from this point, during which period papyrus codices were favoured and dominate the record. Towards the beginning of the fourth century, however, there was a shift in the type of manuscript produced. The Romans under the Emperor Constantine adopted Christianity as a religion of Empire and this generated increased demand for bibles incorporating books of both the Old and New Testaments.

It would have been hard to produce these using papyrus, where it was only practicable to write on one side of each page. The books would have been bulky and unmanageable. In addition to which, unutilised space adds considerably to the overall cost.

So, although making books using parchment was also laborious and expensive, this was the method increasingly adopted. There is a record of Constantine in 330 or 331 CE requesting his Bishop Eusebius in Caesarea to produce 50 copies of the scriptures for churches being built in Constantinople, the Emperor's newly created capital for the Roman Empire. The two copies mentioned earlier, Codex Sinaiticus and Codex Vaticanus are parchment codices dating from about this period. These are significant in that they provide, in contrast with the earlier papyrus fragments, the first complete or nearly complete records of the New Testament.

It may well be wondered how these manuscripts can be dated with such apparent confidence. Radio carbon dating may be an effective tool for, say, a Bronze Age femur or a Neolithic post. But, for objects so relatively recently created, it usually gives too wide a margin to be useful, or much different from intelligent guesswork.

It is, however, possible for some of the documents from this period to be dated with confidence and a degree of accuracy. This is when the text itself contains dates or references to events that can be pinpointed by reference to the historical record. Sometimes, the reverse side of a papyrus scroll, though hard to write on, will have subsequently been used for some other purpose such as providing accounts. If the latter is dated, then the original text must have been written earlier. Similarly, if the original is dated, then anything subsequently written on the back will be later. In other instances, worn papyrus or parchment used for binding must predate the book being created and by a number of years, allowing for the time it will have taken for the old book to wear.

The more accurately dated documents provide a framework for comparison, making it possible to assign approximate dates to other manuscripts. Such documents also make it easier to identify and define a developmental process in writing, in which variations in the style of lettering give clues as to when something was written. Occasionally, it must be said, the evidence is conflicting, with various clues pointing in different directions. And, of course, account needs to be taken of such factors as local tradition, cyclical patterns or a scribe's possible deliberate choice of an archaic style.

So, the dates determined for codices are usually not precise and may be a few decades or more out from the point of actual writing. This will not affect the areas of interest in this book: the changes made from sources in writing the first gospels and then the changes made in copying gospels. In the first case, there will be no direct evidence unless an original, quite likely in Aramaic, is miraculously found. So any modifications made to an original message must be deduced. In the second case, there is most certainly abundant evidence. What may be most important here is sequence, rather than precise dating – whether, for example, one manuscript or piece of writing precedes or succeeds another. It can only incorporate changes to another text, if it was written later in time.

There has been much speculation as to whether or not Codex Sinaiticus and Codex Vaticanus may have been among the copies requested by Constantine from his Bishop Eusebius. It is unfortunately not possible to date them with sufficient accuracy to link them positively with this order. But there is certainly some intriguing evidence, including pointers within the text of Sinaiticus, and this will be discussed in Chapter 3.

It would certainly be surprising if these codices had nothing to do with the decision at around this time to create more bibles for an expanding Church. As will be seen, there are some clues and a strong inferential case as to what the two documents were for.

What is very interesting is that the codices appear to be linked, despite some differences in their presentation and what is known of their origins.

Because all the texts and fragments of text that we have differ from each other, due to the myriad errors and alterations that have over time been introduced, there is no one text that can be said to be an authoritative copy of the bible, Old Testament or New. Bibles used today are the product of a committee, or rather a series of committees over time, who have scrutinised the records and decided to take one reading from a particular source, another from a second, and so on. But, while differing on many readings, Codex Sinaiticus and Codex Vaticanus also show a high degree of correlation. They have more in common with each other than they have with many other ancient parchment codices. There is also a high level of agreement with some of the earlier papyrus codices, particularly **P66** and **P75**. The codices also share a chapter division in Acts, which is found in no other Greek manuscript, although present in later Latin manuscripts, and this also indicates some strong, common link.

The link could be, as many have speculated, that they share a common source from as early as the second century. We have been able in our research to establish that the link between the two books is direct, as opposed to mediated through a number of intermediary sources, and offer some possible explanations that are both surprising and exciting (see Chapters 3–6).

Codex Sinaiticus and Codex Vaticanus do also agree in many other respects. Both omit the story in John's gospel of the woman accused of adultery and threatened with stoning. Differences in style and language indicate that this was an insertion to an earlier text, though there remains the possibility that an original story was deleted and then subsequently refashioned and reinserted.[2]

Both books omit the last twelve verses of Mark that deal with post-crucifixion appearances of Jesus. There are differences in languages and other pointers indicating that these verses are a later addition in those texts where they have been included.

There are a number of other verses that are absent in these two codices, though present in some later manuscripts. It is notable that the vast majority of such omissions in either codex are shared with the other.

Both have an addition to Matthew 27, 49, 'another took a spear and pierced his side, and out came water and blood' which parallels John 19, 34. This may be the result of the scribes making these gospels conform, again indicating that the codices were written, either one in the knowledge of the other, or from a common source, or possibly both.

The texts share a number of smaller omissions and variations. For example, in Matthew 15, 6 'or his mother' is missing in both, but present in other manuscripts. Instead of 'to discuss with each other' in Mark 1, 27, both have 'to discuss other', missing out the Greek letters ΠΡΟΣ Ε.

Like other early bibles, the codices are handwritten in columns of 'uncial' text made up of small Greek capitals. The letters are close written and evenly spaced. There are no gaps between words and the writing is carried up to the end of the line and on to the next, so that words are often split. There is little or no punctuation. The impression presented is that of a solid block of text (Fig. 1).

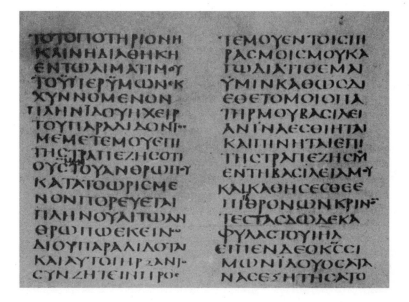

Fig. 1. Extract from Luke chapter 22, Codex Sinaiticus Q79F5V

Each bible would have been produced in a scriptorium, possibly even in this case the same scriptorium. For such an immense undertaking, the work was divided between a number of scribes. Handwriting style identifies particular scribes, so that it is often possible to say how many were involved and which passages each wrote.

The scribes corrected their own work and correctors also went over the work to check for and correct mistakes. Subsequently, other correctors made changes after the texts had left the scriptorium and had come into use, sometimes many years later. It has also been possible, in many cases, to distinguish the different hands of those who made the alterations at different times.

Mistakes were certainly inevitable with lengthy books, copied out by hand from originals that may have suffered from the ravages of time. Spotted early, while the ink was still wet or scarcely dry, an error might sometimes have been seamlessly eradicated by washing out the offending text from that point and then later rewriting it.

Once the work had moved on, however, it was simpler and more expedient to make a written correction at the appropriate point or as a marginal note. Alternatively, letters were scratched out, crossed out or overwritten. Dots were sometimes placed over characters to indicate that the text so marked was deleted and should be disregarded.

No codex from the period is therefore perfect, and perfection is not something that would have been expected. On the other hand, for a book that would have been in daily use as the prized possession of a community, a good standard of presentation would have been required. Codex Vaticanus, like many other parchment codices, does stand scrutiny on this ground. It is neatly and tightly written. There are overall relatively few corrections.

The same cannot be said of its fellow from the early to mid fourth century, Codex Sinaiticus. Throughout the text, there are scattered tens of thousands of corrections, ranging from the alteration of single letters to the insertion or, less frequently, deletion of lengthy passages. Many of the changes were made by the original scribes and correctors at the time the manuscript was produced.

Given the very substantial costs of production, the question arises as to how the project was allowed to continue to the bitter end when – if it was intended as the bible for a particular community – it was clearly a mess, not up to standard and possibly not even fit for purpose (see Chapter 3).

Various estimates have been put on the cost of making a book that required the slaughter of around three hundred animals, lengthy preparation to convert skins to parchment, the labour of scribes and other correctors over many weeks, stitching and binding and the use of other materials. One is that a single book cost the equivalent of the lifetime's wages of one individual. In current terms, the cost for just one book could have been over half a million dollars.

So, when Constantine ordered 50 copies of the scriptures for churches in his new capital, this would have been a major undertaking. This is even if these were not full bibles, but portions such as the gospels together with Acts and some of the epistles.

It is highly improbable that Bishop Eusebius could have gathered together the necessary skilled manpower and resources swiftly to fulfil the Emperor's order. To keep costs within bounds, skins might well have been used from animals slaughtered in the normal course of food production. Even so, it would have meant a significant diversion of hide normally used for other products.

So, it would have taken some time. Other bibles would have been required for other parts of the Empire outside the capital. Perhaps as many as one hundred or even two hundred were produced during the fourth century.

Provided enough competent scribes and parchment could be assembled in one place, one way of speeding up the process might possibly have been by the use of dictation. As with copying by sight, this would also have induced errors, as different scribes heard or thought they heard different things, or whose thought processes modified what was transmitted in going from brain to pen. Given that silent reading had not yet been developed, production might have been a noisy process, whether it involved dictation or copying. No two books so produced would have been exactly the same.

In constant use for reading and services, as in most cases the only bibles in their communities, the bound Greek parchment codices so produced would have been durable enough to last a century or two. But, when these came to the point of falling apart, it is unlikely that many were ever replaced, like for like.

The reason is that there had, in the meantime, been another significant development. Pope Damasus I had commissioned one of his priests, Jerome, to revise the existing Latin translation of the Greek bible. This Jerome did by going back to the original Hebrew for the Old Testament and to the Greek texts to produce a better translation for the gospels. The resulting early fifth century Latin version of the bible became increasingly popular, as the commonly used version ('versio vulgata', or eventually 'Vulgate'). So, for the bible at least, one of the languages of Empire came to supersede another.

What happened to the consignment of the scriptures, ordered by Constantine, which were written in Greek, the language of at least some of the original gospel authors, and which were a continuation of the early texts? These have apparently not survived. Over time and with much constant use, they would have become worn and needed to be replaced. It may also be that some of the survivors were recalled or ordered to be destroyed, when it was decided to adopt the Latin Vulgate bible as the officially sanctioned version for the Catholic Church.

After the passage of centuries, the Vulgate even came to be regarded as preferable to or even superior to the old Greek texts (from which it had in part been copied!). The history, the real connection was lost.

It was only during and after the Reformation period that interest in the early versions of the bible in Greek revived. In the nineteenth century, Christian scholars, keen to discover what they perceived would be the original and authoritative word of God and story of Christ, began to go in search of this early testimony.

Some came knocking at the doors of the Vatican, including the Protestant evangelist Samuel Tregelles, whose frustrations in his effort to study Codex Vaticanus are quoted at the beginning of the Introduction. The Vatican was possessive about its manuscripts, and possibly also obstructive towards scholars from a rival Christian tradition.

Others went in search of early documents known to be, or rumoured to be, lying neglected on the shelves of long-established Christian monasteries. One biblical scholar Constantin Tischendorf made several trips between 1844 and 1859 to the isolated, fortified monastery of St Catherine's on Mount Sinai. The monastery housed a large collection of ancient relics, including icons and illuminated manuscripts. Among the latter, Tischendorf discovered the document that is now called Codex Sinaiticus. He persuaded the monks, some suggest by devious means, to part with the precious manuscript. To this day, monks at the monastery allege that it was a loan for the purpose of study and, because it was not returned, it was therefore stolen. Tischendorf claimed that it was either a gift or a purchase, funded by a payment in roubles from the Russian government.

As a result of this activity, the codex came to be divided between four locations. Some leaves Tischendorf deposited at Leipzig University, where he was a professor of theology. The bulk of it was sent to the Russian government, under whose patronage Tischendorf was acting. This was later sold, as part of a fund-raising exercise, to the British Museum in 1933. It was then transferred, forty years later, to the British Library.

A few pages still remained in the Russian National Library and a few more pages and fragments were uncovered later in a wall at the monastery at St Catherine's.

Through an unprecedented exercise in cooperation between the four institutions that now have parts of the codex (the British Library, the University of Leipzig, the National Library of Russia and St Catherine's monastery), experts created in 2009 a digital online version of the entire codex. This offers a faithful reproduction of the handwritten original and alongside a printed version in Greek, both with marks and corrections made in the text in place. At different parts of the text, there are also translations of the codex into other languages. A variety of techniques, including examination under ultraviolet and infrared light, were used to identify erasures and reconstruct overlying corrections to the text.

It is, of course, not possible to assess at first hand the judgements made by the team in deploying their techniques. It is also hard to evaluate the assignment of the very many corrections in smaller handwriting to the different, identified correctors. The digital recreation is nonetheless as astonishing tool for analysis, the next best thing – and better in some respects – to having the actual manuscript available in the office or at home.

The existence of Codex Vaticanus in the Vatican's extensive library has been known for some time. It was indeed included in the library's first catalogue made in 1475. Where it may have originally come from is unknown; there is the possibility that the Vatican has had it for many centuries longer. It was for some time regarded as a Greek manuscript dependent on the Vulgate, rather than vice versa. But then, as it began to be inspected and analysed, its importance as a source prior to the Latin Vulgate began to be realised. Some of the Vulgate bibles do indeed have the same chapter divisions for Acts. This suggests that Jerome, in preparing his Latin bible, used one or both of the codices, Sinaiticus and Vaticanus, or a related codex that now no longer exists.

The Vatican almost grudgingly allowed access to its codex in the earlier part of the nineteenth century, while nevertheless still putting obstacles in the way of scholars such as Tregelles and Tischendorf. An edition in several volumes was finally published between 1886 and 1881 and the first facsimile in black-and-white produced between 1889 and 1890.

While this was certainly an advance, lack of access to the original still makes it difficult to analyse corrections, especially where several successive changes may have been made to the same text. In addition to this, the manuscript has a very distinctive characteristic. At some point in its history, the original lettering has, with few exceptions, been traced over. Only at points where an original scribe had repeated some letters, a mistake known as dittography, was text left intact. The overwriter had saved himself the bother of copying the same text twice.

Another facsimile of Codex Vaticanus, this time of just the New Testament, was issued shortly afterwards between 1904 and 1907. Then, for a century, the Vatican sat on its asset, while the study of ancient texts elsewhere became more open and cooperation between scholars increased. The ultimate response to this is instructive. Rather than allow access to the codex for the purpose of scientific study, directly or through reproduction online, the papal authorities produced in 1999 an elaborate colour facsimile. This is calf bound with gold and gilt lettering and pages reproduced down to the ragged edges, marks and even small holes in the parchment.

Apart from deflecting interest in the original, its purpose (at a current asking price per copy of around US $6500) is all too evidently to swell the papal coffers. But it is nevertheless a distraction and no real improvement on what had already been produced. It is still not possible to examine the original text beneath the overwriting. Corrections may be hard, or on occasion impossible, to disentangle without access to the original.

Interestingly enough, even 14 years on, not all of the 450 numbered copies have been sold! Libraries, with limited budgets, have realised that there are greater priorities. For most purposes, the black-and-white facsimiles will do just as well. It is, moreover, possible to examine and download a black-and-white facsimile of the New Testament for free, online. And, of course, with documents produced over sixteen centuries ago, there is certainly no moral case, and probably no legal case, for anyone nowadays to claim copyright.

Having thus set the scene, we propose first of all to take a look at Codex Sinaiticus, a manuscript that is more accessible for study and appears to be the end product of many hands. The corrections or alterations are, as will be seen, a great help in determining just how the document originated and for what purpose it was made. Then, in later chapters, text and corrections will be examined for clues to the deliberate alterations that were made to put doctrine and dogma into the record.

However, before all of this, we propose to embark on a small – and we trust entertaining – diversion to look at some of the kinds of mistake that the scribes regularly made.

This will be useful to gain an understanding of the text and how different documents related to each other. Pay attention, though! For now, this exercise will be in English. To make sense of the situation, it will be unavoidable later on to carry out similar procedures on the Greek originals.

CHAPTER 2

Scribal errors and amendments

Weary scribes in the fourth century, as much as weary writers today, made mistakes of all kinds. Words were missed out, or the wrong words put in, when transcribing a text, sometimes through simple negligence. If there is a way that the human brain can, by making the wrong association or wrong connection, make a mistake – then somewhere or other there will be an example of it! Certain types of mistake however occur regularly, possibly because the type of process involved in transcribing the text makes these more likely. The study of such errors can provide some insight into the conditions under which a manuscript may have been produced and the mind-set of the scribes themselves. Sometimes, they may even provide clues as to where and when a manuscript may have been produced, or from what source.

When copying is by dictation, errors may often arise through words that are spelt differently, and have different meanings, nevertheless sounding the same (for example, in English, 'see' and 'sea' or 'threw' and 'through'). Imagine a teacher dictating to the class a passage that includes the following sentence, 'Whether or not he decides to right the wrong, it will still create a bad impression.' A student might copy down, 'Whether or not he decides to write the wrong, it will still create a bad impression'. The error arises because 'right' and 'write' sound the same. It may not seem a very likely mistake. Indeed, the outcome is hardly plausible as a piece of coherent English. It might just about make sense if 'the wrong' is considered to be in inverted commas!

So the student ought perhaps to have avoided the pitfall. It is possible, however, to envisage circumstances that could conspire against him.

The teacher may for example have said, as he commenced dictation, 'Will you please write this down?' Now, when the student gets to the word 'right', the seductive homophone 'write' is freshly in his mind. Alternatively, it might be that the student is preoccupied with the fact that he still has an essay to write, or that he must later write a long-overdue letter. With the in-context, incorrect word already in his mind, the mistake is more likely.

It need hardly be said that more such errors may occur, if either the person doing the dictation or the student writing it down is in a great hurry.

The inadvertent substitution of a similar sounding word or syllable is described as iotacism. This is a word that derives from the Greek, iota (I or i) being a letter of the Greek alphabet. In its origin, it related to the substitution of plain vowels (for example the sound 'i' represented by iota) in place of diphthongs, as pronunciation changed.

An up-to-date example of this could run as follows. Let us imagine that our teacher is in America and dictating to his class part of a story for children written by an author brought up in England. The teacher comes to the sentence, 'Andrew suggested that red would be the best colour to paint the tree house'. The class to the last boy or girl are likely to write 'color', instead of 'colour', because that is the American way of spelling the word.

The sound is the same, or nearly the same. The spelling is different because Americans have substituted a plain vowel for the 'ou' diphthong. If there were only one correct version of English, then this would be an error of iotacism. It is in fact a reflection of the fact that languages evolve, to give variation between societies and also over time. Since American is in many ways a more dominant culture, the English have in some instances tended to adopt American-style spellings and grammatical constructions. It is not a process that happens, to the same extent, the other way round.

To add a little confusion to the picture, let us imagine that the teacher instead writes the story involving Andrew and the tree house up on the board, and invites the class to copy it down. So it is no longer an instance of dictation but of students transcribing by sight. Despite the fact that the children can see the word 'colour' on the board, most if not all may still write 'color'. There are several reasons. First, it is likely to be assumed that the teacher has simply made a mistake.

Second, the human brain tends to see what it expects to see. If it expects 'color', then it may well see 'color'. More subtly, the mind tries to resolve dissonance, in this case between what the child 'knows' to be right and what it perceives as being wrong. Resolved, perhaps even unconsciously, the child writes 'color'.

The point of this is that, with fourth century manuscripts, we cannot call up the 'teacher' giving a dictation or the 'class' of scribes receiving it to give an account of what may have happened. Errors of apparent mishearing might turn out instead to have been either errors (or deliberate changes) made in visual transcription. But we cannot find out by asking. It will have to be deduced.

When it came to copying text visually, a critical point occurred at the end of each line being copied. The scribe would see and write the last word, syllable or group of letters of the line in his text. Then, he would look back, his eye using the end letters just copied as a marker to identify the next line. All well and good, except when there happened to be a line a little further on that ended in precisely the same way.

The scribe might well pick up on this ending and move on to the next line after this, in so doing missing out one or more whole lines of text.

This type of error is called homeoteleuton, from the Greek for 'same ending', and is comparatively common among copied manuscripts of the time. Lots of chances were certainly presented for this type of aberration, given that there were often several columns of text to a page (typically four in Sinaiticus and three in Vaticanus). More line endings gave more possible repetitions. In addition, certain words occurred frequently, for example KAI for 'and', EV for 'in' or 'on', AYTON for 'him' and TON for 'the'.[1] So again this increased the chances of lines with the same ending.

Here is a piece of text in English, constructed not for its elegance or for the case it presents, but purely to illustrate the points we have been making:

> *As an accusation or as an accolade, both enemies and followers described Jesus as 'King of the Jews'. Pilate even had this posted on the Cross. Jews, however, recognised many as potential Messiahs, liberators who might free Israel by beating the Romans. Any 'Messiah' who did this could thereby become a 'King of the Jews'.*
>
> *Romans were aware of the threat that this posed to their rule, in times of great tension.*

Now let us turn this, as far as is possible without the Greek, into a column of text simulating its appearance in an early parchment codex. We are going assume for the purposes of this demonstration that the column width corresponds on average to about 20 characters.[2]

Out will go the punctuation, including quotes. Out will go capitals offering title distinctions, since all the text will be in capitals. Out will go the spaces between words and in this instance the paragraph break. Out will go the lack of justification right, which allowed all lines to end in whole words.

Sacred names (nomina sacra), like 'Cross' and 'Jesus' that tended to be abbreviated – presumably by Christian scribes – will, for present purposes, be retained in full.

The result looks like this:

```
ASANACCUSATIONORASAN
ACCOLADEBOTHENEMIESA
NDFOLLOWERSDESCRIBED
JESUSASKINGOFTHEJEWS
PILATEEVENHADTHISPO
STEDONTHECROSSJEWS
HOWEVERRECOGNISEDMA
NYASPOTENTIALMESSIAH
SLIBERATORSWHOMIGHTF
REEISRAELBYBEATINGTHE
ROMANSANYMESSIAHWH
ODIDTHISCOULDTHEREBY
BECOMEAKINGOFTHEJEWS
ROMANSWEREAWAREOFTH
ETHREATTHATTHISPOSED
TOTHEIRRULEINTIMESOFG
REATTENSION
```

What strikes us most forcefully is how difficult this is to read, even though we have only just invented and written the text and the full version is given above. Is it 'then' in line 2, 'asking' in line 4, 'don't' in line 6, 'tent' or even 'a spot' in line 8, 'berators' in line 9, 'answer' in line 14?

The difficulty arises no doubt largely through unfamiliarity with this type of presentation and it would diminish with practice. It is nevertheless worth recognising that a reader or copyist of text 1,600 or so years ago would often have needed his intelligence and knowledge of context to make sense of what he read. The same type of visual illusion generated by groups of letters may at times also be there in the Greek texts.

Now let us suppose, continuing the thought experiment, that we have a scribe reading and copying this text. He is near the end of his work. It has been a long day and he is both hungry and tired.

We will assume, as indeed often happened, that he is using a different format for his new copy, with in this instance around 24 characters per line. When he gets to the end of the fourth line to be copied, he writes JEWS, dips his reed pen in his ink and looks back again for the word to mark the next line. But, unfortunately, his eye then alights on JEWS at the end of line six, and he prepares to continue from the beginning of line seven, inadvertently missing out lines five and six.

At this point, there are a number of possibilities. He might realise that a sentence apparently beginning, 'However recognised many as potential Messiahs ... ' does not entirely make sense (and we are, for the purposes of this exercise, assuming an English word order, as it is actually an English text!). Alerted to the possibility of an error, the scribe reads back over the text, spots the error that might have led to the omission of two lines and carries on from the beginning of line five. All is then well, the mistake has been avoided.

But let us assume that, because he is tired and maybe under pressure to get on with the job, he fails to spot what has happened and, though a little puzzled, continues writing until he finds a convenient place to stop, perhaps at the end of his page. The text that he has copied will look like this:

```
ASANACCUSATIONORASANACCO
LADEBOTHENEMIESANDFOLLOW
ERSDESCRIBEDJESUSASKINGOFT
HEJEWSHOWEVERRECOGNISEDM
ANYASPOTENTIALMESSIAHSLIB
ERATORSWHOMIGHTFREEISRAEL
BYBEATINGTHEROMANSANYMES
SIAHWHODIDTHISCOULDTHERE
BYBECOMEAKINGOFTHEJEWSRO
MANSWEREAWAREOFTHETHREA
TTHATTHISPOSEDTOTHEIRRUL
EINTIMESOFGREATTENSION
```

Next day, he begins again afresh and glances in his own copy back to the place where he had trouble. What he reads is:

> *As an accusation or as an accolade, both enemies and follow-*
> *ers described Jesus as 'King of the Jews'. However, recognised*
> *many as potential Messiahs, liberators who might free Israel by*
> *beating the Romans. Any 'Messiah' who did this could thereby*
> *become a 'King of the Jews'.*
>
> *Romans were aware of the threat that this posed to their*
> *rule, in times of great tension.*

Clearly, something has gone wrong, but what?

Again, there are a few possibilities as to what will happen next. For example, the copyist sees what appears to have been his mistake. The scribe who wrote the passage had evidently got his word order wrong: it should have been 'However, many recognised as potential Messiahs, liberators who might free Israel by beating the Romans.'

So, the copyist now carefully scrapes out (or washes out, if it is still possible) 'recognised many' and replaces it with 'many recognised'. Alternatively, he puts in marks to show that the words should be transposed or crosses them out and writes the words again, in the presumed right order, in the margin alongside. However it is done, this adds a subtle change of meaning to the original error of omission of text. It does certainly sometimes happen in this way; one error acts as the springboard to create another.

The problem lies is identifying what has happened. As more stages are involved, so it gets harder to work out what may have gone on.

The scribe copying the text might alternatively gain no sense of what has happened and simply proceed with his work. If no one, starting with the scriptorium's corrector whose role it is to go over all the text, subsequently spots the error, then it will stand. The homeoteleuton will go unrecognised, unless it can some time later either be deduced from the reinstated faulty text or by comparison with the exemplar or another copy of it.[3]

For the purposes of this demonstration, we are going to assume that the scribe or a subsequent corrector does identify the mistake, work out what is missing by comparison with the exemplar and make a correction in smaller lettering, after marking the spot in the text. In our example, as indicated overleaf, the correction is written in the margin at the bottom of the column:

ASANACCUSATIONORASANACCO
LADEBOTHENEMIESANDFOLLOW
ERSDESCRIBEDJESUSASKINGOFT
HEJEWSHOWEVERRECOGNISEDM
ANYASPOTENTIALMESSIAHSLIB
ERATORSWHOMIGHTFREEISRAEL
BYBEATINGTHEROMANSANYMES
SIAHWHODIDTHISCOULDTHERE
BYBECOMEAKINGOFTHEJEWSRO
MANSWEREAWAREOFTHETHREA
TTHATTHISPOSEDTOTHEIRRUL
EINTIMESOFGREATTENSION

`PILATEEVENHADTHISPOSTEDONTHECROSSJEWS

In fact, in many of the Greek codices, homeoteleutons like this did crop up and were corrected. These mistakes have a number of distinct characteristics that provide help in understanding how the text was written. In the first place, these are errors that arise from visual transcription. While such an error might arise in dictated text as a freak coincidence, or because the text being dictated had the error already, the presence of a number of homeoteleutons[4] is a sure indication that the text was visually transcribed from an exemplar, rather than dictated.

Secondly, because of the process involved in which the eye skips to a word repeated later in the same place, for simple homeoteleutons (which most are), a whole number of lines will always be involved in the omission.

Then, thirdly, because we are dealing with blocks of text with most lines at around the average length, the number of characters in each omitted passage is likely to be a simple multiple of the average character length of the line in a column of text in the *original* text. Let us assume that the example just given, where there is an omission of 37 characters, is one of many for a section of the codex and that these come in clusters averaging around 20, 40, 60 and 80 characters in length. It is then a reasonable inference that the average line length for the exemplar is the lowest of these – 20 characters.

In practice, the outcome may not be quite so neat, taking account of the fact that even in block form the number of characters per line may vary considerably around the average, this then being reflected in the omitted text.

The passage provided above has a further repetition that could like-wise generate an error of homeoteleuton. Let us assume that the eye of the weary scribe, having written JEWS for the first time, then alights not on the next occurrence of the same word at the end of a line but the one afterwards at the end of line 13. He then writes as follows, having omitted a whole block of text:

ASANACCUSATIONORASANACCO
LADEBOTHENEMIESANDFOLLOW
ERSDESCRIBEDJESUSASKINGOF
THEJEWSROMANSWEREAWAREO
FTHETHREATTHATTHISPOSEDT
OTHEIRRULEINTIMESOFGREATT
ENSION

Now, this generates text that, as it happens, more or less makes sense. So the error might or might not be missed by the scribe, in checking his work, or by another corrector. In this instance, 175 characters are omitted. If the omission is found and indicated, or can be deduced, it will be found to conform well to an assumed average line length of around 20 characters for the exemplar, and an omission of nine whole lines.

Of course, some insertions of sizeable passages as corrections might have occurred for other reasons. The copyist could, for example, have omitted a section through sheer carelessness, without being prompted by identical words or letters at the end of lines. Or he (or a corrector) might have found an additional passage in another source. This extra passage is believed to be authentic and so it is added.

With a particular passage difficult to understand or capable of ambiguity, the copyist or corrector might have come to the conclu-sion that the scribe for the exemplar had made a mistake. Drawing the conclusion that something has been omitted, which would clarify the situation, the copyist or copyist reconstructs what he believes is missing and then adds it as a correction.

In all such cases, the relationship found between the number of characters omitted and the original line length will not in general hold good. It could do so by pure chance for one example, but would not do so for a number of examples. If these are mixed in with genuine errors of homeoteleuton, it becomes more difficult to use the informa-tion to deduce what may have been the line length or column width in terms of characters of the exemplar.

There is, however, a way in which an error of homeoteleuton can be distinguished from other possible errors and amendments that also lead to the insertion of text. The error has a distinctive characteristic, the repeated word or group of characters that helped cause it to arise. If it is assumed that the copyist writes these key characters down, skips by mistake to the next occurrence of the same characters in finding his place and proceeds from there, then what he will have omitted is a piece of text that occurs after the key characters and also ends with these same characters. This provides a means of identification, made easier if the corrector has marked the place in the text where the omission occurred.

So, for example in our original example, the omission in the new text comes just after JEWS and the last word of the omitted piece is also JEWS. The same is true for the error which could occur through the copyist's eye running on nine lines instead of two.

We suggest that this way of putting back the omitted text reflects the manner in which the error will most probably have occurred, as a result of the copyist seeing key characters as a marker and then coming back to the same characters in the same position later on in the text.

The situation is complicated by the fact that there is a second way in which such omitted text can be put back in and still accurately restore what was in the exemplar. The corrector, whose primary concern is likely to be to fix the mistake, rather than to identify and flag how it originated, could just as easily put the omitted piece back in *before* the key word, though now making his insertion begin rather than end with the key word.

In our original example, he would now make his correction mark between 'King of the' and 'Jews' and insert 'Jews Pilate even had this posted on the Cross'. The possibility is of more than passing interest, in that the correctors of the Greek manuscripts often did restore the text this way. It means that some vigilance needs to be exercised in the task of identifying errors triggered by the repetition of characters in the text.

A similar type of error called homioarcton (from the Greek for 'same beginning') can occur when lines have identical beginnings and the eye skips on. It has the same effect on the new copy being made and so cannot in practice be distinguished from an error of homeoteleuton, unless the exemplar is known and available to be examined.

It can be argued that the point at which the copyist is most likely to lose his place is at the end of a line in the text, when his eye has not come to a new word or characters to give him a guide as to where to go next. This would argue for errors of homeoteleuton being more common than ones of homioarcton. But it would require the study of a number of exemplars and their copies, were these to be available, to establish this point.

It should also be borne in mind that errors of omission, arising from the eye skipping on to a repeated word, could in theory originate at other points in a line of text. But a mid-line skip forward would probably be more likely to occur where the key word, or group of characters, was repeated in exactly the same position in a later line. On the whole, it appears from our analysis of text that most skips involving lines of text do involve repetitions of key words located either at the end or at the beginning of lines.

Going back to our original demonstration text (see above), let us assume that our scribe, in starting line eleven, is distracted. He writes ROMANS but then realises his reed pen has run dry. He looks down at the ink well, while dipping in the pen and then looks over to ask the scribe at the next table to be a little quieter (silent reading not at that time having been invented!). By the time he turns back to the text, he's forgotten what he had been writing and picks up after ROMANS at the start of line 14.

The outcome does not make sense and he, or another corrector, picks up the mistake later in rereading the new copy and adds a correction:

ASANACCUSATIONORASANACCO
LADEBOTHENEMIESANDFOLLOW
ERSDESCRIBEDJESUSASKINGOFT
HEJEWSPILATEEVENHADTHISPO
STEDONTHECROSSJEWSHOWEVE
RRECOGNISEDMANYASPOTENTI
ALMESSIAHSLIBERATORSWHOM
IGHTFREEISRAELBYBEATINGTH
EROMANSWEREAWAREOFTHETH
REATTHATTHISPOSEDTOTHEIR
RULEINTIMESOFGREATTENSION

ANYMESSIAHWHODIDTHISCOULDTHERE
BYBECOMEAKINGOFTHEJEWSROMANS

The insert is 58 characters and it ends with the same word as the word which precedes the insertion mark in the text. With our example, this is an error of homioarcton. We know this because we have created it. But someone just reading the copy above, without access to the exemplar, could only conclude that this was an example either of homeoteleuton or homioarcton.

As with errors of homeoteleuton, homioarctons can also be corrected in one of two ways, with the omitted copy reinserted either before or after the key word. In this example, the alternative would be for the corrector to put the correction just before the key word, 'Romans', beginning his correction with 'Romans' and then ending it with 'the Jews'.

Another type of error is called dittography (from the Greek for 'double writing'). Instead of text being omitted, a letter, syllable, word or groups of words is repeated twice. If the repetition is more than a letter or two, the scribe must not only be distracted but then fail to recall that he wrote a moment or two ago the same passage that he is now writing. As has been noted, the mind especially when tired plays tricks and almost anything is possible. However, it would seem from common sense that this type of error might be less likely to occur, and so in fact crop up less frequently in the text than errors of homeoteleuton and homioarcton. This appears often to be the case when ancient texts are examined.

A dittography might occur in our piece of constructed text if, on reaching the end of line six and the word JEWS, the scribe's eye unwittingly travels back to JEWS at the end of line four. He might then write the passage, 'Pilot even had this posted on the Cross. Jews ... ', a second time. That is, providing he is sufficiently sleepy, distracted or unaware! This is what the outcome would look like:

ASANACCUSATIONORASANACCO
LADEBOTHENEMIESANDFOLLOW
ERSDESCRIBEDJESUSASKINGOFT
HEJEWSPILATEEVENHADTHISPO
STEDONTHECROSSJEWSPILATEE
VENHADTHISPOSTEDONTHECRO
SSJEWSHOWEVERRECOGNISEDM
ANYASPOTENTIALMESSIAHSLIB
ERATORSWHOMIGHTFREEISRAE

If picked up later, the error would be indicated either by putting marks above each repeated word, to signify that it is redundant, or by crossing the words out.

It is worth noting that it is found that scribes sometimes repeated blocks of text, without apparently the repetition of key characters to trigger the mistake. In these cases, the repeated text will not usually reflect the exemplar in terms of a multiple of whole lines. For this reason, and also because of their comparative rarity, the examination of dittographies may prove to be less useful as a way of finding information about the earlier text.

This example concludes our curent exercise in exploring possible scribal error. Using a constructed passage in English, we have sought to demonstrate the characteristics of certain types of common scribal error and show how these can come about. This will certainly help in looking at the same phenomena in the early Greek texts.

The analysis of examples of homeoteleuton and homioarcton, can give evidence on a source – specifically on the average number of characters per line that it contained in each column. If there is a potential exemplar available, it could also be possible to rule this in or out, on the basis of (a) the average line length and (b) seeing where the pieces omitted by the process of homeoteleuton or homioarcton occur in the presumed source text.

The frequency of errors of different types can show whether the scribes were being careless or hurried or both. The degree to which errors were then picked up and corrected can provide an indication of how vital it was considered to get the manuscript right.

As will be seen, patterns of errors and the treatment of the text by different scribes give important information on the manner in which the manuscript was prepared and on how it may have been changed. The texts have to be examined in Greek since the origin and form of the errors would otherwise be masked in translation.

There are, as we have noted, two early surviving copies of the bible, Old and New Testaments, which many experts believe on the basis of the writing style and other factors belong to the mid fourth century. These are Codex Sinaiticus and Codex Vaticanus.

Two other ancient Greek bibles, Codex Alexandrinus and Codex Ephraemi Rescriptus, are dated somewhat later, to the latter part of the fourth and to the early fifth century respectively. There are also copies of parts or the whole of the New Testament, including Codex Bezae and Codex Washingtonensis, that date from around this period.

Later manuscripts may sometimes provide texts that go back to sources by routes the authors of earlier manuscripts may have been unaware of or neglected. So, despite being written later than our early fourth century codices, these could in theory still be closer to an original text for certain passages and so more authentic. Codex Bezae, for example, has much in common with Codex Sinaiticus and Codex Vaticanus while deviating through a number of added interpolations, omissions and changes to verse order. It is believed to have been written some time later, perhaps in the early fifth century. But it also shows evidence of its authors having had access to an earlier source in providing a shorter version of the eucharist in Luke (see Appendix X) and in its portrayal of an angry Jesus in Mark (see Chapter 7).

In general, however, earlier codices are likely to have been closer to source. The chances are increased if these were produced, as seems to have been the case with both Codex Sinaiticus and Codex Vaticanus, by an authority able to store, control and access its manuscripts.

Of all the ancient Greek bibles, Codex Sinaiticus has by far the greatest frequency of errors and alterations. So in this respect it offers the greatest scope for analysis. It is also one of the earliest surviving bibles, closely related to both Codex Vaticanus and, in the gospels of Luke and John, to the second century papyrus codices P66 and P75.

Taking into account these considerations, the study of this codex should provide a good starting point.

CHAPTER 3

Scribes and conjecture

Initially rediscovered by Constantin Tischendorf, the bulk of Codex Sinaiticus passed first into the hands of the Russian government. It was then sold to the British Museum in 1933 where a young man, Theodore Skeat, was working as an assistant keeper. Along with a colleague, Herbert Milne, Skeat was responsible for the codex. The two of them turned to analysing its contents, publishing their findings in 1938 under the title *Scribes and Correctors of the Codex Sinaiticus.* Skeat also helped in editing another important acquisition, the Egerton papyrus which appears to be part of a previously unrecorded gospel, published in 1935 as *Fragments of an Unknown Gospel.*

These studies established Skeat's reputation and he rose eventually to be become Keeper of Manuscripts. When he retired after 41 years at the Museum, he continued to study and make contributions to the analysis of early manuscripts. Due partly to his reputation and possibly partly to the unrivalled access that he had to Sinaiticus, the field was to an extent left to him. He certainly made major contributions. Some of his ideas, however, may not have been subject to sufficient scrutiny and so have been allowed to go unchallenged.

The format of the codex is unusual with pages measuring 38 cm by 34.5 cm, which is large when compared with other codices including Codex Vaticanus from around this period. There are generally four columns to a page, with usually 48 lines per column and an average of around 13 letters per line. It was put together in quires usually of four sheets, giving eight leaves (folios) written on both sides (recto and verso) to make a total of 16 pages per quire (see Fig. 2 overleaf).

Using the abbreviations Q for quire, F for folio, R for recto and V for verso, it is possible to identify any page precisely. So, for example, the

Fig. 2. Format of standard quire, Codex Sinaiticus

page in Codex Sinaiticus containing the penance that Paul is ordered to undertake for teaching 'all the Jews living among the Gentiles to forsake Moses' (Acts 21, 21), can be described as Q88F4V. This is more succinct than writing or saying, 'the verso of the fourth folio of quire number 88'.

The numbering used by the scribes involved in preparing the document indicate that there was a now-missing quire numbered 73 between the end of the Old and the beginning of the New Testament. It is possible that this was simply lost. Milne and Skeat suggested it may have been intended to contain tables devised by Eusebius (the Eusebian canon tables) to make it easy to cross-relate similar passages in the gospels.

References with section and table numbers do indeed exist in the margins, which refer back to the canon tables, making it possible for a reader to identify very swiftly other parallel passages. For each gospel, such passages were numbered in sequence (with the section number), together with a number that related to the canon table in which parallel passages in the other gospels would be listed. To identify these for a particular reference, all that had to be done was look up the appropriate numbered table, find the section number for that gospel and the section numbers of parallel passages in other gospels would be found alongside (Fig. 3).

The section numbers, related to particular passages, that Eusebius used are believed to be adapted from a reference system used by an earlier Alexandrian writer, Ammonius. So the section numbers are sometimes called Ammonian section numbers. It was, however, someone a little later, most probably Eusebius, who came up with the improvement of using tables to enable the cross comparison of similar passages.

Eusebian Canon table 2: for parallels in Matthew, Mark and Luke
(Ammonian section numbers for parallel passages on each line)

Mt	Mk	Lk	Mt	Mk	Lk	Mt	Mk	Lk	Mt	Mk	Lk
15	6	15	94	86	97	179	99	197	251	146	255
21	10	32	94	86	146	190	105	195	253	148	204
31	102	185	103	1	70	192	106	216	258	150	257
32	39	79	114	24	41	193	107	121	259	151	258
32	39	133	116	25	42	193	107	218	264	155	156
50	41	56	116	25	165	194	108	152	269	154	228
62	13	4	116	25	177	194	108	219	271	42	230
62	13	24	121	32	127	195	109	220	278	160	263
63	18	33	122	33	129	198	110	221	281	163	268
67	15	26	123	34	147	199	111	173	285	166	265
69	47	83	130	35	82	201	112	222	285	166	267
71	21	38	131	36	76	203	114	270	296	177	280
72	22	39	135	38	78	205	116	224	296	177	284
72	22	186	137	44	167	206	117	232	301	182	286
73	23	40	143	57	90	208	118	233	308	189	305
74	49	85	144	59	12	217	127	240	312	193	299
76	52	169	149	66	35	219	128	241	316	197	293
79	29	86	149	66	43	223	130	243	317	198	295
80	**30**	**44**	153	69	36	225	134	245	322	202	309
82	53	87	164	79	144	226	133	244	338	218	322
82	53	110	168	83	95	229	135	137	339	219	325
83	54	87	168	83	206	229	135	246	340	220	327
83	54	112	170	85	96	242	137	237	342	222	323
85	55	88	172	87	98	242	137	248	344	224	328
85	55	114	174	91	99	243	138	249	346	225	330
88	141	148	176	93	101	248	143	209	353	232	337
88	141	251	178	95	102	248	143	253	354	233	338
92	40	80	178	95	217	249	144	254			

Fig. 3. Eusebian canon table 2

Here is an illustration of how the system works, using as reference Codex Sinaiticus online. Having say come across the passage in which Jesus' core followers are named in Matthew, assume that we now wish to find parallel passages if any in the other gospels. The relevant passage, Matthew 10, 2, is at the head of column three of Q74F5V. In the margin alongside there are two letters. These are from the Greek system in which letters are used to represent numbers.

The first letter Π, representing 80, is the section number. The number below is B, representing two, and refers to canon table number two. This canon table is for convenience given in Fig. 3 on the previous page in full. The tables contain references for the four canonical gospels in varying combinations. This particular one has references for Matthew, Mark and Luke. So we know already that there is, at least according to Eusebius, no parallel passage in John.

We look down the column for Matthew to find the number 80 and the corresponding numbers in the same row, which we have highlighted, for Mark and Luke. The number 30 for Mark can be found in sequence in the margin of the last column at page Q76F3V at Mark 3, 16, correctly marking the point where the naming of the twelve disciples begins. The marginal reference is Λ B (section number 30 in canon table two). Similarly, the number 44 for Luke, can be found at page Q78F1R, with the marginal reference μΔ B (section number 44 in canon table two). This identifies Luke 6, 13 as the passage that introduces the naming of Jesus' followers.

It is a simple cross-referencing system, imperfect in that the comparisons are neither fully comprehensive nor at times entirely comprehensible. And, indeed, the scribes sometimes made mistakes in applying it, by for example putting the marginal references in the wrong place or omitting them altogether.

We have described it in some detail because the subject of the tables will crop up again and the way the references are applied is of some significance in the analysis of the text.

These references in Codex Sinaiticus would, however, have served little purpose if the tables themselves were not included. This provides support for the idea that the missing quire 73 did contain, or was intended to contain, the Eusebian canon tables. The marginal references were imperfectly applied, in that they do not appear in part of Luke and in some other places. Skeat's case is that the plan had initially been to include the tables, but this was then changed after most of the references had been put in.

Milne and Skeat revised Tischendorf's appraisal that provided for four scribes, as authors of the manuscript. They established that Tischendorf had been misled by the distinctive format of the poetical works of the Old Testament into believing that these were the work of a separate scribe, described as scribe C. They were able to reattribute the work to two of the other identified scribes, A and D.

As well as identifying corrections that the scribes made to their own work as it progressed, Tischendorf identified a number of other correctors who made changes or corrections. It is presumed that these were undertaken after the manuscript had left the scriptorium and possibly in some cases centuries later. With no accurate means of assigning dates, it is hard to decide just when corrections were added, particularly when the same style of uncial writing was used. In some instances, sequence is suggested by one identified corrector making a subsequent correction to another identified corrector's work.

There are altogether about 24,000 corrections throughout the manuscript. It is not possible to be precise, given that some leaves of the Old Testament are damaged or in fragments and others lost. One corrector, designated Ca and presumed by many textual analysts to be from the fifth or sixth century, is responsible for a very substantial part of this total.

It can be hard to identify the hand of a particular corrector, often on the basis of a small amount of text. So, some of the earlier assignments have been modified on further scrutiny by Milne and Skeat and subsequent scholars.

The international team involved in putting Sinaiticus fully online has more recently suggested that the work attributed to scribe B might have been done by two separate scribes, denoted as B1 and B2. However, as there some recognisably common features such as the relatively poor quality of the work and because it does not affect the present analysis, we shall stick with the existing framework of just three scribes: A, B and D.

It is plausible, given societal organisation at the time, that the scribes were all men. But that cannot be known for certain. In what follows, masculine nouns and pronouns should be taken in a general, rather than a gender-specific, sense.

The identification of the three scribes is made possible through observed, consistent differences in their handwriting, layout of text and spelling. Scribe D, for example, made greater uses of fillers (diples). Scribe A's K (kappa) used as an abbreviation for KAI, the kai compendium, is particularly distinctive, with its acutely swept-back tail. Scribe B used a 'superline' at the end of a line in place of the final N, detached from the text, whereas in the case of the other scribes this abbreviation overlapped the preceding vowel. Scribe B appeared to make more spelling mistakes.

If all the features that distinguish the scribes are applied to the text, it becomes possible to see what passages were written by each of the scribes. This helps considerably in gaining an understanding of how the scribes worked as a team and, as will be seen in later chapters, how they dealt with difficulties and problems.

Of the three scribes, B appeared, in terms of the corrections made to his copy, to have been most prone to error. Scribe A made more nonsense errors than scribe D and also had a greater frequency of iotacisms, especially in terms of using E in place of AI and I instead of EI. The differences between the scribes in respect of iotacisms may, however, in part reflect some flexibility in the language. It is also possible that the scribes varied in their approaches to the manuscript from which they were copying, written at an earlier time and with possibly different rules for spelling.

Scribe B was allocated a block of work consisting of a section of the Old Testament and the Shepherd of Hermas at the end of the New Testament. There is no indication that the other scribes amended his work. However, scribe B worked together with the other scribes on supplementary material such as titles and page headings, sometimes providing these for sections written by A and D.

So the three scribes worked as a team, even if B might have been seen as less reliable or in some way more junior. Because the quality of scribe D's work is arguably better, and because it is assumed that some of scribe D's interventions were to remedy mistakes by scribe A, it has been speculated that he was the more senior of the three.[1] Scribe A was, however, the real worker, taking on huge sections of both the Old and the New Testaments.

Scribe A is defined as having written most of the historical and poetical works of the Old Testament, almost all of the New Testament and the Epistle of Barnabas. Scribe B wrote the Prophets and the Shepherd of Hermas. Scribe D was responsible for Tobit, Judith, the first half of 4 Maccabees, two thirds of Psalms, most of the first five verses of Revelation and, judging from fragments, at least some of Genesis.

It should incidentally be noted that the books included in the Old Testament vary from those accepted today, the order in which books appear differs from that in modern bibles and there are two books added to the New Testament, the Epistle of Barnabas and the Shepherd of Hermas, that have long been rejected as part of the accepted canon.

Three whole sheets in the New Testament have been attributed to scribe D and, as with the Old Testament sections, this was done on the basis of the analysis of handwriting. These are:

(a) the second sheet of quire 75 (folios 2 and 7) Matthew 16, 9 to 18, 12 and Matthew 24, 35 to 26, 6;

(b) the fourth sheet of quire 77 (folios 4 and 5) Mark 14, 54 to Luke 1, 56;

(c) the third sheet of quire 85 (folios 3 and 6) 1 Thessalonians 2, 14 to 5, 28 and Hebrews 4, 16 to 8, 1.

Because the fourth sheet of a normal quire is the inner sheet, the text is continuous for this whole sheet. So it is possible that, in the second of these three instances, scribe D simply took over from scribe A towards the end of Mark's gospel, carried on for four pages and then handed the work back. However, in the other two instances the sheets involve text that is separated by a substantial gap. It is hard at this point to see what reason there might have been, in terms of cooperation between the scribes, for a second scribe to have written one folio and then the second folio that completed the sheet.

Milne and Skeat described all of these sheets as 'cancel leaves', undertaken by scribe D to replace sheets that had already been written. According to these authors, the objective would have been to correct some major blunders by scribe A, requiring text to be rewritten, added or deleted. This explanation, which is widely accepted, will be examined in detail in Chapters 11 and 12. However these sheets came to be generated, they do certainly provide evidence of a high level of interaction and cooperation between the scribes.

The best illustration of such teamwork is provided by the alternation of work between scribe A and scribe D in the historical books of the Old Testament. For the examples that follow, we are indebted to the analysis of Dirk Jongkind, published in *Scribal Habits of Codex Sinaiticus*. As the diagram shows, first one scribe wrote a substantial section, then the other took over, then it was back to the first and so on (Fig. 4).

	35	36	37	38	39	40	41	42		43
scribe: A			D		A			D	A	B
2 Esdras			Esther	Tobit	Judith	1 Maccabees		4 Macc		Isaiah

Fig. 4. Alternation of scribes, Codex Sinaiticus Old Testament

Rather than working in shifts, although this is feasible at some points, it looks as if the scribes were dividing up the work between them. This meant that they would have been working simultaneously on different parts of the text. In order to do this, they would have needed first of all to decide where a second scribe should start while a first was still working. Then they would have needed to count or, more likely, estimate the number of characters in the intervening text in the original manuscript or manuscripts from which they were copying and work out how many columns and lines of text this would require in the format they were using, based on an average of around 13 characters per line. This would give a starting point – folio, recto or verso and column – for the second scribe.

Given that this was based on an approximation and given there would be factors hard to take into account, for example paragraph breaks and corrections, it is very likely that the first scribe would then have had to make adjustments to fit his remaining text into the space now allocated. There was always the possibility that he might fail.

Both these considerations are illustrated by the transition from Judith written by scribe D to 1 Maccabees written by scribe A. Having (it is hypothesised) allowed an amount of space for scribe D to complete Judith, scribe A began to copy 1 Maccabees, starting on the second column of the recto of quire 39, folio 3. Scribe A had, however, badly miscalculated and been far too generous. As a result, scribe D realised that much too much space had been allocated for him to finish the book of Judith. If he continued as usual, it would have led to two or even three blank columns left at the end before 1 Maccabees, which was already underway.

So scribe D began to make some strenuous adjustments. Starting at folio 2 of quire 39, he cut the line length per column to 46 or 47, ignoring the rule marks set for the normal 48 lines. He made his lines shorter, decreasing the average number of characters per line. He put in more filling marks (diples) that served no function other than to pad out the text. As a result of these efforts, he stretched out the text by at least a column to finish in the last column of the verso of quire 39, folio 2. But it was not quite enough. This still left the unfortunate oddity of a blank column on a new page before the start of 1 Maccabees, something that occurs nowhere else in the manuscript. Elsewhere, a column is only left blank where it is the last column on a page and serves to allow the start of a new book on a new page.

In the next transition, between 1 Maccabees and 4 Maccabees, the desired adjustment appeared to have been to allow the latter to start at the beginning of a new quire. The first book however provided insufficient copy for a full quire. So a quire of two sheets was used instead, making a total of eight pages. Scribe A completed his task neatly within this remit, finishing in the last column, to allow his successor scribe D to start 4 Maccabees in the first column of quire 42.

This latter book, which is divided between scribes D and A, illustrates the converse of the problem experienced in the transition between Judith and 1 Maccabees. Scribe B started Isaiah, the next book after 4 Maccabees, at the beginning of a new quire, maybe to mark the transition from the historical to the prophetic books. Or it may be that it had been calculated, wrongly as it turned out, that this was the right place to start given the quantity of material in the source for the previous book, 4 Maccabees. Either way, it was realised from about the middle of this book that there was just too much copy to fit easily within the frame of a single quire. So Scribe D began to make space by adding first two lines and then three lines, to run the text at 50 to 51 lines per page. When scribe A took over, on the verso of the fourth folio of quire 42, he continued with the unusually extended page length of 50 lines started by scribe D. Finally, as it became clear that enough has been done, A reverted to the standard page length of 48 lines for three folios to finish comfortably within the last column of the quire.

The other example in the sequence of swaps between the two scribes suggests a case where the scribes may have got their counting just right. In the transition between Esther and Tobit, scribe A finished in the second column of the recto of folio 3, quire 37, and scribe D started at the top of the next column. There is no indication of scribe A's text being either stretched or crammed. So either scribe D waited for scribe A to finish before starting in this case, or the two of them calculated the right amount of space to leave for scribe A to finish his work.

These examples demonstrate both the close working relationship between the scribes and the processes involved in cooperation. This will prove helpful later in seeking to understand some of the more difficult issues thrown up by an examination of the text. The involvement of several scribes working together indicates that Sinaiticus may have been a piece of commissioned work, written to a deadline. But just when was it undertaken?

The existence of section and canon numbers, relating to the Eusebian canon tables, in the margin of the gospels is an indication that the codex must date from a point in time after the early fourth century, when these tables were first created. Comparative analysis of the handwriting of this and other early Greek texts suggests that the manuscript was written during the fourth century. This is supported by the plain titles used for the gospels, for example KATA MARKON (according to Mark), as opposed to the more elaborate titles, for example EUAGGELION KATA MARKON (the gospel according to Mark) used later. The inclusion of Barnabas and the Shepherd of Hermas, which have long been treated as non-canonical, also suggest an early date.

Constantin Tischendorf, who found the codex at the St Catherine's Monastery, believed that it was one of 50 copies of the scriptures, recorded as having been ordered in 330 or 331 CE by the Roman Emperor Constantine for churches in his new capital Constantinople, formerly Byzantium. The order was placed with Eusebius who was Bishop of Caesarea. This was a view supported by Skeat who, late in his life, generated an elaborate analysis (*The Codex Sinaiticus, the Codex Vaticanus and Constantine*) linking the production of Codex Sinaiticus to the Emperor's order. Skeat argued that the codex may already have been in production. At any rate, it was created under a situation of intense pressure, hastily put together as evidenced by the large number of mistakes and consequent corrections.

Eusebius would have had great difficulty assembling enough competent scribes and sufficient animal skins for the parchment to complete the entire order. Yet it would appear that Constantine expected 50 copies to be prepared simultaneously and within a reasonably short period of time. Since that was clearly not going to be feasible, Skeat suggested that Eusebius compromised by undertaking to prepare the bibles in batches of three or four.[2]

Sinaiticus must have been one of the very first, according to Skeat, but was rejected before it was finally completed because its large format would have led to a high proportion of waste in the use of animal skins. This is compared with other codices such as Codex Vaticanus, which Skeat believed was also one of the bibles included in the original order but not rejected. Nothing, of course, would have been saved at such a very late stage by not including Sinaiticus in the order. The damage had already been done, Skeat argued, in terms of using too many skins. But it was a format that could not have been applied, with economy, to 50 bibles and possibly even more if the Emperor subsequently made a further order.

The other bibles would have had to be produced in a format resembling that used for Codex Vaticanus. The almost completed Codex

Sinaiticus was not included, according to Skeat, because the Emperor Constantine would have expected a degree of uniformity in his consignment of bibles. Skeat argued that, in struggling to make the format used for Sinaiticus viable, Eusebius decided to leave out his newly devised canon tables. If so, this must have been a last-ditch effort, since the canon table references were for the most part included in the margins of the gospels. The page numbering had also been completed, indicating where the omitted section (quire 73) containing the tables would arguably have been.

As a further consideration, Skeat contended that Eusebius was aware that he could not complete the order as specified, swiftly and in a single consignment. If Eusebius had included his own work, however little extra time this took up, it might not have been viewed very favourably by the Emperor in view of the perceived delay in the project as a whole. So, Skeat suggested, Eusebius chose diplomatically to leave it out.

This is, all in all, quite a complex and detailed theory based on a number of suppositions. What evidence is there to support it? There is, as has already been noted, no direct evidence either way to link the production of the codex with the order by Constantine. The date which most experts assign to the manuscript of around the mid fourth century does however make a link possible. There is also a case based on probability. It was an enormous enterprise to make a full handwritten copy of the bible, and very few were produced at around this time. So it can be argued that there is a good chance that any surviving example would have been one of the fifty.

There is also evidence that links Sinaiticus with Caesarea where there was a library organised by Caesarea's Bishop Eusebius. Such a library, with resources for referencing and cross-checking, would have been an appropriate place for the production and copying of texts. It would also have acted as a scriptorium. The most striking piece of corroboration comes in notes by a corrector, presumed to be from about the sixth century, at the end of the books of 2 Esdras and then Esther. The first of these reads:

> *Collated against a very old copy corrected by the holy martyr Pamphilus, which has at the end a signature in his own hand, reading thus:*
>> *Copied and corrected from the hexapla of Origen.*
>> *Antoninus collated; I, Pamphilus, corrected*

The second note is more expansive:

> *Copied and corrected from the hexapla of Origen, as corrected*
> *by his own hand. At the end of this very old book (which begins*
> *with the first book of Kingdoms and ends at Esther) is the*
> *distinctive signature of Pamphilus himself, reading thus:*
>> *Antoninus, the confessor, collated. I, Pamphilus, corrected*
>> *the volume in prison, with God's great favour and enhance-*
>> *ment. And, if it is not too boastful to say, it would not be*
>> *easy to find a copy that comes close to this copy.*

Origen's hexapla was an edition of the Old Testament produced in the early third century with six different versions in Greek and Hebrew, placed side by side for comparison.

Pamphilus was a patron of the library at Caesarea and Eusebius' teacher and mentor. There are colophons, similar to the ones given above, in other manuscripts which record that Pamphilus and Eusebius worked together on the correction of Old Testament texts. Pamphilus was killed during the persecution by the Emperor Diocletian in 309 CE.

Jerome recorded in his collection of biographies, *On Famous Men*, written towards the end of the fourth century, that Pamphilus copied the majority of the works of Origen and that these copies could be found in the library at Caesarea. Moreover, as earlier noted, Jerome also stated that a few years previously papyrus documents in the library, which had become worn, were replaced with parchment copies.

So, what does this add up to in assessing the evidence provided by the colophons at the end of 2 Esdras and Esther? It seems clear that, in the sixth century, the original hexapla created by Origen was no longer available. If it were, then the corrector would surely have used it. He did have access to a copy of all or part of the hexapla, with an autograph note indicating that it had been made by Pamphilus with the help of another Christian scribe Antoninus. Since, as Jerome recorded, copies of Origen's work that Pamphilus made were lodged in the library at Caesarea, this would suggest that the corrector was working in this library a century or so later, checking Codex Sinaiticus against the annotated hexapla. However, this presumes that the corrector had a Pamphilus autograph original, and not a copy that someone else had made of that. If the chain of reasoning is correct, then it places Codex Sinaiticus in the library at Caesarea around the sixth century, strengthening the presumption that this is where it may have been made.

There are some other intriguing clues, first picked up by Milne and Skeat in *Scribes and Correctors of the Codex Sinaiticus*, which indicate that the codex' place of origin may have been Caesarea. There is a unique reading (Matthew 13, 54) that appears in context and in comparison with other manuscripts to have been a scribal error. The text reads, 'And when Jesus had finished these parables, he left that place [beside the Sea of Galilee] and coming to his hometown [possibly, Capernaum], he taught them in their synagogue ... ' In Codex Sinaiticus, scribe A initially wrote in place of PATRIDA, ('his hometown'), ANTIPATRIDA, that is Antipatris, a place that Herod had named in honour of his father and a considerable distance from where the action was taking place in Galilee. The reading was corrected to PATRIDA, possibly by scribe A himself. The error suggests that scribe A had in his mind, at the time of writing, the name of a place familiar to him. Since Antipatris is about 38 miles south of Caesarea, this provides a helpful, though by no means conclusive, pointer as to where the manuscript was being written.

In another instance, the same scribe made what appears to be a revealing mistake in describing preaching by evangelists, following the persecution that came after the death of Stephen.[3] Acts 8, 5 reads, 'Now, Philip went down to a city of Samaria, and proclaimed the Messiah to them.' But scribe A has, in place of SAMARIAS (of Samaria), KAISARIAS (of Caesarea), which is wrong in respect of the sense, context and the witness of other manuscripts. It would seem that in writing the name, the scribe had 'Caesarea' in his mind, quite likely because that is where he was at the time.

Neither of these examples of course entirely proves the case. It has been pointed out, for example, that Antipatris is roughly equidistant from Jerusalem and Caesarea. So the argument that Milne and Skeat deployed (and which Skeat reiterated and expanded in his later article) could also be used to suggest that the scribe might have been working at a scriptorium in Jerusalem. In Chapter 8 of Acts, Caesarea is mentioned at the end as the place that Philip reached in his preaching in Samaria. The scribe could possibly have read ahead, or been familiar with the text, and so in that way have come to write 'Caesarea' when he should have written 'Samaria' earlier in the chapter.

It is nevertheless hard to contend that these alternative explanations are any more convincing. Confusion with Caesarea because the scribe was familiar with the place, or operating there, seems just as likely. If the notes at the end of 2 Esdras and Esther are also taken into account, and the historical evidence that the Bishop of Caesarea, Eusebius, was around the same time involved in a major exercise producing bibles for Constantine, then it is at least plausible that the Codex Sinaiticus was in some way connected with this order.

Skeat's later theory of Sinaiticus as a rejected prototype does, however, suffer from some major drawbacks. In the first place, far from being abandoned, the project was effectively completed with both the Old and New Testaments as these were conceived at the time fully written out. It really is a strange presumption that, having reached such a point at very substantial cost, the book should then have been discarded and not put to the use for which it was intended. It also seems hardly likely that it would only have been realised, at the point at which this bible was almost finished, that many more such bibles could not be completed in the same way to make up Constantine's consignment.

It is not even certain that it would have been more wasteful to produce bibles in the bulky format used for Sinaiticus as opposed to, say, operating with the much smaller page size used for Codex Vaticanus. Skeat based his argument on measurements cited by another author[4] for the usable areas of skin for parchment from mature goats in ancient times. Applied to a specific fourth century codex, this sort of calculation can at best be approximate. Moreover, when the international team commissioned a study of the type of animal skin used for a sample of the Codex Sinaiticus leaves, it was found that those that could be identified came from sheep and calf.

Possibly the greatest confusion arises as a consequence of the realisation that dictation would have speeded up the process of production, providing enough competent scribes could be assembled in one place and providing a steady supply of parchment sheets could be guaranteed. An original exemplar, even if carefully divided, could only have served one or two scribes copying by sight at once. Copying in this way would have entailed making perhaps only one bible at a time, and then repeating the process for another. If each took several weeks, then the whole project could possibly have been spread over a period of years. So, dictation would arguably have been needed to get the task done speedily, as Constantine required.

Milne and Skeat put forward the case for dictation in *Scribes and Correctors*. This was then heavily criticised, such that Skeat gave it less emphasis in his much later article on Codex Sinaiticus and Codex

Vaticanus. But he did not abandon the idea, as he believed it was essential for a theory that embraced a link between these manuscripts and the order by Constantine.

However, as far as Codex Sinaiticus is concerned, dictation is not compatible with another of Skeat's theories, that the codex was a prototype, rejected when it was decided that it would be wasteful to complete the whole order to the same format. There would have been no need for dictation, in other words no need to involve an extra person in the task, if Sinaiticus had been produced just on a one-off basis. If, on the other hand, it was decided to use dictation and make a few other copies at the same time, then this raises the question of the format used for the other copies.

If these were made in the same way as Sinaiticus, oversized and presumed to be unacceptable to Constantine, then what happened to them? It is increasingly unlikely that there were perhaps four bibles each produced at a cost of around half a million dollars, in today's terms, and then left to go to waste. If, on the other hand, the others (arguably, simultaneously produced by dictation) were in at least roughly the same format as Vaticanus, then it must have already been realised that smaller was more economic – and Sinaiticus would not have been needed at all!

Milne and Skeat argued that dictation must have been used because of the frequency of spelling mistakes. They maintained that that there would have been far fewer errors, if the scribes had had the exemplar in front of them as opposed to having had it read to them. When it comes to vowels and combinations of vowels, all of the scribes exhibit a degree of fluidity with their spelling. On balance, scribe D is more consistent than either scribe B or scribe A. There is considerable variation, although it would appear from Jongkind's research and our own analysis that this is more often in the direction of EI–I and AI–E, rather than vice versa. These differences, or arguably mistakes, were put down to errors by the scribes in hearing what was being dictated to them.

It needs to be remembered that the Greek language was in the process of evolution, with some diphthongs being gradually displaced by single vowels. Hence, for example, HOI POLLOI meaning the many or the majority, and later used derogatorily in English to denote 'the common people', became I POLI in modern Greek. So there was certainly a degree of flux and this would have been accentuated by the fact that the scribes were working from an older exemplar or exemplars, written perhaps more than a century previously.

It is possible that the scribes did not operate a fully consistent approach to an older exemplar that made greater use of diphthongs. At some points, these may have been 'corrected' to vowels and, at other points, copied as they were. As well as variation within the work of each scribe, there was also variation between scribes. So, for example, scribe A appears more often to have used the spelling with which he was familiar, as opposed to sticking precisely to the exemplar.

Another factor is that, whereas now in many languages spelling is regarded as more-or-less fixed, in earlier times this was often not the case. In England, we only have to go back 400 years to Elizabethan times for a relaxed approach to orthography. Shakespeare's name provides an example of a word often spelled in different ways. Besides other variations, sometimes the first, second or third 'e' in Shakespeare was missed out and sometimes the last 'a'.

It would not be surprising if, in Jerusalem or Caesarea 1700 years ago, there were alternatives for the ways words were spelled. So a scribe might have read a word and written down the same spelling and on other occasions used another form, and neither would have been wrong. Or he might have chosen to use a spelling with which he was more comfortable, perhaps even unconsciously, as in the hypothetical case in the previous chapter of an American child copying from an English text in which the word 'colour' was used. The variation in the scribes' treatment of vowels and diphthongs certainly does not prove the case for dictation.

Neither, for many of the same reasons, do the few examples of whole word deviations (technically, harmonisations) that Milne and Skeat provided. We agree that scribe A most probably wrote ANTIPATRIDA instead of PATRIDA in Matthew 13, 54 and KAISARIAS instead of SAMARIAS in Acts 8, 5, because the wrong names happened already to have been in his head. But this could equally have arisen after having seen, as opposed to having heard, the correct word. Copying, according to Dain (*Les manuscrits*) involves a number of stages: reading the text, retaining it, internally dictating it and then writing it down. It is quite possible during this process for another retained word, or for that matter a simple misspelling, to creep in.

As evidence of internal dictation, it is quite common even today for people to mouth or speak aloud words when they are reading. At the time Sinaiticus was prepared, silent reading was probably not the norm – and indeed a scriptorium, whether scribes were reading to themselves or writing from dictation, could have been a noisy place! A far cry indeed from modern public libraries.

Milne and Skeat provided an example, from 1 Maccabees 5, 20, which they felt strongly supports the case for dictation. Here, the authors interpreted letters used by scribe A as representing alternative numbers, 'either six thousand or three thousand'. They supposed that the reader of the text, unable to decipher the original, inadvertently exclaimed what he was thinking – and the scribe duly wrote it all down. This seems a little far-fetched, especially as the text as written down by the scribe makes no real sense, and cannot be assumed to be a garble of 'either six thousand or three thousand'.

Even if it did mean this, a correction *written* in the exemplar, from six thousand to three thousand or vice versa, would have been just as likely as the source of error. Unable to decide which was right, scribe A in doing the copying might have decided to write down both. Or he could have incorporated in his text what had in the original been intended by a corrector as a query written in the margin: 'or three thousand?'

It could be said that there should have been more uniformity in the styles of the three scribes, in for example the use of abbreviations for sacred names (nomina sacra) and in making paragraph breaks, had they each had text from the same source in front of them. But this is a weak argument, given the freedom that the scribes evidently had in presenting their text and also given the choice that, it can be seen, they had in using variant spellings.

Milne and Skeat certainly did not prove their case. The evidence that they presented can at best be taken either way. By contrast, the general arguments that can be advanced against dictation and in favour of copying by sight are much more compelling. It has already been noted that the theory of dictation is inconsistent with the evidence presented, and with which as it happens we concur, of Codex Sinaiticus as a singular case, a very much one-off production.

In addition, Jongkind makes some powerful points arising from his research. Dictation as a theory does not work well against indications that the scribes worked together to keep text within certain limits, by counting the original and making adjustments in spacing and the number of lines per column in the new text. This certainly happened with 4 Maccabees, where a concerted effort was made to keep the book just within the bounds of a quire. It could only have happened, if the scribes were able to see and appraise the text from which they were working. In other words, they had to be operating by sight.

Dictation must also be ruled out from the evidence of the instances where a second scribe went on ahead, having counted how much space would be needed, to write another book or section while the first scribe was finishing his work. Given the difficulty in predicting exactly how much space to leave, it was inevitable that the scribe following on, and needing now to fill a fixed space precisely, would have had to make adjustments. This is clearly demonstrated in the sequences described above between Judith and 1 Maccabees and between 4 Maccabees and Isaiah. In these cases, the following scribes would have needed to see and count the remaining copy and measure it against the space that had to be filled.

Another point is that dictation to a number of copyists only works if all are reasonably competent and able to work at about the same speed. There would be not much gain, if there had to be a pause every time a particular scribe made a mistake and if such errors were frequent. But there are indeed are a lot of errors in Sinaiticus and, while many may have been corrected later, there is also evidence that the scribes corrected their own work as they went along. Once again, this is an argument for the manuscript having been copied by sight rather than taken down from dictation.

We are not aware of any manuscript from this period that can be shown to have been produced by dictation. There is by contrast plenty of evidence, particularly in the form of skip errors (see Chapters 4 and 5), that texts were frequently and perhaps therefore generally generated by visual transcription.

Skeat's promotion of a theory of dictation in *The Codex Sinaiticus, the Codex Vaticanus and Constantine* is thus faulty on two grounds. While it supports one part of his argument, that it would have been desirable if not essential to speed up production, it ran counter to another of his proposals, that Codex Sinaiticus was a one-off, rejected prototype. Even more crucially, the evidence from the ways in which the scribes worked and the mistakes they made point decisively towards visual copying.

The proper course, we suggest, would have been to re-examine the theory of dictation in the light of the evidence, and perhaps see what else could be gleaned from a study of the interaction between the scribes and the text. This is what we have begun to do in this chapter, from the foundation provided by Jongkind's research.

Further analysis in Chapters 4 and 6 will show that Codex Sinaiticus may well have been connected to the order by the Emperor

Constantine, though not quite in the way that Skeat proposed. For the moment, these are our conclusions:

1. **There are indications within the text of Codex Sinaiticus that link the manuscript with Caesarea and to the library and scriptorium there in the fourth century CE.**
2. **The evidence produced by Milne and Skeat in *Scribes and Correctors of the Codex Sinaiticus* does not substantiate their case that the manuscript was produced from dictation.**
3. **Other evidence indicates that the manuscript must have been generated through visual transcription from one or more original sources.**
4. **Skeat does not establish that the manuscript was intended to be one of 50 copies of the bible commissioned by the Emperor Constantine.**

So far, only possible iotacisms and more general errors of mishearing or misreading have been considered in seeking to understand how Codex Sinaiticus came to be written. There are other avenues still to be explored, means of dissecting the text that will reveal some of the surprising secrets of this ancient manuscript.

CHAPTER 4

Secrets of Sinaiticus

Because substantial parts of the beginning of the Old Testament have been lost or remain only in fragments, it is hard to arrive at a precise figure for the number of corrections and alterations throughout Codex Sinaiticus. Judging from the bulk of the manuscript still intact, which is in parts very heavily corrected, our own estimate is that over 24,000 changes were made. This would accord with the listing by Tischendorf of 14,800 corrections in the portion of the codex held in St Petersburg, comprising about two-thirds of the whole.

Many of the alterations are quite small. A large number involve alterations to vowels and diphthongs, discussed in the previous chapter, which to some degree reflect differences in style and the evolution of language over time. There are insertions and deletions of single words or letters, minor substitutions, corrections and alterations to spelling, changes to accentuation and the modification of marks used to denote words which have been abbreviated. Substantial changes involving the substitution, deletion or addition of large changes of text are fewer. But there are still several hundred of these, the count depending on where the cut-off point is chosen for the number of characters involved. Milne and Skeat do not appear to have analysed these more substantial changes, it may be because they did not see why this might be important. They had a theory and perhaps no motivation to look for evidence to challenge it.

The examination of corrections involving a number of characters, to see how many were homeoteleutons or homioarctons, does however provide a good means of testing whether the codex was copied by sight or produced from dictation. The error arising from skipping text through visual copying generates a result with characteristics that are diagnostic. Because the eye of the scribe has skipped from a group of characters to the repetition of the same group of characters later, and so eliminated text that includes these characters, the correction then needed will be formed and placed in one of two ways. It will either be made after these characters and end in the same characters. Or it may be placed before the characters and begin with the same characters. This is an important diagnostic characteristic that makes it possible to identify these errors and thus also to decide whether or not a piece of text has been copied by sight.

It should be noted that, whichever option the corrector chooses, the effect in terms of restoring the original text is the same, with both errors of homeoteleuton and homioarcton. It is not possible to deduce from the characteristics of the correction, how it is formed and where it is placed, whether an error was one of homeoteleuton or homioarcton without access to the exemplar from which the copy was made.

We will use the term, 'skip error', which is less cumbersome, to cover both types of error. The repeated word or characters that trigger a skip error we will define as the 'key word' or 'key characters'. It should be noted that the term dittography (or 'repeat error') is already all-embracing, covering repeats where the key word is at the end or at the beginning of a line and indeed cases where there appears to have been no trigger for the repetition at all.

The second diagnostic characteristic is that pieces of substituted text will have characters which in number are approximate multiples of the average line length of the exemplar, that is the manuscript from which the copy was taken. Unless something unusual has happened, in each case a whole number of lines will have been omitted.

These diagnostic characteristics arise as a result of the way the errors are generated. The eye of the copyist runs from a group of characters at the end of a line, or at the beginning for an error of homioarcton, to the same group of characters in the same position later in the text, so missing out on the intervening portion. It is much more likely that such an error will occur when the key characters are in these positions, rather than in different positions on the line. The letters act as identifiers, guiding the scribe's eye back from the copy he is making to the original text.

The most striking finding is how common skip errors are in both the Old and New Testaments. There are 300 or more scattered liberally throughout the surviving text. It has already been found (see previous chapter) that Milne and Skeat's case for dictation was weak and subject to serious objections, arising from the manner in which the manuscript would have had to be produced and the pattern of cooperation observed between the scribes. The numerous skip errors found in Codex Sinaiticus now provide proof positive that it was copied by visual transcription from one or more exemplars and not produced by dictation. As will be seen, many of the omissions reduced the text to incoherence. These could hardly have all been generated by a reader giving dictation, as Milne and Skeat suggested for all visually generated errors, and then copied without question by the scribes.

We decided first of all to look in detail at a small selection of skip errors from different parts of the Old and New Testaments, not it should be emphasised a statistically valid sample, the purpose being to see how these are presented in practice and the sort of information that can be gleaned from them. Full details of the 12 examples chosen are given in Appendix I. Though the principles are the same as in the English demonstration text used in Chapter 2, we are now dealing with text in Ancient Greek.

To avoid confusion and for the sake of accuracy, we will keep to the lettering as it appears in the original text, chiefly in uncials (capitals). There are a number of differences between the Greek alphabet and the modern Latin-based English alphabet. It should, for example, be noted that Π will appear for P, C usually for S and P for R. In the previous chapter, following Milne and Skeat, English equivalent lettering was used, as in ANTIPATRIDA for ΑΝΤΙΠΑΤΡΙΔΑ and SAMARIAS for CAMAPIAC.

In each example, the text is given as it appears, with the error mark and the correction, usually in the margin or at the top or bottom of the page. An English translation is also provided with the initially omitted, and then subsequently inserted, text shown in brackets. The book and chapter reference is given first followed by the number of characters in the insertion, and the identified corrector.

Our second immediate observation from this preliminary survey is how difficult it will be to draw conclusions about an exemplar on the basis of the skipped text. Even if only one exemplar were involved, one-line skips would still vary a little in length. This is because an exemplar in block column format will have lines varying in length, for a variety of factors including the characters (themselves of varying width) that happen to be in a particular line. This is even though the average could remain fairly constant from page to page. The reader can verify this by taking any typical page of Sinaiticus online and counting characters. If the frequency with which different line lengths occur is plotted, it will be found that the distribution peaks at

13, with most of the lines falling between 11 and 15 characters width. A smaller peak should also be found around five to six characters, representing shorter lines that are at the end of paragraphs. Two-line skips could possibly have an even wider range.

There are a variety of factors that could muddy the picture still further, including the existence of more than one main exemplar and our own possible misidentifications of skip errors. One possibility is that an omitted section might have contained a shorter line at a paragraph break, so that the count of characters omitted no longer fairly represents a multiple of the average line length. Corrections already existing within the omitted section in the exemplar, either as insertions or deletions, could also have had an impact. When the scribe or corrector came to put right the skip error, by writing the omitted section in the margin, he will likely have incorporated these. But he will, in making good an omission within the skipped text, have generated copy of greater length and thus more than would be expected as a multiple of line length. Similarly, by omitting text which has been marked for deletion, he will have generated copy that is shorter than would be expected. He may also have altered spelling or failed to follow the exemplar, when it came to abbreviations for sacred names. Such factors as these will come into the discussion, as the analysis proceeds.

There is a further, practical consideration that arises with multiple-line skips. This can be demonstrated by a consideration of the skip, 42 characters as corrected, in the New Testament Letter to the Galatians 2, 8. Here, Saul/Paul is staking a claim for a mission to the gentiles.

Galatians 2, 8 (42 characters, scribe A, correction by S1)
ΤΗС ΠΕΡΙΤΟΜΗС ˆ Ε
ΝΗΡΓΗС ΕΝ ΚΑΙ ΕΜΟΙ
ˆ Ο ΓΑΡ ΕΝΕΡΓΗСΑС ΠΕΤΡω ΕΙС ΑΠΟСΤΟ ΑΗΝ ΤΗС ΠΕΡΙΤΟΜΗС
' ... to the circumcised. (For he who worked through Peter for the apostolate to the circumcised) worked also through me ... '

It is most definitely a skip, based on a clear key word ΠΕΡΙΤΟΜΗС (circumcised) and with the text reduced to nonsense by the omission. Assuming the skip does reflect the source text, is this an example of a four-line skip from an exemplar of around 10–11 characters line length or an example of a three-line skip from an exemplar of around 14 characters line length?

Of course, an exemplar of around 21 characters or 42 characters line length is theoretically possible from this one example. However, even at this stage, the latter seems most unlikely and the former unlikely, given the consideration in Chapter 2 of the pattern produced by skips of varying line length and evidence of shorter line length skips existing in Codex Sinaiticus.

Our next example from the Old Testament book of Jeremiah appears to show what may have been a simple one-line omission, involving 10 characters. Jeremiah has been given a message to proclaim at the temple.

Jeremiah 8, 9 (10 characters, scribe B, initial correction by Ca)
KAI
ΕΠΤΟΗΘΗCAN ˆ ΟΤΙ
ΤΟΝ ΛΟΓΟΝ ΚΥ ΑΠΕ
ΔΟΚΙΜΑCAN
ˆΚΑΙ ΕΑΛωCAN
' ... and shall be dismayed (and shall be taken) because the word of the Lord they have rejected ... '

The error appears to have occurred because 'dismayed' and 'taken' end in the same letters 'CAN' and the scribe's eye ran on, missing a line. But the text reads quite well without the corrector's addition. So did the scribe simply delete a phrase he thought redundant or the corrector add an elaboration, that in either case just happened to end in the same three letters as the previous piece of text? We shall, in engaging in a more substantive analysis, have to make a rule and stick to it, so as to avoid conscious or unconscious bias, while bearing such possibilities in mind.

Next, in the book of Judges, an angel from God has appeared to Gideon.

Judges 6, 21–22 (49 characters, scribe A, correction by S1)
KAI Ο ΑΓΓΕΛΟΝ ΚΥ ˆ
ˆ ΟΥΤΟC ΕCΤΙΝ ΚΑΙ
ˆ ΕΠΟΡΕΥΘΗ ΑΠΟ ΟΦΘΑΛΜΟΝ ΑΥΤΟΥ Κ(ΑΙ) ΪΔΕΝ ΓΕΔΕωΝ ΟΤΙ Α
ΓΓΕΛΟΝ ΚΥ
'And the angel of the Lord (vanished from his sight. Then Gideon realised the angel of the Lord) this was. And ... '

Here the key word, in the original text is KY (of the Lord). As an abbreviated form of a sacred word, it has in the text a bar line above it. The scribe's eye, in returning to the page of his original, this time ran possibly four or five lines to the next KY and so a much larger chunk of text is missed out. The length of the omitted section in the original will have been four characters longer, if KYPIOY were written out in full.

The generators of Codex Sinaiticus online have in this case identified the correction as being by 'S1', that is one made in the course of production. The text without the omitted piece makes nonsense, which is why possibly the scribe himself recognised that he had made an error and then later went back to the text to deal with it.

In many instances, however, the error was not picked up by the original scribe but identified later and put right by a corrector. Here is part of John's vision of heaven, in Revelation:

Revelation 4, 3–4 (41 characters, scribe A, correction by Ca)
KAI
ÏEPEIC KYKΛOΘEN
TOY ΘPONOY ˆ ΘPONOYC
EIKOCI TECCAPEC
ˆ OMOIωC OPACI CMAPAΓΔINO K(AI) KYKΛOΘEN TOY ΘPONOY
' ... and a rainbow around the throne (in the likeness of an emerald; and around the throne) twenty-four thrones ... '

The omission occurred because the scribe's eye ran on probably either three or four lines from 'throne' to 'throne'. But, in this instance, the scribe failed to pick it up, even though the text without the omitted words does not make sense. The correction was then made by the corrector Ca.

It is not possible on the basis of this preliminary survey to establish the likely average line length of an exemplar for Sinaiticus. The scribes may have used more than one exemplar, perhaps checking one against another for the same book, or they may have used a different main exemplar for some sections of text.

Along with Codex Vaticanus, Codex Sinaiticus is the earliest surviving complete copy of the bible. The possibility has to be entertained that these were among the first attempts to incorporate the Old and New Testaments into one book. In which case, a minimum of two exemplars would have been needed to make Sinaiticus.

One notable factor is that the error of omission involved in a homeoteleuton or homioarcton quite often reduces the remaining text to incoherence, as in two of the examples given above, Judges 6,

21–22 and Revelation 4, 3–4. In the case of the former, the correction is attributed to S1, indicating that it was picked up by one of the scribes in the course of production. But, in the latter case, the correction is attributed to a corrector, identified as Ca.

It is surprising that the scribes would have allowed text that was clearly garbled to pass, without investigating and then identifying and correcting the error. There are in fact a large number of such instances, and this is a factor that deserves further investigation.

Another area of interest is provided by the insertions, made by scribes and correctors, which are not the result of a skip error. Are these also corrections to mistakes in the text and, if so, how did the mistakes occur? If, on the other hand, any were deliberate changes to the exemplar, then how and why were they made?

The gospels of Mark and Matthew provide a potentially fruitful source of study given that these appear, even on superficial investigation, to have a high frequency of corrections involving a number of characters. Mark is also held with justification (see Chapter 7) to be the first of the synoptics written and Matthew replicates large sections of the Markian text.

Based on our provisional conclusion, and after examining these two gospels, we decided that we would not miss any skip errors by concentrating on insertions in the text of these two gospels involving a net increase of eight characters or more. This would also have the benefit of avoiding the large number of small corrections often made to spelling and accentuation.

From Tischendorf onwards, corrections have been identified as having been made by the scribes themselves and by group of around eight or so later correctors. The international team, which generated the online replication of Sinaiticus, noted that some of the correctors (for example Cc and E) confined themselves to certain parts of the text. The team identified a principal 'C' group of correctors who, it says, revised the manuscript between the sixth and seventh centuries.

The team noted that the great majority of changes are to spelling. As already discussed, there was an ongoing evolution of the language, as well as variations in individual style. So that, rather than being corrections of real errors, these may sometimes have been the imposition of the corrector's preference or a reflection of current practice at the time the manuscript was being read.

In all, 58 pieces of text of eight characters net or more inserted by a corrector were identified in Matthew and Mark. These are listed and analysed in Appendix II. For convenience, these insertions are identified sequentially with H and M respectively denoting skips and other errors in Matthew, h and m respectively denoting skips and other errors in Mark. Many of these can be identified as skip errors, on the basis of the presence of a distinct repeated key word or group of characters. Some care was required in identifying skip errors given that there are, as already noted, alternative ways of reinserting the omitted text.

A conservative approach was taken towards identifying skip errors. There were three likely skip errors, where the potential key was a single character. These were provisionally excluded on the grounds that they might have originated by chance. In one case (M1), the key character O ('he' or 'the one') was also a complete word (see Appendix II).

Correctors were, of course, just as human as the scribes themselves. So they could well on occasion have compounded our task now of identifying the type of error by adding their own additional mistakes. Thus it may be that example m1 (see Appendix II) is an example of a skip error where the corrector accidentally omitted the key word KAI in his correction. This again has been conservatively identified as the correction of an error of unknown origin. With example H15, however, it is clear that the corrector must have accidentally omitted the final ME from his correction.

It is quite possible that corrector Ca altered the spelling of an omitted word in example M4, thus disguising what may have been a a possible skip error. Because there is now no match with what could have been the key characters, this was classified as a simple omission or elaboration. In the case of m8 (Mark 14, 7), there is uncharacteristically no correction mark indicating where the insert should be made. This could have been a skip error, if it is assumed that the correction is positioned misleadingly. With a third 'always', which the corrector indicated was in the original, the text gains enormous poetic force:

> *For you always have the poor with you and, whenever you*
> *will, you can always do good to them; but you will not always*
> *have me.*

We have however treated this once again as a correction resulting from an error whose cause is unknown.

Even after these cautious decisions, what comes out compellingly is the frequency of corrections resulting from skip errors, as against other instances where a corrector felt it necessary to insert text. There were 19 found in Matthew and 18 in Mark, about two thirds of the total in each case. Mark is a much shorter work, so the frequency of insertions of substantial quantities of text by correctors is therefore greater in this gospel.

We also examined the text of New Testament Codex Sinaiticus, against other sources, for omissions to see whether there were any that were uncorrected by the scribes or correctors. We found 30 examples of passages entirely omitted, mostly substantial and ranging from the very large (the longer ending of Mark) to the fairly small ('or his mother' omitted at Matthew 15, 6). The bulk of these omissions were shared with Codex Vaticanus. Most could be explained as harmonisations, repetitions, interpolations and explanatory text. Some of the passages may have been known to the Sinaiticus scribes but deemed at the time to be unnecessary or unsound. This is notwithstanding the fact that, in a third of these cases, the repetition of a group of characters or a word could have indicated an error of homeoteleuton or homioarcton.

The doubt surrounding many of these examples, indicating that there is probably a better explanation, is illustrated by the text omitted at Luke 17, 36, 'Two will be in the field: one will be taken and the other left.' This looks like the third part of classic threefold repetition, of one taken and another left, with 'the other left' as the key words generating the homeoteleuton. However, this verse was also omitted in the late second or early third century papyrus manuscript **P**77. In addition to which, the second part of the threefold repetition, verse 17, 35, was also initially omitted in Codex Sinaiticus and corrected in-house by the scribe as presumably a skip error. With his attention thus drawn to the passage, it does seem unlikely that the scribe should have picked up on one verse missed out and not the next. It would therefore appear that either a deliberate decision was made at the time not to include Luke 17, 36 or that the verse was simply not present in the exemplar.

There were two examples (Matthew 15, 6 and Mark 10, 7) that had all the characteristics of skip errors and, in each case, the missing passage was needed to make the surrounding text coherent. These two examples have therefore been included as uncorrected skip errors in Appendix II. It was found that the insertions by correctors increased significantly in frequency in the third and fourth columns of the folio verso. This may indicate that the scribes were motivated to complete a whole folio comprising two pages before taking a proper break, though perhaps pausing briefly to let the ink dry on one side before going on to the next. They would have been more tired by the time they reached the end of such a session and thus more prone to make mistakes.

It is already well established that the corrector described as Ca was responsible for a large number of corrections within the codex. This is reflected in the findings in relation to Matthew and Mark. Ca was involved in correcting 19 of the 37 identified skip errors. Others were corrected in the course of production by the scribes, either A or D or 'S1' where no specific scribe was identified. Just two examples of skip error can be attributed to another corrector, Cb2, although in each case there may be some doubt. In one case, H14 (Matthew 23, 35), the corrector may have put in an explanatory elaboration – indicating that Zechariah was the son of Barachiah. In the other, h16, the corrector may possibly have been harmonising Mark 13, 8 with Matthew 24, 7. If these were not in fact skip errors, it has to be presumed that the repetition, at the end of the correction, of a group of characters located just before the correction is a coincidence.

Cb2 proved to be the only other corrector involved in making substantial insertions to the text of Matthew and Mark. Whereas Ca for the most part dealt with mistakes, including a number of skip errors, Cb2 amended the text and made changes to harmonise text with parallel or related passages elsewhere in the gospels. Thus, in the story of the boy cured of convulsions, Cb2 added the statement attributed to Jesus that 'this kind can only be driven out by prayer' in Mark 9, 29 to Matthew's version (Matthew 17, 21). He also amended both by adding 'and fasting'. In the story of the rich man who had followed the commandments, Cb2 transported the phrase 'from my youth' in Mark 10, 20 to same story in Matthew (Matthew 19, 20), creating a degree of discordance since Matthew's character *is* a young man. In another instance (m7), he made a minor change to harmonise Mark's version of what will happen in the last days (Mark 13, 18) to that in Matthew (Matthew 24, 20).

That Cb2 is a later corrector is demonstrated by changes he made to many other corrections by scribes or by Ca. So, for example, in the story of the boy cured of convulsions in Mark 9, 20, Ca corrected the text, 'And after crying out and convulsing him terribly, it [the evil spirit] came out and the boy was like a corpse', by removing the word 'him'. Ca's alteration may have been an attempt at clarification. Cb2 overrode Ca's correction marks to restore 'him' (AYTON), to conform with what scribe A had written and presumably also with the original exemplar.

In another example, Ca removed a likely alteration to the text of Mark, made by scribe A to harmonise with a passage relating to the same incident in Matthew. The mother of James and John has been canvassing for her sons to receive high positions in Jesus' coming kingdom. It makes sense to see this as coming from an original story, in which Salome and her sons were haggling for something tangible. They were thinking not so much of places in heaven but of positions of authority in an earthly kingdom, once the Romans had been overthrown.[1] The text (Mark 10, 40) reads: 'Then Jesus said to them, "The cup that I drink you will drink and the baptism, with which I am baptised, you will be baptised. But to sit at my right hand or at my left is not mine to grant, but it is for those for whom it has been prepared."' This is the diplomatic response that appears in most versions, including Codex Vaticanus.

The author of Matthew has the words 'by my Father' (ΥΠΟ ΤΟΥ ΠΑΤΡΟϹ ΜΟΥ) at the end of the equivalent passage (Matthew 20, 23). The Sinaiticus scribe, however, also added these words to the story in Mark, it can be presumed to harmonise with Matthew. Ca deleted the harmonisation and Cb2 then restored scribe A's version. This is an example, not included among the examples of insertions because no text is added and the end result, after Cb2's intervention, is for the passage to remain in Sinaiticus as the scribe had written it.

There are many other examples of such alterations made by Cb2. These demonstrate not only that Cb2 is a later corrector but *how* it can be shown to be so: by the corrections made to the work of earlier revisers. It is significant that the same approach yields no result when applied to Ca. We can find no example of Ca changing the work of another corrector, other than that of scribes altering their own work, despite the many thousands of points at which Ca has corrected the text. It is a reasonable conclusion that Ca preceded the other correctors.

Taking changes to the text not positively identified as skip errors, the 21 examples divide three ways. About a third may actually have been skips, either based on one character or with their origin obscured. Another third appear to have been clarifications or elaborations by the corrector, possibly in some cases to restore a phrase the scribe may have seen as redundant. The final third consisted of text inserted, chiefly by Cb2, to harmonise with other passages, usually from Mark to Matthew or vice versa. (See Appendix II for more detail.)

This more detailed examination of Mark and Matthew indicates a possible main exemplar somewhere between 9 and 15 characters average line length. Such a spread, though fairly wide, suggests that there was an exemplar, at least for parts of the New Testament, which had about the same line length as Codex Sinaiticus.

It was decided to explore the situation further by examining a much larger quantity of text. The whole of the New Testament in Sinaiticus was chosen in preference to the Old Testament, which is incomplete and also has its poetical books in a different format, in sense lines over two columns instead of four. Each and every correction in the New Testament was examined to see whether or not it was the result of a skip error. Since there are many thousands of corrections, this proved to be an exacting task, made feasible however by the efforts of the British library-led international team in putting Codex Sinaiticus online. A substantial part of the last book in Sinaiticus, the Shepherd of Hermas, is missing. In the text that remains, 152 examples of skip error have been identified where the key is a group of characters. A further 25 possible examples involve a key which is only a single character.

The references for these are set out in Appendix III. In Appendix IV, we provide a plot in the form of a histogram showing the frequency of skip error, based on a key of more than one character, by number of characters for the four gospels. Appendix V provides this data for the whole of the New Testament. Appendix VI shows the frequency for possible skip errors based on a single character key. In Appendix VII, this data is combined with that for the skips based on a key of multiple characters. Note that, for reasons of space, it was not practicable to include data for a few very large skips on the charts.

This more extensive data does now allow us to draw some conclusions. In the first place, it appears from the concentration of examples in the range 9–15 characters, that single-line skips represent by far the biggest category. Thus it seems that the skip error, which the copyist is most likely to make, happens when two lines are adjacent with characters at the beginning or end of each that are the same.

Secondly, though it is not very clear, a pattern can be discerned (see Appendix VII) of recurrent peaks around 25, 35, 44 and 53/54 characters. Taken together with the initial concentration in the histogram around 9–15 characters, this is consistent with the existence for Sinaiticus of one or more exemplars of 11 to 13 characters average line length. The longer skips may indicate that there was an exemplar that had *either* 11, 12 or 13 characters, but not say 15 characters, average line length. This is because the latter does not fit so well with the pattern generated by the data, as presented in Appendix VII.

One way of examining the robustness of our conclusions so far is to look critically at the main assumptions that have been made.

In looking at Matthew and Mark, it was decided that an insertion with an identified key of only one character could not reliably be assigned as a skip error. So, three possible skip errors were excluded. The reason for excluding them was that the repetition of the key character in conjunction with an omission might have occurred by chance, given the limited number of characters available, rather than as a consequence of the scribe's eye skipping on to a line ending or beginning with the same character. It is also likely that verbalisation, internal or actual, will have played a part in copying. In which case, groups of characters representing syllables or words will have been more likely to have acted as keys than single characters which often do not.

In the New Testament as a whole, we identified 25 such examples. But, as can be seen from Appendix VI, the pattern for these conforms well with the pattern for skip errors based on more than one character. This suggests that many of the single character examples may also have been generated as skip errors. So, we in fact erred on the side of caution in making our initial assumption.

A second assumption was that the word KAI (and), although commonly abbreviated to K in corrections, was written out in full in the original exemplar. The evidence suggests that this was simply shorthand used by correctors to save time and space, especially since the abbreviation is not usually found in the main text in this and other similar manuscripts. We therefore believe the assumption is justified. But, even if it were not, counting the abbreviated KAI as one letter would not have made a significant difference to the overall pattern.

The third assumption was that, when scribes or correctors abbreviated sacred names (nomina sacra), they were reproducing what was there in the exemplar. The justification for this was that the vast majority of the earliest surviving texts of the Old and New Testaments, from the second to the fourth centuries, do make at least some of these abbreviations.

The evidence suggests that the scribes used one main exemplar for the gospels, and possibly also for much of the rest of the New Testament. Given that the gospels were not produced together as one book until the late second or early third century, it is unlikely that its main exemplar could have been from a period earlier than this. If later, as this suggests, the exemplar could well have used some nomina sacra.

The effect, of deciding that the nomina sacra in corrections reproduced what might have been in an original text, has been to exclude two possible examples of skip errors. In Romans 1, 8, there is an insertion by S1 after MOY of ΔIA IY XY (though Jesus Christ). As a seven-letter insert, this has simply to be an elaboration by the scribe to the text. Written in full as ΔIA IHCOY XPICTOY, this could be the correction of an error resulting from the scribe skipping on from the key characters OY to OY and so missing some text. Similarly, in Philippians 1, 27 after EYAΓΓEΛIOY there is an insert by S1 of TOY XY (of Christ). This is either a five-letter insert or the correction of a skip error of text, written in full as TOY XPICTOY.

Excluding these two possible skip errors, of 15 and 10 characters respectively, however, makes no difference to our main conclusion, since these are within the spread that might be expected for an 11 to 13 character average line length exemplar. There is no early papyrus witness for Romans 1, 8. But the mid second century manuscript P46 does contain Philippians 1, 27 with τοy χρυ, indicating that in this instance the Sinaiticus scribe may just have accidentally missed out this text.

In a few other instances that were identified as skips, Luke 24, 51, 1 John 4, 8 and Revelation 4, 5–6, the possible full use of nomina sacra in the exemplar would have made for a slightly longer passage of excluded text. But once again, this is within the expected spread, in these three cases for multiple-line skips.

There are a few surviving papyrus manuscripts containing passages which in Sinaiticus have skip errors involving nomina sacra. These bear out the argument that the earlier manuscripts, and thus probably also the exemplar for Sinaiticus, did use the most common abbreviations. So, for example, P75 which dates from the late second or early third century, abbreviates the word for 'God' to θυ (lower case) in the passage in Luke 14, 15 where it is also abbreviated to ΘY (upper case) by S1 and Ca in Sinaiticus in correcting a skip error. As we have noted, 'of Christ' is likewise abbreviated in Philippians 1, 27.

Of the three assumptions used in calculating skip errors, only the initial exclusion of those that could be based on one key character had a significant impact. Including these strengthens still further the conclusion, based on the distribution of skip errors, that there was at least one main exemplar for Sinaiticus New Testament with an average line length of the order of 11 to 13 characters.

There is a further possibility that needs to be considered. This is that those making corrections may have routinely shortened the diphthongs of an original archaic text from, say, the second or third century to conform with the current practice in the fourth century or later. The passages skipped and then reinserted as corrections could thus have been longer in the original.

The effect would have been greater in terms of characters lost from the original in longer passages, containing more vowels that might originally have been diphthongs. The general pattern (of recurring peaks) that would have been produced by plotting the frequency of characters of these hypothetical originals would then have been much the same as in Appendices IV to VII, except that the values of the medians for one-, two-, three- and four-line skips would be moved on to represent a greater average line length.

There is some evidence that the spelling was changed in copying sources. For example, the text in Mark 4, 28 runs as follows, with the inserted correction in brackets:

ΠΡѠΤΟΝ ΧΟΡΤΟΝ [ΕΙΤΑ СΤΑΧΥΝ] ΕΙΤ' ΕΝ ΠΛΗΡΗ СΙΤΟΝ ΕΝ ΤѠ СΤΑΧΥΙ
(first the shoot/stalk [then a head of grain] then the full head of wheat)

Ca inserted the missing text and put a mark to indicate that the scribe had foreshortened the second ΕΙΤΑ (then) to ΕΙΤ.[2]

There are also instances in the text where diphthongs may have been used in place of vowels. For example, in correcting the skip error in Revelation 19, 9, Ca used ΛΕΓΙ for 'says' instead of ΛΕΓΕΙ. Similarly in making an insertion, not in this case the correction of a skip error, at Hebrews 2, 18, Ca put in ΠΙΡΑСΘΙС for 'having been tested' when he could arguably have used the alternative ΠΕΙΡΑСΘΕΙС.

An examination of the skips of eight-character length shows that some of them may have originated from lines in an exemplar that had one extra character, in ΕΙ diphthongs shortened to Ι by Ca.

It is clear that some of the corrections used spellings that short-ened the length of the omitted original. But there is no evidence that this was on a sufficiently large scale to disturb our findings in respect of the likely average line length of an original exemplar. In many instances, it is now difficult to see from looking at a correction what opportunities there may have been for shortening an original skipped passage. If there has been a slight impact, it will have been to push the direction of the histograms slightly more in the direction of supporting a smaller average line length exemplar. Thus, we can say that the occurrence of such iotacisms marginally increases the chances that an original exemplar was 13 characters average line length as opposed, to say, an exemplar of 11 characters average line length.

We carried out a further check, comparing passages from early papyri that have text corresponding with the skipped passages in Codex Sinaiticus. For the four gospels, 38 corresponding passages were found in examining the text of early papyri fragments dating from the second to third centuries. In 25 of these, the spelling was exactly the same. The 13 exhibiting differences were mostly long passages and in most cases this was a result of corrector Ca using an I for the diphthong EI. But there were also instances where Ca used AI in preference to E. These early papyri texts could be indicative of the format for the main exemplar for Codex Sinaiticus in terms of spelling and abbreviation. What they do not point to is substantial change by the corrector, sufficient to warrant modifying our conclusion as to a possible average line length for a main exemplar.

This now brings our analysis to an interesting point. Given that the average line length for Sinaiticus is 13 characters and given the indications of an exemplar of somewhere between 11 and 13 characters line length for the New Testament, it needs to be considered whether the Sinaiticus scribes were at times seeking to replicate an exemplar, line by line. This might have been seen as an aid to copying. The reason is that, whenever a mistake such as the omission of a word is made, this would be likely to show up through the source and the copy no longer matching. The scribe would thereby have a warning system, alerting him to stop, check, identify and then remedy his mistake. It has however to be said that, if copying were taking place in this way, it did not apparently have a great impact in reducing the number of errors. Codex Sinaiticus has possibly the greatest frequency of corrections among all the New Testament Greek manuscripts.

There is a source of information that could however add some further clarity. It arises from a consideration of just where the skip errors are found, not in the original but in the text as copied by the scribes.

Imagine that an attempt is being made to copy a text exactly, character for character and with the same column width/line length. The scribe succeeds, we will suppose, though just occasionally missing a line or so due to a skip error. As far as he is concerned, the text he is copying and the copy he is making look just the same. The check provided by following the exemplar line by line shows up small mistakes, such as the omission of letters or words. These, the scribe stops and corrects. The skips are, however, not so highlighted because they involve whole lines and so many are missed.

The original we postulate is lost, as is the case with Sinaiticus, and now we are examining the copy. Because the scribe followed the original exactly, and pulled up every time that he could see he would be varying from it, the skip errors will be located in the same place in his copy as the omitted text was in the exemplar.

But now let us suppose that the scribe is not always able to reproduce the text exactly and is also under some pressure, as may well have been the case with Sinaiticus. He cannot afford the time to go back and check whenever he comes off the original, in terms of being in exactly the same place in every line. He will have wandered off at times for several reasons: by accidentally omitting a word, by correcting a dittography in the original, by incorporating a marginal note, by using a different spelling, by adding something to make the text (in his view) read better, by correcting a mistake or by making a change against another exemplar. The pressure he is under, of course, will contribute to the frequency with which he makes mistakes. He does, of course, return to replicate the exemplar exactly every time he follows the original text in starting a paragraph at the beginning of a new line.

The different outcomes, which we have identified, afford the possibility of a diagnostic tool. If text is being reproduced successfully line by line, then a skip error correction will always be situated after the key characters at the end of the line in the copy, as well as the source, in the case of a homeoteleuton. For an error of homioarcton, the correction should likewise always be situated after the key characters at the beginning of a line. This is in either case if the correction ends with the key characters. If the correction is made so as to begin with the key characters, then it will have been inserted before the key characters.

The skip error corrections, when text is being transcribed exactly line by line, should in theory be placed as we have described 100 per cent of the time. However, in the real world, this will be reduced because of errors, corrections and modifications by the scribe transcribing from the source, as well as through the incorporation of marginal material and marked deletions in the exemplar. All of these will have the effect of throwing the source and the copy at least temporarily out of line. A skip error made at such a point would not necessarily occur after or before the key word at the end or beginning of a line in the copy, except by pure chance.

In addition to which, a minority of skips might not have been generated at the end or the beginning of a line. There is also the possibility that we may have misidentified a small number of additions as the correction of skip errors, when these originated in another way, for example as corrector elaborations. The combined effect of these factors will be to reduce from 100 per cent the proportion of cases where, in the copy, the skip is appropriately located after or before the key characters at the end or beginning of a line.

What would be the situation in the case where the copy has a different line length from that of the exemplar? We should then expect that there would be no correlation between the position of the skipped text in the exemplar and the correction in the copy. There are, however, a number of factors that could lead to key characters being located at the end or beginning of a line, even though an exemplar was not being copied line for line. There are, first of all, only so many positions in a line. So, in a small proportion of cases, the key characters might end up in the skip positions by chance.

Keys consisting of a lot of characters, possibly even a group of words, offer more points at which the skip can occur. So these too will increase the odds of possible key characters ending up in the right positions by chance. Keys involving whole words also increase the odds, given a slight tendency by the scribes to avoid where possible splitting words between lines.[3]

Paragraphing also has an impact. If the repetition of the key characters happens to occur at the end of a paragraph (homeoteleuton) in the exemplar, then the scribe will continue after the omission in his copy at the beginning of a new line. If the first occurrence of the key characters happens to occur at the beginning of a paragraph (homioarcton) in the exemplar, then the scribe will continue from this point after making the omission.

Where a list is involved, each item will often be given a separate line almost regardless of the available column width. When
transferred as a whole, any skip errors will then naturally occur at
the end of the line or beginning of the line after the key characters in the copy. A good example is provided in Mark 10, 19 where
Jesus recites commandments that the young man seeking eternal
life should follow. These are each given a separate line in Codex
Sinaiticus, even though they vary from 8 characters for 'do not steal
(MH KΛEψHC) to 17 characters for 'do not bear false witness' (MH
ψEYΔOMAPTYPHCHC). The latter is positively crammed in to fit
the column width.

It does seem probable that separate lines were in this instance also
used in the exemplar. Since all the commandments and therefore
all the lines end in HC, and for that matter begin with MH, this is
a likely place for a skip to happen. And, indeed, the scribe did miss
out on 'do not commit adultery', an error that he did then pick up
and correct.

We cannot, however, deduce from this that an exemplar was being
followed line by line elsewhere than in the list itself. Nor can this
predict the exemplar's average column width in terms of characters
per line since, in this instance as with the copy, the exemplar's scribe
may have been fitting each commandment regardless of length into
a separate line.

If all the various factors are taken into account, then it could be
that key characters in the copy would fall in the positions expected
for a skip error a significant proportion of the time even when no
attempt was being made to reproduce the exemplar exactly. From
the low percentage that might be expected by chance, this could
possibly be as much as a third of the time.

To test our predictions, we made a detailed examination of the
position of all of the skip errors found in New Testament Sinaiticus.
It was found that the key characters for these appeared at the end or
at the beginning of a line in over 60 per cent of cases. This is above
the percentage that might be expected by chance, even allowing for
factors that could increase the percentage.

It is more consistent with what would be expected if text were
being transcribed line by line. It thus supports the proposition that
the main exemplar for the New Testament of Codex Sinaiticus was
written to the same average number of characters per line and so
could have been followed, with at least partial success, by the scribes.
It is also consistent with the distribution of skip errors found,

indicating a main exemplar with an average line length within a narrow range of around 11 to 13 characters.

This examination of the position of skips now adds strength to the argument that a major part of New Testament Sinaiticus may have been copied from an exemplar that had on average the same number of characters per line. The suggestion is that the scribes took the easiest path most of the time, and copied their exemplar as it stood, line by line. But sometimes the source and the copy would have got out of phase, by for example the scribe incorporating a marginal correction in the source. But the scribes would have returned to the format of the exemplar whenever this required a new line. At other points, the scribe making the copy may simply have not felt the need to conform and ended the lines to suit his own preference and style. But the consequence of copying line by line, at least some of the time, would have been skip errors located at the end or beginning of a line, after or before the key word or characters, more frequently than would have been expected by chance. This is indeed what we have found in examining the data. The two uncorrected skip errors identified, Matthew 15, 6 and Mark 10, 7, fit in particularly well as blocks of text precisely matching an exemplar.[4]

Although this is limited progress, it is very illuminating. Our analysis of skip errors has enabled us to find out something about a possible main exemplar for Codex Sinaiticus. But will the same prove to be the case for the type of error that might, in some instances, prove to be the exact converse: where the scribe repeats, instead of missing out, a piece of text?

There are relatively few examples of dittographies involving more than a few characters, as compared with skip errors, throughout Codex Sinaiticus. The comparative rarity of this type of error may reflect the fact that the scribe not only has to make the mistake, in this case skipping back one or more lines, but fail to realise that he is then writing again what he moments ago had already written.

Dittographies could in theory, like skip errors, have characters that are from one or more whole lines, and therefore be a multiple of the exemplar's average line length. This is, it needs to be cautioned, assuming that similar mental processes are at work in both these types of error.

We have identified six cases of dittographies in New Testament Sinaiticus. In two cases, where key words causing the dittography can be identified, the numbers of characters are: 1 Corinthians 1, 8 (60), 1 Thessalonians 2, 13–14 (126). In four other cases, where no key word or characters are apparent, the numbers of characters are: Luke 17, 16 (71), Ephesians 6, 3 (42), Revelation 6, 10 (18) and Revelation 7, 13 (25). See Appendix IX.

It is worth noting that the dittographies tend to be longer than skip errors. This may well be because the copyist is more likely to remember what he has just written in the previous one or two lines, and so avoid repeating it, than if his eye has wandered back several more lines of text. Because there are so few examples and only two of the six examples have identified key words or characters, this limits the scope for drawing conclusions about the exemplar. However, some more may be learned from the examples in Codex Vaticanus (see Chapter 5).

Despite the general likelihood of a scribe remembering what he had just written, there are a few cases where he has accidentally repeated a single word. For example, at Luke 4, 2, scribe A repeated ΟΥΔΕΝ (nothing). At some point in the course of production, this was recognised and dots placed over the repeated word to indicate its deletion. In Luke 21, 30, the repeated word was ΓΕΙΝѠϹΚΕΤΕ (you know), again indicated by deletion dots.

Correctors, just like the scribes, can however occasionally trip up. In the story of the storm on the lake (Luke 8, 24), the disciples alerted Jesus with the cry, 'Master! Master! We are perishing!' Ca deleted the second ΕΠΙϹΤΑΤΑ (master), presumably as an apparent dittography. But the word was probably repeated in the text for dramatic emphasis and as one might, faced with the imminent prospect of drowning. The repetition, also present in **P75** and Codex Vaticanus, was subsequently restored to Codex Sinaiticus by corrector Cb2.

It is possible that, in the longer examples listed above where there is no apparent key, the dittography occurred because the scribe took a break, failed to note properly where he was at in the exemplar and so began again in the wrong place. In Luke 17, 16 and Ephesians 6, 3, the scribe repeated a whole verse and in the two cases in Revelation he repeated a phrase.

In the examples where there is a key involving a group of characters, the scribe's eye appears to have skipped back to these same characters earlier on. A substantial amount of text may in this way be repeated. Here is an example from one of Paul's letters:

1 Corinthians 1, 8 (60 characters, scribe A, corrected by S1)
ΠΟΚΑΛΥΨΙΝΤΟΥΚΥ
ΗΜωΝΙΥΧΥΟCΚΑΙ
ΒΕΒΑΙωCΕΙΥΜΑCΕ
ωCΤΕΛΟΥCΑΝΕΓ
ΚΛΗΤΟΥCΕΝΤΗΗ
ΜΕΡΑΤΟΥΚΥΜΗω(Ν)
ΙΥΧΥ'**OCΚΑΙΒΕΒΑΙ**
(ωCΕΙΥΜΑCΕωCΤΕ
(ΛΟΥCΑΝΕΓΚΛΗΤΟΥC
)(ΕΝΤΗΗΜΕΡΑΤΟΥΚΥ
(ΗΜωΝΙΥΧΥΠICΤΟC
' ... revelation of our Lord Jesus Christ. He will also strengthen you
to the end, so that you are blameless on the day of our Lord Jesus
Christ. **He will also strengthen you to the end, so that you are
blameless on the day of our Lord Jesus Christ.** Faithful ...'

The corrector marked the point (in our copy above with ') in the text
where the dittography began and put brackets alongside the next four
lines where it continued, to signify deletion. The mistake appears to
have been triggered by a group of characters ΤΟΥ ΚΥ ΗΜωΝ ΙΥ ΧΥ
(our Lord Jesus Christ) repeated at an interval in the original exemplar.

As with the other dittography at 1 Thessalonians 2, 13, which also
has an apparent key, the mistake does not appear in the copy as a
block of whole lines. It may be that the visual cue of having a group
of characters repeated at the end or beginning of lines in the exemplar, while being crucial for skip errors, is not always what triggers a
dittography.

The circumstances in which this error is more likely to occur may
be different. So too may the processes in the scribe's mind. It could
simply be that, in these two instances, the scribe had for one reason
or another, fallen out of line in copying from his exemplar. So, while
the key words are not repeated at the ends or beginnings of lines in his
copy, they may have been in the exemplar. With just two examples, it
is hard to draw a conclusion.

Some further insight may be gained from our analysis of dittographies in Codex Vaticanus. But there remains a need for a wider study
embracing more manuscripts and thereby more examples.

The example of repetition from Luke, which has no apparent key, is
interesting because it consists for both copies by the scribe of a whole
block of lines:

Luke 17, 16 (71, scribe A, corrected by Ca)
ΔΟΞΑΖωΝΤΟΝΘΝ
ΚΑΙΕΠΕCΕΝΕΠΙ
ΠΡΟCωΠΟΝΠΑ
ΡΑΤΟΥCΠΟΔΑCΑΥ
ΤΟΥΕΥΧΑΡΙCΤωΝ
ΑΥΤωΚΑΙΑΥΤΟCΗΝ
CΑΜΑΡΙΤΗC
ΚΑΙΕΠΕCΕΝΕΠΙΠΡΟ
CωΠΟΝΠΑΡΑΤΟΥC
ΠΟΔΑCΑΥΤΟΥΕΥ
ΧΑΡΙCΤωΝΑΥΤω
ΚΑΙΑΥΤΟCΗΝCΑ
ΜΑΡΙΤΗC
ΑΠΡΙΘΕΙCΔΕΟ
ΙCΕΙΠΕΝΟΥΧΙΟΙ
' ... glorifying God. And he fell on (his) face at his feet thanking
him. And he was a Samaritan. **And he fell on (his) face at his feet**
thanking him. And he was a Samaritan. But in answer Jesus
said, 'Were not ... '
key: no apparent key

If the scribe were here trying to reproduce his source line for line, then he failed one or both times since the copies do not match each other. The lack of correspondence might in this instance have also been caused by a marginal correction in the source, incorporated by the scribe in different ways each time. Or it could be, as we have suggested, that the adoption of line by line copying from a source in similar column format was uneven and happened not to occur for this particular passage.

The unravelling of skip errors and dittographies in Codex Sinaiticus is proving to be a challenging exercise. But we believe it to be worthwhile if even a small amount of information can be gleaned. Codex Sinaiticus and Codex Vaticanus are the two earliest surviving Greek manuscripts that originally contained the whole of the New Testament and are in large part still intact. While the manuscripts from which these were copied most probably no longer exist, it would be useful to know more about them.

We have deduced that a main exemplar for Codex Sinaiticus had about the same 13 characters average line length. It is thus likely to be later than the earliest papyrus manuscripts that tend to have many more characters in each column line. It may be that the scribes used an exemplar that already contained the gospels, and possibly some of the rest of the New Testament, bound in together. A likely date for this would have been about the end of the second century.

If the scribes did not use even earlier sources for individual gospels, comprising single column papyrus codices of wide column width and so line length, this could have been because these were simply no longer available. By the early fourth century, most will have been destroyed or replaced. Remains of some of the old texts, along with other unwanted paperwork, ended up being discarded as rubbish. One site, excavated by archaeologists at Oxyrhynchus in the Egyptian desert, has yielded a significant proportion of all the papyri now available to us.

If the papyrus manuscripts did not survive long and needed frequent copying, there would have been more opportunities over time for changes to creep in. The picture may then have been one of fairly dynamic evolution, with older copies of texts being discarded and possibly even suppressed when these seemed to conflict with the current theology or interpretation of events.

The question of the column width/line length of the exemplar will also throw some light on the relationship between Codex Sinaiticus and the other early fourth century bible, Codex Vaticanus (see Chapter 5).

The impression conveyed by Skeat's analysis is that Sinaiticus was left as an incomplete manuscript, littered with uncorrected errors, a project abandoned when it was realised that a full production run could not be contemplated with such a large page size. The analysis is faulty, not least because Sinaiticus was produced by copying (as the skip errors and cooperation between scribes powerfully demonstrates) and not by dictation. The project was also completed, apart from the addition of some of the canon table references.

It is just incomprehensible that the largely finished manuscript could have been left to waste, after so much time, effort and use of resources, costing in today's terms possibly around half a million dollars. Yet, it does appear that Sinaiticus was never put to use as a bible for daily reading. The international team examining it found neither the page wear nor the candle wax stains that would have been associated with such use. Why then was it kept for centuries?

The key to the mystery may lie in the identity of the correctors and the timing of the corrections. Although nine or so different correctors have been identified, just one corrector Ca was responsible for the vast bulk of the corrections throughout the Old and New Testaments. Ca made about two-thirds of all the changes to the text. Ten per cent or more were made by the scribes in the course of production. That leaves a relatively small minority for all the other correctors put together.

This general picture, which we arrived at by examining samples of text throughout Sinaiticus, is most definitely confirmed by the analysis of the New Testament skip errors, the most common form of error resulting in the omission of substantial portions of text. Two-thirds were corrected by Ca, just under a third were remedied by scribes in the course of production and only 7 out of the 150, identified as corrected, were put right by other correctors. Two skip errors, we have noted, remained uncorrected.

The sheer number of corrections that had to be made and the cooperation by the two scribes A and D, with sometimes one going ahead in the Old Testament while the other was working on earlier text, suggest that Sinaiticus was being written to a deadline, under pressure of time. There would of course have been plenty of opportunity for the scriptorium's corrector to work on earlier chapters that the scribes had completed, while they were still copying some of the later text. Indeed, if time were a crucial consideration, it would have been imperative to do this.

In a major library and scriptorium, like the one at Caesarea, there would certainly have been someone assigned to the task. Had this person been at any point temporarily unavailable, then a substitute would have been arranged for any project of great significance – such as the production of one of the first complete bibles encompassing the Old and the New Testaments.

The scriptorium corrector (διορθωτής or diorthotes) would have scrutinised sections completed by the scribes and made amendments across the whole of the manuscript. It is thus very puzzling that there is no place for such a person in the schemes posited by Milne and Skeat and by others later. It is especially tantalising, in view of the fact that many of the skip errors generated outcomes that were pure gibberish. This must in general have been apparent to the scribes, pressing on to meet their deadline. They did not fix all the errors, which they knew had taken place, presumably in many instances because they simply did not have the time. This would have been the job of the scriptorium corrector following on closely behind. Indeed, they would surely have alerted the corrector whenever a problem was identified but the cause was not immediately apparent. When they could fix it immediately they did, as evidenced by corrections attributed to the scribes themselves in the course of their work. Otherwise, it was work left to be done.

So, where in the scheme of things is the scriptorium corrector?

There is no certain way of dating either the correctors or their corrections to the text. Ca is accepted as being the earliest, given there is evidence that subsequent correctors like Cb2 overrode or altered his corrections and given the fact that there is no identified instance of Ca changing the work of another corrector. He did however occasionally amend corrections made by the scribes themselves, in the course of producing the manuscript.

Ca is usually assigned to the fifth century CE. This is very much an arbitrary attribution; he could not have been working much later than this because the evidence indicates that his work predates that of the other correctors.

It is an assumption that also adds considerably to the oddity of the situation. We already have to believe that Codex Sinaiticus was inexplicably abandoned after a huge expenditure of time and resources, wilfully left by the scribes full of what were clearly nonsense errors and then retained, even though its utility would have been much reduced by being in such a state. We now have further to believe that it was kept for another 50 or even 100 years and then, and only then, was it subject to the careful and extensive correction needed to turn it into something that could be of use. Why?

There actually is no reason, of style or substance, why the corrector Ca might not have been working much earlier than the fifth century, say in the early or middle part of the fourth century. And that suddenly offers a solution, one which not only satisfactorily resolves a problem but also unlocks the secrets to Sinaiticus' very existence. There would certainly have been a scriptorium corrector and there is only one way, on the evidence, that this could have happened. *Ca must have been the scriptorium corrector!*

As is clearly apparent, he did fulfil this role. He dealt with the work of the scribes across the whole manuscript, providing the detailed scrutiny that was a counterpoise to the need for the scribes to get on swiftly and complete the task, even if it meant making mistakes. As a result of this team effort, the task was effectively completed in the scriptorium and at the time.

To keep the pace, the scribes may have sometimes alerted the corrector when they could see that something did not make sense but could not fathom out immediately what was wrong. Quite possibly, they each kept a record, making notes of passages where there was something apparently wrong that could not immediately be resolved. This would explain the existence of skip errors that produced a nonsensical reading but were left in and then corrected by Ca (as, for example, in Revelation 4, 3–4, p 65 above).

It made no sense assuming that the scribes left uncorrected a number of nonsense errors, which would have been apparent to them at the time, if there was no one available to correct them. But, having identified both the scriptorium corrector and his visible interventions, it now does all make sense. They may have left some such errors unresolved, in order to get on with the work and while leaving Ca to clear them up.

As the scriptorium corrector, Ca did actually do a brilliant job. Taking the New Testament as a whole, he did pick up and correct all of the very many skip errors, bar four attributed to Cb2 and two we have identified as uncorrected. He took a break when it came to Barnabas (so there are no corrections here by Ca) and he left the duplicated section of I Chronicles untouched. Of the four skip errors which we have identified as having been corrected by Cb2, in three cases the correction may instead be an elaboration by Cb2 and in one case an attempt at harmonisation. That is despite the inserted text meeting the requirement for a skip error of a repeated key word or group of characters in the right place.

So Ca, the scriptorium corrector,[5] may have done a near perfect job. As well as putting right the skip errors, he identified and marked a number of dittographies. He corrected other mistakes. He arbitrated, when it came to spelling that reflected differences of style or the evolution of the language over time. It is possible that Ca also introduced a few alterations to make the text conform with another exemplar or source.

The outcome of Ca's efforts was that, when Sinaiticus was completed either to leave or be kept in the scriptorium, the vast majority of the corrections to the text had been made. Instead of around 24,000 corrections, there were maybe only 3 or 4,000 changes made after this point. Some of these were not made to rectify mistakes but to harmonise with other text. Cb2 made a lot of changes of this kind. Some were made to conform with a later corrector's views on grammar, word order, accentuation or spelling. Some represented deliberate alterations to the text, perhaps in the light of another exemplar or the then current doctrine.

Discounting all of these and aside from individual spelling variations, this would have left only a few hundred or so actual errors remaining to be corrected in the codex. The scribes and the scriptorium corrector had done their work. When they had finished, the codex was a fairly accurate document in relation to its sources. It was not however in terms of appearance a tidy document.

The scribes made mistakes, some of which they corrected themselves. Ca did the vast majority of the rest of the corrections in a different coloured ink, which may originally have been red but which has now faded to rust brown. By this means, the accomplishment of each of the scribes was pointed up. They could readily see and learn from what had been their mistakes. It is even possible that their payment might have been adjusted accordingly.

The finished manuscript was undoubtedly untidy, with its many alterations and corrections. But, on the other hand, it was certainly not left brimfull of major mistakes; these had by and large been identified and corrected by the scriptorium corrector. On this issue, Skeat was wrong, as he also was on the question of dictation and the theory of Sinaiticus as a rejected prototype.

But what then *was* the purpose of the codex? The overriding concerns were clearly speed of production and accuracy. This was achieved by the scribes cracking on and the corrector clearing up afterwards. Appearance was evidently less of a consideration, so much so that the finished manuscript, littered as it was with corrections, would probably not have been seen as fit to use as a church bible. The lack of page wear and wax stains from candles also suggest that it was not used in this way.

If accuracy were the most important consideration, and appearance did not really matter, then it may well be that the codex was constructed itself to be an exemplar. Its main source or sources for the Old and New Testaments would have been much earlier, some perhaps in a fragile state. So, Codex Sinaiticus may have been made in order to have a source document, robust enough to be handled and used many times to make more copies.

As a further and no less vital consideration, other source material apart from the main exemplars may have been incorporated in order to have the authorised and approved version all in one book and all in one place. As will be seen, this could mean that some sections of text were edited at this time.

Sinaiticus could have been used to make further copies by direct visual transcription or by dictation. Either way, it would have been an enormous advantage to have such an exemplar, newly made from parchment and strong enough to last for many such exercises over a period of time. Ironically, the manuscript that Skeat wrongly believed was produced by dictation could just possibly have been used subsequently as an exemplar to make copies by this method.

This might explain the one way in which Sinaiticus was not completed, in missing some of the marginal canon table references and omitting the Eusebian canon tables whose intended inclusion was indicated in the quire numbering. It might have been realised that the positioning of the marginal references would be hard to convey by dictation. At the point that it was decided to omit the tables, the scribes stopped putting in the marginal references, since there was no longer any need to complete the exercise.

There is, on the other hand, no direct evidence that dictation was ever used to make copies of the bible to meet the demands of an expanding Church. It is a method, as we have earlier noted, subject to some very severe drawbacks. So it may instead be that it was decided not to include the tables, in copies made using Sinaiticus as an exemplar, in order to make savings in parchment and scribal time. In which case, tables were removed from Sinaiticus and the insertion of marginal references discontinued when this decision was made.

If a large order, such as the one commissioned by the Emperor Constantine, needed to be completed, this could explain why Sinaiticus was apparently generated at such breakneck speed. It was needed as an exemplar that could be handled and it was needed immediately, before any further progress could be made.

Various methods could have been used to speed up the process of copying from Sinaiticus. Even with direct visual transcription, two or more scribes could have worked on an unbound manuscript at the same time, providing they kept to the same format and managed the text so that what was produced filled each sheet and did not run on into another scribe's work.

So it seems that Codex Sinaiticus did after all have a life after its birth in the scriptorium and was not just abandoned as an enormously wasteful and wasted project. It would have continued to be used as a master from which to make further copies for many years, before finally losing its purpose and falling back into disuse and neglect.

How the codex may have related to the history of the time will be considered in Chapter 6. Some of its further secrets will then be teased out in later chapters. For the time being, these are the conclusions reached in this chapter:

- The investigation of skip errors demonstrates that at least one exemplar was used for Codex Sinaiticus with an average line length in the range of 9–15 characters.
- Other evidence indicates that the main exemplar for the New Testament had an average line length of about 13 characters, the same as Sinaiticus itself.
- The codex, far from being abandoned as Skeat has argued, was largely completed.
- Errors were dealt with at the time, either by the scribes or by the scriptorium corrector (Ca), until now wrongly identified as a later corrector, so that what was produced was a reasonably well-finished document.
- Speed and ultimate accuracy, as opposed to appearance, were the prime considerations in creating the codex.
- The codex could have been constructed to act as a robust exemplar, from which to make further copies.

So far, Sinaiticus has held the stage. It is time now to look in more detail at the other early Greek manuscript, Codex Vaticanus, which vies with Sinaiticus in the claim to be the earliest existing complete bible. It will be a task made no easier by the Vatican's refusal to open up the codex for detailed, scientific analysis – in contrast with the approach of the international team headed by the British Library that has put Sinaiticus online. It should nonetheless be possible to throw some light on the provenance of this ancient codex which has been locked away for at least six centuries, possibly even since it was first compiled some 1,700 years ago.

CHAPTER 5

Vaticanus unveiled

It was probably not until the end of the third century or the beginning of the fourth, that an attempt was made to collate the books of the Old and New Testaments. Codex Vaticanus shares with Codex Sinaiticus a particular distinction; these are the two earliest surviving copies of a largely complete bible. They have been dated by handwriting and other aspects of style to the mid fourth century.

As with other ancient manuscripts, there are missing sections especially from the beginning and the end which are most prone to loss and damage. While Sinaiticus has lost a large section from the start of the Old Testament, Vaticanus has suffered most at the end of the New Testament. The Pauline epistles end abruptly at Hebrews 9, 14. As a consequence, most of Hebrews is missing, as well as 1 and 2 Timothy, Titus, Philemon and the Book of Revelation. There are also parts missing towards the beginning of this bible, including most of the book of Genesis.

In its construction, Vaticanus is generally similar to Sinaiticus. It is made up of quires of parchment sewn together and it is written throughout in small Greek uncials, that is upper case lettering. The blocks of text are continuous, apart from paragraph breaks, without spacing between words or punctuation.

However, it differs considerably in the detail. There are generally three columns instead of four to a page and there are more characters on average per line, 17 as opposed to 13 with Sinaiticus. The quires are made up of five sheets of 10 leaves or folios, instead of four of eight leaves.

Fewer scribes have been identified. One scribe, designated as hand B, wrote the whole of the New Testament and worked with one other scribe, hand A, on the Old Testament. There was one contemporaneous corrector and two or three others who made changes to the text later.

There are far fewer corrections and, in consequence, the manuscript generally looks much neater and more presentable. So it might, unlike Sinaiticus, initially have been intended as a working copy to serve a particular Christian community.

One of the oddities of Vaticanus is that at some point in its history the text was carefully written over in its entirety. However, the copyist saved himself the trouble of tracing wording that had been accidentally repeated, that is wherever there were dittographies. So, at these points the underlying apricot coloured writing can been seen against the darker overlay for the rest of the text. There can be no certainty when this was done or why. It would certainly have been a major task, requiring a lot of time.

Like Sinaiticus, the codex is for its age in good condition, exhibiting little sign of the wear and tear that might be expected to have accrued from general use. So it was either made for a church and relatively soon afterwards withdrawn from use. Or it was intended from the outset to be a reference copy. Some support for this idea comes in the form of a number of pairs of horizontal dots (umlauts) spread throughout the margins of the text. It has been argued that these marks were made to indicate the existence of alternate versions of the text in other sources.

The codex could have been kept mainly for reference purposes, but used occasionally for readings. This would account both for the limited wear and the presence of lectionary references in the margins of Acts, which may date from a few centuries after the manuscript was written. The relative paucity of corrections indicates that the manuscript was worked on slowly and carefully to achieve a good result. This contrasts with the conditions under which Sinaiticus was written, where the scribes were apparently in a great hurry. The manner of working also suggests this, with two individual scribes working their way separately through huge portions of text. In Sinaiticus, the scribes often worked together on the same text, with sometimes one going on ahead leaving space for the other to catch up.

Codex Vaticanus has the same simple chapter headings as there are in Sinaiticus. This is indicative of a very early date, earlier than other surviving fourth and fifth century Greek manuscripts. It has less ornamentation which some have argued means that it was written before Sinaiticus. But there is no sure rule that plainer means earlier, particularly with manuscripts that could well have been written within a few years of each other. If the two were in effect contemporaneous, this would indicate that the difference in presentation was a matter of scribal choice, rather than a reflection of period style.

Vaticanus lacks both the Eusebian canon tables and marginal references. Sinaiticus by contrast has most of the marginal references, and the canon tables can be presumed to have originally been in, or intended for, a now-missing quire.

Can Vaticanus be regarded as earlier than Sinaiticus on the evidence of this missing material? Once again, the difference provides no sure test. The presence of part of the Eusebian apparatus means that there is a terminus a quo for Codex Sinaiticus of around 325 CE when the apparatus was first introduced. Sinaiticus could not have been written, with the marginal references, before this time.

But while Vaticanus might have been written earlier, it could just as easily have been produced a few years later. The canon tables were apparently considered and then rejected for Sinaiticus, at a point when the marginal references were still incomplete. The same reasoning that led to this decision could equally well have led to the tables and references, even though at the time available, being excluded from Vaticanus. There is nothing here to prove which manuscript was written first.

In terms of content, these two codices are more similar to each other than they are to other biblical Greek manuscripts from the fourth to the fifth centuries. A number of similarities, such as the omission of the story of the woman taken in adultery (the adulterae pericope) and the use of an abbreviated ending for the gospel of Mark, demonstrate that these are closely related manuscripts. Nearly all the passages that are found to be omitted in Codex Sinaiticus, though included in some later manuscripts, are also excluded in Codex Vaticanus.

Two parallels in particular have led analysts to conclude that they may have been produced at about the same time and even in the same scriptorium. One is the chapter division in Acts which is common to both and used in the Latin Vulgate but found in no other Greek New Testament manuscript. The second is the similarity in writing style between scribe D in Sinaiticus and hand A in Vaticanus, noted by Milne and Skeat. This extends to the decoration (coronis), which amounts to the scribe's signature, used in the colophon at the end of chapters. As can be seen from the reproduction of the coronis for Vaticanus Deuteronomy and for Sinaiticus Mark,[1] these are so similar as to be almost identical – and this suggests that one individual did the work attributed to scribe D and hand A (Fig. 5).[2] Since a scribe can be identified, who may well have worked on both codices, this in turn indicates that these were produced at roughly the same time and in the same place.

colophon Deuteronomy (Codex Vaticanus)

colophon Mark (Codex Sinaiticus)

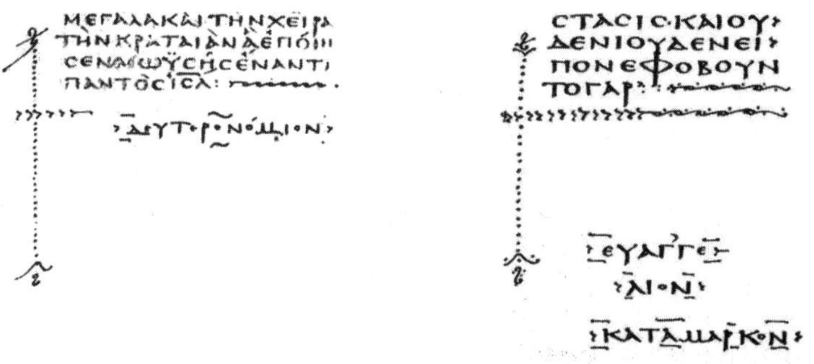

Fig. 5. *Comparison of colophons for hand A in Codex Vaticanus and scribe D in Codex Sinaiticus*

As was noted earlier in Chapter 1, there are also errors common to both manuscripts that are hard to explain as the outcome of coincidence. The best explanation is that there is a link which led to the errors being reproduced in both. But what kind of a link this was, whether for example there might have been a common source for these codices for all or most the New Testament, still needs to be explored.

The examination of spelling variations has been shown to be a method fraught with difficulty when applied to the problem of relating manuscripts to each other and to putative sources. Milne and Skeat failed to demonstrate that Codex Sinaiticus was produced by dictation rather than by visual transcription. Indeed a variety of considerations, including as Jongkind found the working practices of the scribes and our own study of skip errors, indicate strongly that Sinaiticus was in fact directly copied.

Jongkind explored the relationship between the scribes in terms of factors that include the frequency of errors of iotacism, some of which may however reflect permitted variation or the evolution of the language over time. It certainly appears to be the case that the scribes deviated at times from conventions, which had been decided for spelling, in copying from an older exemplar.

It would need a study beyond the scope of this book to determine just what were genuine mistakes and what were the product of a dialogue over orthography between scribes, correctors and the source authors. An investigation of spelling could produce some useful evidence on the relationship between Codex Vaticanus and its possible exemplars. For the present, the emphasis will be on the identification and examination of skip errors that, in the case of Sinaiticus, did throw some light on the format of its exemplars. As already noted, Codex Vaticanus is a more polished document with fewer mistakes and corrections. Its presentation is indicative of a conscious effort made to produce a book that would both look well and read well.

There are, as a consequence, relatively few errors of homeoteleuton/ homioarcton. In New Testament Sinaiticus, 152 instances were found, together with a further 25 possible skip errors based on only one key character. In what survives of New Testament Vaticanus, we found just 14 possible skip errors. In the Old Testament, there were 11 such errors corresponding with passages that are also present in Sinaiticus. For reasons, which will be become clear, these proved to be of more interest than skip errors located where there was no equivalent surviving passage in Sinaiticus.

These examples are set out in Appendix VIII. Although some skips may have been missed, the total number in comparison with those found in Sinaiticus gives an idea of the different circumstances in which the two manuscripts were produced. Greater care may have been exercised, or there may have been less time pressure in producing Vaticanus, such that there were in general fewer scribal errors and so less work for the scriptorium corrector. It may be, as we have suggested, that while Codex Sinaiticus was intended to be an exemplar from which other copies would be made, Codex Vaticanus was intended to be a bible for a church or a reference copy. In either case, appearance as well as accuracy will have been an important consideration.

In 1881, Fenton Hort and Brooke Westcott published an edition of the New Testament in Greek, using the earliest Greek manuscripts then available including and heavily based on Codex Vaticanus and Codex Sinaiticus. In an introduction published the following year, the authors noted that, in the case of Vaticanus, when the scribe made large omissions these were typically between 12 and 14 characters long or multiples thereof. They also noted that that this could often be linked to an error of homeoteleuton. Their deduction was that the scribe for the New Testament was using an exemplar that had lines of this length, that is between 12 and 14 characters. They had also concluded, on the basis of the considerable amount of text the two codices had in common, that Vaticanus and Sinaiticus had a common ancestor.

We have shown how, in principle, omissions due to skip errors should reflect the exemplar's average line length and we have so far applied this to an analysis of skip errors in Codex Sinaiticus. If Vaticanus had been copied from an exemplar of between 12 and 14 characters line length, then the reinstated skip omissions should be around the same length or multiples of it. This would provide support for Westcott and Hort's assertion.

The 25 examples of skip errors listed in Appendix VIII for Codex Vaticanus are unfortunately too few to provide a basis for the type of analysis carried out on Sinaiticus in Chapter 4. But the numbers are consistent with an average 13 character line length exemplar for most of these, taking into account the possibility of skip errors of two, three or more lines.

There are five examples from Isaiah that do not fit into the pattern. The numbers of characters involved are more consistent with an average 17/18 character line length exemplar, the same as Codex Vaticanus itself. This impression is supported by other examples from Isaiah, which are harder to identify as skip errors, but where the text omitted is also a multiple of 17 characters. So, a different exemplar with a larger average line length of around seventeen characters is indicated here.[3]

At this point, some powerful parallels have been thrown up. Codex Sinaiticus has an average thirteen characters line length. It was derived from a main exemplar for the New Testament that, on the evidence, had about the same average line length. Codex Sinaiticus and Codex Vaticanus date from the same period, are textually very similar and have a number of peculiar features in common, including some unique errors and a distinctive chapter organisation for the book of Acts. They can be placed even more firmly in the same context, through the possibility that they shared a scribe. These parallels and association suggest that they may have had a source in common.

But was this a remote source, in each case at a number of removes? Or did they, more simply and directly, share a common exemplar – the same source document for both codices. This would explain features shared by the two codices. The fact that there are also differences would not rule out a main, common source. The scribes and in-house correctors for each could occasionally have used other exemplars, introduced harmonisations, removed errors and repetitions, made mistakes and at points even have consciously moulded the text. The resulting differences that each then share with other, usually later manuscripts, would not preclude a common exemplar for a large part of the text.

There is an even more intriguing possibility. We know that Codex Sinaiticus was not copied from Codex Vaticanus. This is because the length and positioning of skip errors in Sinaiticus indicate an exemplar of 13 characters line length, whereas Vaticanus has an average line length of 17 characters.

But could it be that Codex Vaticanus, with skip errors for the most part (it is hypothesised) of multiples of around the average 13 characters line length for Sinaiticus, was copied at least in part directly from Sinaiticus? It would account for Sinaiticus having the right line length profile for a Vaticanus exemplar and also explain the many features the two codices have in common. Either theory could be right, or possibly to some degree both if the original exemplar and Codex Sinaiticus were available to the Vaticanus scribes. We do, as it happens, have evidence that can throw some light on these ideas.

We have Sinaiticus, which is proposed either as the exemplar for Vaticanus or as a sibling text derived from a common exemplar. We can see if it demonstrates the characteristics to fit either of these theories, in looking at the passages corresponding with those having skip errors in Vaticanus. As would be expected the passages, corresponding to the five examples from Isaiah, which indicate an exemplar of around 17 characters average line length, do not occur in Sinaiticus as whole lines of text. This indicates that in these instances, and thus probably for the writing of the whole of the book of Isaiah, there may have been no direct connection between the two codices.

There is also a passage from Tobit, with a skip of 13 characters, that cannot be expected to be represented as a whole line of text in Sinaiticus, skipped in copying either from Sinaiticus or its exemplar. This is because Codex Vaticanus and Codex Sinaiticus used different Greek versions of this book. The Vaticanus scribe was therefore using a different source and, as would be expected, the skipped passage does not correspond to a whole line of the Sinaiticus text.

Of the five remaining Old Testament examples, there are two with reinserted skips that correspond precisely to whole lines in Codex Sinaiticus. The first of these, from 2 Esdras, 12, 10, appears as an error of homioarcton. This is the text, as it reads in Sinaiticus:

ΚΑΙΗΚΟΥCΕΝCΑ
ΝΑΒΑΛΑΤΘΑΝΡω   (Ca corrects Θ ΑΝΡωΝΕΙ to Ο ΑΡωΝΕΙ)
ΝΕΙΚΑΙΤωΒΙΑΟ
ΔΟΥΛΟCΑΜΜω
ΝΕΙΚΑΙΠΟΝΗΡΟ
ΑΥΤΟΙCΕΓΕΝΕΤΟ
‘ ... and heard it Sanaballat the Haroni and Tobia the slave, the Ammoni, and it was very bad to them ... ’

In Codex Vaticanus, the scribe's eye runs on from the 'NEI' of ΑΡωΝΕΙ (Haroni), which is at the beginning of a line in Sinaiticus, to the same three characters two lines later in ΑΜΜωΝΕΙ (Ammoni) missing out two whole lines, shown above in bold:

ΗΚΟΥCΕΝCΑΝΑΒΑΛΛΑ
ΤΑΡωΝΕΙ ^ΚΑΙΠΟΝΗΡΟ
ΑΥΤΟΙCΕΓΕΝΕΤΟΟΤΙ
^ Κ(ΑΙ)ΤωΒΙΑΟΔΟΥΟCΛΑΜΜωΝΕΙ

The corrector followed the exemplar and found the mistake. The skipped text is two complete lines from Sinaiticus.

It is worth noting that, assuming no direct connection between the two manuscripts, it would be an enormous and unlikely coincidence for such precise correspondence to have happened, even for this one example. What is required is that, not only the skipped passage in Codex Vaticanus happen to start at the beginning of a line in Codex Sinaiticus, but that the passage happen to finish precisely at the end of a line in Codex Sinaiticus. As will be seen, there are so many examples, where the text in Sinaiticus appears exactly as a source would need to be for a skip in Vaticanus, that coincidence as an explanation has to be ruled out.

The second Old Testament example (Judith 8, 6) offers an equally precise match. Translated literally, the extract below from Sinaiticus reads ‘ ... and the Sabbaths, and the eves of the new moons and the new moons and solemn days ... ’

CABBTωNKAICAB
BATWNKAIΠPONOY
MHNIωNKAINOY
MHNIωNKAIEOPTω

In Vaticanus, 'moons and the new' is missed out, and then reinserted. This could either have been a homeoteleuton based on NOY or a homioarcton based on some part of MHNIωNKAI. Shown below is how the text and the correction appear in Codex Vaticanus:

KAICABBATWNKAIΠPO NOYμHNIωNKAI
NOYMHNIωNKAIEOP

The corrector reinserted the omitted text before the key word, for an error of homeoteleuton, and so has the correction beginning, rather than ending with the key word which is, in this case, NOY. He has also used a lower case μ for M. Once this is taken into account, it can be seen that the skipped text again corresponds with a full line in Sinaiticus, with the key words causing the skip positioned at the end of successive lines.

Note that for the present example, while the text in Sinaiticus is coherent, it would also make sense without the second 'moons and the new'. So, the text as it is now in both codices could have originated in an earlier source as a dittography.

In a third example from the Old Testament, a passage was omitted as an apparent skip error in both Sinaiticus and Vaticanus. This is how the text of Nahum 1, 2 appears in Sinaiticus:

CEOYΘCZHΛωTHC
KAIEKΔIKωNKC
METAΘYMOY^EKΔI   ^KAI (added by Ca)
KωNKCTOYCYΠE
NANTIOYCAYTOY
' ... God is jealous and the Lord avenges with wrath. (And) the Lord avenges (against) his enemies ... '

Note that 'the Lord avenges' appears twice, providing dramatic emphasis. But in Vaticanus the phrase is squeezed in a third time, as a correction, into this short passage! And it is this version that has survived into the received text:

ΘCZHΛωТНСКАIЕКΔΙΚ ωNKC EKΔΙ
ΚCΜΕΤΑΘΥΜΟΥΕΚΔΙ
ΚωNΚCΤΟΥCΥΠΕΝΑΝ
'God is zealous and the Lord avenges. (The Lord avenges) with
wrath. The Lord avenges (against) his enemies ... '
key characters: KC

One possible explanation is that the exemplar for Codex Sinaiticus
had deliberately either repeated EKΔIKωNKC (The Lord avenges)
in building up to a climax with a threefold repetition or had simply
repeated the phrase in an error of dittography.

The Sinaiticus scribe (scribe B) then missed out EKΔIKωNKC
(The Lord avenges) from just before 'with wrath', perhaps in
the belief that it was an accidental dittography. The Vaticanus
scribe took the same view, which suggests that he may have been
following Sinaiticus rather than their common exemplar at this
point, while leaving off ωN from 'avenges' at the end of the first
line given above.

A Vaticanus corrector later checked against the exemplar, or
another source, and decided that the repetition could have been
intended and reinserted it. He added the missing ωN, while then
omitting KωN from 'avenges' in his correction.

There are two further examples from the Old Testament where
there is no correspondence between the skipped text and whole lines
in Codex Sinaiticus. These are from Esther which, in both codices, is
the Septuagint version of the original Hebrew text.

Although the number of examples is small, it is surprising to find
two where skips in Old Testament Vaticanus are reflected precisely
in the text in Sinaiticus and a third that appears to be either a skip or
deleted dittography in both codices. The odds are low of this level of
correspondence having happened by chance.

In fact, the six examples from Isaiah, where an average 17 character
line is indicated, and Tobit, known to be from another Greek version,
better reflect what would be expected: that is, no correspondence
at all.

The 14 examples of skips found in New Testament Codex Vaticanus
demonstrate even more powerfully the connection. Where perhaps
one chance example, where the skipped text matched whole lines in
Sinaiticus, might just have happened, there are a total of six including
two in two stages. There are also two examples where the same

passage was skipped in both codices and another where a skip seems to reflect awareness of a correction in Sinaiticus.

The text of Matthew 25, 40 reads literally in Greek as, 'In as much as you did (it) to one of these of the brothers of me the least, you did it to me.' In Vaticanus, 'brothers of me the' is missed out, a skip error based on TWN (the) that greatly reduces the sense of the passage. The error was, however, found and corrected. The corresponding passage from Sinaiticus is shown below:

ΕΦΟϹΟΝΕΠΟΙΗϹΑ
ΤΕΕΝΙΤΟΥΤωΝΤω
ΑΔΕΛΦωΝΜΟΥΤω
ΕΛΑΧΙϹΤωΝΕΜΟΙ
ΕΠΟΙΗϹΑΤΕ

This is how the passage appears in Codex Vaticanus:

ϹΟΝΕΠΟΙΗϹΑΤΕΕΝΙΤΟΥ
ΤωΝΤωΝ^ΕΛΑΧΙϹΤωΝ
ΕΜΟΙΕΠΟΙΗϹΑΤΕ
^ ΑΔΕΛΦωΝμΟΥΤωΝ

As can be seen, the omitted passage in Vaticanus fits in exactly as a one-line skip, an error of homeoteleuton, in Codex Sinaiticus. Two successive lines end in 'the' (TωN shortened to Tω, with the abbreviation indicated by a bar line over the ω). The eye of the Vaticanus scribe skipped between these key letters in returning to the text.

In the second New Testament example, from Mark 10, 19, Jesus is quoted as listing the commandments to the man who wished to inherit eternal life. Here is part of the list in Codex Sinaiticus:

ΜΗΨΕΥΔΟΜΑΡΤΥΡΗϹΗϹ
ΜΗΑΠΟϹΤΕΡΗϹΗϹ
ΤΙΜΑΤΟΝΠΡΑϹΟΥ
'Do not bear false witness. Do not defraud. Honour the father of you ... '

In Vaticanus, the scribe's eye skips from PHCHC to PHCHC and so 'Do not defraud' is missed out:

ΧΕΥϹΗϹΜΗΚΛΨΗϹΜΗ
ΨΕΥΔΟΜΑΡΤΥΡΗϹΗϹ ^
ΤΕΙΜΑΤΟΝΠΑΤΕΡΑϹΟΥ
^ ΜΗΑΠΟϹΤΕΡΗϹΗϹ

While it might be contended that almost any source would have the commandments in the list each given a line, regardless of the column width, that is in fact not the case. In Vaticanus itself, these commandments are allowed to run on and are not on separate lines. It is worth noting that the Sinaiticus scribe, in copying from his source, missed out 'Do not commit adultery' in Mark and 'Do not commit adultery. Do not steal' in the parallel passage in Matthew.

The omitted passage in Codex Vaticanus fits exactly as a skip, a homeoteleuton, in copying from Codex Sinaiticus or its exemplar.

The next example in Acts, involves a quote from a letter sent with Paul to the Roman Governor Felix (Acts 23, 28). Here is the text in Sinaiticus:

ΗΝΕΝΕΚΑΛΟΥΝ
ΑΥΤωΚΑΤΗΓΑΓΟΝ
ΕΙϹΤΟϹΥΝΕΔΡΟΝ
ΑΥΤωΝΟΝΕΥΡΟΝ
' ... for which they accused him. I brought (him) to the Council of them, I found that he ... '

In Vaticanus, 'I brought (him) to the Council of them' is missed out and then reinserted as a correction:

ΑΙΤΙΑΝΔΙΗΝΕΝΕΚΑΛΟΥΝ
ΑΥΤω^ΟΝΕΥΡΟΝΕΓΚΑ (Γ corrected from Ν)
^ ΚΑΤΗΓΑΓΟΝΑΥΤΟΝΕΙϹΤΟϹΥΝΕΔΡΟΙΝΑΥΤωΝ

It does appear as if the copyist's eye has skipped from ΑΥΤω (him) at the beginning of one line to ΑΥΤω at the beginning of a line, two lines later, in an error of homioarcton. The second ΑΥΤω has Ν as an ending, making it 'them', which the Vaticanus scribe may have unconsciously missed out for the text he was copying to make sense. Or he may have considered that the Ν was a scribal slip in the exemplar since, 'As I wanted to know the charge for which they accused them ... ' is clearly wrong, given that only Paul is being accused. With the skip, and as written it reads, ' ... for which they accused him. I found that he ... '

Another example occurs in Romans 9, 3. Sinaiticus reads:

ΓωΑΠΤΟΥΧCΥΠΕΡ
ΤωΝΑΔΕΛΦωΝΜΟΥ
ΤωΝCΥΓΓΕΝωΝΜΟΥ
ΚΑΤΑCΑΡΚΑΟΙΤΙΝΕC

' ... separated from Christ on behalf of the brothers of me, the kinsmen of me according to flesh who ... '

In Vaticanus, the scribe's eye runs from ΤωΝ to ΤωΝ and so misses out a whole line, 'the brothers of me' in another error of homioarcton:

ΥΠΕΡΤωΝ ^
CΥΓΓΕΝωΝΜΟΥΚΑΤΑ
^ ΑΔΕΛΦωΝΜΟΥΤωΝ

The skipped text is here one complete line from Sinaiticus.

Besides these four examples of straightforward skip errors in New Testament Vaticanus, which link to Sinaiticus, there are two possible, more complicated two-stage examples. This is the 'take up your cross' passage in Sinaiticus, Matthew 10, 37:

ΟΦΙΛωΝΠΡΑΗΜΡΑ
ΥΠΕΡΕΜΕΟΥΚΕC
ΤΙΝΜΟΥΑξΙΟC
ΚΑΙΟΦΙΛωΝΥΙΟΝ
ΗΘΥΓΑΤΕΡΑΥΠΕ
ΡΕΜΕΟΥΚΕCΤΙΝ
ΜΟΥΑξΙΟCΚΑΙΟC
ΟΥΛΑΜΒΑΝΙΤΟΝ

'The one loving a father or mother more than me is not worthy of me. And the one loving a son or daughter more than me is not worthy of me. And the one who does not take up the ... '

As shown above, the passage omitted in Vaticanus, 'And the one loving a son or daughter more than me is not worthy of me', while starting at the beginning of a line in Sinaiticus, does not take up a whole number of lines. But it appears nonetheless to have been a two-stage skip error derived from Sinaiticus.

In Vaticanus, the text is as follows:

ΥΠΕΡΕΜΕΟΥΚΕΣΤΙΝΜΟΥ
ΑξΙΟΣ ^ ΚΑΙΟΣΟΥΛΑΜΒΑ
ΝΕΙΤΟΝΣΤΑΥΡΟΝΑΥΤΟΥ
^ Κ(ΑΙ)ΟΦΙΛωΝΥΙΟΝΗΘΥΓΑΤΕΡΑΥΠΕΡΕΜΙΟΥΚΕΣΤΙΝμΟΥΑξΙΟΣ

It is possible that, in reading Sinaiticus or a matching exemplar, the scribe's eye skipped from OC of AξIOC to OC four lines on. So he should then have missed out four whole lines. However, he would have realised that this could not be right since it would lead to the next sentence starting with OY ΛΑΜΒΑΝΕΙ ΤΟΝ CΤΑΥΡΟΝ ('Does not take up the cross'). This would simply not make sense.

He has just written MOY AξIOC (worthy of me) and sees that phrase on the line he believed he was on (line seven in our extract from Sinaiticus above). So he thinks that, in reading, he has accidentally skipped forward a few characters from OC to OC *on that line* (instead of skipping on four whole lines) and continues with 'And the one who does not take up the cross ... ' What he has now copied does make sense, albeit with some text omitted.[4]

The second possible two-stage homeoteleuton from John 17, 15 is very well-known. This is the text in Sinaiticus:

ΤΟΥΚΟCΜΟΥΟΥΚΕ
ΡωΤωΙΝΑΑΡΗCΑΥ
ΤΟΥC**ΕΚΤΟΥΚΟCΜΟΥ**
ΑΛΛΙΝΑΤΗΡΗCΗΑΥ
ΤΟΥCΕΚΤΟΥΠΟΝΗ
ΡΟΥΕΚΤΟΥΚΟCΜΟΥ
ΟΥΚΕΙCΙΝΚΑΘωC
This reads as, ' ... the world. I do not ask that you take them out of the world but that you keep them from the Evil One. Of the world they are not, just as ... '

There are a lot of repeated words in the text, such that it must have been easy to make mistakes. One phrase EK TOY is used successively with slightly different senses: as 'out of the', 'from the' and then as 'of the'. The error of omission in Vaticanus has been ascribed to the scribe accidentally skipping ahead to the second of these, so that he shockingly writes 'I do not ask that you take them ( ) from the Evil One', missing out 'out of the world but that you keep them'. It is in fact not quite so simple. Here is the text, as it appears in Vaticanus:

MOYOYKEPωTωINAA
PHCAYTOYCEKTO YK OCμOY AΛΛA INA THPHCHC AYTOYC
. . . . .   Π NHP
NHPOYEKTOYKOCMOY EK TOY KOCμOY
OYCEICINKAΘωCEΓω

What we have in this passage is a remarkable record, showing just how the scribe made his mistake and the mental processes he went through. In the first place, rather than skip from EK TOY (out of) to EK TOY (from the), he has accidentally begun to skip from KOCMOY ('world') to KOCMOY, also at the end of a line four lines ahead in Sinaiticus. But he is reading ahead, and the text with the skip makes no sense at all to him as, 'I do not ask that you take them out of the world they are not just as I am ... ' This realisation forces him to an abrupt halt and he pauses. He *does in fact pause* in writing what is usually continuous text, *very* uncharacteristically leaving a gap between letters in the word TOY (the). He writes the first letter K of KOCMOY, while realising that the text as he perceives it cannot be right. He looks to see where he might have gone wrong. Remember that, as far as the scribe is aware, he is on the penultimate line of the text as it is quoted in the extract from Sinaiticus above. He has just written EK TOY (of the) and he can see that this phrase occurs on the previous line (line five in Sinaiticus above). So he assumes that this is the point he had actually reached and that he had inadvertently skipped forward a few characters (from EK TOY to EK TOY), missing out ΠONHPOY ('Evil One'). Reading the text this way, 'take them from the Evil One. Of the world they are not ... ' at least makes grammatical sense.

The scribe's intention is to scratch out the K, the last letter written on the previous line, and replace it with ΠO, the first letters of ΠONHPOY. So he writes NHPOY on the next line. But then he is beset with doubt. Can the passage in John really be, 'I do not ask that you take them from the Evil One'? But he is pressed for time and needs to get on. So he alerts the scriptorium corrector, who will be following on checking all of the text, or he makes a note to go back and sort the matter out later. Or possibly, he left the uncharacteristic gap in the text as a pointer to alert the corrector.

When the offending text is later examined carefully against the exemplar, the real error is spotted. And it is corrected by a series of wholesale alterations. NHPOY is marked with dots to show it is deleted. KOCMOY is changed to ΠONHPOY by writing new characters over the ones to be changed. New text is written in smaller characters in the margin alongside the two altered lines. The K of KOCMOY is retained and the rest of the word is continued in smaller letters, though using a lower case μ in place of M. This restores the passage to match the text in the exemplar – to match in fact Sinaiticus, or an identical version of it.

The text in Vaticanus, with its progressive errors, hesitations and alterations, provides against Sinaiticus an enlightening record of the processes the scribe and his corrector went through to generate what is there in the text now. It shows what the exemplar was and it only really makes sense against what the exemplar was, which is what the text in Codex Sinaiticus is now.

In addition to the examples of skip errors matching the text in Codex Sinaiticus, there are two cases where it appears, as in the passage from Nahum, that a piece of text has been skipped in both codices. In Matthew 15, 5–6 (which follows Mark 7, 11–13), Jesus is given to attack the Pharisees and scribes for concocting a scheme, to avoid financial responsibility for their parents, by designating some of their funds as 'korban', that is sacred and not available for personal use. This is the text from Sinaiticus:

ΥΜΙϹΔΕΛΕΓΕΤΕΟϹΑ
ΕΙΠΗΤⲰΠΡΙΗΤΗΜΡΙ
ΔⲰΡΟΝΟΕΑΝΕ𐅷Θ
ΜΟΥⲰΦΕΛΗΘΗϹ
ΟΥΔΕΝΕϹΤΙΝΟΥΜΗ
ΤΙΜΗϹΗΤΟΝΠΡΑΑΥ
(ΤΟΥΗΤΗΝΜΡΑΑΥ)
ΤΟΥΚΑΙΗΚΥΡⲰϹΑ

'But you say, whoever says to his father or his mother whatever from me you might have benefited from is korban. Anything is. By no means, does he honour his father (or his mother). And you nullify ... ' ('Anything is' was deleted by S1)

In this paragraph and in the preceding paragraph, 'father or mother' is referred to three times. Yet the conclusion 'by no means does he honour his father' refers to only one parent. So, towards the end, 'or his mother' (H THN MPA AYTOY) appears to have been missed out. This is a conclusion reinforced by the fact that the missing words do appear in this position in the parallel passage in Mark, on which Matthew is based.

In Codex Vaticanus, the same uncorrected omission is made. The relevant text reads, with the omitted text indicated in brackets:

ΜΗϹΕΙΤΟΝΠΑΤΕΡΑΑΥ (ΤΟΥΗΤΗΝΜΡΑΑΥ)
ΤΟΥΚΑΙΗΚΥΡΩϹΑΤΕ

Other, later texts do have 'or his mother'. It would be an unlikely coincidence if this phrase were present in a common exemplar for Sinaiticus and Vaticanus, but in both cases the scribes happened at this point to make the same error, skipping from (say) TOY to TOY to miss one full line of twelve characters.

It is possible that a common exemplar for the two codices missed out the phrase and that this was then copied for both codices, given that the passage with the omission though it is awkward still makes sense. Alternatively, the Sinaiticus scribe did make a skip error. The Vaticanus scribe would then have been copying from Sinaiticus, rather than the exemplar that had the missing phrase, and that would be why he also missed it out.

The omitted text fits in perfectly in Codex Sinaiticus as a 12 character error of homioarcton, shown in the text above in brackets. This gives support to the idea that this was a skip error by the Sinaiticus scribe in copying from his exemplar, in the same line format, that was then copied from Sinaiticus by the Vaticanus scribe. We would otherwise have to presume that, by an extraordinary and unlikely coincidence, the scribe for the exemplar for Sinaiticus was also copying from an, at this point, identical exemplar and made the skip, which was then copied in both Codex Sinaiticus and Codex Vaticanus.

A similar, possibly even more compelling, example is provided by a phrase omitted in both codices from Mark 10, 7. Jesus is here given to reply to testing questions from Pharisees on the question of divorce. This is how the text appears in Sinaiticus, with the missing lines of text in brackets:

ΚΑΤΑΛΙΨΙΑΝΘΡѠΠѠ
ΤΟΝΠΡΑΑΥΤΟΥΚΑΙ
ΤΗΝΜΡΑΑΥΤΟΥΚΑΙ
(ΠΡΟCΚΟΛΛΗΘΗCΕ
ΤΑΙΠΡΟCΤΗΝΓΥΝ
ΑΙΚΑΑΥΤΟΥΚΑΙ)
ΕCΟΝΤΑΙΟΙΔΥΟΕΙC
CΑΡΚΑΜΙΑΝѠCΤΕ

' ... a man will leave his father and mother and (he will be joined to his wife. And) the two will be one flesh. For this reason ... '

Without the omitted passage, the text makes no sense. It lacks the necessary reference to the joining of a man to his wife to explain the reference to two becoming one flesh. The omission occurs in Codex Sinaiticus and it is repeated in Codex Vaticanus. The uncorrected omission is given below the text in brackets:

ΕΝΕΚΕΝΤΟΥΤΟΥΚΑΤΑ
ΛΙΨΕΙΑΝΘΡѠΠΟCΤΟΝ
ΠΑΤΕΡΑΑΥΤΟΥΚΑΙΤΗΝ
ΜΗΤΕΡΑΚΑΙ( )ΕCΟΝΤΑΙΟΙ
ΔΥΟΕΙCCΑΡΚΑΜΙΑΝѠC
(ΠΡΟCΚΟΛΛΗΘΗCΕΤΑΙΠΡΟCΤΗΝΓΥΝΑΙΚΑΑΥΤΟΥΚΑΙ)

The omission fits perfectly as a 38-character three-line error of homeoteleuton in Codex Sinaiticus, committed by the scribe in copying from his exemplar of average line length of around 13 characters, just like Sinaiticus. It occurs as a block of text of one or more lines from the exemplar omitted at the end of a line in the copy, the skip generated by the repetition of the key characters 'ΑΥΤΟΥΚΑΙ'. Positioned in this way, it indicates, just like the previous example, that at this point the Sinaiticus scribe was copying from his exemplar, line by line. This conclusion was also drawn from a wider examination of the position of skips (see Chapter 4).

The repetition of the same, uncorrected nonsense error in Codex Vaticanus can only satisfactorily be explained by the proposition that the Vaticanus scribe was at this point copying from Codex Sinaiticus as his exemplar. It is highly improbable that the scribe could, just by chance, have happened to make precisely the same blunder (though for different reasons) at the same point in the text and left it uncorrected.

It is also unlikely that the error could have occurred in an exemplar at one or more removes from both codices, then to be transmitted uncorrected, despite the obvious unintelligibility of the cut copy, through separate lines to both codices. Such a proposition would, of course, presume another remarkable coincidence: that the source, which had the correct and full version, just happened to be written to an average 13 characters per line and happened at this point to reproduce the exact format of the text in Codex Sinaiticus.

It could be argued that the error was originally a two-line, 19 characters per line skip or even a one-line 38-character skip from a single column papyrus. But this then presumes that, when Sinaiticus was written, the text prior to the omission happened by chance to have gone up to the end of a line, in just the right position for an error of homeoteleuton. It also leaves unresolved the problem of how the obvious error remained over time in two separate lines of transmission, when it could have been resolved either by intelligent amendment or by reference to other sources that had the text in full. It is furthermore not a line of argument that can be applied to the skipped text, amounting to 13 characters, missing from both codices at Matthew 15, 6 in the previous example. As a skip, this can only have been a single line.

The simplest and best explanation, which accords with the other agreements found between skipped text in Vaticanus and the layout of Sinaiticus, is that the Vaticanus scribes were at this point copying from Codex Sinaiticus as their source.

The skip in Codex Vaticanus that seems to reflect awareness of the Sinaiticus text occurs in 1 Peter 1, 1. This is part of a list of the intended recipients of the letter:

ΓΑΛΑΤΕΙΑСΚΑΠΠΑ
ΔΟΚΕΙΑС^**ΚΑΙΒΙΘΥ**   ^ACIAC
ΝΙΑСΚΑΤΑΠΡΟΓΝω
'... of Galatia, of Cappadocia, of Asia and of Bithynia according to the foreknowledge ...'

Ca inserts ACIAC ('Asia') via a correction mark and marginal note, it may well be because the word has been accidentally omitted. It is hard to see a reason why Ca might have inserted ACIAC as his own elaboration. In addition to which, the word was also present in the text of **P**72 that dates from the late third or early fourth century.

The Vaticanus scribe who wrote this passage has the following:

ΠΟΝΤΟΥΓΑΛΑΤΙΑΣΚΑΠ
ΠΑΔΟΚΙΑΣ ΑΣΙΑΣΚΑΤΑ
ΠΡΟΓΝѠϹΙΝΟΥΠΑΤΡΟϹ
correction in left-hand margin: ΚΑΙ ΒΙΘΥΝΙΑϹ
' ... of Pontos, of Galatia, of Cappadocia, of Asia (and of Bithynia)
according to the foreknowledge of God the father ... '
key characters: ΙΑϹ

As with the two-stage skip identified for John 17, 15 (see p 103), there is a highly unusual gap in the continuous text. This points to a place in the text where the scribe paused to consider, and it may be deliberately left a gap to alert the scriptorium corrector or himself following on later to check the text. The gap is before ΑϹΙΑϹ. If we work on the assumption that Codex Vaticanus was here copied from or with reference to Codex Sinaiticus, then we can look at Sinaiticus to see if there is anything that offers an explanation.

In this case, there is a possible explanation. The Vaticanus scribe may have paused before ΑϹΙΑϹ because he was uncertain whether or not to include the insertion among the places for which the letter was intended. Perhaps it was not in the original exemplar from which Sinaiticus was copied. Or possibly the Sinaiticus scribe felt that ΑϹΙΑϹ was an oddity among the places listed. The term may have been applied to a particular region. But it had also, then as now, the connotation of the whole continent. This is why the Sinaiticus scribe may have omitted it, only for it to be reinstated by the scriptorium corrector Ca.

Before incorporating Ca's correction, the Vaticanus scribe had just written ΙΑϹ from the previous word ΚΑΠΠΑΔΟΚΙΑϹ. The pause having deflected him, we suggest that, when he looked back to find his place, his eye alighted on the wrong ΙΑϹ on the next line. He continued from that point, missing out ΚΑΙ ΒΙΘΥΝΙΑϹ, an error that was later corrected. It could be that what induced the skip in Vaticanus here was the problem of what to do with an insert of ΑϹΙΑϹ in Sinaiticus by Ca.

There are thus nine examples of skip errors in New Testament Codex Vaticanus that associate strongly with the text of Codex Sinaiticus: four examples of straightforward skip errors, two examples of skips in two stages, two skips common to both and a skip apparently triggered by a correction. This degree of correspondence, backed by the associations found in the Old Testament examples, could not have happened by coincidence and positively establishes the link between the two manuscripts.

If it is accepted that the connection has been established, the remaining five examples are then not beyond explanation. In Mark 10, 46, the omission and then reinstatement of a sentence beginning with KAI in Vaticanus could well have been the product of different views as to whether that sentence should be included. Skips involving KAI (and) as a key word need to be treated with more than usual caution since this word is frequently used to start sentences. In this instance the sentence, 'And they came to Jericho', was probably deleted by the Vaticanus scribe because nothing is said of what happened in Jericho. The next sentence begins, 'And, having left Jericho ... ' So it may not have been a skip after all.[5]

Other text could similarly have been omitted deliberately while coincidentally giving the appearance of a skip error. This could be what happened with text missing from John 1, 13, 'nor of the will of a husband'. Since this is apparently already covered by 'not of blood, nor of the will of the flesh', the Vaticanus scribe might have decided to eliminate it but then been overruled by his corrector. The full version also appears in the second century papyrus manuscript P66, indicating that the corrector was probably right and the phrase had been in the exemplar.

The phrase 'and might kill' added or restored to Matthew 26, 4 might have been, instead of the correction of a skip error, harmonisation by the corrector to Mark 14, 1 and Matthew 12, 14. The phrase is, however, present in the early third century papyrus manuscript P45.

The omission in Luke 22, 40 is just one word, ΕΙΣΕΛΘΕΙΝ (to enter) and could have happened as an inadvertent skip within a single line of the exemplar. Finally, 1 John 4, 21, could provide an example of a mid-line skip where the key word ΤΟΝ (the) occurs in the same position in successive lines in Sinaiticus.

We are not suggesting these five examples should be explained away, though it does appear on reflection that the one from Mark was not a skip error. We are arguing first of all that the other nine examples furnish a compelling case for a direct link between the two codices. While the other five cases do not provide any positive support, neither do they render the case for a direct link between the two codices invalid.

The 14 skip errors found in New Testament Codex Vaticanus are included for reference in Appendix VIII.

The link between the two codices, which we have established, is much more than the possibility of a common ancestor that Hort suggested. The Vaticanus scribes were copying directly from a manuscript that, in many places, precisely matched Codex Sinaiticus or were copying from Sinaiticus itself. It is not likely, especially from what we have observed of the processes involved, that the scribes for these two codices were copying in each instance from separate, though precisely corresponding, exemplars. It is far more likely that they had to hand and used the *same* common exemplar, that is the same physical manuscript. It was what Westcott and Hort termed a proximate source. This would fit with that we know about the codices, including their similarities in content and style and extending to the possibility that one scribe was involved in both projects.

If the codices had the same common exemplar, for Vaticanus to generate skip errors that replicated lines of Sinaiticus exactly, then this means that Sinaiticus was reproducing not merely the text but in many places line by line the format of its exemplar. In the last chapter, we concluded that Sinaiticus had an exemplar of about the same average line length of 13 characters and found evidence to indicate that its scribes were, for at least some of time, reproducing it line by line.

Codex Sinaiticus, as we have found, is full of mistakes and corrections: changes to spelling, harmonisations to other text, additional flourishes by the scribe, accidental omissions and repetitions. In addition to this, it is probable that the exemplar was not perfect and may have had unrecognised errors as well as marginal notes and corrections of its own to be incorporated. All of these would have had the effect of throwing Sinaiticus off track in copying from its postulated same-format exemplar.

So, lines of characters would match only some of the time. That in turn would be enough to explain why Codex Vaticanus, copied from the same exemplar, might not always have generated skip errors that matched lines in Codex Sinaiticus.

The match is, however, extraordinarily close, with even the exceptions for the 14 examples from the New Testament capable of explanation. Instead of using a common, proximate exemplar, the Vaticanus scribes could well have been copying from Codex Sinaiticus itself.

Errors that the manuscripts have in common tend to support this as an explanation. For example, in Mark 1, 27 both codices have 'to discuss other' instead of 'to discuss with each other'. It is possible that this arose in their common exemplar, where it was unnoticed and uncorrected, and was then separately copied into Codex Sinaiticus and Codex Vaticanus, where in both cases it was also unnoticed and uncorrected. However, this involves three stages. The two-stage explanation, that the error occurred in Sinaiticus and was copied into Vaticanus, is less complicated and seems more likely.

The two pieces of omitted text discussed above, from Matthew 15, 6 and Mark 10, 7, also lend support to the idea of direct copying. Not only are fewer stages involved, but in these cases the evidence is that these were skip errors that occurred when the Sinaiticus scribe copied from his exemplar. The full text would thus have been in the exemplar for the Vaticanus scribe to see. It is much more probable that this scribe copied the text with the omission from Codex Sinaiticus, than happened by pure fluke to make the same mistake at the same point in copying from a common exemplar. It is, if anything, even more improbable that the skip, involving a previous source, was already in a common exemplar and happened then to show up with all the features of a skip generated in line-by-line copying in Codex Sinaiticus.

One small variation from other, later Greek manuscripts, the absence in both codices of EIKH, 'without cause' from Matthew 5, 22, could reflect an error made in Codex Sinaiticus in copying from the exemplar, followed by the Vaticanus scribe. Alternatively, both may have been true to their common exemplar, especially given that the earlier papyrus manuscript P67 also lacks EIKH, 'without cause'. Later copyists might simply have decided that 'Everyone who is angry with his brother will be subject to judgment' was, without qualification, unduly harsh. A later corrector, Cb2, added EIKH to the text of Sinaiticus Matthew.

It will be demonstrated later (see Chapter 13) that changes were introduced for some of the sheets of Codex Sinaiticus, possibly through a second exemplar. Given that the Vaticanus scribe followed Codex Sinaiticus for these passages, it is apparent that he was also aware of what was happening with Sinaiticus. There are also instances (see discussion of 1 Peter 1, 1, p 108 above) where the Vaticanus scribe appears to be responding to a correction made in Sinaiticus. In the case of the amendment to Matthew 27, 56 (see pp 188–194) the corrector was making changes to what was in the exemplar used by scribe A. So, here again the Codex Vaticanus scribe, in following the corrected copy, demonstrated his awareness of Codex Sinaiticus.

The corrections in both these instances were made by Ca. Given that the Vaticanus scribe generally followed Ca's changes, both here and elsewhere, this establishes that the changes by Ca were made in the period after Codex Sinaiticus had been drafted and before Codex Vaticanus was written. There are strong links between the two codices, indicating that they may well have been written in the same place and with a scribe in common. So the time gap, during which Ca could have made his corrections, is likely to have been fairly short. This reinforces the case (see Chapter 4, p 85) that Ca was in fact the scriptorium corrector for Codex Sinaiticus.

It is notable that, where the scriptorium corrector Ca made changes to the text of New Testament Codex Sinaiticus, the text of Codex Vaticanus often followed these, especially for substantive modifications. So, for example, in Luke 23, 34, the cry from the cross attributed to Jesus was included by scribe A but deleted by Ca. The version with the deletion is followed in Codex Vaticanus, in line with both the earlier papyrus manuscript P75 and Ca's amendment of Sinaiticus. The same goes for the note in Luke 23, 38 that the inscription on the cross was given in three languages: included by scribe A, deleted by Ca and absent in Codex Vaticanus and P75.[6] The description of the agony at the Mount of Olives in Luke 22, 43–44, was likewise included by scribe A, deleted by Ca and absent in Codex Vaticanus and P75.

We established, through the pattern of skip errors in Codex Sinaiticus and the average line length in terms of number of characters for Codex Vaticanus, that the former could not have been copied from the latter. The detail of the Codex Vaticanus skip errors, on the other hand, indicates that this codex must in many places either have been copied from a common, proximate exemplar, or alternatively, with reference to Codex Sinaiticus itself. There are errors and other common features that lend strong weight to this latter explanation.

The agreement of Codex Vaticanus with Ca, rather than with scribe A, especially where this corrector has made substantive changes, raises some interesting questions. If scribe A, who wrote most of Sinaiticus, deviated at times from a form of text finally adopted in both codices, why did he do so and from where did he get his information? This is a question that will recur in Chapter 10, in a consideration of significant changes to a verse in Matthew describing the women present at the cross.

Our conclusion, reached on separate grounds in the previous chapter, that Ca must have been a contemporary, would resolve the issue. The manuscript of Sinaiticus, which the Vaticanus scribes likely had available, would have included corrections by the scriptorium corrector Ca. The latter would likewise have had access to the exemplars used by the Sinaiticus scribes. We will be suggesting (see Chapters 11–13) that some of the text in scribe A's exemplar, or exemplars, was excluded in favour of other versions. Corrections by Ca could thus have been part of the means by which this text was modified.

The links between Codex Vaticanus and Codex Sinaiticus operate powerfully on several levels: through unique errors and common styles, including the chapter division in Acts, through the many omissions that the codices share in contrast with other manuscripts and through the replication of the format of Sinaiticus in the skip errors by Codex Vaticanus. We have noted also that Vaticanus adopts some substantive editing by the scriptorium corrector Ca and also, as will be concluded, by a second Sinaiticus scribe. All of this means that the Vaticanus scribes must have had Codex Sinaiticus available to them. They clearly at times used other exemplars, for example for Tobit where a different Greek source can be identified and for Isaiah where the skip errors indicate an exemplar of around 17 characters line length. They may well have checked the text of Sinaiticus against other sources.

Analysis of handwriting and content indicates that the codices date from the same period, that is mid fourth century CE, and similarities of style indicate that they might have been produced in the same scriptorium. There are indeed parallels in the design of the decorative coronides at the end of chapters and in handwriting, indicating that one scribe may have worked on both codices. So it is more than possible these two manuscripts were produced in the same place and within a short time of each other. The scribe for Codex Vaticanus could thus have had the advantage of Codex Sinaiticus as an exemplar, for the core of the New Testament, as well as the source manuscripts for Sinaiticus to use and check against to resolve any difficulties.

The finding that Codex Vaticanus was, at least in part, most probably copied from Codex Sinaiticus is important though not, as might seem on first reflection, unlikely. We have already established that Codex Sinaiticus may well have been constructed as a robust exemplar, from which to make further copies. Possibly, no more than 100 complete bibles were generated, at some substantial cost, during the fourth century. So it is not against the odds that, of these, a main exemplar was cherished and survived and that the other surviving copy is related to it.

Errors of dittography, as was pointed out in the previous chapter, could also in theory provide a means of identifying the average line length of an exemplar. This is because the error can occur when the scribe picks up on characters that had previously occurred in the same place at the beginning or end of a line, and so inadvertently repeat several whole lines of text. As with skip errors, the number of characters should then be a multiple of the exemplar's average line length.

There are, however, a number of problems with using this as a diagnostic tool. In the first place, dittographies embodying portions of text are usually very long, so that it becomes more difficult to decide what the multiple of the exemplar's average line length may have been. These errors are also found to occur less frequently than skip errors. So it is hard to make deductions with any degree of confidence.

Of the six dittographies found in New Testament Sinaiticus, only two were identified with repeated characters that could have triggered the scribe's eye wandering back to repeat a portion of text. This compares with twelve examples found in the New Testament of Codex Vaticanus (see Appendix IX). Here, there were eight cases, mostly outside of the gospels, identified with repeated groups of characters or whole words, associated with the skip back to repeat a portion of text.

If the numbers for both skip errors and dittographies are considered for these two codices, it is possible to draw some conclusions. One is that the Codex Vaticanus examples bear out the conclusions from the previous chapter that dittographies tend on average to involve more copy than skip errors. In terms of pieces of text, as opposed to a few characters or a single word, these errors were found to be far less common than skip errors in Codex Sinaiticus.

This is in line with the conclusion reached by Colwell, from his examination of the papyrus manuscripts P45, P66 and P75, that the scribe seeking to find his place looked ahead three times as often as he looked back.[7] In other words, he found errors of homeoteleuton and homioarcton (skip errors) to be roughly three times more common than errors of dittography.

In Codex Sinaiticus, this is a position that is even more exaggerated. Skip errors in the New Testament are of the order of 20 times more common, even assuming that we have in our investigation failed to identify some errors of dittography. We suggest that this is a product of what we have deduced from the evidence, particularly the frequency of mistakes and the appearance of the manuscript, that the Sinaiticus scribes were under some pressure and pressing on to complete their task. They were quite literally looking ahead, and thus more likely to skip text when their eyes returned each time from the copy they were making to the exemplar.

In the case of Codex Vaticanus, the circumstances must have been very different. There are relatively few skip errors or dittographies. The outcome is a much better looking manuscript. We suggest that here, accuracy and presentation were the most important considerations, as opposed to completing the task to a deadline.

In New Testament Vaticanus, there are about as many of each type of error. This suggests that, while focus and methodical working may have made it less likely that a scribe might accidentally skip ahead, this did little or nothing to help reduce the number of dittographies or skips backwards. Indeed, in comparison with Codex Sinaiticus and bearing in mind that the numbers involved are small, it could even have made such errors marginally more likely.

The likely mental mechanics involved in dittographies does throw some light on these considerations. About half of the examples in Codex Sinaiticus and Codex Vaticanus did involve a key word or group of characters that the scribe's eyes skipped back to, so causing him to repeat some text. It may be that this happened in the normal way of copying the text. However, it could on occasions have been that the scribe took a break, making a note of the characters at the end of the line he had reached in the exemplar, and then found the wrong line with the same characters at the end, on returning to the text. He could even have followed some other means of marking his position and got it wrong, such that no key characters were involved. These processes mimic to some degree those involved in skip errors, except that the skip is backwards instead of forwards.

There is, however, a crucial difference between the two types of error. This is that, with a dittography, the scribe is actually repeating text he has already written. That he should remember this, and so realise and abort his error, may be the reason that these errors are in general less frequent. As Dain has noted, copying proceeds through a form of internal dictation. Indeed, with silent reading probably not at the time established, the scribe may well have been reading the text to himself. He has to remember what he has just read, and then said, copy it and then wipe the information from his mind so as to accommodate the next piece of text. What we suggest may happen, especially with some of the dittographies not based on any key characters, is that the scribe fails to clear his mind and so writes a piece of text a second time.

In the case of Codex Vaticanus, we suggest that the scribes were under instruction to get it right if at all possible the first time, so as to produce an accurate copy that also looked good. So they were forced to go slowly and deliberately, looking hard at the text and even looking back at the text. The task must have been experienced as tedious and repetitive and not surprisingly their minds must have wandered some of the time. Under such conditions, we suggest, a scribe might have been less likely to identify that he was semi-automatically repeating what he had already just written.

Given that there are few examples and given that four of the 12 identified dittographies do not have any apparent repeated key characters to trigger the error, the scope for examining the text of Vaticanus for these errors against Sinaiticus is limited. It is difficult to assess the remaining eight examples, not knowing the degree to which a visual cue or verbal repetition may have been responsible for repetition of text.

In 1 Corinthians 13, 7, the dittography is likely to have been generated through a succession of lines beginning with the same word ΠΑΝΤΑ (all things). This is how the text appears in Codex Sinaiticus, with the line that is repeated in Codex Vaticanus given in bold:

ΤΗ ΑΛΗΘΙΑ
ΠΑΝΤΑΣΤΕΓΕΙ
ΠΑΝΤΑΠΙΣΤΕΥΕΙ
ΠΑΝΤΑΕΛΠΙΖΕΙ
' ... the truth. It bears all things, believes all things, hopes all things ... '

With four lines in all beginning with ΠΑΝΤΑ, the error of skipping back a line from one ΠΑΝΤΑ to the previous one would have been easily induced. This is what is likely to have happened with the Vaticanus scribe copying from Codex Sinaiticus or another exemplar that had the text laid out in precisely the same way.

There are no other examples that are so clear. But in one case, in Romans 4, 4–5, lines beginning with the same characters in Codex Sinaiticus may have been what guided the scribe's eye back, so helping to generate the dittography:

ΕΙΣΔΙΚΑΙΟCΥΝΗ
ΤΩΔΕΕΡΓΑΖΟΜΕΝΩ
ΟΜΙCΘΟCΟΥΛΟΓΙ
ΖΕΤΑΙΚΑΤΑΧΑΡΙΝ
ΑΛΛΑΚΑΤΑΟΦΙΛΗ
ΜΑ
ΤΩΔΕΜΗΕΡΓΑΖΟΜΕ
ΝΩΠΙCΤΕΥΟΝΤΙ
' ... as righteousness. Now, to the one working, payment is not reckoned as a gift but as something due. Now, to the one not working, though believing ... '

In Codex Vaticanus, the scribe repeated the text shown in bold. If his exemplar were laid out in the same way as Codex Sinaiticus, what could have led him back, having just written ΕΡΓΑΖΟΜΕΝω (working) a second time was the coincidence of a previous line also beginning with the characters Τω ΔΕ (Now to).

In another instance, in Romans 9, 18, the repeated key characters in Codex Sinaiticus as possible exemplar are located above each other on successive lines:

ΑΡΑΟΥΝΟΝΘΕΛΕΙΕ
ΛΕΕΙΟΝΔΕΘΕΛΕΙΣΚΛΗ
ΡΥΝΕΙ
' ... So then, (on) whom he wills he has mercy and whom he wills he makes hard-hearted.'

It is possible that this layout induced the Vaticanus scribe to skip back from ΘΕΛΕΙ (he wills) to the same word immediately above on the previous line and so write 'he has mercy and on whom he wills' a second time.

These few examples of dittographies from Codex Vaticanus do not provide the same convincing support for a common exemplar in the same format as Codex Sinaiticus, or direct copying from Sinaiticus itself, that we found in the analysis of skip errors. However, there are enough parallels and links not to rule out these possibilities.

A further conclusion is that the processes involved with dittographies, of both visual copying and verbally repeating text, may lead to outcomes that do not obviously relate to the original exemplar. There is a need for an examination of a wider range of manuscripts. It would certainly be useful to look at more cases where the identity of an extant exemplar is either suspected or known.

We have made some substantial progress in reaching this point. In the previous chapter, we were able to test theories relating to the Codex Sinaiticus. We were also able to learn something about its construction and purpose. In this chapter, we have put Codex Vaticanus under similar scrutiny and determined the nature of the relationship between the two codices. These are our conclusions:

- **The core of the New Testament and some books of the Old Testament in Codex Vaticanus were copied, visually rather than by dictation, from an exemplar that had the same average line length, about 13 characters, as Codex Sinaiticus.**

- The strong correspondence of skip errors in Codex Vaticanus to text in Codex Sinaiticus, as it would have appeared in an exemplar, establishes a direct link between the two manuscripts.
- The finding that Codex Sinaiticus also had an exemplar of the same average line length as that for Codex Vaticanus, and was in places attempting to follow this exactly (see Chapter 4), makes it possible to explain the skip error correspondence in terms of a common proximate exemplar. This cannot, however, be easily explained in terms of a remote common exemplar at one or more removes.
- The alternative, simpler explanation is that the Vaticanus scribes were using Codex Sinaiticus directly, as its main exemplar.
- The characteristics of some errors held in common, together with other common features, support the proposition that the Codex Vaticanus scribes did use Codex Sinaiticus as a direct source. Of the two alternatives – common proximate exemplar or Codex Sinaiticus as exemplar – the latter is then to be preferred.
- Correspondences in style indicate that the codices were produced at around the same time and possibly in the same scriptorium. The Codex Vaticanus scribes could therefore have had access both to Codex Sinaiticus and to a common, proximate exemplar.
- The book of Isaiah was copied from a different exemplar, of the same average line length of 17 characters as Codex Vaticanus.
- The Codex was produced with care, either as a reference copy or for use in a religious community or both.

We have so far been looking at the two earliest copies of the bible in terms of their content and their relationship with each other and with other biblical sources. But these were generated in a historical context and that context was the Roman Empire which under the Emperor Constantine had recently adopted Christianity as an official, state religion.

Understanding these manuscripts better will certainly have helped towards seeing where and how they may fit in with the history of their time.

CHAPTER 6

The Emperor's order

Power was divided in the Roman Empire at the beginning of the fourth century. At any one time, there were up to six claimants taking the highest title of Augustus or Emperor, exerting control over different regions and competing with each other.

The man who rose through the turmoil to become the sole ruler and unite the Empire was Flavius Valerius Constantinus. As Emperor, he was known as Constantine. He was the son of a high-ranking military officer Constantius, who himself had succeeded to the title of Augustus, on the retirement of Diocletian and Maximian. But a year later Constantius died while on a campaign with Constantine against the Picts in Britain.

Besides having the military skill, Constantine displayed a high degree of political acumen. He built alliances, marrying the daughter of one of his rivals, Maxentius, and marrying his sister to another, Licinius. He managed from the outset to demonstrate tolerance for Christians, who were by then an influential minority, but without alienating the pagan majority.

Constantine defeated his rival Maxentius in a battle near Rome to take control of the Western half of the Empire in 312 CE and then later defeated Licinius in 323 CE to become sole Emperor. The first of these events is credited with Constantine's conversion to Christianity. However, some caution need to be observed with regard to what is supposed to have happened.

In an account by Lacantius, tutor to the Emperor's son Crispus, Constantine had a dream the night before the battle that he should order his soldiers to put the cross of Christ upon their shields. This he did and, when Maxentius' forces were routed, Constantine took it as an auspicious sign and so became a Christian.

Eusebius, who was Bishop of Caesarea, wrote a life of Constantine after the Emperor's death in 337 CE. There is unfortunately no other comprehensive record available and Eusebius' account is certainly unreliable. He had good reason to be grateful to Constantine who had adopted Christianity as a religion of Empire and later begun to favour this religion over paganism.

Eusebius presents a biography which is far more than appreciative; it is uncritical, as well as embroidered and fanciful. Constantine is presented as a man without any blemish, who was really a Christian throughout his rule. In Eusebius' version of the omen before the crucial battle of Milvian Bridge against Maxentius, Constantine saw a cross of light above the sun with an inscription 'conquer by this'. Following this, he had his dream in which Christ instructed him to go into battle with standards made in the form of a Christian cross.

But, far from abandoning the old ways, Constantine retained the title of pontifex maximus as the High Priest in charge of supervising and coordinating the worship of pagan gods. While relaxing restrictions which had been imposed on Christians and restoring their property, which had been confiscated during the Diocletian persecutions, he was also careful not to offend the pagan majority. He ordered the restoration of pagan temples. He used pagan rites as well as Christian rites in dedicating his new capital, which became known as Constantinople, built on the ruins of Byzantium.

Indeed, if there is some truth in the 'cross of light' story before the battle near Rome, then it almost certainly reflects Constantine's consummate diplomacy, as opposed to a sudden, Damascene conversion.

The cross, as well as being significant to Christians, was also an important Mithraic symbol. It features in a number of drawings and carvings relating to Mithraic ritual, from about the same period. No written record survives to indicate what the cross was supposed to represent. Suggestions include a sword, possibly for justice and retribution, or alternatively the intersection of celestial spheres. One illustration shows followers taking part in a ritual meal with wine and small loaves marked with a cross. This is quite striking in that these are also key elements in the Christian communion service. It may be that early Christianity borrowed some ritual trappings from its pagan converts.

What is clear is that both religions did at the time attribute symbolic significance to the sign of the cross. The followers of Mithras would thus, just as much as Christians, have had no problem marching to battle with a cross marked on their shields.

Portrayed as the outcome of divine instruction, the Emperor's action might have been more the product of his own careful calculation. Constantine was, at a stroke, able to unite his own forces – by using one symbol with alternative meanings. His careful cultivation of the Christians did indeed pay dividends. Constantine's appeal to them would have had the effect of undermining the unity of his opponents who controlled territories in which Christians were more numerous. Licinius in the east had, at this time, begun to renew the persecution of Christians and this may have contributed to his downfall.

It appears that, rather being a Christian by conviction, Constantine took a pragmatic view, recognising that the religion could help to unify his empire. He would have seen the parallels with paganism, particularly Mithraism, from whose beliefs and rituals Christianity had borrowed. He did eventually become a Christian, through baptism, though only on his deathbed. This was apparently to ensure that the rite would definitely cleanse him of his sins and ensure entry into heaven (there being no time left to commit any more).

Far from being a model of perfection, Constantine had like other Roman Emperors acted arbitrarily and at times cruelly. He had his eldest son Crispus and his own wife Fausta killed, it was rumoured because of an alleged illicit relationship between them. He had others executed who stood in his way. These are details which Eusebius failed to mention in his life of Constantine.

Eusebius also wrote about the Council of Nicea, which Constantine convened in 325 CE, but without even mentioning the man whose views were the main focus of debate. This was an Egyptian priest Arius who had argued that, while Christ and God were both divine, they were not consubstantial. Christ, he maintained, was created at a moment in time and therefore could not be coeternal with God. Furthermore, if Christ were created, then it was from nothing and therefore not from the substance of God.

Constantine was disturbed at the disagreement over this issue. He saw it as threatening not just the unity of the Church but possibly, in turn, order within his Empire. He convened the Council with the aim of getting the Christian bishops to decide on a view and end the argument.

The outcome was that Arius lost on a vote and, together with two dissenting bishops, was sent into exile. The Church adopted the Nicene Creed, encompassing the majority view that Christ was 'of one substance with the father'.

Eusebius' purpose, as he frankly admitted, was to suppress anything that might discredit the Church, rather than to present an absolutely accurate record. This is why he offered such a rosy account of the Church's patron Constantine and why he refrained from mentioning discord or disagreement.

So Eusebius cannot therefore be relied on as a chronicler. But there is no doubt that, as Bishop of Caesarea, he was a key player with regard to the Church record. He had inherited, from his predecessor and patron Pamphilus, a great library at Caesarea that contained many early and original documents. It was to Eusebius that Constantine turned when he wanted 50 copies of the holy scriptures for the churches of the city he had built and dedicated as his new capital in 331 CE.

Eusebius had the resources at his disposal, possibly the best library then available anywhere of biblical and other Christian material. He was able to use this to effect in, among other projects, compiling the first history of the Christian Church. But he was, at times clearly purposefully, not wholly accurate. Can his account of Constantine's order of a major consignment of either whole bibles or collections of books, and his own response to it, be trusted? It could be, for example, that Eusebius exaggerated the number requested in order to enhance his own importance. Certainly, this was large for just one city. The details, which Eusebius records, do however accord in some respects with what is known of the circumstances at the time.

Constantine had, during his long reign, increasingly begun to favour the adherents of Christianity as opposed to the older, pagan religions. So it is entirely plausible that he would have required a number of bibles for use in churches at Constantinople and probably subsequently also for other parts of the Empire. It is also likely that he would have turned to Eusebius who controlled a library housing the necessary source material, and where there would also have been a scriptorium for the copying of manuscripts and the production of new books.

Constantine was, as Emperor, used to instigating vast construction projects and major military campaigns – and to having the necessary materials and manpower made available to him without question. So, again, it is entirely likely that the Emperor made an order for a substantial number of bibles, which he expected to be provided immediately. But, as Eusebius records, there was simply not the means to do this at such short notice. So what he did do was complete the order in batches of three or four, in the hope that Constantine would be placated as the bibles began to arrive.

In his *Life of Constantine*, Eusebius quotes the letter, giving the details of what was required in the order. It is hard to see a reason why Eusebius might have entirely forged the letter. As Skeat notes in his article, *The Codex Sinaiticus, the Codex Vaticanus and Constantine*, there is one independent check. Eusebius quotes several letters and edicts. For one of them, Constantine's edict to the Eastern Provincials, a fragment of what appears to be a contemporary manuscript has survived and this agrees with the version that Eusebius gives.

Eusebius' dilemma, faced with a request for 50 bibles and neither the trained staff nor sufficient parchment immediately to fulfil it, is also entirely plausible. Again, as Skeat notes, another order at around this period requiring just ten scribes brought all other copying to a standstill. Where was Eusebius going to get as many as fifty skilled copyists? And where was he going to get the necessary parchment, without slaughtering animals not needed for food and without cutting off the production of hide for other purposes?

It would certainly have been an immense undertaking. It was also one that marked a turning point both in the organisation of the Church and the production of its literature. This latter had evolved over a period of two hundred years according to the needs of its members and current technology. By the end of the third century, the means had become available for making long manuscripts in the form of a codex. Surviving fragments indicate that the gospels were by then regularly produced together, rather than as individual books. But there are very few references to whole bibles, encompassing both the whole of the Old and New Testaments, and none survive from before the time that Codex Sinaiticus and Codex Vaticanus were written.

The analysis of handwriting, style, materials and method of production indicate that these manuscripts were produced towards the early part of the fourth century. The plain titles used for the gospels, for example KATA LOYKAN for the Gospel of Luke as opposed to EUAGGELION KATA LOYKAN used later, are indicative of an early fourth century date. Barnabas and the Shepherd of Hermas are present in Sinaiticus, and may have been present in Vaticanus which is missing the last part of its New Testament. These books were excluded from the accepted canon early on. So again this suggests that the two codices are of very great antiquity.

Sinaiticus cannot however date from earlier than 325 CE because it contains marginal references for the Eusebian canon tables and this is the date when these were first introduced. So there is a relatively narrow time frame in which it can be calculated that the two codices were produced. Their creation comes within the period in which the production of Christian literature was increased under Roman patronage, beginning with the order from the Emperor Constantine around 331 CE to his Bishop Eusebius. In addition to which there are unconscious mistakes in Sinaiticus, ANTIPATRIDA for PATRIDA and KAISARIAS for SAMARIAS, suggesting a link to Bishop Eusebius' territory and specifically to Caesarea. There are also notes by a corrector at the end of the books of Esdras and Esther, which indicate cross checking against a manuscript by the previous Bishop Pamphilus who founded the library at Caesarea. Furthermore, the notes indicate that Pamphilus was using a handwritten copy of Origen's hexapla, which it is believed was kept at Caesarea.

If all this is taken into account, then there is some support for the argument that Codex Sinaiticus at least was produced at the scriptorium at Caesarea and, because of its imputed date, linked in some way to the order for copies of the scriptures made by the Emperor Constantine. But, as we have found (Chapter 3), Sinaiticus was not produced by dictation as Milne and Skeat contended, but was visually transcribed. As we also found (Chapter 4), far from being abandoned as an incomplete copy, it was finished for all practical purposes. It was not left littered with errors, but thoroughly checked by an individual (Ca) wrongly believed to be from a later period but who was in fact the diorthotes, or scriptorium corrector.

Because speed of production appeared to be a main objective, the scribes worked on Sinaiticus fast and made mistakes which the corrector Ca and sometimes the scribes themselves later picked up. It meant that the manuscript, though fairly accurate, was not particularly presentable, certainly not of a standard required as the focus, in most cases the only focus, for reading and study in a church. So it was not, as Skeat believed, intended to be part of Constantine's order. But it did fulfil the requirements of a master copy or new exemplar, hurriedly generated for the purpose of creating further copies either by dictation or by visual transcription.

If we turn to the circumstances in which Eusebius found himself, this may have been what he needed in order to do what was asked of him. He had to act quickly because this was what the Emperor expected. He might well have needed to create one robust master copy from one or more older, and quite probably fragile, source documents that would not have been able to withstand being handled time after time. It would not have mattered much what such a master copy looked like, only that it be produced with all due speed and accurately and thoroughly corrected. So it is quite likely that he produced a master copy on strong parchment, which could then have been used in assembling the current order and for other orders in the future.

A single exemplar, made possibly from several sources, would also have served another purpose. It would be the definitive source, replicated many times and effectively displacing all earlier and any alternative versions. Eusebius, who was concerned with holding to doctrine and preserving the reputation of the Church, must have seen this as a pivotal moment and a key opportunity. If he could control the process (and he was in charge of the exercise) and if he could mould the contents where it appeared necessary and was feasible, then he could fix the message as he wished for all time in the future. Whether this was done and, if so, how it was done are issues that will be considered in later chapters.

It would have been very costly to produce such a document, as indeed it would have been to make further copies from it, even assuming some economies of scale. As Eusebius himself noted, he could not assemble the resources to make 50 copies all at once. So he produced the bibles in batches of three or four.[1] For such an exercise, it would have been feasible to use an exemplar that was unbound and rotate the leaves (bifolia) around a table at which the copyists were working. There would be a break in the text, given the way sheets were bound together, for all of the sheets except the one making up the middle of a quire. So, for the sake of clarity and ease of working, whole quires might have been circulated instead. Alternatively, the same layout could have been followed for the copies, allowing the scribes to work with confidence on whole sheets, often requiring starts at new points in the text. Either way, this would have allowed for some degree of simultaneous working, so speeding up the production process.

Using the same exemplar over a period would have made sense from the point of view of saving time and money. It would also have been important to keep the same exemplar if possible, as a check against errors leading to alternative readings of the same text in different copies. In the event of future disagreement as to which was the correct version for a particular passage, this could then have been settled by reference back to the exemplar. Keeping the same exemplar would also have helped to ensure that, as far as possible, future copies from new orders matched those that had already been made.

The Bishop of Alexandria, Athanasius, mentions that in 341 CE he sent copies of the holy scriptures to Constans, one of three sons who succeeded Constantine. By this time, Eusebius had died. There is thus one other mass production of scriptures at around this time and there may have been others, not recorded.

It is probable, for the reasons given, that there were not many master copies created as a means to aid the production of bibles on a large scale during the fourth century. Sinaiticus, we have already deduced, was such an exemplar produced at about the right time and, it appears from what scant evidence there is, created and kept at the library and scriptorium at Caesarea. So could it be that Codex Sinaiticus was an exemplar that Bishop Eusebius produced under great pressure for his undertaking to fulfil the Emperor's Constantine's order? It is certainly possible. But the evidence for such a direct link is only slight and circumstantial. It can, furthermore, be argued that Eusebius might have been reluctant to devote time to generating a master copy, given the pressure he was evidently under. He could therefore have worked from the exemplars he already had in fulfilling Constantine's order.

Some lessons would have been learned from such an exercise. It would have been evident, in view of likely continuing and expanding demand, that method and order would be required for future production. Codex Sinaiticus could well fit as being a master copy created for an expansion of production and distribution of bibles, just a few years later. So, even if not made specifically to cater for Constantine's order, it would as an exemplar have played a role in the wider dissemination of Christian texts. It would have been seen and treated as a precious asset, to be retained as a reference and brought out for use as and when more copies were needed for decades, possibly even more than a century. It would also have been used as a means of arbitrating when, inevitably, differences were found in the books produced by copying. Eventually as the Latin version of the bible, produced by Jerome, came into general use and gradually came to replace the Greek texts, there would have been a decreasing need and then finally no need for an original Greek exemplar.

Codex Sinaiticus and Codex Vaticanus share a chapter division in Acts that is unique among the Greek texts, though also found in the Latin Vulgate. This indicates that Jerome may have used one of these or alternatively a copy made from one which has since been lost. It is known that Jerome did consult the old Greek texts in producing his Latin bible.

Sinaiticus might have continued to be consulted for a while as a venerated, ancient source. But, once Greek was superseded, in its initial role it was redundant. Once the majority of old Greek texts had been replaced, it was simply no longer needed. It was then no longer brought out in order to generate more copies or as a reference against which to check for errors or adjudicate conflicting text.

These exercises would have served both as a graphic demonstration and reminder of Sinaiticus' purpose. Without them there was an increasing likelihood that, over time, its purpose would no longer be remembered. The story of Sinaiticus' origins may have been retold for a while. But, over generations, as the job of keeping the ancient manuscripts at Caesarea passed from hand to hand, the original role of Codex Sinaiticus was eventually forgotten.

Codex Vaticanus, also written in Greek and from the same period, has suffered a similar fate. It has been in the Vatican library for over five centuries and possibly much longer. It is hard to decide the circumstances in which it was created.

The New Testament and part of the Old Testament of Codex Vaticanus was, as we have demonstrated from the analysis of skip errors, quite likely copied both from a common exemplar and also with reference to Codex Sinaiticus itself (see Chapter 5). The same order is followed for the books of the New Testament in both codices, except that Acts and the letters attributed to James, Peter, John and Jude have been brought forward in sequence to follow the gospels in Vaticanus. For Acts, as we have noted, the codices share a chapter division not found in any other Greek manuscript.

In the Old Testament, there is much greater variation, though by and large it is by virtue of blocks of books being put into a different sequence. So, if Codex Vaticanus were, as we have concluded, copied with reference to Codex Sinaiticus, it would indicate that a degree of flexibility was nonetheless allowed for the ordering of the books, especially in the Old Testament.

The similarities between the two books extend to the decorative designs with which the scribes signed off their work at the end of chapters. These are so similar in some instances as to indicate that one scribe (described as scribe D in Sinaiticus and as hand A in Vaticanus) may have worked on both manuscripts. This in turn suggests that the production of both occurred within a fairly narrow time frame. The evidence (see Chapter 5) is that Codex Vaticanus was copied for much of the New Testament using both Codex Sinaiticus and its main exemplars to check against. It could therefore be that it was created as a reference copy, perhaps as insurance against damage to the master copy, Sinaiticus.

So, what eventually happened to the bibles that Constantine ordered and how did Codex Sinaiticus and Codex Vaticanus come to end up where they did, one in a monastery on Mount Sinai and the other in the Vatican library? These two survived, we suggest, because they were not used in the same way as the bulk of the bibles produced at this time.

Each bible among those ordered would have been a precious asset, serving a particular Christian community as one of its main textual sources. Handled frequently, on a daily basis for readings and services, the bibles would have soon begun to suffer some wear and tear. After a century or so, they would have begun to be replaced by Jerome's new Latin version (the Vulgate). At some point, it may have been decided to recall the remainder. Redundant, and to those unfamiliar with Greek unreadable, these copies would likely have been left to disintegrate, taken apart and recycled or destroyed. It is no surprise that, after almost 17 centuries, it is hard to find anything that can be identified as one of the bibles from among the copies ordered by the Emperor Constantine or from other similar orders made during the fourth century.

The exception is Codex Vaticanus, which may have been one of the fifty or part of another similar order. It could have been kept, simply because it happened to be in very good condition when the Vulgate came into general use. As Skeat speculates, it may ultimately been sent to Rome as a gift. It is recorded in the Vatican library's first catalogue in 1475 but it could have been there centuries earlier.

An alternative explanation is that Codex Vaticanus was made as a reference copy, specifically for the papal authorities to keep. In which case, it could have reached Rome not long after it was made, in the fourth century. That would certainly account for the manuscript's good condition and relative lack of wear.

Codex Sinaiticus, we have deduced, was created as an exemplar from which to make further copies, rather than as a copy for use by a particular church. So it was not handled on a daily basis over a long period, and it too escaped much of the wear that would otherwise have been expected. The evidence, although slight, indicates that it may have originated from the scriptorium attached to the library at Caesarea. It would have been held at the library while copies were made from it, kept for reference and retained to help fulfil new orders. Notes by a corrector at the end of two Old Testament books in Sinaiticus, Esdras and Esther, indicate that it was there later and being actively cross-checked against other manuscripts held in the library.

If the codex had remained at Caesarea, it would have been at risk and possibly destroyed when Muslim Arabs in the early seventh century took over Palestine and other eastern areas that had been under Roman rule. By the time Jerusalem was captured in 638 CE, it had probably been removed together with other precious relics, ultimately reaching the place where it was discovered by Constantin Tischendorf in the nineteenth century. This was the monastery of St Catherine's on Mt Sinai. The monastery was, and still is, heavily forti-fied. Even until the twentieth century, it was only accessed by a door high up in the outer walls. Supplies and visitors were pulled up to the entrance by means of a rope.

The monastery's formidable defences are probably the main reason it was never sacked. Reputedly built on the site where Moses saw the vision of God in the burning bush, it was regarded as a sacred site by Muslims as well as Jews and Christians. So this also provides a reason why the monastery was left untouched. Codex Sinaiticus had found a safe haven and was preserved as a link with the past.

The survival of the two codices from the mid fourth century, Codex Sinaiticus and Codex Vaticanus, may well be no accident. Related to each other and with related functions, one as a reference copy and the other as an exemplar, these had more chance of being retained. The copies in daily use in church communities from the same period will, by contrast, have vanished long ago.

Our conclusions in this chapter are:

- As a likely master copy, Codex Sinaiticus could have been created to help with the production of bibles for distribution within the Roman Empire during the fourth century.
- Codex Sinaiticus is associated in several ways with Caesarea, where there was a library and scriptorium under Bishop Eusebius, towards the beginning of the fourth century. So it is possible that Codex Sinaiticus was used as an exemplar from which to make copies to fulfil an order by the Emperor Constantine.
- Codex Vaticanus, derived in many parts from Codex Sinaiticus and their common exemplar, is most likely to have been gener-ated as a reference copy.

It is worth noting that our findings are at variance with the theory put forward by Skeat (see Chapter 3) that Sinaiticus was simply intended to be one of the 50 bibles that Constantine ordered for his new capital.

Codex Sinaiticus and Codex Vaticanus provide the earliest surviving records for the gospels and indeed the New Testament in its entirety. There are earlier papyrus sources, from the second and third centuries, that do cover some of the text including, for example, large parts of the gospels of Luke and John. But, for the most part, these sources are incomplete and fragmentary. For many passages, there is no earlier surviving record.

We reached the conclusion that, although both codices were produced at about the same time and using a common exemplar for at least parts of the New Testament, Codex Sinaiticus is nearer to source and was created first.

Taking Codex Sinaiticus together with other evidence, we shall next examine how some essential elements of the Christian message may have come to be incorporated into the text. But, in order to do this, it will help to establish a sequence for the gospels.

The question is: which came first?

CHAPTER 7

The primacy of Mark

The gospels of Mark, Matthew and Luke have a great deal of material in common and for this reason are described as 'synoptic'. That there are common passages, sometimes with little or no alteration, suggests a degree of borrowing. But the evidence needs to be examined to discover in which direction the borrowing went. Which, in other words, preceded the others? We will be arguing in this chapter that primacy rests with the gospel of Mark.

There is a fourth canonical gospel that stands apart in that the greater part of its material is unique. This is the gospel of John, which gives evidence of having being written with access to an additional source. Its author appears to have a theological objective to counter the argument, which had begun to develop among some Christian groups at the beginning of the second century, that Jesus was simply a man on whom the spirit of God had descended. He was special, it was contended, though by virtue of having been chosen. When Jesus died, the spirit left him.

Taking the argument to its conclusion, there would then have been no need for a resurrection. Jesus as a man died. The spirit remained untouched and eternal. John's counter in his prologue is the argument that Jesus was in fact all along the divine essence, the word or 'logos'. His death was then a sacrifice, but a triumph because Jesus as the word was then resurrected. The remainder of the gospel is in part an attempt to demonstrate Jesus' special status through his deeds, including the miraculous raising of Lazarus.

Since John is very clearly set in the context of a period later than the other gospels, there have been few attempts to argue that John was, notwithstanding the evidence, the earliest. Jesus, though a

Jew himself, is constantly represented as being in opposition to 'the Jews'. Thus, for example, in John 9, 28, the Jews say to a man Jesus has healed, 'You are his disciple, but we are disciples of Moses'. This statement is understandable in the light of the conflict between Jews and Christians from the end of the first century. But it does not reflect what was going on in Jesus' lifetime or in the period immediately following his death. Mark by contrast, while at times portraying Jesus in opposition to scribes and Pharisees[1] has Jesus interacting with and at ease with those who were clearly his fellow Jews.

The writer of John used some material from the other gospels and he appeared to have access to a second source for the passion story. From this source may have come the detail of a soldier plunging his spear into Jesus' side.

The other three canonical gospels of Mark, Matthew and Luke have many passages that parallel each other. While the wording may differ, it is often clear that these represent versions of the same sayings or the same narrative. There are long accounts in Mark and Matthew that follow each other in close agreement or even word-for-word. The correspondences indicate that the gospel authors used other gospel material for reference and also copied out passages. The question is to decide in which direction the copying was done.

Many writers have looked at this issue. A strong consensus has developed that Mark was the earliest of the three gospels and a major source from which the others borrowed. It is apparent that Matthew and Luke had access to other material providing sayings attributed to Jesus. However, what is not clearly established is whether they accessed this independently or the extent to which they have may have been dependent on each other. The hypothetical common source of sayings has been designated as the Q document, from the German 'Quelle' for source. The argument for the primacy of Mark can be summarised as follows.[2]

Common content

There is very little in the gospel of Mark that is not also found in Matthew. Over 90 per cent is shared with Matthew and some 60 per cent with Luke. There are two possible explanations, given the scale of the overlap: that the other two gospels were in large part an elaboration of Mark or that Mark itself was an attempt to provide a collation and summary of the other two.

THE INVENTION OF JESUS

The major problem, with any argument that Mark is derived from the other two, comes from the amount and type of material that the author of Mark would have had to pass up in writing his gospel. It is hard to see why, presented with these other gospels as a source, he would have left out the Sermon on the Mount or the infancy stories of Jesus. What motivation could he have had to miss out the Lord's prayer, the birth of John the Baptist or the death of Judas? Why, for example, in the passion sequence is there no mention of the guard placed on the tomb?

Jesus' role as a teacher features at several points in the narrative in Mark. Given that the writer is keen to emphasise this why, given the opportunity, would the author of this gospel have chosen to omit great chunks of teaching present in the other gospels?

Given the material that is held in common and what is not held in common, it is very hard to argue that the author of Mark used Matthew and Luke. The alternative explanation, that Mark was the original, is by contrast logical and understandable. The extra material in these other gospels would have come from other sources, including a collation of sayings, and possibly legendary accretions and elaborations by their writers. It is apparent that the author of Mark did not include this material for a straightforward reason; he did not have it.

It is also significant that, while Matthew and Luke contain much of Mark and are overall longer, the passages that are equivalent to ones in Mark are often shorter. The explanation for the missing bits is, in each case, better in going from Mark to Matthew and Luke rather than vice versa. It is, for example, hard to see why Mark in copying might have wanted to add some new and inessential detail, such as that Jesus slept on a cushion in the boat while the storm was raging (Mark 4, 38) or that four men carried the pallet on which the paralytic man lay (Mark 2, 3). It is more understandable to see this as Matthew, in copying from Mark, leaving out these details to concentrate on the essentials.

Other omissions can be seen to have been made in order to change the picture being presented. Did Mark gratuitously insert the detail that Jesus' relatives thought he had gone mad (Mark 3, 21)? Or did the later writers simply decide to eliminate this detail because it gave a poor impression of their character?

Some omissions seem to indicate a degree of carelessness. For example in Mark, the men carrying a paralytic man for healing cannot reach Jesus in his house (Mark 2, 1–5). So they make a hole in the roof and let him down. In response to the action, Jesus marvels at their faith in going to such trouble and this version is repeated in Luke. But

Matthew omits to say that the paralytic was let down through the roof (Matthew 9, 2), while retaining the statement about their faith by Jesus, for which there is no longer any apparent reason! It makes sense, however, if in abbreviating Mark's story, Matthew has left out this crucial detail. It seems less likely that Mark made it up in copying a version in Matthew that did not have it.

In similar vein, it is very unclear in Luke's version of the trial of Jesus (Luke 23, 18) why the crowd should be demanding the release of 'Barabbas', when there would be no reason for Pilate to do this. But Luke has, in taking from Mark the details of a prisoner who had committed murder in an uprising (Mark 15, 7), omitted the information in Mark's previous verse about a custom of releasing one prisoner of the crowd's choice at every Passover. That would certainly make more sense of Luke's story. The omission is an indication that Luke copied from Mark and not vice versa.[3]

Another, slightly more complicated example, comes in the incident when the disciples of John and the Pharisees are described as fasting (Mark 2, 18). In Mark, in the next sentence, 'they' ask Jesus why his disciples do not do the same as the disciples of John and the Pharisees. The subject of this sentence has to be someone other than the disciples of John and the Pharisees; it could be either Jews in general or perhaps the scribes mentioned in previous paragraphs. Matthew omits the sentence that sets the scene and so is able to represent the question in another way, as the disciples of John asking (Matthew 9, 14), 'Why do we and the Pharisees fast, but your disciples do not fast?' It is difficult to get from this to Mark but easier to see how Matthew could have reached his version by a process of omission and conflation.

The evidence from content thus indicates that Mark was a major source for, and not a summary of, the other synoptic gospels. If the gospel had been just a later attempt at synoptic harmony, it is also difficult to see how it would have achieved and retained its standing. It could indeed, like Tatian's *Diatessaron* that did represent an early effort to harmonise the gospels, have been excluded from the accepted canon.

Harder readings

The argument with respect to harder readings is that, where there are two versions in manuscripts relating to the same text or alternatively two versions of the same story in different texts, the one that is harder to explain is likely to be earliest. The reason the rule generally holds good is that, while the existence of a more difficult reading provides a good reason for the existence of an easier one, the same would not apply the other way round. The one that can explain why the other came into being will generally be earlier.

It is easy to see how this happens. Faced with a reading that does not match prevailing theology or his preconceptions, a scribe engaged with copying text will look for some sort of explanation. And one line of reasoning is likely to be that the scribe who created the exemplar made a mistake. If an alternative reading can be imagined as having been behind the text, one that does not present the same difficulty, then the copyist may assume that this was the real reading that the original scribe misrepresented.

If he then changes the text in copying to what he assumes may have been the original, the second scribe will be creating a new version. If copies of the old one remain in circulation, there will be two competing versions. If, as is quite possible, the new version is preferred when further copies are made, the original version may become the minority text. It follows that the majority text is not always the one that is more reliable or original.

An example of this is provided by the story of Jesus approached by a man with leprosy in Mark.[4] The majority of the surviving manuscripts portray Jesus as 'feeling compassion' when he stretches out his hand to heal the leper (Mark 1, 41). This is what might have been expected. It is appropriate to the general view of Jesus presented in the gospels and to the particular situation.

But one Greek text, Codex Bezae, supported by three Latin manuscripts, has Jesus 'feeling angry'. This is at first sight puzzling. Why would Jesus have felt angry in carrying out an act of healing? Surely this reading must be wrong? But, adopting the rule of the harder reading, it is possible to see how this reading gave rise to 'feeling compassion', though not the other way round. The alternative words in the Greek are similar and have the same ending. At some point, a copyist must have felt that the 'feeling angry' in this part of Mark was wrong and altered it to what he felt must have been the correct and original text. The 'feeling compassion' version was accepted, copied and recopied, leaving just a few remaining alternative (and, as is argued here, likely more authentic) texts.

Codex Bezae is probably fifth century, but is believed to be based on at least one source going back to the second century. It is possible that the codex had a source with some variations that predate those in the exemplar used for Codex Sinaiticus, even if in other respects it was subsequent to and dependent on the line of textual transmission engendered by or represented by Sinaiticus.

There are, as it happens, other clues supporting the interpretation that the 'feeling angry' version in the story is earlier. In the same passage in Mark in which Jesus performs his act of healing, he is given to rebuke the leper severely and cast him out or send him on his way. This is moreover a picture of Jesus that is not untypical, especially in Mark's gospel. Jesus is often shown as angry, impatient or exasperated. The picture provided by such incidents accords with the character given to Jesus in Mark of a charismatic prophet, battling with Satan and wild beasts in the desert, emerging to cast out demons and call people to repentance.

In the same story related in the gospels of Matthew and Luke, the wording is almost exactly the same for the equivalent passage, except that there is no word to describe Jesus' response, neither compassion nor anger. Nor do these versions have Jesus rebuking the leper and casting him out. So, did an author of Mark copy one of these and add the note of anger that is found in the Bezae text? The reading is difficult because of the Christian theology that has developed of Jesus as a perfect man. If he were perfect, if indeed he were a godman, then he should not have been prone to outbursts of anger, especially where these appeared from the text to have no justification. Though he is portrayed as having healed the leper, he is also shown as having treated him in an abrupt and dismissive manner. The difficult reading in Bezae we suggest is the original one because it explains the other version, where anger was changed to pity because it conformed with what was expected in this instance as appropriate and acceptable behaviour.

It is also the case (the argument from content) that the image of an 'angry' Jesus is what is otherwise consistently portrayed in Mark and eliminated when the same stories are told in Matthew and Luke. In the story of the man with the withered hand, Jesus looks round angrily at onlookers hoping to report him for breaking the Law in respect of the Sabbath (Mark 3, 1–6). Matthew and Luke tell the same story, almost word for word, but omit the reference to anger (Matthew 12, 10–14; Luke 6, 6–11). The angry reaction of Jesus to the money changers in the temple (Mark 11, 15–17) is similarly diminished by process of omission in these other gospels (Matthew 21, 12–13; Luke 19, 45–46). These are by no means the only examples of common stories where the element of anger is present in Mark, but missing in Matthew and Luke.[5]

There are other instances where there are readings in Mark, apparently contradicting the Christian image cultivated of Jesus, which cannot then be found in closely worded parallel accounts in the other synoptic gospels. A particularly crucial one comes in the story of a rich man seeking to ensure that, through his conduct in this life, he gains eternal life in the next (Mark 10, 17–22, followed in Luke 18, 19). The man has kept the commandments from his youth. He asks what more he should do, addressing Jesus as 'good teacher'. Jesus is given to respond sharply, 'Why do you call me good? No one is good but God alone.'

Now this is a statement that is clearly at odds with the theology concerning Jesus that the Church developed from very early times: that he was a perfect man, the son of God, indeed indivisible from God. It is a difficult case to make that Jesus was really perfect, really God, but just in this instance being modest. The author of Matthew felt the need to alter the text. In his version (Matthew 19, 16–22) the words are shifted around to change the meaning. So instead of asking, 'Good teacher, what must I do to inherit eternal life?' the man asks, 'Teacher, what *good deed* must I do, to have eternal life?'

It is in this version rather a shallow question, with the idea of goodness no longer dangerously applied to Jesus but to some single action the man might have to do. Thus Jesus' reply can be directed to this, rather than to himself, though the outcome in the text is not at all coherent. He is made to draw a conclusion about God, even though there is now really nothing in the man's question to suggest it: 'Why do you ask me about what is good? One there is who is good.'

There is much less in this to offend Christian theology. This version, the easier one in relation to doctrine, does not however suggest a means by which Mark's version if subsequent and dependent came about. But going from the harder version in Mark is understandable and easier to explain. It was changed to reduce the force of Jesus' statement and its implications. This implied firstly that Jesus was not good since only God was good. Secondly, it suggested that Jesus, not being good like God, could not therefore be God.

The words put into the mouth of Jesus in Matthew are more ambivalent and could simply be taken to mean, 'Ask the fount of all goodness, that is God.' It should be noted that this example is really no different in its dynamic from the one where two versions came about of the story of the leper cured in Mark's gospel. It was only at a later date that distinct identities and authors were attributed to the synoptic gospels. In the first production of Matthew, and quite possibly subsequent rewrites, the author would no doubt have seen himself as producing 'the gospel' from a number of sources including a passion sequence. This then ultimately survived as a separate gospel with authorship attributed to Matthew.

The gospels are distinct because we perceive them to be so. In reality, there was at first no separate Matthew, just an edit of Mark. Or it could be taken the other way round, that Mark was effectively the first draft of Matthew's gospel which was then edited and expanded with additional sayings. Only, the draft also survived to take on a life of its own.[6] With the focus shifted to Matthew's gospel, Mark for a long time was seen as secondary and perhaps not given similar critical attention. By the time it was incorporated in a canon of four gospels within the New Testament, there may have been too many existing copies of Mark for it to have been feasible to make changes. Or, if there were changes to be made, dealing with this particular discrepancy was not seen to be the most pressing.

Mark as a whole made it, with its 'No one is good but God alone', variation. Codex Bezae did not become popular as a source for the New Testament. Hence it has many readings of the gospels that may be early but are either unique or not represented in other witnesses.

The significance of language

There are a number of instances in the gospel of Mark where words or sayings are given in Aramaic, with an accompanying translation into Greek. In most of these instances, the words are given as those directly spoken by Jesus.

The other synoptic gospels deal with the same situations but lack these Aramaic words and phrases, except for the cry from the cross, 'Eloi, eloi lama sabachthani' (Mark 15, 34) which in Matthew is rendered as 'Eli, eli ... ' as in the Hebrew of Psalm 22 of the Old Testament (Matthew 27, 46). The words from Psalm 22, 'My God, My God, why have you forsaken me?' which Jesus is given to quote is put first in Aramaic or Hebrew and then followed by a translation into the Greek in these two gospels.

The other usages of Aramaic words in Mark are 'boanerges' for 'sons of thunder' (Mark 3, 17), 'talitha cumi' for 'young woman arise' (Mark 5, 41), 'korban' for 'gifted (to God)' (Mark 7, 11), 'ephphatha' for 'be opened' (Mark 7, 34), 'bartimaeus' for 'son of Timaeus' (Mark 10, 46) and 'abba' for 'father' (Mark 14, 36). As with the cry from the cross, and with the exception of the name of the blind beggar, Bartimaeus, these are the words that the author of Mark is quoting Jesus as having spoken.

There is no doubt that Jesus, as a Palestinian Jew, would in ordinary conversation have spoken in Aramaic. Mark is writing in Greek so his intended audience must have been Greek speakers. He is translating the Aramaic words he uses and this must mean that it could not at the time be presumed his intended readers would know this language. The gospel was therefore written in this form for people outside of Palestine.

But why would the author of Mark have taken the trouble to include words that he would then immediately have to translate? Why did he not simply leave them out? It is, of course, tempting to quote from a source in another language. Many writers do this. Mark may have added the Aramaic phrases for colour and dramatic effect. It may also have been done to enhance his claim to be authoritative. By using words attributed to Jesus, Mark is in effect saying that he had access to an original source, an eyewitness account: someone who was there and remembered or wrote the words down.

Matthew and Luke do not do this and so, on this general count, could be presumed to be later. Also, since Aramaic was the language of Jesus, material in Aramaic might be considered to have a better chance of being closer to source and so earlier than material translated into Greek. But this latter is, it should be noted, a question of probability; it is not necessarily the case.

Looking at the issue from a different point of view, if the other synoptics were earlier and the author of Mark copied from either or both of them, then where did he get the actual words supposed to have been spoken by Jesus? It does not seem likely that Mark merely made them up. He could, of course, have had a separate source. In which case, we are back to the same argument. There is a good chance that such a source, with the Aramaic words of Jesus, would have been earlier than Matthew and Luke. And thus Mark itself would have primacy.

The assumption that Matthew and Luke copied from Mark, however, appears to run up against a different kind of problem. Why would these gospel authors have left out the important evidence of the actual words claimed to have been spoken by Jesus? This was surely something to be accorded respect and reverence and preserved for the benefit of future generations of believers?

The answer to the question is the key to this conundrum. Matthew and possibly also Luke did in fact preserve the words spoken by Jesus. But they wrote their gospels initially in Aramaic, using a collection of sayings in this language and also the gospel of Mark, written in Greek for communities of early Christians in the diaspora. Translating Greek with Aramaic quotations and parallel translations into Aramaic would have produced a confusing redundancy[7] with the same words spoken twice over in the same language.[8]

So the translations of these words, which would consequently have been needless repetitions in the same language as the rest of the text, were eliminated. In the process by which the gospels evolved, the Aramaic versions of Matthew and Luke were then translated into Greek which then came to dominate. But these then differed from Mark, which was first created in Greek and retained the quotations in Aramaic.[9]

When it comes to place names, the evidence for transmission of text is less clear since the name of a place in a local language will often stand when that place is written about in another language. Hence Gethsemane, in origin an Aramaic place name derived from 'wine press' or 'wine vat', is recorded as such in the Greek in Mark, Matthew and John. All four gospels record the place of crucifixion as Golgotha which may derive from Hebrew, as stated in John. Except for Luke, the gospels record this as meaning 'place of the skull', although there is reason to believe that this may not be accurate (see Appendix X p 340).

The one Aramaic word that Matthew records is 'bariona', as a nickname in reference to Simon Peter (Matthew 16, 17). It means outlaw. When this gospel was translated back into Greek, the copyist was doubtless uncomfortable with the implications of this and so left it in its Aramaic form. Subsequently, the word was taken to mean 'son of Jona' and by a circuitous route transmuted into 'son of John' in the gospel of John (see Appendix X pp 337–338).

As well as the Aramaicisms in Mark, there are a number of instances where the author uses colloquial language that is rendered in the other synoptics into better Greek. One example is where Mark uses KRABATTON for the stretcher on which the paralytic man was lowered down from the roof into the room where Jesus was. Matthew and Luke use KLINH which is more exact.

Events in sequence

In Mark's gospel, stories are usually presented in a logical and coherent sequence. Sometimes, there is a shift in the middle of the narrative to relate a different event, before going back to the main story. In this way, the writer manages to convey the passing of time. In some cases, when the same stories are presented in Matthew and Luke, the sequence is lost and there are omissions. This leads to details that are perplexing and unexplained as well logical inconsistencies.

At the beginning of Mark in chapter 1, after Jesus comes out from the desert, events as they are related rapidly unfold. He took on his first disciples, entered Capernaum, preached in the synagogue, healed a man there with an 'unclean spirit' and immediately went to the house of Simon's mother-in-law who had a fever. Jesus healed her. Then, people brought their own sick friends and relatives to the door of the house to be healed. It is made explicit that this was after the Sabbath had ended, 'in the evening, when the sun had set'.

Matthew describes the recruitment of Jesus' disciples early on in chapter 4 and then later the healing of Simon's mother-in-law at Simon's house. Matthew includes the observation that after this, 'that evening', people brought to Jesus their own sick to be healed. The detail, that it was in the evening, would appear to be irrelevant. This is because Matthew has not included the specific incident of healing in the synagogue on the Sabbath and linked it, in sequence, so that it is made clear that the healing of Simon's mother-in-law was also on the Sabbath. The crowd of callers respectfully waited until sundown, when the Sabbath had ended, before bringing other people to be healed. The detail is thus highly relevant, even though Matthew missed out the information that would enable the reader to judge that it was so.

It is hard to explain Mark's version as the creation and positioning of an incident in a tight sequence so as to create a meaning for Matthew's otherwise inexplicable detail. Rather, it is evident that the author of Matthew had before him a version of Mark when he wrote and that he reworked and repositioned the text, losing some information entirely and consequently the relevance of other detail that he did include.

Another story, that of the death of John the Baptist, perfectly illustrates the way in which the omission of a part of a crafted narrative renders it unintelligible. In Mark, this story is told as a retrospective (Mark 6, 7–32). Jesus has sent out the twelve apostles on a preaching and healing mission. The author next reports that Herod (Herod Antipas), when he heard of it, began to wonder whether Jesus was John the Baptist raised from the dead.

He then tells how Herod had imprisoned John the Baptist, offering as the reason for it John's criticism of Herod's marriage to Herodias.[10] Herod is portrayed as not at all hostile to John, indeed respectful of him as a 'righteous man' while perplexed by his teaching. Mark explains how Herodias successfully schemed to get John killed. He notes that John's disciples came for the body and buried it.

Having concluded this retrospective story, explaining Herod's reaction to Jesus, Mark then picks up the main narrative. The insertion has provided a break, so indicating the passing of time. The apostles are described as returning weary from their mission. Jesus suggests they go somewhere where they can enjoy some privacy and rest (a lonely place). But they are then spotted leaving by boat and followed to their landing place. So they get no peace.

In his version, Matthew records the mission of the apostles at the beginning of chapter 10 and then follows with other material, culminating in Jesus' preaching and rejection in Galilee which in Mark is placed just before the apostles are sent out. Matthew then includes the reaction of Herod and story of John the Baptist's death, also told in retrospect (Matthew 14, 1–13).

This is presented in abbreviated form, as is a lot of material parallel with Mark, and is in comparison somewhat confused. Now, it is Herod who wanted John the Baptist's death; it is only the potential wrath of the populace that held him back. But, as in Mark, it is Herodias who secured the death of John. But Herod is reported as being sorry afterwards, a reaction that is hardly comprehensible in the light of Matthew's earlier statement that Herod wanted John dead. It does, however, make sense in the light of the observations by Mark that Herod, though fearing John, had heard him 'gladly' and kept him safe. This is one indication that Matthew has copied Mark.

There are others. Matthew continues with the information about John's disciples coming to fetch and bury the body. But he then fails to include the note about the apostles returning from their mission which would have framed the retrospective story of the death of John the Baptist. He continues instead with the story of Jesus withdrawing to a lonely place, as if it were part of the interspersed retrospective commentary on Herod's previous actions and also as a consequence of hearing of John the Baptist's death. Since there is nothing, as there is by contrast in Mark, to bring the narrative from the flashback to the current sequence of events, it would in effect make the rest of Matthew part of the retrospective on Herod. This would clearly be nonsensical and not what the author intended.

The confusion has to be a consequence of the author of Matthew failing to observe the form in Mark of narrative framing the retrospective commentary. However, not only does Matthew fail to say that the apostles returned, he also displaces information about the start of their mission to an earlier point. There is therefore nothing to frame the story about Herod at either end.

Matthew could have done so by recommencing at 14, 13, with a statement, 'Now, Jesus decided to leave his own country and preach in another place'. This would have related to his text just prior to the story about Herod and John the Baptist. But he doesn't do this. What he has done is juggle the text that is in Mark to produce a result that does not make sense.

If it is accepted that Matthew meant the narrative to resume with Jesus responding to John the Baptist's death by trying to withdraw to somewhere secluded, this raises another problem. Herod is given to say of Jesus, just before the retrospective story, 'This is John the Baptist, he has been raised from the dead.' So, the death of John had happened previously. Jesus could not in the sequence, as it is presented, at that moment be making an immediate response 'when he heard it'.

It is really very hard to see how Matthew could have got where he did without chopping up Mark's text and losing the sense and sequence of it. It is likewise difficult to imagine how Mark could have written his account on the basis of Matthew. This example, like the previous one, provides powerful evidence for Matthew being dependent on and secondary to Mark, rather than vice versa, where they have text in common.

The placing of one story within another one at other points in Mark also causes problems when the text appears in Matthew. In a story of the relatives of Jesus (Mark 3, 21–35), another incident is interspersed in which the scribes also accuse him of being possessed. The structure is that Jesus' relatives go out to find and restrain him. Then, in the meantime, he has an altercation with the scribes. So time has passed and his mothers and brothers finally find him engaged in preaching. But it is apparent that Jesus, from his response, is disinclined to see them.

Matthew has the same story but, as already noted, misses out the first part about his relatives seeking to restrain him (Matthew 12, 22–50). Though he still prefaces it with narrative containing the accusation of demonic possession by his critics, that he is possessed, the reason for his later apparent discourtesy to his relatives is no longer apparent. In Mark, it is clearer. They want to stop him preaching, and that is why he will not see them. Once again, it is possible to see how Matthew got where he did from Mark, but hard to see how Mark by elaborating might have created the cohesion that is lacking in Matthew.

The examples chosen to represent the case for the primacy of Mark have come under four headings: content, difficulty of readings, language and sequence. These examples, and others like them, establish that Mark (or an earlier version of Mark) provided the source on which Matthew and Luke based their accounts for passages that are held in common.

Other arguments have been adduced, for example that the theology contained in Mark is less developed than in the other gospels and so must be more original. The problem with this line of reasoning is that the gospels provide the prime evidence for the early stages in the development of doctrine. So whichever is found to be earlier offers, through its content, evidence of a 'less developed' theology.

We have established the primacy of Mark through internal evidence, by way of what are primarily textual arguments. We can now relate this understanding to the text of the other gospels, to see how certain key concepts and descriptions may have changed during transmission. This will be our objective for the following three chapters, with reference to the early Greek New Testament sources.

The texts that we have for Mark do of course originate from a period later than the time when the gospel was first drafted. So it is possible, for example, that Mark will at some points have subsequently been edited to conform with later thinking in Matthew and Luke. We will demonstrate some striking examples of this in Chapters 8 and 10.

With the focus back on our sources, we will then examine how these fit into the process and give evidence of it. Finally, we will be back to the immediate level in the production of the gospels, the scribes themselves, where we see a struggle for accuracy, honesty, integrity and control.

First, however, we look at a question which may at first glance not seem all that important. Jesus is described as a Nazarene. Why has there been an enormous anxiety, during almost two thousands years of Church history, to convey that this means that he came 'from Nazareth'?

Our main conclusions from this chapter are as follows:

- **From a variety of considerations relating to content, harder readings, language and sequence, it is established that the gospel of Mark preceded that of Matthew and that the author of Matthew copied from it.**
- **Mark is by the same criteria the earliest of the four canonical gospels.**

CHAPTER 8

Nazarene or Nazareth

Old Testament writers predicted and yearned for a time when a man, a 'son of David' descended from the old kings of Israel, would free the Jews from occupation by foreign powers. This man would be a great warrior,[1] anointed as a king and hence described as 'masioch', anointed one, or as it has been transliterated, a messiah.

There is nothing in the texts to indicate that these writers expected the prophecy to apply to anything other than their own circumstances. But the Christian sect established in a break from Judaism, as far as can be ascertained under Paul,[2] adapted the idea of a messiah to apply to a wider context. This would be someone who would liberate all of mankind and it would be a form of spiritual rather than physical redemption: liberation not from the chains of slavery but from the fetters of personal sin. This fitted rather well with the situation in which Christianity found itself, that of having to accommodate to the reality of Roman power, the same power which had so recently crushed the Jewish liberation movement.

There were elements of the messianic message that the early Christians took with them, in part because it gave the new religion a respectable pedigree. Their adopted Jewish messiah, Jesus, could also be a 'son of David', whom the Old Testament prophets had predicted would one day arise. So there was no inhibition in describing Jesus as a 'son of David' and indeed history was manipulated[3] to have Jesus born in Bethlehem, traditionally believed to have been King David's birthplace.

Jesus lived when Judea was under direct Roman rule and in the context of a struggle during the first century to achieve freedom from Rome and a succession of Herodian client kings. Jesus was a Jew and shared this context and heritage. To appear authentic, Christianity needed to reflect at least some of this reality, while at the same time avoid dangerous associations with the Jewish messianic movement. Jesus could not be bracketed with those who sought to throw off the shackles of Roman, imperial power.

It was a delicate balancing act to achieve, one likely to lead to a lot of semantic if not theological confusion. One straightforward theory is that there was a messianic movement, broadly one entity though possibly linking several discrete groups with common aims, fostered by insistence on the fundamentals of Judaism, notwithstanding the fact of pagan occupation. So, at the core was an unflinching religious nationalism, 'righteous' leaders prepared to stand up and refuse to compromise and for whom, and for whose beliefs, many others were at times prepared to fight. At times of increased oppression, including direct Roman rule in Judea at the time of Jesus, people turned in increasing numbers to this fundamentalist core.

It was not necessarily something as concrete as a separate sect or tendency, since no religiously observant Jew could really argue with the requirements to observe the Jewish Law (the Torah), practise circumcision, meet dietary requirements, disavow forbidden sexual relationships (fornication) and avoid the accumulation and love of wealth for its own sake. In addition to all this, there was a more general prohibition against the corruption of the temple by foreign, pagan influence. This in effect meant resisting the imposition of the symbols of Roman power which, of course, led to intermittent clashes since the Romans were equally determined to insist on it. It was, it appears, the refusal to continue sacrifices on behalf of the Roman Emperor that precipitated a bid for liberation in the first great Jewish uprising, just a few decades after Jesus' death.

The fundamentalists may thus have seen themselves as within the mainstream, as Pharisees, and have been regarded by others as such. As this movement grew in strength, it may have come to dominate, to speak not just for itself but for Jews as a whole. Indeed, it did speak for the Jews as a whole who yearned for liberation and who had a messianic agenda as part and parcel of the framework of their religion.

Labels were applied to it, or at least to some of the groups that made up the movement. The 'Essenes', described by the contemporary Jewish historian Josephus, appear to have been the group responsible for scrolls deposited in caves by the Dead Sea and rediscovered nineteen centuries later. In the scrolls' unreconstituted message, the Romans, the 'kittim', were the enemy, to be defeated in a final apocalyptic battle. The 'sons of light', Jews who had kept to God's covenant, would in this way overcome 'the sons of darkness'.

Josephus describes other uncompromising groups, including a 'No Lord but God' movement arising a few years before Jesus under someone described as Judas the Galilean. Judas and his followers advocated refusal to pay Roman-imposed taxes. Then, there were 'zealots', either purely religious or militant. Josephus describes the 'sicarii', definitely a militant group, so named after the short 'sicae' daggers that were used to assassinate political opponents, those it would seem they regarded as collaborators. In his account of the Jewish War, Josephus alternates between describing the rebels as zealots and as sicarii. It may be that these groups were not in practice all that distinct.

Herod (the Great), the first of a family of Herodian client kings, had secured Palestine for the Romans and, in so doing, had displaced a short-lived dynasty of Jewish Maccabean kings. Herod engaged with them for as long as he needed to, and then he ruthlessly disposed of them and all other political rivals.

During the first century those who claimed to be 'sons of David' and thus the rightful inheritors of the throne of David were forced at the very least to become more circumspect. Some of them went to ground and, it has been argued[4] were harboured within the broad limits of the messianic movement, to 'come out' from time to time, proclaim the message of liberation and then perish in a series of ill-fated rebellions.

While Jesus is described in the gospels as being based in Galilee, his brother James subsequently emerges in Acts and in some of the letters attributed to Paul as head of a movement based in Jerusalem. From the dialogue with Paul and the description in Acts, it is apparent that James and his followers were strictly observant Jews. A bitter debate arose over the requirements for non-Jews who wished to join the movement. While James insisted on the dietary observances and other rules set out for gentile 'godfearers', Paul was advocating abandoning the Torah entirely and with it the ideal (for perfection) of circumcision. The outcome was that Paul and his followers ultimately split away to form their own sect, involving a new covenant with God, centred on the figure of Jesus and without many of the requirements of Judaism.[5]

There are some disparities between the gospel accounts and that in Acts. How, for example, did the action that was so firmly based in Galilee in the gospels appear a few years later entrenched in Jerusalem where James and his followers were based? The answer to this may be that a messianic line, including Jesus and therefore also his brothers, was kept safe within a religious movement located at or near Jerusalem. So this was the place to which James, claiming not the kingship of Israel but apparently just its religious leadership,[6] ultimately returned.

The other apparent oddity is that the issues between the followers of James and Paul seemed to be all about requirements for membership and nothing about Jesus. Once a new 'Christian' sect had been created, the crucial dividing line then came to be the character of Jesus. This may well be because, at the time that James and Paul were at odds, no one was arguing a case for the divinity of Jesus (see Chapter 9, pp 171–172). It did not come up because it was not at that time a point at issue.[7] Christianity gained the doctrine of a sacrificed godman as it absorbed former followers of Mithraism, its rituals and some of the concepts of pagan religions.

So what labels were applied to the movement led by James, which it can be argued had come to be a dominant force within Pharisaic Judaism? It seems they may have seen themselves as 'the poor', a designation subsequently applied to the 'Ebionites' (from the Hebrew, Evyonim, meaning 'poor ones'), Torah-abiding Jews who revered James. This was also one of the chief self-designations of the group responsible for the Dead Sea scrolls, which in its organisation and practices in many ways mirrored those of the Jerusalem community under James.[8] Paul, it will be recalled, records that he was asked 'to remember the poor' (Galatians 2, 10), that is that he should collect funds for the community in Jerusalem. In fact, this is precisely what he is described as doing in Acts and his letters to the Corinthians.

Another description that can be applied to the movement under James is that they were guardians or keepers of the Jewish Law and Covenant. James certainly does appear in this role in Acts, in seeking to enforce minimum requirements for gentile converts to Judaism. Other early references describe James as righteous, leading a highly ascetic life and often praying to God on behalf of the people.[9]

It is with James' movement that Paul, as his earlier or alter ego as Saul, sought to ingratiate himself. Though to an extent rebuffed, he persisted and took on a mission to gentiles. However, Paul was teaching that the Torah was redundant and that circumcision was no longer required even for Jews. When word of this reached Jerusalem, Paul was twice summoned to account for himself. On the second occasion, a riot broke out and Paul was arrested and taken before the Roman governor, Felix. This action shortly preceded Paul's final break with the Jerusalem community of Torah-observing Jews under James.

Paul was accused by the High Priest and Jewish elders of being 'a pestilent fellow, an agitator among all the Jews throughout the world, and a ringleader of the sect of the Nazoreans' (Acts 24, 5). Paul admitted to being a member of 'the way, which they call a sect' but, according to Acts, tried to argue that he was really being put on trial on the basis of a difference over whether or not God would resurrect the dead.

What is clear, from the narrative and the timing of events, is that Paul/Saul was being accused of stirring up trouble among Jews in the diaspora on his preaching and fund-raising mission. Further, it was as a prominent member of the group to which he had attached himself and still belonged, that is the movement under James in Jerusalem. It was not just the High Priest but James and his followers who were unhappy over the discord that Paul was causing. So, while Paul's followers may already have begun to diverge in their practices, it was as a member of James' group that Paul was accused. Thus, the term 'Nazorean' was a label applied to this strict, Torah-abiding movement within Judaism.

It is a conclusion that fits in strikingly with the most likely derivation of the word Nazorean, which is from the Aramaic and Hebrew base NTZR (natzar) meaning to watch, keep or guard. James and his movement saw themselves as defending and keeping the covenant between the Jewish people and God. So they might well have been called 'keepers' which became in one variant 'Nazoreans' and in another 'Nazarenes', in effect the same word since written Hebrew and Aramaic did not use vowels.[10]

Another possible derivation or association is with the Hebrew word 'netzer' meaning 'branch' which has exactly the same Hebrew base as 'keep'. If applied to the movement led by James, this could relate to an Old Testament messianic prophecy in the book of Isaiah. The writer looked back to the calling of King David, who was the son of Jesse, and also forward to a future gathering in of dispersed Jews and the re-emergence of Israel and Judah: 'there shall come forth a shoot from the stump of Jesse, and a branch shall grow out of his roots' (Isaiah 11, 1). The Nazorean movement, we have suggested, harboured messianic claimants including John the Baptist and Jesus. In the case of the latter, the claim is supported by genealogies going back to David in the gospels of Matthew and Luke.[11]

It is less likely that Nazorean was derived from 'nazir' meaning consecrated or apart, which was applied to those who took a vow for a period typically to abstain from wine and other products from grapes and to avoid cutting their hair. Hence, the term, 'Nazirite'. Here, however, the Greek letter zeta is rendering the Hebrew letter zayin. So the base is N Z R, as opposed to N TZ R for Nazarene where confusingly the same Greek letter zeta renders the Hebrew letter tzaddi.

A further confirmation that the term Nazarene/Nazorean was applied to the movement under James comes in the writings of a fourth century bishop, Epiphanius. In a treatise against what he saw as various heresies (*Against Heresies*, originally titled *Panarion*), he noted that 'all Christians were called Nazarenes once. For a short time they were also given the name Iessaeians [likely – 'Essenes'], before the disciples in Antioch began to be called Christians.'[12]

Epiphanius also described Nazarenes in his time as following a heresy because, while believing in Jesus, they also followed the Jewish Law and practised circumcision. He recorded that Nazarenes lived in the region of Pella in Perea and he related this to the flight from Jerusalem to this area, when the city was under Roman siege during the Jewish uprising. Eusebius, writing his Church history earlier in the fourth century, described the Jerusalem Church, warned by revelation, as fleeing to Pella to avoid the siege.

The siege and fall of Jerusalem took place in 70 CE. James had been killed shortly before the uprising and the Nazarenes who managed to escape to, or reestablish themselves around, Pella were initially led by another brother of Jesus, Simon or Simeon.[13]

The evidence of the early sources establishes that the use of the designation 'Nazarene' or 'Nazorean' preceded that of 'Christian', as applied to Paul's sect at Antioch. It was applied to the movement under James of which Paul was accused of being a member. This was a movement within Judaism that continued to observe the Laws of Judaism, including attending the temple (Acts 2, 46; 3, 1).

With the crushing of the Jewish revolt in 70 CE, coupled with the destruction of the temple and the elimination of the priestly class, there was a need for Judaism to reorganise. It did so around a council of rabbis who began the task of formulating the oral law. But there was no longer a central focus for worship.

The Nazarenes, who had been at the heart of religious messianism, became increasingly marginalised. They were then actively persecuted after they failed to take part in the uprising led by Simon ben Kosiba from 132 CE to 135 CE. Simon had taken on the name 'Bar Kochba', meaning in Aramaic 'Son of the Star'. This was after the messianic 'star prophecy' (Numbers 24, 17), that 'there shall come a star out of Jacob and a sceptre shall rise out of Israel ... ' It may simply be that the Nazarenes rejected Simon's claim because he was not in their own Davidic line.

By the second century, Christians were a growing sect, which had not only abrogated the Torah and other Jewish practices but had also embraced Jesus as the son of God. They were treated by Jews as heretical on both of these grounds. The Nazarenes and later Ebionites may well have taken some of this stigma because they accepted Jesus as God's prophet and were thus seen in the same light as Christians. They also came to be regarded as heretical by Jews. This dual perspective is encapsulated in the modern Hebrew word for Christian, which is 'Notzri'.

Regarded as heretical by both Christians and Jews, the Ebionites dwindled in numbers over the years and had increasingly less influence. Banned and burned, their writings for the most part disappeared. What was left was a one-sided, though also revealing, account of the original fracture between the followers of Paul and those of James.

The objective of Acts was at least partly to paper over the cracks. Not only did the account fail to do this satisfactorily, it also drew attention to the differences between Paul's followers and those of James who attended the temple, just like other Jews (Acts 2, 46). Moreover, the label Nazarene/Nazorean hangs heavily over the narrative: as applied to the pestilential sect that Paul sought to join (and was accused of being prominent in) and to the early followers of Jesus led by James. In bringing forth sons of David, potential claimants to the throne, this was messianic, anti-Roman, zealot.

It might plausibly be argued that Jesus was none of all this, if it could be shown that Paul's representation of Jesus, or indeed that of the gospel authors, was nearer to historical reality than the presentation of James and his followers in a variety of sources including Acts. These people had been the close followers of Jesus. Indeed, there is strong evidence that many of them were kith and kin, and in particular that the term 'brother' applied to James meant precisely that and was not some honorary title or vague kinship designation.[14]

The evidence is that these very same people, after the death of Jesus, went on behaving as observant Jews. They came into conflict with Paul in insisting on all the fundamentals of Judaism. Furthermore, in providing the 'zealous' backcloth for messianic nationalism[15] if not harbouring claimants such as Jesus, they really did fit with a label which suggested this, in context and through its likely roots. Nazarenes: keepers of the covenant, branches from the line of David.

How improbable it is then that Jesus, *one of them*, should just a few years previously have been promoting a quite different kind of pan-universal messianism, nothing at all to do with the objective of removing the Romans and restoring Jewish national sovereignty and a

Jewish monarch. A messianism based on a new and innovative agenda that they completely ignored or had completely forgotten once Jesus was dead, executed by the Romans. It should be added, how really improbable, given that the representation of Jesus in the gospels is both internally inconsistent and not consistent with the Christian doctrine subsequently developed.

It is clear, for example, despite some obfuscation that Jesus was executed as a failed messianic contender. That is what Pilate had posted on the cross. The gospels of Matthew and Luke moreover give genealogies supporting Jesus' messianic credentials. Though given in the gospels to promote a message of compliance and personal redemption, there are moments also when Jesus is presented as defending Jewish Law in all its details.[16] Just like James.

We have suggested (and the evidence suggests) that Jesus, instead of being in a completely different mould from his family and followers, would have been more like them. And this, indeed, is how he is described, as a Nazarene. Just like them. Allowing for the path the text may have taken, from Aramaic to Greek and then to other languages, it seems that he was really described as 'the Nazarene' rather than as 'a Nazarene', implying that he was seen by others as a leader, of or within the sect. This could well be news to anyone familiar only with a translation of the New Testament, and without knowing the original Greek. This is because 'Nazarene' and 'Nazorean' are often rendered in translation, with what little justification it will be seen, as 'of Nazareth'. So, for example, the blind beggar who was the son of Timaeus was told in the original Greek, not that Jesus of Nazareth was on his way but that Jesus the Nazarene was coming (Mark 10, 47). Or, in Luke's version of the same story, it was Jesus the Nazorean (Luke 18, 37). From the narrative, it appears that this was enough to tell the son of Timaeus that it was Jesus (Yeshua), heir to the throne of Israel, whom he then addresses as 'son of David'.

Similarly, when a snatch force of Roman soldiers and Jewish civil police went up to Gethsemane, they demanded not Jesus of Nazareth but Jesus the Nazorean (John 18, 5 and 7). What might otherwise be puzzling, the message that Pilate had posted on the cross 'the King of the Jews' (Mark 15, 26; Matthew 27, 37; Luke 23, 38) is explained by further information provided in John. Here, the title on the cross is described as 'Jesus the Nazorean, the King of the Jews', though not as the critical text states 'Jesus of Nazareth, the King of the Jews' (John 19, 19).

The objection by 'the chief priests of the Jews', to the title or charge on the cross is that it appeared almost as an accolade, suggesting that Jesus *was* rightfully King of the Jews (John 19, 21). But the gloss provided in John has subtly altered the message. It can now be read as, 'this is what happens to Nazorean leaders claiming to be King of the Jews'. In the underlying story, which early Christian authors borrowed, the crucifixion was not just a punishment but an object lesson intended to deter any other would-be messianic, nationalist claimants.

Another interesting reference comes in the statement attributed to the man with an unclean spirit in the synagogue (Mark 1, 24), 'What (have you come to do) to us, Jesus the Nazarene? Have you come to destroy us? I know who you are, the holy one of God.' As in the other instances, 'the Nazarene' is misrendered in translation as 'of Nazareth'. The term 'holy one', ΑΓΙΟC, is precisely that used in Paul's letters to describe the Nazoreans in Jerusalem (2 Corinthians 9, 1; Romans 15, 26; *et al.*).[17] Thus, the man with the unclean spirit was able to use 'Nazarene' and 'holy one' as alternative descriptions for Jesus who was, as the brother of James, one of the Nazarenes or holy ones.

There are altogether twelve references to Jesus as Nazorean/Nazarene in the gospels and eleven to Nazareth as a place where it is claimed he had once resided. With one exception (Matthew 21, 11), these latter are in introductory passages. In Mark, established as the earliest of the gospels (see Chapter 7), there is just one reference to Nazareth.

Christian interpreters have difficulty dealing with the idea that the immediate followers of Jesus belonged to a group within Judaism that was zealous in its religious observance, messianic in a Jewish sense, nationalist and anti-Roman. The difficulty is compounded when it comes to the fact that the same label, applied to this movement within Judaism, was applied to Jesus himself. The difficulty is that, though it accords with the evidence of what the title meant and the expectation that Jesus would have much in common with other related and successive leaders from John the Baptist through to James and Simon, it is at odds with the Christian theology that has been built around a fictionalised version of the Jewish Jesus.

The way that this has been dealt with by successive writers, starting with the author of Matthew, in his rewrite of the gospel of Mark, is this. Matthew claimed that Nazorean/Nazarene really meant 'from Nazareth', a place that exists nowadays about 25 miles south of Capernaum. In modifying Mark, Matthew added a number of additional sayings attributed to Jesus, summarised some of the text and cut other bits that he did not want to include. He began with an added genealogy and nativity account, at the end of which he provided his explanation for the connection (Matthew 2, 23):

> *There he (Joseph) settled in a town called Nazareth, so*
> *that what had been spoken through the prophets might be*
> *fulfilled, 'He will be called a Nazorean'.*

The first, compelling objection to this is that the label Nazorean/ Nazarene was applied to the movement run by James, and to which Paul aspired to belong and to which he was accused of belonging. This has a very good derivation from the Hebrew and Aramaic roots for 'to keep', as in keeping the Jewish covenant, or 'branch', as in a line of descent from David. The name of the town, Nazareth, is not only less likely in terms of providing a root, it is also highly implausible as an ascription applied to a whole group of people, zealous about keeping to the fundamentals of Judaism, troublesome to the Roman and the collaborating Sadducee authorities. They will not all have come from Nazareth. Indeed, given that the group had considerable appeal, according to the account in Acts and other records,[18] it is likely that the vast majority would have come from elsewhere.

If the narrative of the New Testament is examined as a whole, it will also be seen that people are most often identified by their roles – what they do for a living or their place in society – or by their relationship to someone else, rather than by their place of origin. Hence: John the baptiser, Jairus who was a ruler of the synagogue, Matthew the tax collector, James the son of Alphaeus, Mary the mother of James, Andrew the brother of Simon (Peter) and so on.

Sometimes, the two types of reference are combined in order to be more specific. The person who accosted Jesus beside the road from Jericho is described as a blind beggar, the son of Timaeus. There could well have been many such blind beggars, and Timaeus may well have had more than one son. The description, by using two designations, thus pinpointed the person involved. When another person was being introduced to a story it was, however, usually sufficient to relate them to someone with whom the audience was already acquainted.

The person healed in Simon's house is described as his mother-in-law (Mark 1, 30). Since we already know who he was, we now also know in general terms who she was.[19] It is the case that only rarely were people defined by the specific place from which they came. What people did, or to whom they were related, was usually more important, and where they had lived was usually not relevant to the narrative.[20]

Thus observation gains added significance from instances where the description of a character has been altered, from something unacceptable to the narrator, to a place description. This is the way the Greek gospel authors sometimes dealt with telling original Aramaic descriptions. A good example is provided by the apostles lists: in Luke there is a disciple Simon called a zealot, for which the Aramaic is 'cana', while in the equivalent passages in Mark and Matthew the same disciple is described as coming from the town of Cana in Galilee. The gospel authors were accustomed to such semantic smoke screening,[21] for which the effort to portray Nazorean as meaning that Jesus came from Nazareth, initiated by Matthew, is a further example.

It would be very odd indeed if this were the way that Jesus was universally known, given that Nazareth is only briefly mentioned and that a huge section of the narrative takes place in and around Capernaum, by the shore of the lake of Galilee. In Mark, Jesus is described as frequently going back and forth from Capernaum, his 'home' town, where he was indeed at home and where his family was also living. Oddly, although there is just one reference to Jesus coming from Nazareth in Mark, within the initial sequence relating to John the Baptist, there is then no mention of how Jesus almost immediately came to be living in Capernaum.

This gap is filled out in Matthew but without proper explanation. After John had been arrested by Herod the Tetrarch, Jesus returned from the desert, left Nazareth and settled in Capernaum (Matthew 4, 12–16). This could not have been to escape to a safer place, since Capernaum is not far from Nazareth and in any case both places were within Herod's jurisdiction. Jesus was then, according to the gospels, living for the crucial part of his adult life in Capernaum. The response or associations evoked by the description Jesus the Nazorean, if Matthew's explanation were correct, should have been quite muted. Jesus, Yeshua or Joshua in the language used then, was a relatively common name. There must have been many people called Yeshua who were living in, or had lived in, Nazareth at any one time. Yeshua from Nazareth. So what?

In fact, the association generated by the phrase, 'the Nazorean', was immediate and dramatic and meant to be. The blind beggar, on being told that Jesus the Nazorean was coming, knew immediately that this was the current messianic claimant. He called out to him, 'son of David', the title given to the descendants of Jewish kings. Such messiahs were expected to reveal themselves through great signs and miracles. Therefore, in the story, the blind beggar, son of Timaeus, could ask and expect to be healed.

Similarly, Pilate had put on the cross the words Jesus the Nazorean, associated with the title King of the Jews. He would hardly have put up something of little consequence, that Jesus had once lived in Nazareth. The message was, 'here is the leader of the Nazoreans, executed for claiming to be King of the Jews'.

There are other instances where the references to Jesus as the Nazorean were significant, for example when Simon Peter was accused, after Jesus had been arrested. The point is that Nazorean, as applied to Jesus, fits perfectly well with the meaning that the term is known to have had from other contexts. It simply did not mean that Jesus came from Nazareth.

Matthew sought to suggest that the term itself and his quoted statement, 'He shall be called a Nazorean', were based on statements by 'the prophets' (Matthew 2, 23). But there is nowhere in the Old Testament a statement like this, no linking of the place Nazareth to a future Messiah and no correlation between the place name and possible roots with messianic implications. Even if there were, it would not establish that Jesus had ever lived in Nazareth. The evidence in Mark, the earliest of the gospels which the others used as a base for their narratives, is very slim: just a single reference.

The use that the author of Matthew made of Mark's gospel is illuminating in this respect. It was established in Chapter 7 that Matthew made use of Mark, rather than vice versa. Matthew added sayings from a separate source, he elaborated on Mark's narrative and he omitted small portions, either carelessly or possibly deliberately in some instances. The gospel of Mark is, however, very tightly written and the author of Matthew used most of it as it stood, as much as 90 per cent, in what was in effect a version of Mark as opposed to a completely new gospel.

We give below the first 15 verses of Mark which are also the narrative of Matthew. Additions by Matthew are shown in square brackets, while any text that Matthew deleted is shown in italics. Matthew added a genealogy, nativity story and the justification for regarding 'Nazorean' as meaning 'from Nazareth', at the beginning of his account. This translation is from the Greek of Codex Sinaiticus, though it could equally have come from the critical text that follows Sinaiticus closely.

The beginning of the good news of Jesus Christ.
As it is written in the prophet Isaiah,
> *See, I am sending my messenger ahead of you who will prepare your way.*
> The voice of one crying in the wilderness.
> Prepare the way of the Lord, make his paths straight.

John the baptiser appeared in the wilderness [of Judea] proclaiming a baptism of repentance *for the forgiveness of sins.*

And people from the whole Judean countryside and all the people of Jerusalem [and all the region along the Jordan] were going out to him, and were baptised by him in the river Jordan, confessing their sins.

Now, John was clothed with camel's hair, with a leather belt around his waist, and he ate locusts and wild honey.

[But when he saw many Pharisees and Sadducees coming for baptism, he said to them, 'You brood of vipers! Who warned you to flee from the coming wrath? Bear fruit worthy of repentance. Do not say to yourselves, "We have Abraham as our ancestor", for I tell you God is able to raise up from these stones children to Abraham. Even now, the axe is lying at the root of the tree; every tree that does not bear good fruit is cut down and thrown into the fire.']

He proclaimed, 'the one who is more powerful than me is coming after me. I am not worthy to stoop down and untie the thong of his sandals [Matthew: carry his sandals]. I have baptised you with water for repentance but he will baptise you with the Holy Spirit [and fire].'

[His winnowing fork is in his hand, and he will clear the threshing floor and will gather his wheat into the granary. But the chaff he will burn in unquenchable fire.]

In those days, Jesus came from *Nazareth of* Galilee and was baptised by John in the Jordan.

[John would have prevented him, saying, 'I need to be baptised by you, and you come to me?' But Jesus answered him, 'Let it be so now; for it is proper for us in this way to fulfil all righteousness.' Then, he consented.]

And [having been baptised] immediately coming up from the water, he saw the heavens torn apart and the spirit [of God] descending like a dove on him.

And a voice came from heaven, 'You are my son, the beloved,

with you [Matthew: whom] I am well pleased.'
And the spirit immediately drove him out into the wilder-
ness. He was in the wilderness forty days, tempted by Satan;
and he was with the wild beasts, and the angels waited on
him.
[Matthew 4, 2–11 describes temptations instigated by Satan.]
Now, after John was arrested, Jesus came to Galilee.
[He left Galilee and settled in Capernaum by the sea. Matthew
4, 14–16 continues, relating this to a prophecy in Isaiah.]
[From that time] He proclaimed *the good news of God saying,*
'The time is fulfilled and the kingdom of God has come near,
repent and believe in the good news.'

There are three parts to this opening passage. John is introduced. He baptises Jesus. Jesus begins his preaching mission.

What is immediately apparent is how much Matthew is dependent on Mark. He uses virtually all of Mark and what he adds makes little material difference to the action. He fills out the temptations by Satan and there also some slight changes to wording or sentence construction.

Two passages were added to serve a theological purpose, to show Jesus attacking the main Jewish groups and to set him apart from them. There is a further addition to explain why, though Jesus was baptised by John, it was Jesus who had precedence. These derivative Christian preoccupations, it must be said, do not disguise an under-lying substance: one messianic contender dies and then another, related to him, replaces him.

There are very few deletions. The elimination of the introduction is straightforward in that the author of Matthew had provided his own and no longer needed it. That Jesus was 'with the wild beasts' got lost in the elaboration of the temptations by Satan, or was seen as inap-propriate for a figure deemed divine.

There are three theologically motivated omissions. John is being portrayed in Matthew as 'making the way' for Jesus. But the first part of the quote from Isaiah talks of someone coming to prepare the way for the people. So this piece of the quote, which did not fit in, was cut out.

It was believed that only God (or a son of God) could forgive sins. But John was described as 'proclaiming a baptism of repentance for the forgiveness of sins'. And he was depicted as a mere mortal, paving the way for Jesus. So the latter part of this, 'for the forgiveness of sins', was cut out.

In Mark, Jesus is described, when he began his mission, as proclaiming the good news: the imminent fulfilment of the kingdom of God. By the time that Matthew was writing, it was evident that this apocalyptic vision had not been and probably was not about to be fulfilled. In any case, the intent of the gospel was to portray Jesus *as* the good news. And that's aside from the possibility that far, far back in the original, the good news was to be the fulfilment of an original messianism, the establishment of a Jewish kingdom of God on earth. So, no imminent kingdom of God; that too was cut out.

The remaining omission that the author of Matthew made is very puzzling. The three elements of the preface that he added to Mark indicate his concerns. These were, firstly to demonstrate a respectable Jewish pedigree for Jesus by recounting a Davidic pedigree. Secondly, he offered a birth story that integrated Jesus with the pagan myths of gods inseminating mortal women to generate a heroic, semi-divine God-man. Thirdly?

Thirdly, his concern was very much to counter the impression from Mark that Jesus was associated with, or even leader of, a troublesome zealous anti-Roman movement. That is why, among all the other things he could also have put in his preface, he included as his final item a justification, albeit strained, for regarding the term 'Nazarene', amply used in Mark, as indicating that Jesus came from Nazareth.

So, *why* then did he cut out the single reference that there is in Mark to Jesus having lived in Nazareth? It cannot have been done with deliberation, as with the many small out-takes that Matthew made to suppress doctrinally inconvenient facts (such as that John was also preaching the forgiveness of sins). The idea that Jesus came from Nazareth is something that Matthew positively wanted to encourage. It can hardly have been an accidental omission, since this was evidently for Matthew and indeed for others at the time a major preoccupation. The author of Matthew made very few cuts, and this was one of the things he really would have made sure stayed in the text. It cannot be because Matthew has transferred the relevant passage to his preface. The passage is in fact still all there, except for the reference to Nazareth, in Matthew's text: 'Jesus came from Galilee to John at the Jordan to be baptised by him'. There could be no motivation to keep all of this in, yet omit 'Nazareth of' before 'Galilee', something strongly needed there to reinforce Matthew's case.

There is only one explanation that holds. And this is that, in the text of Mark that the author of Matthew had before him, in making his amplified version, *there was no reference to Nazareth*. There was just a reference to Jesus coming from Galilee and it is the reason that, at this point, Matthew also has no reference to Nazareth.

We do not, of course, have this very early version of Mark or indeed any version that includes the first part of this gospel (and indeed other key passages) before Codex Sinaiticus, that is before about 330 CE. In the meantime, the gospel of Mark had been copied and recopied and at some point, the reference to Nazareth was put in to harmonise with the later synoptic gospels and with Christian doctrine – that Nazarene/Nazorean was, despite all the counter-indications, just a safe way of saying that Jesus came from Nazareth.

The insertion, not surprisingly, jars with the context. An editor, acting at a later point in time than when the surrounding text was written and later in time of course than when the first draft of the derivative gospel of Matthew was written, made an addition to Mark to place Jesus in Nazareth. But the place where all the action takes place, the place that is home to Jesus (Mark 2, 1; 3, 20) and to his family (Mark 3, 21) and supporters (Mark 1, 29) is Capernaum. There is nothing in Mark to indicate how or why Jesus might have moved to Capernaum from Nazareth, where he so recently was supposed to have been.[22] The reason is that the author of Mark did not have to get Jesus there. Jesus lived where the action took place in Capernaum and (unless by an enormous coincidence, not linked to the issue of the meaning of 'Nazarene') had never lived in Nazareth.

So the author of Mark faced no problem. There was no Nazareth in his story and no Jesus in Nazareth. Without this reference, the narrative is coherent and makes sense. With it, it does not. And with it, the reference would then have been transported in its context into Matthew where it is in fact missing.

Having in his preamble introduced Nazareth as the place where Jesus lived, in order to fulfil a biblical prophecy that cannot be found, Matthew then had to make another addition to the text explaining that Jesus subsequently left Nazareth and also why he did so. This was because the action all too evidently took place in Capernaum, where Jesus lived, and not in Nazareth. Jesus is described as moving to Capernaum not for any practical reason, but apparently to fulfil another, in this case misapplied and misinterpreted, biblical prophecy (Matthew 4, 12–17).[23]

It is possible now to appreciate something of the circumstances in which the gospel of Matthew was written. There had been a split leading to the creation of Paul's gentile-orientated sect. But the Jews themselves only a few years after this had been crushed in a failed uprising leading to the destruction of the temple and Jerusalem, huge loss of life, the dispersal of many Jews and the reduced effectiveness of the anti-Roman messianic movements for another two or three generations.

The author of the gospel of Matthew was writing in the aftermath of all this. He no longer had to contend with the authority of the followers of Jesus and their successors. Displaced from Jerusalem, they were at least for the time, a spent force. He had an account of Jesus' heroic struggle and triumph over, or escape from, death, generated by his followers. This had been incorporated by a Greek-speaking writer, a follower of Paul, into an account giving the 'good news', the gospel of Mark. He also had a collection of sayings in Aramaic attributed to Jesus.

What worried him, in the context of his times, were the liberal references to Jesus as 'the Nazarene'. This epithet was applied, though James was by then dead, to James' followers, dispersed into Perea north of Jerusalem. These people were in fact also the Jewish followers of Jesus.

Had the term Nazarene instead been commonly understood as meaning someone who came from Nazareth, the author of Matthew would not have had a problem.

'Nazarene' or 'Nazorean' was not just a term of reference for the Jewish followers of James. It had also been applied to Paul, in so far as he had associated with this group. It was a word that meant trouble: Jewish religious zealotry, messianism, nationalism, anti-Roman sentiment. For failing to take part in the second Jewish revolt that began in 132 CE, the Nazarenes, it will be remembered, were persecuted by their fellow Jews. But they were not being persecuted at this time – 50 years earlier – because then they *were* part of the wider messianic movement, arguably even its core. They had upheld the sanctity of the temple, deplored the intrusion of foreigners and had done their bit, certainly as a religiously zealous force, and very likely in many instances had fought and died on the zealot side. Despite the death, disruption and dislocation, this would have been common knowledge in Palestine. But not so much outside. And this was where the writer's constituency lay, among more peaceful peoples within the embrace of the empire: Greek- and Latin-speaking pagans, gentiles.

The existing text of the good news was popular and had been copied many times. So it might not have been seen as feasible or expedient to replace it. What the author of Matthew did was produce an upgrade, with all the new sayings, plenty of additions to reflect new doctrine and with explanations to defuse the potentially explosive association of Jesus with a fiercely Jewish, messianic movement. It would have been sufficient for uncritical gentiles who in any case wanted to believe the message they were being given. Matthew cast about and found the name of a place that more or less fitted the term applied to Jesus. He justified the term, in association with the place, on the basis of an invented prophecy. Few who had bought the package would ever question this, as indeed is the case to this day.

But Jesus, as we have shown, did not live in Nazareth.[24] He once lived, as far as the evidence goes, in Capernaum. He was a Jewish messianic leader, a Nazorean.

Here then, is a summary of our conclusions from this chapter:

- The label Nazorean/Nazarene ultimately derives from the Hebrew base NTZR that generated derivations meaning 'to keep, watch or guard' and 'branch'.
- The label was applied contemporaneously to a Jewish messianic movement and to Jesus and James, who were therefore among its members.
- The movement and its label were distinct from the sect Paul formed, that became known as Christians.
- References to Nazareth, in association with the term Nazorean/Nazarene, were included by the author of Matthew to distract from the identification of Jesus with a Jewish messianic movement of Nazoreans/Nazarenes.
- The reference to Jesus living in Nazareth was retrospectively inserted into Mark, the earliest of the four gospels.
- The text indicates that Jesus' home town was Capernaum and, given the previous findings, he most probably never lived in Nazareth.

As a final note, given that that there is evidence of how much Matthew and for that matter Luke and John altered their original text, what credence can be placed on Matthew's main source, the 'good news' of Mark? The answer must be not much more. It would have been altered from whatever was the message generated by Jesus' supporters and brought out from Palestine. It would then have been changed in copying. Teasing out what that original message might have been was the subject of another book.[25]

CHAPTER 9

Son of Man or
Son of God

It is evident where the idea of a mortal man as the son of God came from, just as it is evident that the historical Jesus was not literally a son or the son of God. In the stories of a pre-Christian, pagan world, it was a common theme to have a god consorting with a mortal woman to generate someone who was then half-god, half-man. Another frequent motif was the subsequent death and resurrection of the godman.[1] The difference, which distinguishes Christianity from a host of contemporary pagan sects, is that it swallowed the allegory. It was added to a story with which, just because it was the tale of a mortal man, it was not entirely consistent. Thus, Jesus had a mortal father and his mother would not have been a virgin. He had, in the normal way of things, brothers and sisters and a normal adulthood. This would have meant, in the society in which he lived and through his position within it, marriage and in time (barring fertility difficulties) children of his own. It is not the purpose here to recapitulate this argument,[2] but it may be observed that, when two such disparate accounts are combined, the fracture lines do show.

The idea that Jesus was or might have been the son of God should be seen in the context of the Jews who saw themselves in general as the children of God. Jews prayed every day to God as their father. Indeed, the Lord's prayer in which Christians pray to 'our father' is a typical Jewish prayer that Jesus might have used. God is described in the Old Testament (2 Samuel 7, 12–14) as making a promise to treat David and his offspring as his sons. In one of the Psalms, the connection is made even more explicit. God is to reward David as if he were his own first born, establishing a line of succession to rule Israel for ever (Psalm 89, 26–29).

There was no intention to make a biological connection in these instances, and it was known that there was none. The description of Jesus as the son of God in the New Testament stems then from a background in which the idea was used to express the relationship, as it was conceived, between God and a particular people.

Christians may have needed a literal son of God in accommodating pagan converts along with elements of their old religion. It may have suited some of the Christian writers of the gospels wilfully to misunderstand a Jewish metaphor. Jesus was a Jew and could therefore have been seen as a son of God just like his fellow Jews. In addition to which, he had a further qualification as a claimant to the throne of Israel, with a pedigree that showed descent from David. As a son of David, Jesus could claim to have, or be seen to have, a special relationship with God, as delineated in the Old Testament.

There are a number of references to Jesus as the son of God in the gospels, in most cases in descriptions by others. There are most in John's gospel and few in Mark, as compared with the other synoptics. Given that Mark is earliest of the four gospels, this suggests that the references came to be inserted, at least more frequently, into the gospels as the doctrine of the divinity of Jesus developed and as these books were copied and rewritten.

In Mark, there are three references to human witnesses describing Jesus as son of God. One occurs in the context of his healing mission in and around Capernaum. The evidence is from those who were possessed. We are told that, 'whenever the unclean spirits saw him, they fell down before him and shouted, "You are the son of God!"' (Mark 3, 11).

A second testimony is offered through the centurion at the cross observing, 'Truly this man was a (or the) son of God' (Mark 15, 39). While the author of Matthew followed this (Matthew 27, 54), Luke merely has the centurion observe that, by the manner of his death, 'this man was innocent' (Luke 23, 47). John omits any reference to the incident. It might be thought that the authors of these gospels, who did otherwise represent Jesus as the son of God, would have been keen to report the important testimony of the centurion from the gospels of Mark and Matthew that were available to them. That they did not indicates that the witness of the centurion may not have been present in the early version of the gospel, which became Mark and Matthew,

THE INVENTION OF JESUS

but was inserted later. There are no surviving records predating Codex Sinaiticus for the passages in Mark and Matthew and so a gap potentially of 250 years in which this could have happened.

The third human testimony is provided by an apparent admission by Jesus who, when pressed by the High Priest, 'Are you the messiah, the son of the blessed one?' answered, 'I am'. (Mark 14, 61–62).

In relating stories at the time, it was a common practice to give characters dialogue appropriate to the situations in which they found themselves. But, even if the words of the centurion or a mentally ill person have been accurately reported and transmitted over the centuries, there remains the question of what reliance can be placed upon them. We do not mean in terms of their accuracy as a proposition. This, as we have argued, needs to be evaluated in respect of other considerations, such the evidence of Jesus as a historical character and where the concept originated.[3] The question is whether these statements provide a fair reflection of how people at the time saw Jesus.

Given that the concept of Jesus as the son of God came to be such a cornerstone of Christian belief, it has to be said that the evidence from Mark that he was considered as such is meagre. The evidence that Jesus saw himself in such a light is practically non-existent. It comes in a passage that appears to be have been concocted, given the abundant evidence in Mark and elsewhere in the gospels that Jesus was tried and executed by the Romans for claiming the kingship of Israel, which was treason. Quite possibly, he had also mounted an abortive insurrection in support of this claim.

What the Roman-appointed Sadducee High Priest Caiaphas was concerned about was the likelihood that a messianic claimant would bring Roman retribution (John 11, 50). That, indeed, was what his question referred to. The messiah, a mighty 'son of David', that is someone attributed with descent from David, was expected to come forward and free Israel. At that particular time, this meant removing the Romans.

Just as David was supposed in scripture to have been adopted by God as his first born son, so those in David's line could also be seen in a special, though metaphorical, sense as sons of God. Thus Jesus could, whether he actually did or not, have answered a question such as that put by the High Priest in Mark in the affirmative, without any implication that he was literally the son of God. This is even though such an implication may have been intended by the Christian author of Mark, or by subsequent editors and rewriters, in the words attributed to the High Priest.

The witness of Jesus, as it is conveyed in Mark, is thus not all that it seems. The other claimed witness of Jesus as the son of God in Mark is God himself, who describes Jesus as his 'beloved son' after Jesus has been baptised by John the Baptist (Mark 1, 11) and again later, after the transfiguration (Mark 9, 7). This has parallels with stories in the Old Testament in which God spoke directly to prophets and religious leaders in dreams or in the open, from the heavens, fire or clouds. It was a literary device to provide a charter for actions and institutions such as the occupation of Canaan and the Jewish Law (ten commandments) or, in the New Testament, the special authority of Jesus.

We have suggested that the distribution of references to Jesus as the son of God, with more located in gospels written later, indicates that the concept may have been introduced into the text over time, as it developed as a Christian doctrine.

The opening line of Mark's gospel, quoted in the previous chapter, sets out the author's prospectus, 'The beginning of the good news of Jesus Christ'. Now, this is a statement which of itself is not at odds with a Jewish perspective since 'Christos' is a Greek translation of the Hebrew 'masioch' or messiah, which means 'anointed' as in anyone anointed to high office. The Jews were expecting a messiah to liberate them and indeed several candidates came forward during the first century.

What is missing, as the reader may have noticed, is the ending of the first sentence, as relayed in modern versions of the first sentence in Mark's gospel, 'the beginning of the good news of Jesus Christ, *the son of God*. That is because, in what we have established as the earliest available witness to this statement, Codex Sinaiticus, the last part of the sentence is not there. Jesus was not described in this opening prospectus as the son of God.

It was not in the scribe's own text. It was, however, subsequently added as an insertion by a corrector denoted by the online project team as S1, that is, someone among the scribes in the course of production. The insertion, as an abbreviated nomina sacra, YY ΘY, has only two different letters, making it hard to attribute with confidence to any particular corrector. It might have been scribe A or scribe D as David Parker, who was a member of the team, suggested.[4] But it could just as plausibly have been the scriptorium corrector Ca or a later corrector.

We agree with Parker that the omission by the scribe can hardly have been an oversight. The scribe would have been aware of the importance for Christian theology of the idea that Jesus was the son of

God. So, at the start of the very first verse of Mark, he would not have inadvertently missed this out, had it been present in his exemplar. The conclusion must be that it was not present in the early manuscript from which he was copying.

Its absence from the exemplar was the reason the scribe did not include it. But the statement was then added to the text, for doctrinal reasons, by a corrector and incorporated in Codex Vaticanus and most other subsequent versions of the gospel. It is one demonstration of how in practice Christian doctrine was consciously introduced into the text.

Parker suggested that the addition of the title, son of God, to the opening text at the beginning of Mark represented a move away from an earlier Christian idea that Jesus was 'adopted' as the son of God through baptism, as announced by God in a voice from heaven in Mark 1, 11, 'You are my son, the beloved, with you I am well pleased'. Putting the title up front in the gospel was a means of stating that Jesus had acquired his status by birth.

The situation is even more complex than this since, as Ehrman has pointed out,[5] in an early version of the equivalent passage to Mark 1, 11 in Luke, God is given to announce 'You are my son, today I have begotten you' (Luke 3, 22).

The suggestion is that this more 'difficult' version may have reflected an original in both Mark and Luke. Because it may have appeared too clearly to be adoptionalist, it was changed to the statement attributed to God that now appears in both Mark and Luke. This latter can be read as simply confirming an already given status.

This more usual version, reused again in the story of the transfiguration, appears to have its origins in the first verse of chapter 42 of the Old Testament book of Isaiah, 'Behold my servant, whom I uphold, my chosen, in whom my soul delights.' The more difficult, and therefore possibly the more original version, 'You are my son, today I have begotten you', is a straight steal from Psalm 2, verse 7.

The alteration to this reading of Luke was, like the addition to the beginning of Mark, made for doctrinal reasons. It was part of a process extending over centuries in which the text was gradually transformed to conform with evolving Church doctrine.[6]

It is worth noting that, in the textus receptus or critical text, for the opening of John's gospel there is a similar declaration, attributed to John the Baptist, that Jesus was the son of God (John 1, 34). This may represent a deviation from the archetype text since the wording in Codex Sinaiticus is 'elect (ie chosen one) of God'. The earlier papyrus

SON OF MAN OR SON OF GOD

witnesses, **P5** and **P106**, also have this reading while others, **P66** and **P75**, support the version selected for the critical text, 'son of God'.

There are no surviving, earlier papyrus manuscripts for the very beginning of Mark. However, the opening of the gospel is quoted, without the added words 'son of God', by the second century writer Irenaeus and also by the early third century theologian, Origen. This provides confirmation for a possible exemplar for Sinaiticus that lacked the claim for divinity in the opening of Mark. What cannot be determined is whether the corrector was working from another source or harmonising the beginning of Mark to other parts of the gospels. What, however, is clear is that this was an editorial decision, made at some point, to put up front what had become an important doctrine for the Christian Church.

Another important illustration of this process is provided by the story, discussed earlier in Chapter 7, of the man who wished to gain eternal life. The author of Matthew's gospel altered Mark's original in an effort to remove the direct implication, in a statement attributed to Jesus, that he was not God since only God was good (Matthew 19, 16–17). The outcome is that Matthew's version does not in itself make sense but can be understood as a corrupted version of Mark.

Not only that, but it appears as if Matthew's version was itself created in two stages. In the first stage, the question put to Jesus read, 'Teacher, what good deed must I do to inherit eternal life?' To which the answer would have been, 'Why do you ask me about what is good? One there is who is good, the (or my) Father in heaven.' This garbled satisfactorily, for Christian interpretation, the reference to Jesus as good and his denial of it (Mark 10, 18). But it still left the statement by Jesus that only God was good, that is God the father in heaven. So that, therefore, Jesus was not claiming to be God.

Note that here again there is nothing that is contrary to Jewish belief, since Jews regarded God as their father and, in a special sense of adoption, as father to David and his line. The latter part, 'the/my Father in heaven' is known to have been there in an earlier version of Matthew, since it is cited by early second and third century sources including Justin, Irenaeus and Hippolytus.

It must have been realised that, by excising this, it would become less clear that Jesus was making a statement by implication that he was not God. So the ending was subsequently cut, leaving, 'Why do you ask me about what is good? One there is who is good.' Without Jesus' denial of goodness and without the attribution of this quality to God alone, the explosive quality of the statement is now greatly defused. It must have been considered safe enough in this form to be retained. Indeed, it is what appears in texts from the fourth century onwards; there are unfortunately no earlier surviving manuscripts for this passage.

Another key example, this time of an attempted harmonisation, is provided by the passage where James and John ask Jesus to look favourably on them in dividing up positions of responsibility in his future kingdom. The original context for this story may have been the expectation that Jesus and his followers (on their way to Jerusalem) were about to overthrow the Romans and set up an independent Jewish state.[7] In Mark, as it now reads, this is deflected by an implication that the request actually referred to a heavenly kingdom. Jesus replies that 'to sit at my right hand or at my left is not mine to grant, but it is for those for whom it has been prepared' (Mark 10, 40).

The author of Matthew copied the incident, but had Salome asking for favours on behalf of her sons (Matthew 20, 20–23). He also expanded Jesus' reply to read, 'but it is for those for whom it has been prepared *by my father'*. In the context, where 'our' could just as easily have been used as 'my', this presents a claim of Jesus as literally the son of God. But the original in Mark, from which the author of Matthew copied, remained unchanged. That is until the Codex Sinaiticus was being prepared. The scribe (scribe A) compared Mark with the corresponding passage in Matthew and decided that the author of Mark must have missed out the words 'by my father' and so added them in, when copying from his exemplar.

The diorthotes, the scriptorium corrector Ca, in checking the scribe's work against the exemplar, spotted that an addition had been made to the text and struck it out. Then later, the corrector Cb2, who often countermanded Ca's work and introduced harmonisations of his own, reinstated the addition.

The scribe preparing the New Testament of Codex Vaticanus was, we have established, working with reference to Codex Sinaiticus and to their common exemplar. He would have seen either the original passage in the exemplar, before it had been altered by scribe A, or the passage as written by scribe A with Ca's marks showing that it should be deleted, or both. He did not see Cb2's reinstatement of the passage, as that had yet to happen.

So he went along with the exemplar or Ca's correction, leaving out the additional words. The outcome was that both Codex Sinaiticus, as refined by the scriptorium corrector, and Codex Vaticanus were faithful to the original exemplar. The same course was followed in other manuscripts and this is now the received version, in modern translations of the New Testament.

It is interesting how this one passage presents a timeline, illustrating conclusions that we have reached. There appears to be a remnant of an original Jewish Nazorean story of a move on Rome, with the followers of Jesus jockeying for position in advance of an expected victory. This story, though retained in a Christian rewrite in creating the gospel of Mark, was modified in an attempt to disguise the nature of the event.

The author of Matthew introduced some further changes, including a reference to God as Jesus' father, in line with the developing doctrine of Jesus as the son of God. However, the original version of this rewrite survived as a separate book, the gospel of Mark. When it came to the point of making copies on a large scale for a Roman Church, the scribe noted the difference between the two gospels and attempted to harmonise. But the corrector, whom we have identified as the diorthotes, or scriptorium corrector, decided to reinstate what was in the exemplar. In the next stage, the scribe for Codex Vaticanus followed either the exemplar or the decision of the diorthotes in copying from Codex Sinaiticus. By the time that a later corrector reversed the correction made by the diorthotes, in another effort to harmonise Mark with Matthew, it was too late, in that the version of Mark 10, 40 from the exemplar had become widely established.

As in this example and others discussed, it is possible to see how the doctrine of Jesus as the son of God came gradually to be introduced into the gospels. It is even possible to go back a little further in time through letters written by Paul/Saul, in the mid first century, at a time when he was carrying out missionary activity and in conflict with the followers of Jesus led by James in Jerusalem. We do not have originals, any more than there are surviving originals of the gospels of Mark and Matthew. So these letters may well have been similarly altered in copying. In their original form, however, those that are genuine would have predated all of the gospels.

A core of five gospels are widely accepted as being consistent in style and with what is known from various sources, principally Acts, of Paul's activities at the time. These can be placed from the references each contains in a sequence from about 50 CE to 58 CE. The first two of these were written after Paul had been on one of his early missionary journeys and established a church in Thessalonica in northern Greece.

There is no reference in 2 Thessalonians to Jesus as the son of God. In both letters, there is a conjunction between 'our Lord Jesus' and 'God our father' (1 Thessalonians 3, 11 and 2 Thessalonians 2, 16). In this context, if God is father of Jesus it is in the sense of being the father of all.

In 1 Thessalonians, there is a single reference to Jesus as son of God. This is after a sentence, complete in itself, 'For they themselves report about us what kind of welcome we had among you, and how you turned to God from idols to serve a living and true God' (1 Thessalonians 1, 9). The continuation, 'and to wait for his son from heaven, whom he raised from the dead – Jesus who rescues us from the wrath that is coming', is cumbersome and may have been an editor's later addition.

Both letters to the Thessalonians are however peppered with references to the 'Lord Jesus Christ'.

This is a label that in part accords with Jewish perception: Iesous from Yeshua and Christos as the Greek rendering of the Hebrew masioch or messiah. But the description of Jesus as 'Lord' is alien to the view that Jews took of authority figures, whether their own or those of foreign rulers. The only Lord was God and this indeed was the slogan for one of the uprisings which had taken place under Judas the Galilean, a few years prior to Jesus: 'No Lord but God'. It is also why in Mark, the earliest of the four canonical gospels, there is no reference to Jesus as Lord either from his followers or from other Jews. The distinction is clearly made in Mark 11, 9. Jesus, in his entry to Jerusalem, came 'in the name of the Lord', that is in the name of God who was Lord. But he did not come 'as Lord'; thus the title here did not refer to Jesus himself.

There is just one reference to Jesus as Lord (Mark 7, 28). This was by a non-Jewish woman from Syrophoenicia, a territory to the north of Galilee. The point is that, in the Greek-speaking gentile world, the subjects of Rome were accustomed to referring to their masters as 'Lord'. This, through Paul, then became assimilated into the language used for spiritual as well as temporal power: Caesar as one type of Lord and Jesus as another. The other gospels, which came after Mark, took on this frame of reference.

So, at the outset in Paul's letters, we suggest that Jesus was referred to as Lord but not yet as son of God. In the next letter in the sequence, to the Galatians, there is a progression towards this idea, though it is balanced by a degree of mysticism. While Paul stated that God 'sent forth' his son (Galatians 4, 4), there was also a sense in which anyone could be in this position. Hence, Paul also claimed that God 'was pleased to reveal his son in me' (Galatians 1, 16). He also told his converts, 'for in Christ Jesus you are all sons of God through faith' (Galatians 3, 26).

The next two letters to the Corinthians also contain affirmations of Jesus as the son of God (1 Corinthians 1, 9; 15, 28; 2 Corinthians 1, 19; 11, 31). In the first of these, there is also a statement of another Christian doctrine, that God raised Jesus from the dead (1 Corinthians 6, 14; 15, 4).

Finally, in the letter to the Romans, there is a more complete statement of what Paul meant, or at least the position that he had reached at that point. Jesus was 'descended from David according to the flesh', that is he was fully human in the ordinary, biological sense. But, on a spiritual plane, he acquired or was granted a special relationship with God, that is as his son, by virtue of being resurrected (Romans 1, 4): 'designated son of God in power according to the spirit of holiness by resurrection from the dead'. In other words, Paul claimed that it was the act of resurrection that made or entitled Jesus to be the son of God. This is not the literalist position that had developed a few years later in the Christian Church. So what was going on?

We suggest that a history can be traced in which Paul (as Saul) first of all sought to extend a version of Judaism, mediated by him, to gentiles living outside of Palestine but within the Roman world. He did this through and in conflict with a popular movement within Judaism, Nazoreans or keepers of the covenant, that was strict in interpretation of the Jewish Law.

The people who joined Paul's newly established congregations in Syria, Turkey and Greece brought with them their existing beliefs and myths. It was a process over which Paul was not entirely in control, as the new ideas were merged with the old. One God, it is true, replaced the old pantheon of gods. But Jesus was slotted in to take the place of pagan representations, particularly the godman Dionysus, born out of a union between Zeus and a mortal woman Semele. The rituals of Mithraism were incorporated into the new religion.

According to Acts and the testimony of Paul's letters, Paul had not met Jesus but he had interacted with his followers. He must have been aware that they did not see their fallen leader as a God or son of a God. There were probably no written accounts at this time. But the Nazoreans we suggest were promoting the story that Jesus, though crucified by the Romans, had survived and then been taken directly into heaven like Elijah and many other figures in Jewish myth.

Paul's portrayal of Jesus in his letters can be seen as a progressive response to the rapidly unfolding development of his new communities, amidst a swirl of pagan practices and beliefs. At first, there was no mention of Jesus as son of God. There was no need. Paul's new Judaism, though shorn of the requirement for circumcision and dietary restrictions, was still as he had envisaged it. Then, as Jesus came to be worshipped as a Dionysian-style godman, a son of God, Paul responded by promoting a version in which everybody could be sons of god through belief. Once the idea was firmly established, however, Paul was unable to contain it. But his own view, however, appeared still to be mystical and gnostic as in 'Christ who is the *likeness* of God' (2 Corinthians 4, 4).

There was also a need at this point for a narrative to justify the adopted Mithraic ritual in which wine and bread were consumed as symbols of the sacrificed God. Paul provided it (1 Corinthians 11, 23–26).

His final resolution was to suggest that it was the raising up of Jesus that qualified him as a son of God. It may be, of course, that Paul was helped towards this conclusion by misunderstanding the Nazorean proposition (or propaganda) that Jesus was raised to heaven, which did not necessarily imply that he was raised from the dead.[8] Even at this stage, however, Paul was still acknowledging that Jesus was born according to the flesh and not literally the son of God.

As we have argued, the idea of Jesus as the son of God was not something that was fully established in Mark, the earliest of the gospels, though it did come to be incorporated as new gospels were created, copied and edited. The conscious manipulation of the text to conform with this doctrine can be seen in the earliest surviving manuscript which has the introduction of Mark, Codex Sinaiticus.

While Paul finally reached a position of Jesus qualifying to be in a special relationship with God (as son of God) by being resurrected, in the early gospel he was described as being adopted as such through his baptism. But that was not sufficient as literalist Christianity developed. So the text of Mark was altered to make Jesus son of God from the very outset, and then this was copied in later versions of the New Testament. The concept did not arise from the immediate historical context but was progressively imposed as Church doctrine developed.

If Jesus was not seen by himself or by his immediate followers as a son of God, then how was he seen? What was the title that he used for himself?

The phrase that Jesus used, or is given to use, for himself is 'son of man'. This occurs frequently throughout the four gospels in sayings attributed to Jesus. It is an odd-sounding phrase for an English speaker, in that it has no direct equivalent. However, 'son of man' was commonly used in ancient Aramaic simply to mean human, man or even just 'a man'. It was often used in conjunction with 'man' as an emphatic way of expressing the idea of mankind or an individual human being. Such usages can be found in the Old Testament, for example in Isaiah:

> *Blessed is the man who does this and the son of man who holds it fast, who keeps the Sabbath from profaning it, and keeps his hand from doing evil.*
>
> Isaiah 56, 2

There are similar examples in Psalms:

> *What is man that you think of him?*
> *The son of man that you care for him?*
>
> Psalm 8, 4

This is such a well-established structure that it is hard to tell in some instances in the gospels whether a reference is to 'man' in general or to Jesus himself:

> *And he said to them, 'The Sabbath was made for man and not man for the Sabbath: so the son of man is lord even of the Sabbath.'*
>
> Mark 2, 27

So who is lord of the Sabbath, mankind or Jesus? It seems, on balance, in this context that it was meant to be mankind.

There is a similar usage in Matthew:

> *And Jesus said to him, 'Foxes have holes and birds of the air have nests but the son of man has nowhere to lay his head'.*
>
> Matthew 8, 20

Since Jesus was responding to a scribe who wanted to follow him, 'son of man' should probably be taken from the context as referring to Jesus himself. It could also, by an allusion to man's disposition to wander, have been a means of saying to the scribe: you will have no idea where you will end up.

There are a whole group of sayings where the phrase is clearly self-referential. These are where Jesus is given to predict his death and resurrection, for example in Mark:

> He then began to teach them that the son of man must suffer
> many things and be rejected by the elders, the chief priests and
> the scribes and be killed and after three days rise again.

Mark 8, 31

There are several such passages in the synoptic gospels, all with only slight variations on the same theme. In the way that it is used here, 'son of man' is a roundabout and possibly somewhat self-deprecatory way of saying 'I' or 'me'. There are parallels in Ezekiel where the term 'son of man' was used frequently to refer to the book's author.

There is, however, another overtone to the phrase that could have been intended by the gospel writer. The phrase was used in Daniel, in the context of what came to be seen in Judaism as a messianic prophecy:

> I saw in the night visions, and behold, with the clouds of heaven
> there came one like a son of man. And he came to the ancient of
> days and was presented before him.
>   And to him was given dominion and glory and kingdom,
> that all peoples, nations and languages should serve him.

Daniel 7, 13–14

Since a little later in this passage, it is explained to Daniel, that the 'holy ones of the most high' would receive the kingdom and keep it for ever, it is reasonable to assume that the one who came like a son of man was to be a representative of these beings, perhaps heavenly creatures or God's chosen people. So that argues for a messianic interpretation for the phrase.

However, in the same passage the angel Gabriel explains to Daniel:

> [Gabriel] said to me, 'Understand, son of man, for the vision
> belongs to the end of time'.

Daniel 8, 17

This statement confirms that it was an eschatological vision, but not without throwing some confusion into the messianic interpretation of the title 'son of man'. This is because it was used in this instance to refer to Daniel, with its common meaning of human being or man. The earlier passage in Daniel, on the other hand, has been taken to refer to a figure who would eventually come and unite all people.

This is clearly how the gospel authors intended it. Here is the passage in Mark containing the full saying attributed to Jesus, quoting from Daniel 7, 13 and possibly also Psalm 110:

> *Again, the high priest asked him, 'Are you the messiah, the son of the blessed one?'*
> *Jesus said, 'I am – and you will see the son of man seated at the right hand of power and coming with the clouds of heaven'.*

Mark 14, 61–62

The distinction has to be made between what the gospel authors wrote, reflecting their own frame of reference and belief, and what the characters in their stories may have said. Less reliance can be placed on words than a possibly remembered sequence of events. This is because it was at the time a common practice to give the actors in a story appropriate dialogue, what they might have said in the opinion of the writer rather than what was reported as having been said.

It is thus unsurprising that a Christian writer should have a Jewish high priest describing the messiah, an expected mortal liberator, as a literal son of God, something that no Jew would have done. Likewise, the implication in the words of Jesus that he was the end-of-time divine figure, is something that came from the mind of the author and is unlikely to have been spoken by the captured Nazorean leader. The same can be said for a similar reference, in the little apocalypse:

> *'Then, you will see the son of man coming on clouds with great power and glory ... '*

Mark 13, 26

As we have seen, the description of Jesus by others as the son of God came into the gospels by accretion, as this Christian doctrine developed. We have shown how alterations were made at different points to accommodate this, for example in Matthew's editing of Mark and also in revisions made to the opening of Mark.

In the earliest gospel Mark, even as we now have it, the reference to Jesus as son of God is hardly found and not spoken by Jesus himself. But here in the passage above, admittedly as a reference back to Daniel, what is being attributed to Jesus, Christians would claim, is a statement that he will be there at the end of time, on a par with God.

This does not square with the rest of Mark, in which Jesus did not claim Godlike status. Nor does it square with the way in which the phrase was used at other moments in the text by Jesus, just as a roundabout way of saying 'I' or 'me'.

Just as it is not clear what Daniel intended, because he also used the phrase simply to refer to a man, so it is not clear what in apocalyptic terms the terms 'son of man' or even 'holy ones of the most high' actually mean.

So, how did Jesus see himself? It is hard to deduce that from Christian-constructed and much edited text. But it may well be that he used the phrase 'son of man' to refer to himself since it does appear frequently in the text and it was a polite, slightly self-deprecatory form of self-reference used at the time. He was one of a number of potential Jewish messianic liberators, sons of David, during the first century. As such, he may well also have appreciated the phrase's messianic overtones.

But the evidence is that he did not refer to himself or particularly see himself as a son of God, any more than Judas the Galilean, John the Baptist, Theudas, 'the Egyptian', Menahem and others at the time who put themselves in opposition to Rome.

These are the conclusions from this chapter:

- **Jesus may have spoken of himself as 'the son of man', a phrase which functioned at the time both as a polite form of self-reference and as a messianic title.**
- **Paul helped instigate the concept of Jesus as Lord, a concept at odds with the beliefs of messianic Jews.**
- **Jesus became a godman or son of God as result of a fusion of pagan and Jewish belief in the churches created by Paul.**
- **There is a progression in Paul's letters towards a view of Jesus acquiring the status of son of God by resurrection.**

- The statement that Jesus was the son of God was not in the opening of Mark's gospel in the earliest witness, Codex Sinaiticus, but was inserted by a corrector.
- As more gospels were written and as these were copied and recopied over time, so references directly indicating or supporting the idea that Jesus was the son of God came to be included.

CHAPTER 10

Women at the cross

In the previous two chapters, we looked at the evidence in the New Testament for the titles that were applied to Jesus and their meaning. With a progression established for the creation of the gospels and also for key sources, it has been possible to see how changes were made to make the text fit with developing Church doctrine.

In passing, it has also been noted that quoted speech is often notoriously unreliable. This is the case even for words written down shortly after an event, and it is more so for recollections written down years afterwards. However, some things are likely to have been better or more accurately remembered. These may include the actual framework of events, the names of important personages, structured lists and words spoken at key moments.

There are a number of crucial lists in the gospels – of the disciples, the brothers and sisters of Jesus and the women at the crucifixion who stood by the cross. These latter would have been significant persons in Jesus' life, either accurately remembered or at the very least those people the story writer believed should have been there.

It is curious, as many have noted, that the account of the women at the cross in the gospel of John appears to be at odds with those in Mark and Matthew. The objective in this chapter will be to explore this difference, in the first place purely as an analytic exercise in respect of the received text. This in itself brings some surprising conclusions: that the difference between John and the synoptics is only apparent and that some of the relationships between characters are not as traditionally perceived. Following this, we will see what further insights can be gained through looking at the sources and changes made to the text.

All the gospels describe a number of women who went with Jesus and his band of followers to Jerusalem. Luke does not name the women who 'stood at a distance' at the place of crucifixion. In Mark's gospel, the scene is described as follows:

> *There were also women looking on from afar, among whom were Mary Magdalene, and Mary the ( ) of James the younger (less) and Joses, and Salome who, when he was in Galilee, followed him, and ministered to him.*

Mark 15, 40

The author of Matthew worked from this earlier gospel, quoting many passages with closely similar or identical wording. Here, he follows Mark up to the point of a third woman listed as present, whom he describes differently:

> *There were also many women there, looking on from afar, who had followed Jesus from Galilee, ministering to him; among whom were Mary Magdalene, and Mary the mother of James and Joseph, and the mother of the sons of Zebedee.*

Matthew 27, 55–56

The two Marys were, as would be expected from their place in the story, significant women in the life of Jesus: the first his wife/partner (see following, pp 193–194) and the second his mother (and so also mother of James, the brother of Jesus). The third woman named as present at the scene of the crucifixion should also have been someone of significance. If Matthew is following Mark, as he has been for the rest of the passage, then he is adding further information. Salome is the wife of Zebedee and thus the mother of his sons, James and John.

At this point, it is not clear why the storyteller has placed her there. James and John, 'sons of thunder', have been identified earlier in the narrative as recruits to the cause. But this would of itself scarcely have merited placing their mother at the centre of the action, at the cross, with the wife and the mother of Jesus.

The author of John's gospel presents a picture which, as it is now translated from the Greek, does not seem to make sense:

But standing by the cross of Jesus were his mother, and his mother's sister, Mary (the wife) of Clopas, and Mary Magdalene.

John 19, 25

According to this, there are two sisters present, one the mother of Jesus and the other his aunt, both called Mary. This is improbable, given that families did not then, as now, generate confusion by giving siblings the same forename. Furthermore, John's gospel is at odds with Mark and Matthew in that there is a new character, the wife of Clopas, in place of Salome.

The fourth century Catholic theologian Jerome nevertheless used this reading of the passage in John to put forward a theory which cut Jesus from his natural family. Comparing this text with the parallel passages in Mark and Matthew, he proposed that 'Mary ( ) of Clopas' was the same person as Mary the mother of James and Joses. Given that James was elsewhere (Mark 3, 18; Matthew 10, 3; Luke 6, 15; Acts 1, 13) identified as the son of Alphaeus, this Mary had to be married to Alphaeus. Since this Mary was described as the sister of Jesus' mother, it also meant that James and the others described as brothers were really only Jesus' cousins. Stripped of her other children, Jesus' mother could – since in the case of Jesus it was supposed to be God who impregnated her – be regarded as having remained a virgin. The theory appeared to gain weight later when it was recognised that Clopas and Alphaeus, listed as the father of James in the gospels, are both likely derivations from the Aramaic name Chalphai.

Strained arguments have, however, been introduced to make Mary, a wife and mother, into a virgin. The authors of Matthew and Luke relied on a mistranslation[1] of a prophecy by Isaiah that a young woman would bear a son who would rescue Israel. In their version of the Old Testament, translated from Hebrew into Greek, the young woman became a 'virgin' and this was then incorporated into the nativity stories.

Jerome's interpretation of the passage in John introduced further strains, beyond the implausibility of having two sisters both called Mary and the difficulty of supposed cousins being frankly described as brothers in the gospels and other sources. In John's gospel, Jesus' mother is present at the cross, as would be expected as one of the most significant women in his life. But, if the wife of Clopas/Alphaeus is the sister of Jesus' mother and also the mother of James and Joses, then it is she who is present at the cross, instead of Jesus' mother, in the descriptions in Mark and Matthew. This is inconsistent to say the least. It is not likely that Jesus' mother would have been missing from the scene in these gospels, especially when she is described as present in John.

An examination of the Greek text of John 19, 25, as literally written, shows that the translation usually made is in error and the cause of all the difficulties:

> *But there had stood beside the cross of Jesus the mother of him and the sister of the mother of him, Mary the wife of Clopas, and Mary Magdalene.*

In the Greek used in the gospels, qualifying words are often placed later in sequence, leaving the reader to make a sensible judgement as to what they refer. In another later list (John 21, 2), Jesus appears to his disciples:

> *There were together Simon Peter and Thomas the one called the twin and Nathanael the one from Cana of Galilee and the (sons) of Zebedee and others of the disciples of him two.*

The word 'two', displaced to last position in the sentence, could be taken to apply in several contexts. But 'others of the two disciples' makes no sense. Using it as 'the two (sons) of Zebedee' makes sense, although 'two' is not used in other references to the sons of Zebedee and it leaves the phrase 'others of the disciples' incomplete. The best reading is therefore 'two others of the disciples', which makes sense and gives a sentence that is coherent.

The same logic needs to be applied to the description of the women standing by the cross (see above) where there is, if anything, an easier decision to make. The phrase 'Mary the wife of Clopas' comes after the second of two references to 'the mother of him', where it has been placed for convenience and which we suggest it qualifies. The reading this produces is better because it is more coherent and fits with other evidence:

> *But standing by the cross of Jesus were his mother, Mary the wife of Clopas, and his mother's sister, and Mary Magdalene.*

This now makes sense. Gone is the improbability of two sisters, both named Mary. The *same* three women are present as in the gospels of Mark and Matthew. Mary the mother of Jesus, and also of James and Joses/Joseph, is reinstated in the two synoptic gospels.

There is now also a reason for the third woman in the accounts in Mark and Matthew to be present at or near the cross. Salome, mother of the sons of Zebedee, appears in John as the sister of Jesus' mother. As Jesus' aunt, though ranking third in importance after his wife and mother, she may have been a significant person in his life.

As well as allowing Mary to have had other children beside Jesus, the new reading makes Clopas her husband rather than Joseph. This would accord with the portrayal of Joseph as rather a shadowy figure, not even mentioned in the earliest of the gospels, Mark.

Joseph is introduced in the nativity stories in Matthew and Luke, but then disappears in the passion narrative. Commentators have presumed that this is because he may by this time have died. An alternative explanation, supported by the evidence outlined above, is that he never was the husband of Mary but was introduced to distract from the real family of Jesus involving a mother, father (Clopas) and brothers and sisters.

Some have argued that the versions of the women present at the cross in Mark and Matthew could be taken to indicate that one of the two Marys present was the daughter of James and mother of Joses. Both versions have the same format in the Greek wording. In Matthew, the full description is 'Mary Magdalene and Mary the of James and Joseph mother and the mother of the sons of Zebedee'. The argument is threefold, that 'mother' only qualifies 'Joseph', that there is a word omitted in describing the relationship between Mary and James and that the word omitted is 'daughter'.

The Old Syriac version of Matthew in the Sinaiticus Palimpsest would appear to lend support to this argument. The manuscript dates from around the late fourth century and shows evidence of being translated from a Greek source. It is likely to have been produced in response to need among Eastern Church members, following earlier persecutions in which many Christian texts were destroyed. Here, the description of the women at the cross in Matthew runs as, 'Mary Magdalene and Mary the daughter of James and mother of Joseph and the mother of the children of Zebedee'.

There are, however, strong reasons for believing that this Syriac interpretation from the Greek is mistaken. In the first place, James and Joses or Joseph appear as the first part of the description of four of the brothers of Jesus in both Mark (6, 3) and Matthew (13, 55). Having described the brothers in full, the narrator in each gospel apparently felt no need to do so again. The mother was then subsequently defined in relationship to two brothers, as mother of James and Joses/Joseph (Mark 15, 40 and Matthew 27, 56), or as mother of just one (James in Mark 16, 1 and Luke 24, 10 and Joses in Mark 15, 47) or evasively as 'the other Mary' (Matthew 27, 61 and 28, 1). It is clear from all these descriptions that Mary was recognised as the mother of both James and Joses/Joseph. This evidence is at odds with the supposition that Mary was mother only of Joses and *daughter* of James.

Paul furthermore in his letters recognised James as a brother of Jesus. Several early church authorities also described James as Jesus' brother. He was thus another son of Mary, rather than her father. The description in John's gospel, properly interpreted, has the wife of Clopas as Jesus' mother. Since it is considered that Clopas and Alphaeus are versions of the same name, this makes James the son of Alphaeus[2] in the Apostles lists the same person as the James described in the synoptic gospels as the son of Mary.

There is incidentally a similar problem in interpreting the descriptions in the Greek of 'Mary the ( ) of James' and 'Judas ( ) of James' (Acts 1, 13). Early authorities depicted James as a lifelong celibate. He is likely therefore to have been the son of Mary and brother of Judas, who is described in the gospels as among the brothers of Jesus, rather than the parent of either or both of them.[3]

Having deduced what the gospel descriptions of the women at the cross actually record, it remains to explain how they have come to be in their present form. We suggest that the early gospel writers had little material to go on. There was the Nazorean claim in oral tradition, or possibly in written form, that Jesus had survived crucifixion and had like Elijah been taken up to heaven. There were some sayings, transmitted orally and eventually written down. The author of Luke may have had access to some official Roman records.

There could have been very little else, in view of the fact that some years had passed since the crucifixion and a large part of the population had been killed or dispersed in the Jewish uprising from 66 CE to 70 CE. The gospel compilers were furthermore followers of Paul who had established a breakaway sect, advocating the abrogation of the Torah and in opposition to the Nazorean Jews. This could well have impeded the collection of source material.

But some key facts will have been well remembered, such as the warlike descriptions of Jesus' followers,[4] redolent of the struggles that were actually being conducted against the collaborating Sadducees and occupying Romans. It also seems probable that the gospel writers would have had access to the basic facts about the family of Jesus. When John's gospel was written, early in the second century, there may have been no problem about including straightforward information on Jesus' mother, father and brothers individually and as a family.

Subsequently, a cult of Mary as a virgin and consort of God was developed. The Jewish Yeshua was turned into a Greek Jesus, the product of a union between God and a mortal woman, following the precedent of myths that pagans themselves understood as allegories.

Jesus' actual family as presented could have become an impediment to these new doctrines. So the gospels were re-examined. As a product of the way in which the Greek was written, the description of the women present at the cross in John's gospel *could* be taken to indicate that a sister of Mary was the mother of those generally regarded as her children, though with all the difficulties, drawbacks and inconsistencies hitherto described. On this basis, the passage was retained.[5]

References to Clopas in the synoptic gospels, now inconsistent with this reading, were written out or disguised. References to Mary, when being described in relation to her children were modified to exclude Jesus in every instance.[6] A nativity tale was introduced in which Mary was not even married but betrothed to a new man, safely described as Joseph, so that she could be depicted as a virgin when God supposedly inseminated her. Any direct references there may have been to Mary Magdalene as the wife of Jesus were also eliminated.

What survives first and foremost is a not a record of three women present at the cross, which may or may not be true, but an early storyteller's perception of which three women were the most significant in Jesus' life and therefore to be cast in place at this point in the drama. They were in order of listing in Mark and Matthew, and quite likely in order of precedence, his wife/partner Mary Magdalene, his mother Mary and his aunt Salome. What survive too are the marks of the alterations, the text in John which read correctly gives the game away and the listings of the brothers of Jesus: James, Joses/Joseph, Simon and Judas.

We have so far in this chapter examined the received text, which represents a view of the weight that should be attached to variations in different manuscripts. While this may be sound up to a point, to gain further insight we need to look at the sources.

The earliest surviving witnesses for the passages in the preceding analysis are partial, papyrus documents dating from around the mid second century. These are **P66** for the description in John of the women present at the cross and **P103** for the listing of the brothers of Jesus in Matthew. There are no similar, very early records for the description of the women at the cross in Mark and Matthew. For this, and the list of the brothers of Jesus in Mark, the earliest sources are Codex Sinaiticus and Codex Vaticanus.

The received text relies heavily on these two codices, which are very substantially in agreement with each other and with **P66** and **P103**. It is therefore unsurprising that an examination of these sources confirms the conclusions reached through the study of the received text. These were firstly that the list of women in John, correctly read, gives the same three women present at the cross as in Mark and Matthew. Secondly, it was found that Mary, the mother of Jesus, was married not to Joseph but to Clopas. Thirdly, the mother of the sons of Zebedee was Salome, who was also sister to Mary the mother of Jesus.

There is a disparity between the accounts in Mark and Matthew in that one of the brothers of Jesus is called Joses in Mark and Joseph in Matthew. Similarly, in the description of the women at the cross, Mark has Joses as the brother of James and son of Mary, and thus brother of Jesus, while Matthew has Joseph in the same position.

Given that these accounts agree in other detail, it would seem that the characters are interchangeable and that Joses and Joseph may have arisen as different ways of spelling the name of the same person. This comes across very clearly in the Greek where Joses is rendered as IⲱCH or IⲱCHTOC and Joseph as IⲱCHΦ. But, is it just that Mark opted for Joses while the author of Matthew chose another variant, Joseph? The answer is: only in the received text as it has been devised and not in the original sources.

An examination of the source texts shows that the usages are not consistent in Mark and Matthew, as the received text would have us believe. The usages are in fact intermingled. So, for example, in the 'women at the cross' passage in Matthew, the brother of James is Joseph in Codex Sinaiticus but Joses in Codex Vaticanus. Similarly, in the 'brothers of Jesus' passage in Mark, the second brother is given as Joseph in Codex Sinaiticus and Joses in Codex Vaticanus.

In the 'brothers of Jesus' passage in Matthew, **P103** has Joses as the second brother, at odds with both Codex Vaticanus and Codex Sinaiticus, both of which have Joseph as the second brother. But even that is not without a glitch, since Codex Sinaiticus originally had IⲱANNHC, that is John, as the second brother, corrected in the course of production to IⲰCHⲪ (Joseph). This considerable variation adds weight to the supposition that there was just one character involved, the second of the four brothers listed and bracketed in some passages as the brother of James. For the purposes of the argument so far, we will call that person Joseph, of which an idiomatic version may have been Joses.

So, now to the elephant in the room that textual analysts have tended to ignore. The list of the women at the cross is likely to have been one of the building blocks in the creation of the gospels, something well remembered and not part of the padding and embroidery required to fill out the narrative. It was something of importance. Writers at the time liked such lists, which gave legitimacy and put people in their context in society. It was less a question of who actually was present at the crucifixion, than of who were seen as the most important women in Jesus' life, in order, according to their status. This was remembered; the initial author of Mark had that information. Whether they were there or not, these people should have been present at the cross and so in the story were placed there at the cross. But in the earliest available source, Codex Sinaiticus since none of the papyrus texts for this passage have survived, the list given in Matthew in its original form is markedly different from what we now read for Matthew 27, 56 in the received text.

It is true that the received text follows an extensive correction made by the diorthotes (the scriptorium corrector, Ca). But the correction, as will be seen, does not derive from the altered text; it is not in any obvious sense the modification of a mistake. This is what scribe A wrote in copying from his source:

> And there were many women from a distance observing, who followed Jesus from Galilee, providing for him.
> Among whom was Mary the ( ) of James and the Mary the ( ) Joseph and the Mary the ( ) of the sons of Zebedee.

This is, on the face of it, very strange, given that there are three women described here as present at the cross, all of whom are called Mary.

Corrector Ca, the scriptorium corrector, changed this extensively by making several alterations. He inserted 'Mary Magdalene and' at the start, just after 'Among whom was'. He deleted the second 'Mary the', indicating this with dots over the words. He inserted an abbreviated 'mother' (MHP) after Joseph. He altered the third 'Mary', which was the last word at the bottom of a column, by scratching out the letters and inserting new letters to make the word 'mother'. Finally, he scratched out 'the' (H) at the top of the next column, before 'of the sons of Zebedee'. This made the text read as follows:

Among whom was Mary Magdalene and Mary the of James
and the Joseph mother and the mother of the sons of Zebedee.

For the effect that he appears to have been trying to achieve, the scriptorium corrector Ca should perhaps have deleted 'the Mary the', instead of 'Mary the', so that there would not be a superfluous 'the' before Joseph in this amended version.

It should be noted that the correction that Ca has made here is very unlike the vast majority of the other corrections in Sinaiticus. It is not a question of some simple error by the scribe; the corrector has, by making wholesale changes, moulded the text to some purpose.

The question is: where did the scribe get his text from, which appears so markedly different from the received text, as manifested in Ca's revision and other manuscripts including Codex Vaticanus.

Let us first look at the hypothesis that the version created from it by Ca was the 'right' version, in the sense that it was in the main exemplar from which scribe A was copying. It would then follow that scribe A deviated from it. If so, it could not have been by virtue of a simple scribal error. One aberration might of course be understandable. But for scribe A to have arrived at his copy from the version by Ca, would have entailed him making four or five significant, inexplicable mistakes in just the space of one relatively short sentence. So this theory is not tenable. The changes made by Ca have to be seen for what they are, alterations to a text as opposed to corrections to a text.

So did scribe A deliberately alter an original that corresponded with the version that Ca introduced, on this hypothesis the 'right' version, through wholesale alterations? It is hard to see why scribe A might have, or even could have, invented a new version that then had to be changed by the scriptorium corrector. If he were deviating from the main exemplar here, then it would have been by reference to another exemplar. This is possible, in that there might well have been other manuscripts of Matthew available in the scriptorium.

We discovered through our examination of skip errors, that the scribes were following one main exemplar in New Testament Sinaiticus. What is also well established is that the author of Matthew followed the text of Mark, often in great detail. For this part of the passion story, Mark 15, 33–46 and Matthew 27, 45–60, not only does Matthew follow the same sequence of events but in large part the same wording as Mark.[7]

The description of the women at the cross in Sinaiticus Mark corresponds with Ca's revision of the corresponding verse in Matthew. It is within a bifolium, one of three in the New Testament, copied out by scribe D. On the assumption that Ca's version follows the main exemplar, this would mean that scribe D was also following the main exemplar for Mark and that scribe A used an alternative exemplar for his version of the women at the cross in Matthew. It would also mean that scribe A most probably used this other exemplar for just the one verse. Other discrepancies could otherwise be expected in the surrounding text, which does in fact agree with Mark.

If it is assumed instead that Ca was amending the text to agree with an alternative exemplar, then scribe A would have been following the main exemplar and scribe D would have been following the same alternative exemplar as the scriptorium corrector Ca. Either way, what Ca was doing was harmonising the text of Matthew in Sinaiticus to agree with what scribe D had produced in Mark.[8]

It is possible that the unamended version of Matthew 27, 56 chosen by scribe A, whether following the main or an alternative exemplar, was from a more original source. It therefore deserves closer examination.

The passage does not appear to make sense, particularly in placing three women all called Mary at the cross. But it does have some of the building blocks of the other gospel versions: three women at the cross, one of them related to James and another to the sons of Zebedee, as well as a character named Joseph. It can readily be agreed that scribe A must have made some mistake. But it was in fact just one major error, and not several simultaneously as an uncritical reading of Ca's alterations might indicate.

There were two distinct persons called Mary, though not three, both well attested in the New Testament. And the person related to the sons of Zebedee was not Mary but their *mother*. What we suggest scribe A actually *saw* in his exemplar for Matthew 27, 56 was this:

Among whom was Mary the ( ) of James and the Mary the ( )
Joseph and the mother of the sons of Zebedee.

Having just written 'Mary the' twice, it was in his mind when he began to write the 'M' of mother. He was at the bottom of a column and a little distracted by the need to get the whole word in, rather than have it split between two columns. These are quite likely what caused him to make the mistake, continuing with 'Mary the' rather than 'mother'. He made just one mistake, as opposed to several simultaneously which is just not plausible.

This leaves us with not a mistaken or concocted version, but simply an alternative version of the women at the cross. The two alternative versions may have come about through a struggle, never fully resolved,[9] to reconcile a prototype for the women at the cross in the two synoptic gospels with that in the gospel of John. The prototype, represented we suggest by the uncorrected version of Matthew 27, 56 above, was modified on the basis that the second Mary the ( ) of Joseph was not recognisable as a gospel character and so must have originated as a slip of the scribe's pen. Since there was a Joseph/Joses among the brothers of Jesus, described in other passages, it was assumed that the writer of the prototype must really have intended one Mary, mother of both James and Joseph/Joses. But that would have reduced the number of women at the cross to two, as against three in John. As Mary Magdalene appeared to be missing, though present in John, she was then added in. The changes made gave rise to the current versions in Mark and Matthew.

What we are suggesting is a template generated to resolve an apparent problem. This might have been created at the time that Sinaiticus was written. Or it could already have been fashioned in whole cloth in another exemplar, used by the scribes. As we have seen, in the Sinaiticus Palimpsest, Matthew's description of the women at the cross, is 'Mary Magdalene and Mary the daughter of James and mother of Joseph and the mother of the children of Zebedee'.

The latter part of this list would likely have appeared in the author's Greek source as 'Mary the ( ) of James and the ( ) of Joseph and the mother of the children of Zebedee'. This is very close to what scribe A wrote in Codex Sinaiticus and provides intriguing evidence of another possible early attempt at harmonisation.

The writer would here have been trying to reconcile an exemplar of the type that scribe A had, against the version in John, and possibly also against either Sinaiticus or Vaticanus or a copy of one of these manuscripts. We have argued above that Mary could not have been the daughter of James, as the writer of the Sinaiticus

Palimpsest interpreted his Greek text. A version of his original did, however, survive in an exemplar which found its way into a scriptorium, most probably in Caesarea, where it was used in the preparation of Codex Sinaiticus.

There are good reasons for arguing that the exemplar used by scribe A preceded the alternative version. The first is that it is fairly easy to explain how the apparently more 'difficult' reading came to be transformed into the more understandable reading, in fact precisely as Ca did in making his changes. But it is much harder to generate an explanation as to how scribe A's version might have been derived from the one substituted by Ca.

The second reason is that the scribes working on Sinaiticus would almost certainly initially have sought to use the oldest and thereby more authentic texts, which is presumably what scribe A was seeking to do. But whether or not it was more original, as we have suggested, what remains is the task of deciphering the text. Who was Mary ( ) of Joseph?

The first observation is that it is only in the two synoptic 'women at the cross' passages, in Mark and Matthew, that Mary is defined in relation to two of her sons. But we have deduced that this came about through a reconstruction of text in which there had been two Marys, one related to James and one to Joseph. There was no need to have defined Mary in relation to two people instead of one, and nor was this usual. We can however see how the duplicate definition came to be constructed at this point. We can see also how it should have been from the description, only a little further on in Mark, of the women who went to the tomb early on Sunday morning: Mary Magdalene and Mary the mother of James and Salome.

The next observation is that there are three women at the cross in all of the versions, including the gospel of John. The final point to note is there is a correspondence between John and the prototype of Matthew, just as was found in the exercise conducted a little earlier on the received text. Mary the mother of James equates with Mary, the wife of Clopas, and the mother of the sons of Zebedee (Salome) equates with the sister of Mary, the wife of Clopas. That leaves Mary (of) Joseph, who we suggest will have been Mary/Mary Magdalene. This is an identification that might have been hard to make at the outset, but which is supported by the evidence. It is now not at all surprising.

Our reconciliation has restored to the group present at the cross, characters who would have been, as the original writer doubtless intended, the three most significant women in Jesus' life. These were his mother, his wife and his aunt Salome.

These women were described in Mark and Matthew through a Christian author's circumlocutions, designed to avoid giving information on the real relationships that the Jewish Jesus had. Thus Mary was described as the mother of James. But James was Jesus' brother and Mary was also Jesus' mother. Salome was left as an unexplained female or described circuitously as the mother of the sons of Zebedee. But she was Mary's sister and so also Jesus' aunt.

In John, these relationships were described with greater frankness, though in a Greek construction that allowed for misinterpretation and was so misinterpreted, the reason perhaps that the text survived. But when it came to Mary/Mary Magdalene, even John could not be explicit because this was for the early Church a sensitive topic. It is only because of getting on for two thousand years of habituation to a prudish perception that something so normal and usual, either now or in Jewish society at the time, could still today produce anything remotely approaching a reaction of shock. Jesus would have been married and the strong and most likely candidate as his wife, from the evidence in the gospels, is Mary Magdalene.[10]

So how did she come to be described as Mary the (of) Joseph in the original passage in Matthew? The mother of Jesus is here described sufficiently in terms of just one of Jesus' brothers, James. The name 'Joseph' is attached to the other Mary. The evidence suggests two possibilities.

One is that Mary was the daughter of someone called Joseph. That Joseph, we have argued, may have been Joseph of Arimathea, a corruption of Hebrew/Aramaic Yusuf ab Maria (Joseph, father of Mary). Joseph fits perfectly into this role in the gospel story as the person who provided the family tomb, who stepped in when Jesus' father had ceased to be mentioned and can be presumed to have died and who claimed the body of Jesus, something only a close relative had a right to do. So, if this interpretation is correct, the second Mary present, Mary the ( ) of Joseph, was the daughter of Joseph. This was the man, father-in-law to Jesus, who stood in to take responsibility for claiming the body of Jesus after the crucifixion, in the absence of Jesus' natural father, Clopas.[11]

A second possibility relates to the enigmatic character of the second listed brother of Jesus, variously described as Joses or Joseph. Apart from this reference, he takes no further part in the action in the gospels, unlike James, Simon and Judas. Nor is there even a faint echo of Joses' life in other sources. This again stands in contrast with James and Simon, who in turn afterwards led the Jewish Nazorean community and Judas who as Theuda gets a mention and as Theudas may have led a revolt against the Romans.

Though we have suggested that Joses may have been a variation of Joseph, the confusion over the name indicates something else. Were the Greek translators of an Aramaic original attempting to deal with a name that they were perplexed by, or did not recognise, and coming up with different solutions?

An eleventh century writer, Papias, compiled a lexicon in which 'Mary the wife of Cleophas or Alphaeus' was also described as 'the mother of James the bishop and apostle, and of Simon and Thaddeus and a certain Joseph'. Thaddeus is known from the apostles' lists in the gospels to equate with Judas. So, is Joseph the fourth of the brothers of Jesus? Or he is, since Jesus should be there as one of the sons of Mary, not a brother at all but Jesus himself, at some earlier point mistranslated from an earlier source?

That would clear up a lot of difficulties, including the confusion over the name, either Joseph or Joses, and the lack of any real substance to such a character as a brother of Jesus in any record. It also provides another possible resolution to what was intended by Mary the ( ) of Joseph. If this Joseph were really Jesus, then the Mary here described as Mary the ( ) of Joseph, is Mary the wife of Jesus. This is precisely what has been deduced on other evidence for the role of Mary Magdalene.

So there is one puzzle and two possible solutions. Either of these would adequately explain the original exemplar used in Sinaiticus for the passage relating to the women at the cross. It is also worth noting that the explanations are not mutually exclusive, given that Mary/Mary Magdalene could have been both daughter of Joseph and the wife of Jesus.

Both solutions involve the same group of three women and both are in accordance with the depiction of the women in all three canonical gospels. We have thus satisfactorily resolved the discrepancies, real and apparent, in the descriptions of the women present at the cross.

Scribes, correctors and more recent commentators may have found it difficult to do this, at least in part because of their own preconceptions. It would certainly have been hard even to have embarked on such an exercise from a committed standpoint. There is no escaping the fact that the evidence raises uncomfortable implications for Christian tradition.

We have arrived at these conclusions in respect of the women at the cross:

- **The four gospels all describe, in various ways, the same three women present at the cross.**
- **These women were: Mary Magdalene, Mary (mother of Jesus and James) and Salome (wife of Zebedee, mother of his sons James and John and sister of Mary who was the mother of Jesus).**
- **John's description of the women at the cross has, in translation, been based on a misreading of the Greek. It provides the further information that Jesus' mother Mary was the wife of Clopas.**
- **Codex Sinaiticus has a version of the women at the cross in Matthew that has Mary (Magdalene) described in relation to a character named Joseph.**

We have, in this chapter, reached a point where the battle to control the message, in this instance in deciding which alternative source or version to use, can clearly be seen to have entered the scriptorium. There is a lot more to be discovered in our final four chapters.

CHAPTER 11

The lost ending of Mark

The last twelve verses of the gospel of Mark represent a very big problem for theologians and textual critics. That is because there is a profound disjunction between these verses and the preceding text. There is a consensus view among many scholars that this longer ending is not original, but was added at some later time to fill an apparent gap.

It is a view supported by a number of differences in construction, style and content, indicating that the two portions of text were written by different hands. Not only that, but the earliest witnesses to the last part of Mark, Codex Sinaiticus and Codex Vaticanus, lack these twelve verses entirely as indeed do a number of other later sources.

The question of the ending of Mark has been much debated and at great length. Though we are not proposing to go into the same detail here, we hope to deal with the crucial issues and point the reader towards relevant sources. Having put the matter into context, however, we will be able to proceed to an analysis of the texts. The omissions in Sinaiticus and Vaticanus, far from telling us nothing, do in fact speak volumes.

A degree of caution is advised in examining arguments that may rest on vested interest or predisposed belief. We have, for example, in Chapter 8 summarised the case that Mark was originally written prior to the gospels of Matthew and Luke, which not only use Mark as a source but are dependent on this gospel for much of their narrative. Most scholars accept this. But a few, who have canvassed Matthew as original, may have had ulterior motivation. This is to deal with the problem for Christian theology of the picture presented by Mark, in comparison with the versions in the other canonical gospels.

So, for example, we have in Mark a predominantly 'angry' Jesus who is made to appear more compassionate as a result of changes in Luke and Matthew.[1] We also have in Mark a Jesus who does not acknowledge himself as good, but only God as good, and a garbled version of the same story in Matthew to disguise and blur this message (see above pp 138, 169). We have in Mark a Jesus who is not described by his followers as 'Lord', as he is in the other canonical gospels.

We also have, in the context of the present discussion, in Mark a Jesus missing from the tomb, with no account of subsequent appearances and thus no witness that could be construed as evidence of resurrection. This difficulty would, of course, be obviated if Matthew were a prior source, since this gospel does contain a description of appearances, albeit sparse, of Jesus to his disciples after the crucifixion.

The abbreviated version of Mark, before the addition, ends with the women going to the tomb. They find a young man posted there, telling them to pass on the message to the disciples that Jesus has risen and gone to Galilee where they should go to meet him. At which the women flee the tomb and, out of fear, tell no one what has happened. This is where the story ends. There is, in this first source, no statement of any of Jesus' appearances or his miraculous ascension. There is only the young man's statement that he had gone to Galilee, in which context the word 'risen' is at least ambiguous.

We have argued elsewhere[2] that the oral or written Nazorean testimony from the followers of Jesus, on which the prototype of Mark was based, made a case that Jesus had in fact survived the ordeal of crucifixion. Persisting in Mark are many crucial points to this effect: for example, that Jesus' legs were not broken (the coup de grace required to complete the execution) and that he was on the cross for a comparatively short time.

There is thus, in the earliest available witness, less than compelling evidence on the issue of the resurrection. We give below the text without additions, as it is in Codex Sinaiticus and also in the critical text:

> *When the Sabbath was over, Mary Magdalene and Mary the*
> *mother of James and Salome bought spices in order to go and*
> *anoint him. So, very early on the first day of the week when the*
> *sun had risen, they went to the tomb.*

They had been saying to each other, 'Who will roll away the stone for us from the tomb?' But, when they looked up, they saw that the stone, which was very large, had already been rolled away.

As they entered the tomb, they saw a young man in a white robe sitting on the right and they were alarmed. But he said to them, 'Do not be alarmed. You are looking for Jesus the Nazorean, who was crucified. He has been raised. He is not here. Look at the place where they laid him. But go, tell his disciples and Peter that he is going ahead of you to Galilee. There you will see him, just as he told you.'

They left the tomb and fled for terror and amazement had seized them. And they said nothing to anyone for they were afraid.

Mark 16, 1–8

Codex Bobiensis, an Old Latin source from around the end of the fourth century, adds the following short, summary ending:

And they reported briefly to those with Peter all that they had been told. And afterwards Jesus himself sent out through them, from east to west, the sacred and imperishable proclamation of eternal salvation.

Mark, shorter ending

In other manuscripts, this ending is sandwiched between Mark 16, 1–8 and a longer ending. However, in most of these later sources, this longer ending follows directly after verse 16, 8:

Now, after he rose early on the first day of the week, he appeared first to Mary Magdalene from whom he had cast out seven demons. She went and told those who had been with him, as they mourned and wept. But, when they heard that he was alive and had been seen by her, they would not believe it.

After this, he appeared in another form to two of them, as they were walking into the country. And they went back and told the rest but they did not believe them.*

Later, he appeared to the eleven themselves, as they sat at table. And he reproached them for their lack of belief and

*hardness of heart because they did not believe those who had
seen him after he had risen.*

*And he said to them, 'Go into the whole world and preach
the good news to all of creation. Whoever believes and is
baptised will be saved but whoever does not believe will
be condemned. And these signs will accompany those who
believe: they will cast out demons in my name, they will
speak in new tongues and they will pick up snakes with their
hands. And, if they drink any deadly poison, it will not harm
them. They will lay their hands on the sick and they will
become healthy.'*

*So then the Lord Jesus, after he had spoken to them, was
taken up into heaven and sat down at the right hand of God.
And they went out and preached everywhere, while the Lord
worked with them and confirmed the message through the
signs that accompanied it.*

Mark 16, 9–20 (longer ending)

There is another variation to this longer ending. In Codex
Washingtonensis, a Greek manuscript of the four gospels from the
fourth or fifth century, there is a unique addition after the expression
of the disciples' disbelief (* above):

*And they excused themselves, saying, 'This age of lawlessness
and unbelief is under Satan who does not allow the truth and
power of God to prevail over the unclean things of the spirits.
Therefore, reveal thy righteousness now!'*

*Thus, they spoke to Christ. And Christ replied to them,
'The term of years of Satan's power has been fulfilled, but
other terrible things draw near. And, for those who have
sinned, I was delivered over to death that they may return
to the truth and sin no more, so that they may inherit the
spiritual and incorruptible glory of righteousness which is in
heaven.'*

Addition after longer ending, Mark 16, 14 (Freer logion)

The first question that needs to be considered is whether or not the
verses added in the longer version were original to Mark. The story
without these verses, or certainly some other ending, appears incomplete. It reaches the point where Jesus has been crucified and the tomb

is empty, leaving open the questions of what happened to the body and whether Jesus, naturally or miraculously, might still be alive. The story builds to a climax and that climax, in what we will describe as the abbreviated version, is missing.

The argument, that the verses in the longer ending were nonetheless a later addition, was put very cogently by Bruce Metzger in his *A Textual Commentary on the New Testament*. In terms of the narrative, Metzger makes the telling point that verses 9–20 of the longer ending do not follow smoothly from the previous text; there is a severe dislocation. The subject of the final verse of the abbreviated Mark is the women who ran away, afraid. The subject of the first verse of the longer ending, denoted as 'he', is presumably Jesus. If the narrative had been continuous Jesus should, for the sake of clarity, at this point have been named.

Mary Magdalene is introduced in the opening sentence of the longer ending as if she were a new character, with a qualifying comment 'from whom he had cast out seven demons' to define her. But, in fact, she has already been introduced to the reader, having been mentioned twice in the previous few verses.

In the longer ending, there is no mention of the other women described in Mark 16, 1–8, Mary the mother of James and/or Joses and Salome, although this might have been expected, had this really been a contemporaneous continuation.

The plot is left unresolved at the end of verse 16, 8 and the sentence is left hanging. The final clause, ΕΦΟΒΟΥΝΤΟ ΓΑΡ (for they were afraid) is highly unusual as a means of ending a sentence or paragraph. The women kept silent, except perhaps to tell the disciples as instructed. But we are not told why they were afraid. A clause beginning with 'because' is almost invited at the end of 16, 8 after 'they said nothing to anyone for they were afraid'. The wording of the beginning of 16, 9, 'Now, after he rose early on the first day of the week', does not relate to the previous text. It is unsuited as a continuation.

The added verses, as a whole, do not deal with the climax that is indicated. Peter and the disciples are told to go to Galilee, which presumably they would then have done. But there is no mention in the additional text of the disciples making such a journey or its outcome. There are descriptions of other appearances/meetings. But the only one that is indicated, from what has survived of the original ending of Mark in the shorter version, that is a journey to Galilee, is not dealt with in the additional verses.

The language and style of the longer ending, Metzger points out, are different in some ways from the text of the abbreviated Mark.

The word 'Lord' (KYPIOC), we note, is used twice in the last paragraph, even though this usage is alien to Mark while frequently used in the later gospels.

Some content, such as the appearance to two persons, appear to be summaries of, rather than a source for, material in Luke. The reference to 'seven demons', with regard to Mary Magdalene, appears in Luke 8, 2. Other elements, including the use of speaking in tongues as a sign, may well have originated from Acts.

The case that the additional verses in the longer version were not original is thus quite powerful. Their existence was known to some early patristic sources. In the late second century, Irenaeus appears to have quoted the longer ending and Tatian, writing at about the same time, may have used it in his *Diatessaron*, an amalgamation of the four gospels. But such relatively early use does not necessarily mean that the ending is authentic in terms of being from the same author as the rest of Mark.

Origen, in the third century, in discussing reported resurrection appearances in *Against Heresies*, does not refer to the longer ending. Such a reference might have been expected, if he had access to it and thought it genuinely to be an integral part of Mark's gospel. Later in the fourth century, Eusebius and Jerome, though aware of the longer ending, indicated that they did not believe it to have been original. Eusebius did not include the longer ending of Mark in his canon tables, used as a means of locating comparable passages in the gospels.

The position that has been reached among scholars is a broad consensus, based on good evidence, that the longer ending of Mark was added later. It should be noted that the issue is not a matter of great moment, seen from an objective standpoint. Even had there been an authentic ending to Mark, including post-crucifixion appearances, this would not in any case have added to the case for the resurrection, since abbreviated Mark is still at some remove from the account of Jesus' Jewish followers. This, as we have argued, was Nazorean propaganda, whether or not with a basis in fact, aimed at the Romans and to the effect that Jesus had survived. It was subsequently given a Christian gloss in the gospel written for the Church that Paul had founded.

The absence of an ending to Mark with resurrection appearances was, however, perceived by many of the faithful as a weakness. It led to greater emphasis on other arguments, one of which was that Mark was dependent on Matthew and or Luke, rather than vice versa. If that were the case, then it would be of less consequence that Mark's account is lacking, when it comes to the crucial passage. As we have already demonstrated (Chapter 7), this argument is not supported by the evidence.

Other positions that have been taken include the argument that the truth of the resurrection is supported by Church tradition. Additionally, or alternatively, it has been claimed that later writers were divinely inspired. Thus, even though they may have had no direct evidence, they came to the right conclusions by intuition. It is not just that such reasoning is circular and self-evidently flawed. We are in the realm of conjecture where anyone can say anything and whoever has the loudest voice, or can inspire the most fear or credulity, will be likely to carry the day.

Barring such diversions, there have been one or two attempts to make the case that the longer ending of Mark is in some way valid, despite being clearly secondary on the evidence. So, for example, it has been argued[3] that the original, putative author John Mark was interrupted in writing his gospel (essentially, by going away and in the meantime being martyred). His colleagues, who had access to his notes or his thinking, then finished it. Hence, the stylistic differences in the longer ending and hence presumably the preference that some would have had for the shorter version that John Mark alone had written.

We do not, of course, have reliable early evidence for the authorship of any of the gospels. Names were simply added much later to the texts, according to traditions that had developed over periods of perhaps more than a century. So, any explanation that has reference to specific characters is at least partly founded on speculation.

Aside from this, the chief flaw with the argument is that it depends on a number of quite complicated suppositions, for none of which is there any evidence. The assumptions are that the author was interrupted in his work, that it was his first attempt and so there were no other copies, that there was no exemplar or that this was the exemplar, that he was unable for a specific reason to return to complete it, that his colleagues then added an ending and that this added ending corresponded with what was known or with what the colleagues knew the author intended.

It is also presumed that something like the gospel of Mark, as we have it, was the very first version. This gospel depended, however, on the witness of people who were not Christians but Jewish followers of Jesus. Their account, which we have suggested was fashioned to a particular agenda, was then adapted by Mark's original author. We have evidence of at least one prior version of Mark, that is Secret Mark,[4] and there may have been one or two more stages in arriving at the current version, as it is evidenced in Codex Sinaiticus. Some scholars have argued for a prototype 'Cross gospel', from which came the gospels of Mark and Peter.[5]

In addition to which, had someone else attempted to finish the gospel, they would likely have achieved a better continuation, without for example the clumsy reintroduction of Mary Magdalene or starting the first sentence without naming the subject of it. It is also improbable that its author would have left such an important document unfinished and gone off to do something else, after most of the gospel had been finished and just a few verses from the end, when there was no exemplar and no other copy.

It really is a very weak argument. What is clear is that the longer ending was added later and not as a continuation written to follow on smoothly from the existing text. It appears to have been borrowed from some other document, which had possibly been written as a gospel summation or summary.

This first approach, which we have outlined, advocating an interruption in the compilation of Mark, was taken by an American clergyman, James Snapp. It is matched by a second, this time from an ordained Anglican and one-time Oxford Professor of the Exegesis of Holy Scripture, B H Streeter, in his book *The Four Gospels.* In order, it would seem, to deal with the same difficulty: the lack of any authentic end to Mark and thus the lack of any early witness for the resurrection, Streeter speculated that the gospel *had* in fact been finished by its author. But, almost immediately afterwards and before any copies had been made, he posited that there was some such event as a Roman 'police raid' on the house where it was held, during which the vital last page was torn from the gospel and lost for ever.

Streeter goes on to suggest that someone made a note in general terms from memory of what the gospel ending had contained. This, he argued, then formed the basis for the very sparse account in Matthew, including an 'appearance' to the two Marys in Jerusalem followed later by one to the eleven disciples in Galilee. The longer ending of Mark was constructed subsequently from material already in Luke and Acts.

Streeter's proposal unfortunately suffers from the same fatal defects. It relies on an elaborate construction of hypothetical events, for which there is no factual basis. It is also reliant on an improbable scenario, that the final page of the manuscript was lost just after it had been completed and before any other copies could be made and that its source could not be used to reinstate it. It assumes that that there were no precursors to the present gospel of Mark. It also assumes that, for a very short and significant remaining part of the story suddenly lost, no one who had had access to it could remember anything other than the barest outline.

The two theories, which we have just described, seek in different ways to accommodate a longer ending of Mark despite the evidence that it was added later. In one case, it is suggested that the ending was completed, lost and then summarised in another gospel. In the other, it is proposed that the ending, though not completed by the author, was finished by colleagues.

These approaches may have been motivated by the desire to restore what is in actuality lacking in the earliest gospel, any description of resurrection appearances. Although unsubstantiated, they do however point up one characteristic of the abbreviated ending of Mark. This is that it was written in a way which indicates that there was more to come.

At two points, Jesus is given to say that he will meet up with the disciples in Galilee. The first is in conversation with Simon Peter (Mark 14, 28). Then later, when the women reach the tomb, a young man dressed in white gives them the message that Jesus is going ahead of Peter and the disciples to Galilee (Mark 16, 7). It is a reasonable expectation that the ensuing narrative would resolve this. Since it is predicated in the story up to 16, 8, there should be something to indicate that Jesus did go to Galilee followed by a description of his meeting there with Peter and the disciples.

The story is clearly incomplete and positively begs for this material to conclude it. So, although the longer ending often included with Mark is inauthentic, it appears highly likely that the author did originally add more to conclude his narrative. That conclusion is missing and the question that remains to be answered is: what happened to it?

A number of other accounts fill in these details. In Matthew, the young man in the tomb is transformed into an angel of the Lord who rolls back the stone blocking the entrance to the tomb. In Luke, it is now two men in 'dazzling' clothes and in John two angels in white who appear before the women in the tomb. In the gospel of Peter, two men go into the tomb and help Jesus out of it, providing him with support. Various other witnesses are provided for Jesus leaving or having left the tomb. In Matthew and John, as in the added longer ending to Mark, he is seen outside by Mary Magdalene. Matthew also has Jesus' mother Mary present. In the gospel of the Hebrews, Jesus hands his linen shroud to the High Priest's servant. In the gospel of Peter, soldiers and Jewish elders who were on watch see him being helped from the tomb.

Jesus then makes appearances, or meets with, a number of his family and followers in Jerusalem. In Luke he meets two, possibly his brother James (son of Clopas) and either Simon Peter or another brother Simon (Luke 24, 13–35), on the way to Emmaus, as in the added longer ending of Mark which has 'in the country'. Jesus goes to meet James in the gospel of the Hebrews. He meets the disciples in Jerusalem in Luke and John (twice). Once again, this is reflected in the longer ending of Mark, where Jesus appears to or meets the disciples 'as they sat at table'.

The gospels of Peter and John provide accounts, the former broken off, of a meeting with Jesus and some of the disciples including Peter in connection with a fishing expedition in Galilee. In Matthew, the meeting with the disciples in Galilee is at a mountain, to which Jesus had directed them. Whereas in John's gospel Peter and the others recognise Jesus in Galilee, in Matthew the disciples are described as uncertain.

It has been suggested that elements now in the endings of some of the other gospel accounts might have originally been in a lost ending of the abbreviated version of Mark. There is considerable disagreement in these accounts over the details, which might indicate divergence over time or the lack of a common source or indeed both.

What agreement there is might be accounted for by commonsense expectation. For example, it is related both in Peter and John that some of the disciples went on a fishing trip in Galilee. But a number of them were identified at the outset in Mark as fishermen. Not unexpected, this could easily have been a story line independently developed in Peter and John. Or, alternatively, John might have depended on Peter, or rather an earlier version of the gospel of Peter that we have now, without this being derived from an ending that had been present in Mark.

As already noted, a future meeting in Galilee is twice signposted in the account in Mark up to the break at verse 16, 8. So it was indicated for later gospel writers and might therefore have been imaginatively reconstructed.

We have established that abbreviated Mark almost certainly had a longer ending, but that it was not the ending now added in the longer version. And we have rejected the arguments that it somehow survived, either in the longer version as an addition by the author's colleagues or in Matthew as a remembered summary. There is no clear indication whether or not elements of an original longer ending survived into the gospels of John, Peter or Luke.

What is evident is that, in seeking to make sense of the various source material they had, the gospel writers provided it with structure. This reaches a culmination in John's gospel, whose author appears to have had the synoptics and Peter available, as well as some independent material. He welds the reported appearances into a sequence: at the tomb, in Jerusalem and then finally at the Sea of Galilee.

But what was indicated in the incomplete Mark was specifically a meeting-up in Galilee. The gospel of Peter, available from a large fragment covering the latter part of the passion narrative, does include a description of a fishing expedition in Galilee. Tantalisingly, once this point is reached, the narrative breaks off in mid-sentence, with the rest of the text missing. The gospel of John, which is complete, provides more detail.

Matthew includes in his last twelve verses, after the women have run from the tomb, a subsequent meeting between Jesus and the disciples on a mountain in Galilee. The description is so brief and limited as to indicate that this author only had before him abbreviated Mark, with its announcement of a meeting in Galilee, from which to fashion his own ending.

So what then happened to the original ending of Mark? It is, as we have pointed out, improbable that there was an accidental loss or failure to complete the ending when there was just one original. But if prototype Mark were copied and distributed, then it is hard to see how a truncated version might have completely supplanted the whole, original text. Manuscripts did certainly suffer damage, particular where they were more exposed at the beginning or end. But, if a last page were to become accidentally detached and lost in one copy, then the ending could have been sought out and supplied from other copies known to exist.

The theory of a conscious effort to suppress the ending would seem to suffer from the same defect. It would have been difficult to have sought out and eliminated all rival copies of the gospel with a complete ending. At this early time, the Church lacked the central control that it later developed. There is evidence indeed from Paul's letters, particularly to the Galatians, that he was finding it hard as early as around 55–60 CE to keep the scattered outposts of his new sect in line. So centrally-directed, conscious censorship of this sort might well not then have been feasible.

It is reasonable to suppose that the semi-autonomous, decentralised situation that existed when Paul wrote his letters, continued into the time just a few years later when the first gospel was written. This we suggest was, in Crossan's terms, a Cross gospel or prototype Mark. It was, we have argued, derived from a Nazorean account, a piece of propaganda whether true or not claiming that their man Jesus (Yeshua) had survived a Roman execution. Many elements of this persisted when the story was developed into the prototype gospel of Mark.

It was a good story, but it was not about the central issues that then divided the emerging Christians and their parent Nazorean community: that is, the requirements for circumcision, dietary restrictions and scrupulous adherence to the Jewish Law or Torah.

To understand what may have happened at around this time, between about 70 and 85 CE, it is necessary first of all to get into a different mind-set. There were no gospels written with names attributed to different authors. The names were added later, and very likely without any real evidence that it was someone called John or Mark or Matthew or Peter or Luke who was responsible. It is apparent why names were eventually added; by the time that many different versions of the gospels were in circulation, putative authors' names would have been a useful way of distinguishing them. Until Irenaeus wrote around 175 CE, there is no association of names with gospels.

The prototype Mark (at the time, simply the gospel), with its passion narrative, was written in Greek by Christians outside Palestine on the basis of written and/or oral Jewish Nazorean testimony. It was copied and changed by different communities, forming the basis for a prototype of the gospel of Peter and possibly other versions of which there is no longer any record. Other information may have been added in at this point, or a little later, to generate versions that were later attributed to Luke and John. Prototype Mark may, in a competitive situation, have lost ground to these other versions.

The precise sequence of events is hard to recover, given that the period in question consists of a very few years between about 70 and 85 CE for which there are no direct textual witnesses and little in the way of indirect information. Although copies were made and although competing accounts arose, all in effect versions of the one gospel, the Christian compass was still very restricted. There were relatively few members and so relatively few texts were needed.

A great deal had however been happening over this short and crucial period when the gospel story was being put together. Initially, as can be seen both from Paul's letters and Acts, the divide was between the rules that the Nazorean Jewish community demanded be applied and the new order that Paul and his supporters – without dietary restrictions, circumcision or the Torah – were wrestling to generate, in what would become a schismatic sect. But their gentile converts brought with them key elements of pagan beliefs: a semi-divine man born from the union of a god and a mortal woman, dying to be resurrected.[6] This perception would not have been in the ingenious tale by the Nazorean Jews themselves of a leader, a messianic claimant to the throne of David, captured and condemned to death but surviving his execution.

Paul had perforce to adapt to a process over which he was not entirely in control. His letters (see Chapter 9) over a decade progressively took on the ideas of the resurrection and of a Jesus accorded a special relationship with God by virtue of being raised from the dead.

But the emerging prototype gospel had Jesus subjected to an uncompleted execution, helped from the tomb, given time to recover and then meeting with his family and supporters to do some very ordinary things. It was not an appropriate account in view of the developing doctrine of a miraculous resurrection.

The elements of the story that have persisted indicate that the prototype for Mark provided a record of a man who was only resurrected in the sense that he managed to survive an execution procedure. It may even have indicated that Jesus did what would have been eminently sensible for a Jewish, messianic rebel who, if still alive, was wanted by the authorities. It might have stated that he had then gone into hiding or exile.[7]

We suggest that sometime very early on, the prototype gospel was cut. Probably, this was not in all copies. We agree that the central organisation was not there at the time to ensure conformity through the elimination of all the earlier texts.

But some people had objected to the ending of the gospel (Mark), possibly because it was at odds with developing Christian doctrine, and removed it from the prototype written in Greek, in one or more copies, sometime around 60–70 CE. This would have been among the gentile communities within the diaspora, possibly in Rome, where the new sect had a hold. In the east in Palestine, the new Christian communities were circulating a text of the sayings of Jesus in Aramaic.

At this time, in 64 CE, there was an extensive fire in Rome that the Emperor Nero blamed on Christians. In the ensuing persecution, it is likely that copies were destroyed and the dissemination of the prototype gospel slowed. While this was happening, or a few years afterwards, it was decided to improve the gospel still further by combining it with the sayings of Jesus in Aramaic. This was done initially in Aramaic, using the cut version, and then it was translated back into Greek (see Appendix X). The new version of the gospel proved popular, so that there may in consequence have been far fewer of the old versions (prototype Mark) whether cut or uncut at this time in circulation. There was a perceived better version to supplant the old, as copies became worn out or were discarded.

The opportunity was taken in the improved version to amend Jesus' character, to correspond better with the mythical godman figure that had infiltrated the new sect at its core. The 'angry' elements were filtered out. The saying attributed to Jesus, that he was not good but only God was good, was changed. The title which Jews gave to God only, as in 'the Lord God' was extended to Jesus.

In these ways, and many other small ones, the earlier version of the gospel was censored. The rewrite of the gospel that included more sayings made subtle but significant changes. The new version was eventually attributed to Matthew, still just in Greek 'the gospel'. In Aramaic, it was the gospel according to the language of the Hebrews, rendered as the gospel of or according to the Hebrews.

Matthew's ending is vague, out of keeping with both the robust style of its template, Mark, and with its own colourful storytelling earlier, for example in describing the nativity or the temptation of Jesus in the desert. It shows all the indications of a summary made where there were few or no clues in the original.

The author of Matthew was then, as we have deduced, working from the abbreviated version of Mark. He follows Mark very closely throughout the narrative up to the end of the abbreviated ending at 16, 8. But, after that, his story bears no relation to the longer ending, indicating that the author was either unaware of it or had rejected it. This provides support for the idea that the longer ending of Mark was generated after both prototype Mark and Matthew had been written in the first century, possibly around the beginning of the second century.

The ending of Matthew, from the point in the story after the women have run from the tomb, continues rather clumsily. For example, Jesus is given to meet and tell the women that the disciples should go and meet him in Galilee. This is just after the young man (angel/ messenger of the Lord in Matthew) has told the women the very same thing. It is thus possible that the last twelve verses of Matthew were also added later. So, the elaboration of Mark that originally became Matthew may also have originally stopped short.

Perhaps in belated recognition of its importance as an early witness, interest was at some point revived in the prototype of the gospel, now called Mark. But by this time there were few copies in circulation. The copy that was immediately available was missing its ending. This rediscovered prototype gospel was copied and recirculated. A version with a longer ending, intended to fill in what appeared to be missing, was then generated.

So what then might have been in the lost ending of Mark? One pointer may lie in the fact that the accounts in all of the gospels show Jesus doing some very mundane things after being released from the tomb: cooking food, eating fish, walking about. If these are in any degree a reflection of an original ending of Mark, then they are surviving fragments of a Jewish tale that carried forward the description of Jesus' claimed survival from the crucifixion narrative into the period immediately afterwards. While Matthew appears to have been generated with reference to a cut version of the gospel that lacked an ending, the authors of the other gospels – Luke, John and Peter – might have used elements of the uncut Mark, a few copies of which could at the time have still been available.

It could however be claimed that, on the contrary, the elements of ordinary living were put in as part of a Christian effort to counter the docetist view that Jesus was all along a spirit, and therefore did not die. If he could eat and walk about, then he was not a ghost and had really been resurrected.

However, if these reflect what was in the Jewish Nazorean account, then they ultimately originate from a period from about 50 CE or earlier, preceding the early development of Christianity and the disagreements and schisms (including docetism) that may subsequently have taken place. The message was that, if Jesus could eat and walk about, then he was not a ghost, was still alive and had survived.

If, as is also possible, all the remaining resurrection accounts are intelligent projections from what was left in Mark, then we are still left with the elements of the story in Mark that suggest Jesus may have survived the crucifixion, plus a description of him that suggests he was an ordinary, mortal man. In which case, it is still likely that the missing ending of Mark contained a very prosaic description of what happened next, not at all in keeping with the developing view of Jesus as a god or godman.

We suggest that a combination of factors acted to squeeze out prototype Mark with its original ending. It was generated at a time the Church was small and so few copies were needed. It may have been circulated within a limited geographic area. Copies were probably lost through the persecution initiated by Nero. A rival was created with the ending cut.

The impetus to retain and make new copies was diminished when a perceived better version was created, at the time just 'the gospel', though ultimately with a separate identity and attributed to Matthew. In this climate, earlier versions of Mark with an uncut ending, which sat uneasily with developing doctrine of a resurrected Jesus, would be more likely to have been discarded. They were not in any case needed, since there was on offer what was perceived to be a more up-to-date version.

When later the prototype and the improved versions came to be seen as separate gospels, interest revived in what we now know as Mark, the earlier version. But what was then immediately to hand was the cut version and it was this that was then recopied. The copies of Mark with the uncut ending had been lost or pushed to one side.

By the time that the Emperor Constantine requested 50 copies of the holy scriptures from his bishop Eusebius, two centuries or more later, the canon of accepted gospels had been reduced to four. In the case of Mark, there were in circulation several alternative versions. We know of an abbreviated gospel up to and including 16, 8, a version with an added summary ending, another with the added longer ending and versions with both the summary and the longer endings.

There are two reasons suggesting that Eusebius favoured the abbreviated version of Mark. Firstly, he excluded the additional verses from 16, 9 to 16, 20 from his canon tables. This would suggest that he did not believe these verses to be sufficiently authentic to warrant comparison with any parallel passages in the other gospels.

Secondly, quotations from a now-lost work by him, *Questions to Stephanus and Marinus*, indicate that he did not believe copies of Mark that had the extra verses to be the 'most accurate'. It would also appear that, at least at the time he was writing, the abbreviated version was in the majority, since he is quoted as saying that the gospel of Mark ended at 16, 8 'in nearly all the copies'.[8]

It is the case that, in both Codex Sinaiticus and Codex Vaticanus, the gospel of Mark ends at 16, 8. These are not merely the earliest surviving complete bibles, and possibly among the first ever made. They are also the earliest surviving witnesses to the ending of Mark.

There is evidence that the first of these codices was linked with Caesarea where Eusebius had his scriptorium and library. We have argued that Sinaiticus was produced as a master copy from which to make further copies, possibly to fulfil the Emperor Constantine's order or a subsequent order. We have further shown that Vaticanus was derived from the same main exemplar for the New Testament. It is most likely that it was written at about the same time and that the Vaticanus scribes had access both to Sinaiticus itself and to their common exemplar.

So, if these books were associated with Eusebius, is it merely a matter of their reflecting in their construction his view at the time of the authenticity of the additional twelve verses at the end of Mark? It is not quite that simple. There are some very strange aspects to the end of Mark in both Sinaiticus and Vaticanus that require explanation.

Taking Codex Vaticanus first of all, which in general has three columns per page, there is on the page that contains the transition from Mark to Luke, an entire second blank column following Mark 16, 8. The end of this gospel comes two-thirds the way down the first column. The second column is blank and then the text picks up in the third column with Luke 1, 1. There is no other case in the Vaticanus New Testament where a whole column is in this way left blank.

In the Old Testament, there are three instances but each of these can be explained. A column is left blank at the very end, after the book of Daniel, to allow the New Testament to begin with Matthew on a new page. There is a blank page column between Esdras 2 and Psalms, reflecting the fact that Esdras 2 was written in three columns and Psalms, as one of the poetic works, in two.

There is also a blank column between Tobit and Hosea. This may result from the division of work between two scribes in the Old Testament, one of whom wrote Tobit leaving the other to do Hosea. It may be, just as in similar instances in Old Testament Sinaiticus (see p 48), that the scribes miscalculated when one went on ahead leaving the other to catch up. There is, however, no such explanation for the gap between Mark and Luke, since one of the scribes wrote the whole of the Vaticanus New Testament. The empty column appears to have been left for a reason. But what?

Given that Vaticanus and Sinaiticus are linked, as we have deduced in the particular sense that one was in part copied from the same exemplar and with reference to the other, it is significant that Sinaiticus also shows evidence of a substantial gap at the end of Mark.

There is in this case no blank column. Mark just reaches by four lines into the second column of a page, leaving most of this column blank. Luke then starts at the head of the next column, as shown in the diagram below. But the text of the ending of the abbreviated version of Mark, as it is in Sinaiticus from 15, 6 to 16, 8, gives every indication of having been considerably stretched out.

The scribe did a number of things that contributed to this effect. He made greater use of filler marks (diples), which provide padding, and he extended the text by using more paragraphs breaks. In one instance, wrote out IHCOYN (Jesus) in full when the abbreviated nomen sacrum IN would normally have been used.

The greatest impact came through lines being typically one or two characters shorter than average. The outcome, over a whole column of 48 lines, is that there is much less text than might have been expected.

Whereas the average number of characters per column in Sinaiticus is about 625 over 48 lines, the last five full columns in Mark are substantially below this, at between 566 and 598 characters (Fig. 6).

Q77F4V   Q77F5R

Fig. 6. Transition from Mark to Luke, Codex Sinaiticus

While some degree of variation about the average is normal, in this case it is substantial and very unusual in persisting over five columns.[9] In addition to which it is, as observed, associated with behaviour by the scribe apparently designed to achieve the effect of stretching out the text. The scribe has made his copy fit a space for which it might, written in his usual style, have been up to 15 lines short. The five columns, together with a last short column of 37 characters, belong to the inner bifolium of a quire of eight pages, one of just three sheets in the New Testament written by scribe D.

The best attempt at an explanation for this made so far is that the three were all 'cancel leaves' written by scribe D, presumed to be the more competent and senior, to correct some major blunders by scribe A. The other two presumed cancel leaves, one in Matthew and the other covering the end of 1 Thessalonians and text from Hebrews, do not form part of an inner bifolium. That is, they each comprise two folios of separated text.

The three sheets by scribe D have features in common suggesting that they should be considered together. Apart from one minor inter-polation in Revelation, these are the only contributions by scribe D in the New Testament. Each consists of a single, complete bifolium within a huge extent of work by scribe A. This represents a very unusual division of labour, at odds for example with the pattern in the Old Testament where scribes A and D shared work between them, alternatively writing books or whole sections of books.

There are extensive sections in each sheet where lines have been cramped up, resulting in columns with far more than the average number of characters. While these are not the only places within the New Testament of Codex Sinaiticus where the number of characters per line is increased, they are among a few that stand out from the surrounding text. The compression could indicate that the scribe had too much text for the space available or that he was adding text. In the case of the inner bifolium of quire 77 including the end of Mark and the beginning of Luke, there is as already noted also some stretching out that would indicate insufficient text or the elimination of text.

There are actually two possible, overall explanations that can be advanced for the work contributed by scribe D. One is that these leaves were, as Milne and Skeat hypothesised, correction sheets to cater for some huge blunders by scribe A. The other is these were passages where scribe D took over from scribe A, notwithstanding the apparent oddity of such an arrangement for just one sheet in each case.

We shall consider these explanations in more detail, in the next two chapters, when we look at the three bifolia by scribe D taken together. For the present, we are concerned with what changes may have been made to the sheet containing the end of the gospel of Mark, by scribe D correcting or altering the text he had before him: either the exemplar or scribe A's first attempt at making a copy.

The simplest explanation is that what scribe D was doing, in stretching out Mark from 15, 16 to 16, 8, was making the text fit the space so that there would not be a blank column between the gospels of Mark and Luke, as indeed there is at the same point in Codex Vaticanus. Thus, by stretching the text to extend to about a further 15 lines, he made Mark run into a second column on the recto of folio five of quire 77 (Q77F5R) by just over three lines, as opposed to ending about 12 lines short of this in the first column.

He had, we suggest, a specific space to fill, given that regardless of what was done to the text by way of additions and deletions, the bifolium had to finish at a precise point, Luke 1, 56, so as to match up with the next folios written by scribe A. Whether copying scribe A's sheet, or following an exemplar, the same reasoning applies. Either way, however, it leaves open the question. Just why did scribe D have insufficient text from Mark, unless stretched out, to fill the space?

There are other actions taken by scribe D that are also coherent, if seen as adjustments to working within a fixed extent. The problem is that these either conflict with, or are not immediately explicable in terms of, his actions in stretching out the section of Mark from 15, 16 to 16, 8. Most perplexing of all is that the fact that he only began to stretch out the text on the verso of the first sheet of the bifolium. Before that, on the recto side of folio 4, the first three columns show no signs of being stretched and the fourth, at 708 characters, is well above the average of around 625 characters per column. So, just prior to stretching out the text by 15 lines, scribe D in one column had condensed it by about 6 or 7 lines! This would appear to make no sense.

Broadly speaking, three explanations have been advanced, to which we will add a fourth. It has to be said, at the outset, that none including our own provide a simple explanation of scribe D's abrupt change of direction. But we do at least offer a possible mechanism to explain what happened, albeit in two stages.

1   The spacing of Codex Vaticanus and Codex Sinaiticus simply indicates that the scribes had knowledge of the longer ending of Mark

It has been argued that the gap of more than a whole column at the end of Mark in Codex Vaticanus must mean that the scribe knew of the longer ending, left a space for it but did not include it. The implication is that he did not have access to the longer ending at the time and allowed for it to be included later, even though in the event this never happened.

The problem with this is that both versions of Mark, with the longer and abbreviated endings, were in circulation at the time. Eusebius for example, who died in 339 CE, is quoted as making reference to both. Codex Vaticanus, as an early fourth century complete bible, would have been one among the very first. It was a major project undertaken at great expense and – even if not part of the fifty ordered by Constantine – accomplished under the new order in which it had the backing of both the Christian Church and the Roman Empire. The scribes would have had access to all the resources they needed. It is therefore unthinkable that a copy of a distinct version of Mark, that has persisted until the present time and we know did exist then, would not have been among the books available to them.

Not only this, but the space left at the end of Vaticanus would have been several lines short of what would have been needed to incorporate the longer ending. Having gone to such trouble already, why would the scribes then have either skimped or so miscalculated? They could just as well have left two columns blank and begun Luke on a new page.

The argument, that the gap was there to allow for the known shorter ending, fails for quite the opposite reason. It could quite easily have been included in Codex Vaticanus after Mark 16, 8 in space left over in the first column. So there would, in such circumstance, have been no need to leave a second column blank.

Applied to the ending of Mark in Codex Sinaiticus, the case is also very weak. While there is the best part of a column empty at the end of this gospel, it would likewise have been insufficient for the known longer ending. Nor would the space have been enough, even if scribe D had not stretched the text in Mark 15, 16 to 16, 8 to fill an extra 15 lines.

The argument fails to provide any reason why scribe D might have taken over from scribe A for just one bifolium or, alternatively, what had happened to necessitate scribe D apparently redoing scribe A's work. It offers nothing to account for scribe D making a strenuous effort to condense the text in column four of the recto of folio four before switching immediately to a strategy of stretching it out on the next page, the verso of folio four. Finally, it does not account for another feature, which is that all the first six columns of Luke on folio five are well above the average, at between 679 and 728 characters. The text has here been compressed, saving of the order of 30 lines, by including more characters into each line.

2 The bifolium Q77F4–5 was rewritten by scribe D because scribe A had made a major blunder in the first part of Luke (1, 1 to 1, 56), accidentally repeating a substantial chunk of text

Milne and Skeat argued, in *Scribes and Correctors of the Codex Sinaiticus*, that scribe A must have committed a dittography of immense proportions, repeating a substantial amount of text at the beginning of Luke's gospel. The bifolium was then rewritten by scribe D to deal with it.

According to the theory, Luke in scribe A's postulated initial version originally began at the top of the second column of the recto of folio five. With the repeated text removed and with no other measures taken, it would in scribe D's copy (since he had to make the copy fit the space) either have ended up with a glaring gap in the text at the end of the verso of Q77F5. Or, alternatively, the gospel of Luke would have had to begin about half way down a column.

Since it was a convention, scrupulously followed, that new books began at the top of a column and since a gap mid-text was also undesirable, scribe D would therefore have had a choice of two options in dealing with scribe A's presumed error. He could either have stretched out the diminished text of Luke (minus the repeat) over seven columns of folio 5, so as to fill the space available and tie in with the next page by scribe A. Or he could have compressed the remaining text of Luke to fill six columns and stretch the text of Mark to go into the second column of the recto of folio five, thereby avoiding a whole blank column.

Since the text of Luke is, as we have noted, compressed, and since the text of Mark from 15, 16 is stretched out, Milne and Skeat presumed that scribe D chose this second option in dealing with a massive dittography in Luke by scribe A.

The compression of the text in Luke could, on the same presumption, have been the result of a decision either to add new text or reinstate accidentally omitted text, again on a substantial scale. However, as this would not explain the text stretched out in Mark, Milne and Skeat rejected the idea.

Although an improvement in some respects, Milne and Skeat's theory also suffers from some major drawbacks. One is that they have posited a very large problem with the beginning of Luke, for which there is no intimation anywhere else, instead of first looking at the fact that there was a known problem, even at the time the scribes wrote, with the ending of Mark. This is what could be described as an objection from common sense.

Even more damaging to their case is the fact that, while some dittographies can be found in Sinaiticus, such repetitions on a very large scale are very rare. There is no precedent in the New Testament, as far as we are aware, for a dittography on such a scale. Its size can be calculated the fact that, over six columns, the additional text squeezed in amounts to about 30 lines. Over seven columns, as hypothesised by Milne and Skeat, the text would have been a column of 48 less 30 lines short, that is around 18 lines, the amount of the presumed repeated text. It would have been a very unlikely error for scribe A to have accidentally repeated around 18 lines of text that he may well have been familiar with.[10]

We found six dittographies involving more than a few characters in Sinaiticus, in a search that was admittedly not exhaustive. But the biggest of the six, in 1 Thessalonians, amounts to 10 lines. Not only were Milne and Skeat postulating a dittography, for which there was no evidence, but they were presuming that it had taken place on a scale that far exceeded any other such error by scribe A.

Furthermore, we have to assume for their theory that scribe D did not realise that he could then have embarked on just one operation, instead of two, saving himself a lot of time and bother. That is, if there had been a dittography of around 18 lines in Luke 1, 1 to 1, 56, he could simply have stretched out the text minus the repeated text in the presumed seven columns of Luke in folio five and left the text of Mark as it was, ending in (arguably) column one of the recto of folio five. Instead, he apparently decided to compress the hypothesised leftover 30 lines in column two of the recto of five into the remaining six columns, harder surely than spreading out the text of Luke to extend to an extra 18 lines. Then, he had also to stretch out the text of Mark to fill the gap.

In addition to this, Milne and Skeat's theory fails to account for the substantial compression of text in the final column of the recto of folio four, just before scribe D switched to stretching out the text of Mark.

We can also fault the theory on the basis of what we have found now, but Milne and Skeat did not appreciate at the time. This is that Codex Sinaiticus was intended as a robust master copy or exemplar from which to make further copies. So, while accuracy was important, appearance was not so crucial and compromised in any case by an apparent pressing aim to get the job done swiftly. There were a lot of mistakes, but this was acceptable providing these were remedied either by the scribes themselves or by the scriptorium corrector Ca.

In other words, it would not have mattered much if scribe A *had* unaccountably committed an enormous dittography in Luke. It could have been rectified, in what was intended as an exemplar and not as a copy to adorn a church lectern, simply by putting dots over the repeated section to indicate deletion and making no further adjustment to scribe A's text. There would have been no need for scribe D laboriously to rewrite the whole bifolium, this surely a vital consideration in an exercise in which speed apparently was of the essence. In Codex Sinaiticus, and also Codex Vaticanus, dittographies were simply dealt with in this way by marking the repeated text and leaving it in place.[11]

It also remains to account for the blank column left in Codex Vaticanus, after the abbreviated end of Mark. Milne and Skeat's theory would not extend to explaining this. We have demonstrated that Codex Vaticanus was extensively copied in the New Testament from a common exemplar or from Codex Sinaiticus or with reference to both. The gap left by the Vaticanus scribes at the end of Mark seems to signal that they were also aware that something was missing from Mark.

3   The bifolium Q77F4–5 was rewritten by scribe D because scribe A had omitted a large section in the first part of Luke (1.1 to 1.56)

In examining Milne and Skeat's theory, Jongkind in *Scribal Habits of Codex Sinaiticus* put forward an alternative explanation that Mark had originally ended where it does now in the second column of the verso of folio four. He suggested that scribe A had omitted a large section of text in the opening of Luke and, as a result, the whole bifo-lium was rewritten by scribe D to rectify this. So, scribe D bunched up the six columns of Luke to squeeze in the omitted text. In contrast with the dittography proposed by Milne and Skeat, which could have been dealt with by deletion marks, this could at least explain why the text might have been recopied. Cramming a 30-line insert into the margins of one page would have made the text, which we have deduced was intended as a master copy, hard to read.

The implication, from reading Jongkind, is that scribe A is presumed to have accidentally omitted text in Luke. An unnoticed 30-line omis-sion in the New Testament is, however, improbable, almost as much as an unnoticed 18-line dittography. There is no precedent for an error of omission by scribe A on such a scale.

There are other possibilities, at least in theory. Scribe A might have deliberately left out the text. But, once again, without evidence and in the realm of speculation, we would have to decide what text had been omitted and why. It might alternatively have been decided to add some new text, possibly from another exemplar, and scribe D was assigned the task of incorporating it. Though not envisaged by Jongkind, this is a possibility.

It remains to explain why it was necessary to stretch out the text in Mark 15, 16 to 16, 8 to go into six columns when scribe D rewrote the text. Jongkind offered two ideas. One is based on the fact that there is what appears to be an error of omission in the text of Mark on the verso of folio 4 from 15, 47 to 16, 1. This was corrected by Ca who was, as we have established, the scriptorium corrector. Had scribe D not made this presumed error, he would have had between five and six more lines of copy. The error created the need to stretch out the text.

The second idea, which Jongkind raised and then dismissed, was that scribe A originally wrote the text leaving an empty column at the end of Mark. Scribe D, while dealing with the problem caused in Luke, according to this idea decided at the same time to remove the empty column by stretching out the text of Mark.

The reason that Jongkind gave, for dismissing this second idea of his, was that the stretching out of Mark starts late while the columns of Luke are crowded. Scribe D could then, as we have suggested in relation to (2) above, have simply stretched out Luke to fill seven columns instead of six and thus neatly dealt with both issues. Apart from which, leaving a spare blank column at the end of a gospel would have been just as much out of order in Codex Sinaiticus as it appears now in Codex Vaticanus. So it is much more likely that there was something with the ending of Mark that had to be dealt with, than that scribe A (in a putative first version) had taken the highly irregular course of leaving a blank column at the end of Mark.

As for Jongkind's first idea, the lesser problem is that the presumed skip error does not provide enough to account for scribe D's need to stretch out the text at the end of Mark: only five to six lines lost as against around 15 lines gained by stretching the text to run into column two of the recto of folio five by just over three lines. The greater and fatal problem is that text was lost by a presumed error at the bottom of the last column of the verso of folio four, *after* scribe D had already stretched out four out of the last five columns of Mark. It could therefore have had nothing to do with a decision made earlier by scribe D to stretch out this text, the bulk of which had been accomplished by the time the skip error occurred. It may also be (see pp 224–226) that the material inserted by Ca was not to remedy a skip error, but from a parallel text.

Jongkind's theory thus does not explain the stretching out of text from Mark 15, 16 to 16, 8. Nor does it account for the compacting of text in the fourth column of the recto of folio four just before this and scribe D's change of plan from this point on.

As with Milne and Skeat's theory, Jongkind's ideas do not approach the question of why Codex Vaticanus, a document linked to Sinaiticus, had very unusually a blank column at the end of Mark.

4   *The bifolium Q77F4–5 was written by scribe D primarily in order to substitute a different ending of Mark for the one used in the exemplar*

The theories discussed so far do not explain the very substantial stretching out of copy at the end of Mark's gospel. We suggest that that this must have been associated in some way with the changeover to another scribe for this one bifolium.

Our theory is that what was happening was an alternation of work between the scribes.[12] In the context of major adjustments, it is less likely that the deployment was coincidental, and more likely that scribe D was brought in to change the ending of Mark from what was being used in an exemplar at that point. It is possible that scribe A had already written a first attempt, though there is no evidence for this, and that scribe D was amending it. But it is our view, consistent with what will be found for two other two bifolia, that scribe D was rather working directly from the available sources. In either case, it should be noted, the effect would have been to substitute copy in an exemplar from which the scribes had been working.

The inner sheet of quire 77 is one of three sheets in the New Testament written by scribe D. The arrangement by which a second scribe stepped in to write occasional single sheets, including in this case two with disconnected text, is extremely unusual. So, while it is possible that there are completely separate explanations for each of the three sheets, it is more likely that there is some causative factor in common.

The three sheets need to be considered together, as will indeed be done in the next two chapters. But there is enough information now to get a good idea of what was happening with the bifolium, containing the end of Mark and the beginning of Luke. The clarification of some aspects may have to wait until a consideration of scribe D's overall contribution.

The pattern of interaction between scribe A and D changes significantly in the New Testament. It is not here a case of one scribe going on ahead to speed up the process and help out the other, as happened in the Old Testament (see pp 47–49). The substantial squeezing and stretching of text in folios four and five of quire 77 is indicative of modifications being made, in the context of an effort to keep within the confines of a bifolium.

We suggest, for the reasons already given above, that it is improbable that the bunching up of text from Luke 1, 1 to 1, 56 was to counter a huge, hypothesised 18 line dittography instigated in a first attempt by scribe A. Nor is there any indication that scribe A might have accidentally or even deliberately omitted 30 lines of text from the exemplar, which then had to be restored by scribe D.

The amount of text from the opening of Luke, which scribe D put into his last six columns, is very much greater than would arise from the average density, measured in characters per column, and also out of keeping with the rest of Luke. Text has therefore been squeezed in to fit the given space. It is possible that the space allowed to scribe D was not enough, or that text was added to an exemplar, or even both. This will be explored further in the next chapter.

We are not tied to the idea that there may have been a first attempt at the bifolium by scribe A, especially as there is no evidence for it. Nor do we have to speculate that Luke might have begun in column two instead of column three of the recto folio five of quire 77. There is no evidence of a major dittography. So there is no reason to believe that scribe D had to make an adjustment by squeezing the remnant of a column, after a dittography had been eliminated, into the rest of his bifolium, starting at the beginning of column three. Thus, even in a hypothetical first version by scribe A, Luke would have begun at the head of the third column of the recto of folio five.

If we now go back to the copying of Mark on to the first three pages of the bifolium, we can see that there was not enough material to fill the allocated space, allowing for the bunching and squeezing that have taken place and an error of omission. So we conclude that there must have been some additional text towards or at the end of Mark, from 14, 54 to 16, 8 in the exemplar or scribe A's copy of it. Since that text is no longer there, it must also be concluded that scribe D omitted it.

With the additional text originally present, the gospel of Mark would have come up towards the end of the second column of the recto of folio five, with perhaps a line or two to spare. Given that the abbreviated Mark ends rather awkwardly and given that there exists no indication of other text that might have been present from 14, 54 onwards, it is likely that the additional text constituted an ending of Mark from verse 16, 8. The evidence, as we have found, does indeed indicate that there is an ending missing from abbreviated Mark.

From considerations of space, it is apparent that the ending missing from Sinaiticus was somewhat shorter than the known longer ending of Mark. The number of characters in this longer known ending would have taken the text well into the third column of the recto of folio five, leaving insufficient space for the text of Luke.

Scribe D we suggest was briefed to remove a shorter ending of Mark, from 16, 8 onwards, which we have deduced was there in the exemplar. He calculated that he could do this by substituting the longer ending, which was in common use, from another exemplar. But, in order to do this, he would have needed to save several lines. He began to do this by compressing the text in the last column of the recto of folio four.

But then there was a change of plan. It was decided after all not to incorporate the longer ending, which was (with justification) even at the time not regarded as authentic, and instead opt for the abbreviated version of Mark, which was also in common use. This meant that scribe D would, from then on, have had to stretch out the copy substantially. If he were substituting a sheet first written by another scribe, presumably scribe A, the purpose may have been to avoid having a blank space of well over a column at the end of Mark. If he were working from the exemplar, though within the confines of a bifolium, the purpose may simply have been to compensate for the immediate loss of copy and so avoid possible problems later on.

In either case, he succeeded by extending the remaining text that he had of Mark to run into an extra column. While engaged in this, he may also have substituted a different version of the women present at the cross in 15, 40 on the verso of folio four, to conform with what the scriptorium corrector had already done for the corresponding passage in Matthew (see Chapter 10).

There is some further, intriguing evidence that that there were two or more parallel versions of Mark, available for the scribes at this point. The correction made by Ca near the bottom of column four of Q77F4V can be seen as remedying a skip error based on MAPIAH from 15, 47–16, 1 (h17, Appendix II, p 304).

However, rather than representing an integral part of the text, the material of 15, 47 does appear to replicate with some variation what is presented in 16, 1:

> And he (Joseph) rolled a stone against the entrance of the tomb.
> Now Mary Magdalene and Mary the (mother) of Joses saw where he was laid.
> 'When the Sabbath was over, Mary Magdalene and Mary the (mother) of James and Salome bought spices, so that they might go and anoint him. And very early on the first day of the week, when the sun had risen, they went to the tomb.

Mark, 15, 46–16, 2

In the first place, whenever a character or group of characters is introduced, the writer then uses 'he/she' or 'they' to avoid cumbersome repetition. So, for example, from Luke 23, 55, 'the women who had come with him from Galilee' are spoken of as 'they' right up to 24, 10, when they are more specifically identified. From Matthew 28, 5, 'the women', previously identified as 'Mary Magdalene and the other Mary' are subsequently referred to as 'they'.

It is not consistent for the women to be specifically identified in successive sentences, as they are in Mark 15, 47–16, 1. It is also unclear, if both sentences were part of the same text, how it could have come about that Salome was missed out in the first sentence and one Mary should be variously identified as the mother of Joses in the first and of James in the second. It should have been clear, at least from the script (Mark 15, 40), that the mother of James and of Joses were one and the same.

Furthermore, with Ca's interpolation, it is stated that the women bought spices after the Sabbath, that is after sunset on the Saturday. With the text as it now is, they would either not have had the time to do this or they would have had to make their purchases at night. This is because they are also described as arriving at the tomb very early on Sunday, the first day of the week, as soon as the sun had risen.

There is however no problem without the changes made by Ca:

> *And he (Joseph) rolled a stone against the entrance of the tomb.*
> *Now Mary Magdalene and Mary the mother of James and*
> *Salome bought spices, so that they might go and anoint him.*
> *And very early on the first day of the week, when the sun had*
> *risen, they went to the tomb.*

So, anticipating the need and knowing that they could not buy on the next day, the Sabbath, the women bought the spices late on the Friday. The point is similarly made in Luke. The women prepared spices and ointments, rested on the Sabbath and then went to tomb very early the next day (Luke 23, 55–24, 1).

So this was arguably not a case of an original author of Mark aggregating alternative descriptions of the women, as some have suggested, but of the scriptorium corrector Ca[13] adding a second version to the text, either from another exemplar or possibly to harmonise with Matthew 27, 61. The reason he did this was that, in the version used by scribe D, there was no mention of the women observing where Jesus was taken, and so no explanation of how they knew where to go.

The introduction of a sentence from another version, in order to plug this gap, generated a degree of repetition and conflict in that the parallel descriptions of the women do not fully agree. But Ca may have decided, while making his addition, to retain the description of the women preparing spices from the version used by scribe D because it added more detail. He may even have felt that two slightly different though overlapping groups of women were involved.

In the alternative version available to Ca, there need also have been no issue over purchasing goods on the Sabbath. The text that follows indicates how the passage may have continued:

And he (Joseph) rolled a stone against the entrance of the tomb.
Now Mary Magdalene and Mary (the mother) of Joses saw
where he was laid. When the Sabbath was over ... very early
on the first day of the week ... they went to the tomb/they
prepared spices and went to the tomb ... [14]

According to our theory, a shorter lost ending, if not the lost ending, of Mark was eliminated in making Codex Sinaiticus. Scribe D may have worked from this, or he may have worked from a substitute or both, up to 16, 8 when he stopped. The two texts up to this point may well have been similar. But it seems that they deviated enough for Ca to want to add in a bit from the second exemplar.[15]

Having stretched out the text of Mark, scribe D found that he then had to compress the text of Luke, by a substantial amount, in the remaining six columns of the bifolium. It may be that some copy was added from another source or that, working within the confines of a bifolium, a miscalculation meant that he had limited space.[16]

The most effective strategy might have been to marry the changes made to Mark with the requirements for Luke, dictated by the space available to the bifolium as a whole. Mark, with its reduced ending, could have been written without stretching to fit into one less column. Then, the beginning of Luke in this bifolium could have been written over seven columns instead of six. Even this course of action would not, however, have been without its difficulties. Spread over seven columns, the text of Luke in the bifolium would then itself have been stretched out, below the average in terms of characters per column.[17]

The evidence is also that scribe D, possibly as a result of having to change his plans, was not looking in any detail that far ahead. He had first of all condensed text in order, we have suggested, to accommodate the longer ending of Mark. Had he continued with a plan to have the longer ending of Mark, it would have allowed no scope to save a column and so provide more space for the text of Luke.

But scribe D then switched to an alternative strategy that meant stretching out the text of Mark. The reason for this, we have suggested, was to cut the ending of Mark so that the text ended at verse 16, 8. The abrupt change of course meant that scribe D suddenly found himself having to deal with a different type of problem. He was thus preoccupied. This may explain why he did not appreciate that there could have been a more effective way of dealing with the text.

So why is there a lack of other indications of our postulated shorter, lost ending? It is something that will be considered in subsequent chapters. But the short answer is that Codex Sinaiticus was created as a means of disseminating the Christian bible. If missing in Sinaiticus, such an ending would then be missing in all the copies that followed from it.

There is a further point that needs to be considered. Why did the Vaticanus scribes leave a whole column blank at the end of Mark? This would not have been enough to contain the known, though even at the time apparently discredited, longer ending of Mark. It could, however, have contained a somewhat shorter ending, which we have found may have been deleted at the time from Codex Sinaiticus and to this day is still lost.

We have found that Vaticanus must have been written from the same exemplar as Sinaiticus or copied from Sinaiticus, possibly with the same exemplar as reference. The two manuscripts are linked in many ways, including the characteristic styles of their decorative colophons at chapter ends. It is possible that they had at least one scribe (scribe D) in common. So it may well be that they were produced in the same context and at around the same time as each other.

The Vaticanus scribes could see for themselves what changes had been made from the common exemplar in creating Codex Sinaiticus. They may even have been directly aware of the changes of mind involving scribe D in respect of the ending of Mark.[18]

What they did do was leave space, perhaps to allow for the later insertion of another ending (for example, our hypothesised shorter ending), in the event of another change of mind. Intended or not, the blank column does also serve another function. It points up the fact that something is missing.

Our theory does in several ways represent an improvement on the efforts by Jongkind and Milne and Skeat. We have provided a solution that takes account of the variations, in terms of compression and squeezing of text, in both Mark and Luke. We have not had to resort to explanations involving highly improbable blunders by scribe A, massive accidental omissions or dittographies, for which there is no precedent and no other sign. This has shifted the focus from a distraction, the presumed incompetence of scribe A, to where it should always have been, the text itself.

Scribe D made deletions and possibly additions that represented changes to text and were not corrections of mistakes. If he were changing scribe A's work, then he was at the same time changing the exemplar since this was what scribe A was also following. There is, however, now no need to postulate an initial attempt by scribe A, a phantom sheet for the existence of which there is no direct evidence. This is because we are no longer tied to the theory that scribe A must have made enormous and unlikely errors that scribe D then corrected.

There is no evidence that scribe A made any such mistakes in a now-missing original draft. It is an unnecessary presumption, the product not of the evidence but of a theory that is unsubstantiated. Nor need we assume that there was a decision to make changes to quire 77 after scribe A had already copied it from the exemplar. It is more justifiable to read the situation at face value, that scribe A wrote the first three folios of quire 77 and that scribe D took over for folios 4 and 5. As will be seen in the next chapter, a consideration of other interventions by scribe D in the New Testament will tend to confirm this position.

The evidence is that scribe D eliminated an ending of Mark that extended beyond verse 16, 8 and compressed the beginning Luke to accommodate the text he had to put into the bifolium. From considerations of space, it appears that the ending of Mark eliminated was not the longer ending that was available at the time and is known to us now.

As we noted earlier, the bifolium covering the end of Mark and the beginning of Luke is one of just three in the New Testament, written by scribe D, all of which have substantial sections where the text has been squeezed up.

These sheets do represent a quite different way of dividing up the work between scribe A and scribe D from that which operated in the Old Testament. This raises questions as to the role of scribe D, the type of changes being made and the reasons that there may have been for altering the text. Specifically, the question is whether the change of scribe is coincidental or related to the changes that appear to have been made to the text.

It is time to turn our attention to a more detailed examination of the pattern of cooperation between these scribes in the New Testament.

In this chapter, our conclusions have been:

- **The inner bifolium of quire 77 (folios 4 and 5), which includes the end of Mark and the beginning of Luke, was a sheet written by scribe D incorporating modifications to the exemplar.**
- **The sheet was not written to correct massive blunders by scribe A in a presumed earlier sheet by this scribe, as previous writers including Milne and Skeat have suggested.**

- The evidence indicates that one major change to the exemplar was the removal of an ending of Mark.
- The ending of Mark removed was not the known longer ending but one shorter than this.
- To deal with the eliminated text from the ending of Mark, scribe D stretched out his text.
- Scribe D then compressed text in the last six columns, either to stay within the confines of the bifolium, or to add text to the exemplar or a combination of both.

CHAPTER 12

The reluctant scribe

While scribe A did the bulk of the work in the New Testament he was, as in the Old Testament, helped by the other two scribes. However, scribe D contributed just three sheets and a few lines at the beginning of the book of Revelation. Scribe B wrote the last book, the Shepherd of Hermas. All the other pages were written, or rather copied from the exemplar or exemplars, by scribe A.

For convenience, we list again the bifolia produced by scribe D. These were:

(a) the second sheet of quire 75 (folios 2 and 7) Matthew 16, 9 to 18, 12 and Matthew 24, 35 to 26, 6;
(b) the fourth sheet of quire 77 (folios 4 and 5) Mark 14, 54 to Luke 1, 56;
(c) the third sheet of quire 85 (folios 3 and 6) 1 Thessalonians 2, 14 to 5, 28 and Hebrews 4, 16 to 8, 1.

There is evidence linking Codex Sinaiticus to the scriptorium and library at Caesarea (see especially Chapter 3) and hence to the production of bibles in the mid fourth century. The Roman Emperor Constantine had embraced Christianity as one of the religions of Empire and asked the Bishop of Caesarea and library's custodian, Eusebius, to make 50 copies of the scriptures. There is a case (see Chapters 4 and 6) that Codex Sinaiticus was itself created as a robust exemplar or master copy, conceivably for the purposes of fulfilling either this order or a later one similar to it.

There is also a powerful case that Codex Sinaiticus was, at least for the New Testament, itself copied from a main exemplar with on average the same number of characters per line. This meant the scribes could seek to match their original, line by line. They would at times have been thrown off course by corrections and changes they chose to make or were forced to make. So a perfect copy, though it might have been desirable, would not have been possible.

The case is backed by a number of mutually reinforcing arguments. It was found that the distribution of skip errors indicated a main exemplar for Sinaiticus of between 9 and 15 characters average line length, narrowed to between 11 and 13 characters when the pattern for multiple-line skips was taken into account.

Sinaiticus itself is written with an average of 13 characters per line. So, in copying from an exemplar of between 11 and 13 characters, the scribes must either have chosen to follow it or vary slightly from it. It is hard to see why they might have opted for this latter option when, for no more effort, there would have been some benefit in choosing the same line length in an attempt to make an accurate copy. Mistakes made, while copying in this way, would usually have caused the copy and the exemplar to get temporarily out of line. Thus highlighted, the errors would have been easier to spot and correct.

It was also found that skip errors occurred at the end of a line in the copy, that is in Sinaiticus itself, far more often than would have been expected by chance. This indicates strongly that an attempt was being made as far as possible to replicate the exemplar. The reason is that, where exact copying is successful, skips will be in whole lines in both the copy and the exemplar.

There was furthermore a very high level of correspondence between skip errors in Codex Vaticanus and corresponding passages in Codex Sinaiticus, particularly in the New Testament (Chapter 5). This establishes that, if not copied from Sinaiticus, Vaticanus was copied from the same, common exemplar. In which case, the skip error passages in Vaticanus that correspond precisely to whole lines in Sinaiticus were existing in just this format in the exemplar. The exemplar and its copy, that is Codex Sinaiticus, were thus for much of the time a perfect match. The common exemplar for most of the New Testament had the same average line length of 13 characters as Sinaiticus and, for large parts of the text, the Sinaiticus scribes were able to replicate it precisely.

As would be expected, there is a considerable amount of variation about the average of 625 characters per column. The scribes were constrained by the size of the page and the format adopted within it. There were columns of equal width and standard margins between them. While the scribes would not have been motivated to try to keep to any particular number of characters in a line, they had to stay within the column and for this reason ended up writing around 13 characters, sometimes more and sometimes less.

We have found that the scribes were often matching their exemplar. At these points, the number of characters in a line ultimately derived from decisions made and points of style when the earlier manuscript was created. But, whether at any particular stage deriving from Sinaiticus itself or from an exemplar, the column width was a determining factor.

One of the reasons that the number of characters varied in any given line was that the characters themselves varied in width, from a relatively slender iota to a more chunky omega. So, if a particular bit of text happened to have more bulkier characters, then it would be expected that at that point there would be fewer characters copied into a line of Sinaiticus. The converse, of course, also applies.

There are very many other factors that could have and would have influenced the number of characters per line. Pressure of time, or fatigue, could for example at times have led to characters being less tightly written and so more spread out. The style of the exemplar might have varied and this in turn could have led to variations in the way that the copy was written.

The frequency of paragraph breaks, within or at the end of verses, can be seen to vary and will have had an impact. Given the rule that the new paragraph begins on a new line, this would mean that a particular line could have been short by perhaps as much as 11 characters. More paragraphs in a given column would generally mean fewer characters overall, while fewer paragraphs would have led to columns with more characters.

With 48 lines to a column, writing with just one more or one less character per line would have led to a variation of plus or minus 48 characters from the average over the whole column. Given the number of factors involved, it is reasonable to expect around this degree of variation and at least an approximately normal distribution. In the absence of other evidence, therefore, nothing much should be read into columns with character numbers within these limits.

There are a few passages in the New Testament that have columns substantially outside expected limits and these seem to be disproportionately associated with the three sheets by scribe D. To put this in perspective, it was decided to examine the whole of the New

Testament excluding the last book, the Shepherd of Hermas by scribe B, two-thirds of which is missing.[1]

There are 912 columns, the vast majority by scribe A and just 48 in the three sheets by scribe D. New books always begin at the head of a new column, which means that there will almost always be an incomplete column at the end of the preceding book. There are 28 such columns that, because they are incomplete, are harder to evaluate. Of the remaining 884 columns, there are 26 with less than 580 characters and 44 with more than 670 characters.

Taking the columns with fewer characters first, a significant minority can be explained by the propensity by the authors of different books to create lists and for the scribes then to give each person, quality or other item on the list a separate line. Usually, the separate items each amount to much less than 13 characters. Over several lines, this can lead to a great reduction in the quantity of text within the column, as against the overall average.

The genealogy attributed to Jesus is given in Luke 3, 23–38 and this has affected columns one and two of Q77F7V that have respectively 479 and 401 characters. In Romans 8, 35 and 8, 38, lists of adverse circumstances, created for rhetorical effect, take column four of Q82F4R down to 566 characters. In 1 Corinthians 6, 9–10, there is a list of people the author considers will not inherit the kingdom of God. As a result, column four of Q83F1R has only 530 characters. Later in the same book, at 1 Corinthians 12, 28–29, there is a list of roles within the Church, reducing column two of Q83F4R to 547 characters. Galatians 5, 22–24 has lists of desirable and undesirable qualities (fruits of the spirit and works of the flesh) that impact on column one of Q84F4V, reducing it to 496 characters. Finally, the list of the apostles in Acts 1, 13 leads to column three of Q86F7R being well below average, at only 567 characters.

So, seven of the 26 apparently aberrant columns, with a well below average number of characters, can thus be explained. This leaves 19 columns, of which nine are widely distributed and have causative attributes, such as more frequent use of paragraphs that can sometimes be identified.

There are just two passages associated in the whole of the New Testament with a *sequence* of columns with a well-below average number of characters. One occurs with the last quire of Barnabas, which very unusually has only two sheets. All the columns of the quire are below average, including a sequence of seven consecutive columns and a further column that are all below 580 characters. With the last column partially filled and an empty column at the end, eight out of 14 columns are below 580 characters. The last three books of the New Testament, including Barnabas, appear to have been written in the same cooperative pattern as some books in the Old Testament, with the scribe here stretching out the text within the space allocated to him (see discussion following, pp 238–241).

The other instance of a passage with columns well below average occurs at the end of Mark. The last five complete columns are below average, in terms of number of characters. Two of these, at 566 and 560 characters, are under 580 characters. There has clearly been some stretching of the text at this point which we have argued is associated with a decision to eliminate an ending of Mark in the exemplar, while keeping within the constraints of a defined space. This was the bifolium consisting of folios four and five of quire 77 written by scribe D.

Turning now to columns with an unusually high number of characters, there are 44 of these by our definition, representing five per cent of the total of 884 complete columns. There are just a few places where these are concentrated. One is within the first quire of Revelation where, we will argue, the scribe was motivated at first to save space so as to ensure that this book and the next could be contained within two full quires. This book has columns generally above average, in terms of number of characters, including five within the first quire with over 680 characters.

Another occurrence, hard to evaluate, comes in Acts which is mostly contained within two full quires. The beginning of the second of these quires coincides with a shift, starting at Acts 16, 10, from 'they' as the main subject, denoting the apostles and/or the followers of Paul, to Paul himself and 'we', denoting the followers of Paul and not the apostles. From this point, the text is more densely packed with columns that are generally above average in terms of characters per column. There are seven columns with over 670 characters in the latter part of Acts as opposed to one such column in the first part, towards the beginning.

It seems likely that in Acts two narratives have been combined. It may be that some element of a denser style in the second narrative, the 'we' document, survived being copied from its earlier source to the exemplar for Codex Sinaiticus and then ultimately to Sinaiticus itself. This is certainly possible if, as we have argued, Sinaiticus were being copied for the bulk of the New Testament to match as far as possible, an exemplar of about the same average line length.[2]

The evidence does not give support to the alternative idea, that the scribe was seeking to economise on space to keep within a quire. At the end, Acts runs into another quire by more than two full columns. Had the tactic of compression been used, to keep within a quire, it was not only unsuccessful but could have been seen to be so. In the last page of quire 88, scribe A continued to write at well above the average in terms of characters per column when, at this point, there was no chance that he could have kept Acts within this second quire.

As with the unusually below-average columns, there are a few examples (fourteen in all) scattered throughout the New Testament that have no obvious, immediate explanation. These may simply reflect the outer limits of an expected, normal distribution.

The remaining instances, where a number of very densely packed columns are concentrated, all occur within the three bifolia written by scribe D. There are in fact 17 columns out of a total of 46 by scribe D, excluding two short columns at the end of books, where the number of characters is above 670. Thus, by this rough measure, more than a third of scribe D's text is very densely packed, as opposed to 27 columns, representing just three per cent of the 838 columns in the rest of the New Testament excluding the Shepherd of Hermas. The four columns with the highest number of characters in the New Testament, at over 700, all occur in scribe D's work: in Mark, Luke, 1 Thessalonians and Hebrews.

There are six successive columns at over 670 characters at the beginning of Luke, three such columns in 1 Thessalonians and two pairs of three columns in Hebrews. These are the only three places where text is so concentrated in the New Testament, apart from Revelation and the second part of Acts. All occur within two bifolia written by scribe D. It should be noted that, in scribe D's third sheet in Matthew, the columns also contain an overall above-average number of characters, with one at 682 and one at 670 characters. Our conclusions from this analysis are as follows.

Firstly, there are some major sections of text, where an explanation of a systematic kind can account for concentration or stretching of text. In the case of Revelation and the end of Barnabas, compression or stretching appears to have occurred in a progressive effort to match the text to the space allocated. In the case of the second part of Acts, the concentration of text coincides with a switch in the narrative, so possibly reflecting a difference of style in the original sources.

Secondly, the location of all the remaining sequences of stretching and compression in the New Testament within the only three bifolia written by scribe D is highly significant and cannot be accounted for by chance. It is therefore something that needs to be examined and, if possible, explained.

Thirdly, having taken account of the concentrations of compressed or stretched text that have or need an explanation, the remaining examples of columns with characters well above or well below the average number are relatively few, scattered and what might be expected. That is, given the variety of influences on the scribes, most columns could be expected to cluster about the average, with just a few outriders having very low or high numbers of characters, without there having to be a special explanation for them.

This latter conclusion is very relevant, in view of the attempt by Christian Tindall in *Contributions to the Statistical Study of the Codex Sinaiticus*, to identify specific passages as added in, at the point of copying from an exemplar, on the basis of specific columns with an above average number of characters. As we have found, there are very few at either extreme, outside of some sections accounted for by more general explanations, and these are what might be expected in a normal distribution. So, Tindall's approach is flawed at the outset and fails on this ground.

Tindall described twenty instances where he believed that additional matter had been introduced into the text of Codex Sinaiticus. This is certainly problematical, even aside from the fundamental point that in general the variations are what might be expected. Even if matter were being added, it would be hard to tell what specific passage related to an increased density of text or whether, even, the outcome were the net effect of some text being deleted and some added.

In addition, while it appears scribes were for most of the New Testament copying from an exemplar of the same average line length and so presumably similar column width, there is no evidence that they were constrained to work according to the exemplar's overall page layout.[3] If copy were being added or deleted, it should thus almost always have been possible to keep to the same column width and let the extra be mopped up simply by going on to the next page. The very limited exceptions to this would have occurred when the scribe was seeking to work within a fixed extent, by for example fitting a certain amount of text within a quire. This is the mechanism that could explain the general compression and stretching of text in Revelation and Barnabas.[4]

For the rest of the text, there would certainly have been additions and deletions through for example corrections and the incorporation of marginal notes. But these, as the text flowed from page to page, need not have had an impact on column density as Tindall supposed. The variation observed is primarily the expected, combined effect of the various influences involved.

The sheets by scribe D could provide possible exceptions. These show signs of having been written to a fixed extent and, as we have shown, a cut at the end of Mark did have an impact on column density. Even with these sheets, however, it will be found that there is no necessary link between the observed compression and what is found in the text.

Tindall raised a hostage to fortune in listing his twenty instances, given that there is some much earlier papyrus evidence. If copy were being added in, it might be expected that these earlier sources would lack the passages that Tindall deduced had been interpolated. However, this is found not to be the case. In all four cases, where there is available evidence, the sections that Tindall argued were missing from the exemplar and added to Sinaiticus are present in the earlier papyrus sources.[5]

It could be that the papyrus sources, **P**45 and **P**75 from the late second to early third century, represent an independent strand that generated a secondary exemplar, from which the passages were taken to add to the main exemplar for Sinaiticus. But this is not at all convincing. What we have are the earlier papyrus sources and Sinaiticus, *both* containing the passages that Tindall thought may have been added during the course of production. On this evidence, the simplest and clearest conclusion is that the main exemplar for Sinaiticus contained these particular passages, just like the earlier papyrus manuscripts.

Even if it were not invalid on other grounds, Tindall's method suffers from another, serious imbedded flaw. There is bound to be a temptation to choose cut-off points that make passages, which might be interpolations, fit with the calculated 'excess' text. Tindall did thereby sometimes make unsustainable assumptions. He suggested, for example, that the phrase 'in the presence of the angels of God over one sinner who repents' in Luke 15, 10 is doubtful and may therefore have been added to the exemplar. It has 49 characters and the column in which it is located has 679 characters, between 32 and 49 characters more than the other three columns on the same page. This is all very neat, except that this phrase could not have been a simple addition because it is integral with the rest of the sentence of which it is a part. The opening words of the sentence, 'Just so, I tell you, there is joy ... ' do not stand alone. If the whole sentence were an addition, then it would have been one of 73 rather than 49 characters. The supposed added phrase is, as it happens, also present in P75, undermining still further a very shaky argument.

Tindall likewise may sometimes have chosen passages for comparison, perhaps unconsciously to support what he had already decided was an interpolation. So, for example, he compared the whole of the verso of Q78F4, which has Luke's description of the transfiguration (Luke 9, 31–37), with the recto to come up with a difference in terms of characters to match verses containing an account of a conversation between Moses and Elijah and Jesus. One section, not present in Mark, is thus presumed to have been added to Luke in the course of producing Sinaiticus (though it is also, we note, present in Luke in P45).

The verses in question extend from the bottom of column one to the top of column two on the verso of Q78F4. But it is only the third column that has a number of characters significantly above average. Indeed, the page as a whole is around about the average in terms of characters, while the recto has fewer characters than average – and it might be this that has to be explained.[6]

Jongkind criticised Tindall for showing no awareness of the 'codicological description by Milne and Skeat'.[7] He appears to mean by this the identification of contributions made by different scribes and the interactions between scribes, which Milne and Skeat began and Jongkind himself developed for the Old Testament. Tindall was certainly sceptical about evidence from handwriting and so ignored this aspect.

The argument, that the amount of text in individual columns should necessarily be seen as reflecting additions to or deletions from an exemplar, is thus demonstrably invalid. But it remains to examine in more detail the instances where there is very high or very low density of text sustained over a number of columns. These, we have suggested, may reflect the constraint of working to a given spatial limit and in such circumstances could in theory also reflect the addition or deletion of some text.

For most of the New Testament, apart from the three single bifolium contributions by scribe D, which we shall consider shortly, it was a case of just one scribe doing the work. There is, however, at the very end, a reversion to the pattern of cooperation that Jongkind observed in operation for much of the Old Testament.

After scribe A had done so much, there was suddenly a change in the way of working. The final three books were all started by different scribes, in what may have been a last great push to finish the project. Scribe D began the Book of Revelation, scribe A started (it may be that he intended to start simultaneously) on Barnabas and scribe B took on the last book, the Shepherd of Hermas.

Scribe B began his work at the start of a new quire. In view of this, it could be that the primary objective for Revelation and Barnabas was to make the material fit within the confines of two quires, so as to end if possible without a large gap before the start of the Shepherd of Hermas. It is possible that these books were not a part of the main exemplar for the New Testament from which scribe A had been copying.

The Letter of Jude was completed by scribe A on the recto of the first folio of quire 90. Scribe D began to write Revelation on the verso of the first folio of quire 90 and the aim we suggest was to fill the remainder of this and the next quire with Revelation and Barnabas. However, something soon happened to alter this plan.

Scribe D can be identified from his handwriting as having written the first five verses of the book of Revelation. But he then broke off mid-sentence and mid-line at the end of the phrase 'firstborn of the dead', towards the end of the fifth verse. Scribe A continued from this point to finish Revelation and Barnabas. We can only speculate as to why scribe D stopped so abruptly. Something may have happened to call him away to other work. As he made only relatively slight contributions to the New Testament overall, it does appear that he was at the time occupied with other tasks.

There is another unusual aspect, as will be seen, this time to scribe A's work. It is plain that, by the end of Revelation, the aim was to contain within two quires the remaining work up to scribe B's contribution. The text of Revelation, at well over the average in terms of characters per column, might well have been compressed with this end in mind. As a tactic, it was if anything over-successful. Barnabas was, possibly in consequence, written at below the average in terms of characters per column, so as not to leave too much empty space at the end. Even so, despite considerable stretching, it finished well over a column short of the start of the Shepherd of Hermas.

The oddity is that the last four sheets, containing the end of Revelation and the whole of Barnabas, are divided into two quires of three sheets and one sheet respectively, when both could easily have been incorporated within a standard four-sheet quire. The sheets of the first of these, quire 91, deviate from the normal pattern in which flesh faces flesh and hair faces hair alternatively in the double page parchment spreads. Something must have happened to disturb scribe A from what should have been a routine task of completing his work with a normal quire of eight folios in four sheets.

After completing quire 90, scribe A had another folio or so left of Revelation to complete and all of Barnabas to fit into the next quire. By this time, scribe B would have finished or been well into writing the Shepherd of Hermas, which he had begun on a new quire (Fig. 7).

We suggest that just enough sheets were made, given that the book was an unusually large size and the parchment might not have been easily adaptable for another project. So scribe A had just four sheets left, which he rightly calculated would comfortably take his remaining copy.

He completed the first folio and then began on the second folio, which would have been on his second sheet, to complete Revelation and start on Barnabas. But at some point, he made a mess of the second folio, perhaps spilling ink or making an error that was in his eyes too large to correct. He would not have wanted to waste a whole sheet of valuable parchment. We suggest that he acted promptly to save it by having it washed out. Unfortunately, he could not then wait for it to dry since a degree of urgency was required to complete the task.

(a) theoretical intended regular format for quire 91:

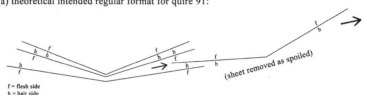

f = flesh side
h = hair side

(b) outcome:

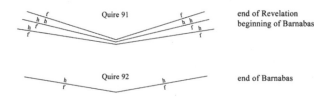

Fig. 7. Illustration of possible genesis of irregular quires 91 and 92

So, he decided to press on as far he could with the remaining sheets, starting from the end of the first folio. This, of course, meant creating a quire of three sheets, as he now had only three sheets with which to work. When he had finished his three-sheet quire, the washed out sheet was dry enough to write on. He then used it to make a single quire to complete Barnabas, the last text of the bible that he had to copy.

The sheets had been stacked ready for use, so that double page spreads of parchment would alternatively have had the flesh side facing the flesh side and the hair side facing the hair side. Scribe A should, after removing the second sheet for treatment and reuse, have turned over the third and fourth sheets to preserve the sequence. But he neglected to do so. This is why the first and second sheets of the three-sheet quire do not face each other in the usual flesh to flesh and hair to hair way.[8]

There was, we have suggested, a pattern of cooperation between the scribes for the last three books of the New Testament, similar to that which had operated for the Old Testament. It was characterised by the abrupt termination of scribe D's contribution in Revelation, by efforts to contain text within a given space and by the adjustments that scribe A had to make to deal with an accident or mistake.

Prior to this point, the work had been done by scribe A, with scribe D coming in to write just three bifolia, in a pattern that is distinctive and different from that which had operated in the Old Testament. The explanation, adopted by Milne and Skeat and followed by Jongkind, was that scribe D's contributions were replacement sheets to correct for some hypothesised faulty sheets with major blunders written by scribe A.

In examining the issue of the ending of Mark in the previous chapter, we found that such an explanation was improbable and at odds with the evidence for the second of the sheets, the middle sheet of quire 77. We concluded that, though much remained to be explained, it was more justifiable to read the situation at face value, as an alternation of work between the scribes.

Neither Milne and Skeat nor Jongkind have much to say about the other two sheets by scribe D that have in one case material from Matthew and in the other from 1 Thessalonians and Hebrews. Jongkind ventured that the first of these does not deviate greatly from the average in terms of characters per line or column[9], a statement that is in fact not accurate. The first page of the sheet from Matthew in particular, the recto of folio two of quire 75, has one column at 682 characters and its four columns averaging 665 characters as against the average of 625 characters per column.

With the second of these other sheets, Jongkind saw the problem as arising from the second folio containing text from Hebrews that has an above average number of characters per column. He suggested that the reason for its presumed replacement was to reinstate a passage that scribe A had here accidentally omitted. However, there is also a very substantial compression in the recto of the first folio of 1 Thessalonians, also potentially indicating omission and reinstatement or the addition of text. From Jongkind's perspective, it is an uncomfortable and unfathomable 'either–or' situation; it is hard to explain possible major errors on *both* folios of a presumed replaced bifolium where the text is discontinuous. Indeed, there is a problem even with the continuous text of the inner bifolium of quire 77. If the main reason for the presumed substitution were a problem with the ending of Mark, why would there coincidentally have also been a major difficulty with the beginning of Luke? And, of course, vice versa.

Jongkind, like Milne and Skeat, treated the other, discontinuous sheets by scribe D only superficially and did not come to grips with what might have been involved in the dynamics of their construction.

The three sheets by scribe D have a number of factors in common. For this reason, it is possible, and perhaps likely, that a valid explanation for their causation and creation will cover them all.

So, what are their common characteristics? In the first place, these all represent isolated instances of work by a scribe, other than scribe A, in the New Testament as a whole before the last three books. At which point, as we have earlier described, there was an attempt at a switch to the pattern of cooperation that pertained in the Old Testament. A second feature is that these sheets were all the work of one copyist, scribe D. The third feature is that they are all single sheets, representing a division of layout that is not merely unusual but without precedent elsewhere in Codex Sinaiticus. It is something that very much needs to be explained.

A fourth feature is that the three sheets all have columns on both folios with a number of characters that is substantially above average. We have found that over a third of the columns are very densely packed as opposed to just three per cent, by the same definition, in the rest of the New Testament. There is no doubt that scribe D's work is here strongly associated with major compression of the text and that this could not have happened by chance.

The conventional theory was that the sheets were replacements to cope with major blunders by scribe A. If these were omissions, this could be taken to explain the squeezing up of the text when scribe D came (it is hypothesised) to repeat the sheets and add in the presumed omitted text.

However, we have already found for the sheet containing the end of Mark and the beginning of Luke that Milne and Skeat's theory of a major dittography by scribe A is untenable and that Jongkind's alternative explanation of an even more substantial error of omission is both insufficient and improbable. What we have proposed, in terms of adjustments made to the text of Mark and Luke, covers the observed features and avoids hypothetical scenarios for which there is actually no evidence (see Chapter 11).

There are similarly insuperable difficulties for regarding these other two sheets as the outcome of huge blunders of omission by scribe A, which had later to be corrected by scribe D. To give an idea of the amounts of text involved, as against the average of 625 characters per column, there are in the first six columns of Luke 405 more characters. The scribe has in effect accommodated in this space an extra 30 or so lines. On the first page of Thessalonians by scribe D, there are similarly 231 more characters that would amount to an extra 18 lines. On the other folio of the same sheet by scribe D, comprising a section of Hebrews, there are 360 characters above the average, that could have made a further 28 lines. In scribe D's sheet in Matthew, there is also compression in both folios, although it is less pronounced. As against the average, 10 more lines have been squeezed into the first folio and seven into the second.

To account for all of these, as the outcome of reinstating text accidentally omitted by scribe A, is so improbable as to be surreal. As can be observed from the text by scribe A in the rest of the New Testament, we know that he was not generally prone to making such mistakes. So, why would he have left out a truly massive amount of text in 1 Thessalonians and then – by pure coincidence – happen to do the same later on in Hebrews in the folio that formed part of the *same* bifolium? Why would he have left out text, though on not such a great scale, in a folio of Matthew and then done exactly the same in another folio later on that also just happened to be part of the same bifolium? Why might he have blundered similarly in Luke, leaving out 30 lines or committed an equally improbable dittography of 18 lines, in a sheet that just happened to have some very substantial adjustments to the ending of Mark?

Furthermore, as far as the sheet in Matthew is concerned, the hypothetical omissions are not so great that they might not have been dealt with by means of marginal corrections. In which case, there would have been no need for scribe D to replace it.

If the sheets were not written, for the reasons we have given, to correct massive hypothetical blunders by scribe A, then the sheets must represent what they give all the appearances of being: an alternation of work between the scribes. We have noted that the middle sheet of quire 77 is associated with adjustments indicating that an ending of Mark has been replaced. We have suggested that the allocation of the sheet involving this work to scribe D may not be coincidental. This is especially given that the division of labour, by which a second scribe wrote single sheets including some with disconnected text, was most unusual and is also in practical terms difficult to explain.

There are possible reasons why one scribe might take a break, allowing another scribe to write a folio. But it is hard to see why the first scribe might, many pages later, have then chosen to stop and let the second scribe write another folio that happened to make up the complete bifolium. Furthermore, having ruled out improbable blunders in two such separated sheets in the theory of replacement, it still remains to explain why there should have been considerable extra text in the two halves of a separated bifolium written by another scribe.

There are, however, the beginnings of an explanation to account for the mechanism of the working arrangement between scribe A and scribe D. There are a number of clues arising from the different ways in which the scribes behaved in the New Testament. Scribe A worked steadily through and must have been, in working hours, on the case most of the time. But scribe D was clearly not so available. He only wrote three sheets. When there was a cooperative effort for the last three books, he only managed a few lines of Revelation before breaking off, mid-line and mid-sentence, to hand the work back to scribe A.

It is thus reasonable to presume that scribe D had an alternative role that was sufficiently important to call him and keep him away. He may have had his own bench somewhere else, possible in another room or even in another building.

So, when the point was reached in Matthew with the first of three bifolia ultimately allocated to scribe D, scribe A found that he had a problem in handing over work. Scribe D was, as at other times, not immediately available or present. So, what we suggest scribe A did, especially as there seems to have been an imperative to get Sinaiticus completed, was make a note of the point he had reached, and calculate the point he would need to start the next-but-one folio.

The sheets were not cut up into halves in production but kept intact for the purposes of binding. We suggest, therefore, that scribe A then took the next *whole sheet*, already marked up and together with the notes he had made, to the place where scribe D would be working when he was able to give it his attention. Having thus missed out folio two of quire 75, and put folio seven at least temporarily out of reach, scribe A pressed on with folio three.

It might be objected that this arrangement would not have been feasible, given that scribe A had the exemplar that scribe D needed to copy. This assumes, however, that scribe D needed to be on the job at the same time. He was in actuality only required to do a limited amount. He could have done this, effectively after hours, or when scribe A was taking a meal break or even much later after most of the project had been completed. He might have used an alternative exemplar, although this is an unnecessary complication. He could have used, and probably would have needed to refer to, the exemplar used by scribe A.

When scribe A finished folio six, he had reached the point at which he should have embarked on folio seven, the second of the folios belonging to the sheet that was now with scribe D. It is possible, this being the first of the three sheets by a second scribe and thus presumably the first instance of a new pattern of cooperation, that scribe A had expected folio two to have been completed and the sheet handed back to him.

He had, however, discovered, what is also apparent to us now, the fact of scribe D's extended unavailability. Folio two, we suggest, had at this point not yet been written. Rather than go and get the sheet, write folio seven and then possibly take the sheet back for scribe D to do folio two, as had originally been planned, scribe A decided to continue with folio eight. He needed, of course, to calculate where to start and also provide a second note for scribe D's benefit as to where to begin and end folio seven.

Precisely the same procedure could have operated with the two other sheets by scribe D. There would, of course, have been a difference in the case of the inner bifolium of quire 77. Since the text is here continuous, scribe A only needed to make one calculation, where to pick up in Luke at the start of folio six. He was then able to take the inner sheet comprising folios four and five to scribe D's work place, with a note of where to start and finish.

This suggestion, as to the way the scribes operated, has the benefit of explaining how some text came to be compressed in all three sheets by scribe D and especially how the text may have come to be compressed in the separated folios of the *same* sheet. With scribe A having gone ahead, scribe D would have been working in each case to a fixed extent. When scribe A miscalculated and allowed insufficient space, scribe D then had to compress the exemplar's text.

Such miscalculation is by no means implausible. In the Old Testament, scribe D took drastic measures to stretch out the text of the end of Judith, cutting the number of lines per column, decreasing the number of characters in each column and using filler marks (diples) copiously. Even with all this effort, he still managed to end nearly two columns short of the beginning of 1 Maccabees. It is evident that, in this latter book, scribe A had gone ahead, since he began in the second column of Q39F3R leaving the first column blank. If by that time Judith had been completed, there would have been no reason for him to have left the first column of the first page of a new book blank. Indeed, there is no precedent for such an action anywhere else in Codex Sinaiticus.

It is reasonable to presume, as Jongkind does, that scribe A began there because he had calculated that scribe D would need to run into the first column of the page to complete his book. But, in the event, scribe A badly miscalculated, leaving scribe D with far too much space to fill and having to take drastic measures to stretch out his text.

In the New Testament, it may be with this experience in mind, scribe A tended to err on the side of allowing his fellow scribe much more limited space. He could not have been too far out in Matthew, as scribe D only had to compress in text by 10 lines and seven lines, as against the average number of characters per column, in the two folios of the bifolium Q75F2/7.

He appears to have been more substantially out in the inner bifolium of quire 77. Here, we have argued, scribe D made progressive adjustments to Mark, ultimately stretching out text to cope with the elimination of an ending that was in the exemplar. Scribe A had, we suggest, initially left scribe D with limited space overall for this bifolium. Once it was decided to cut the ending of Mark, however, scribe D had if anything too much space.

However, the break between books, coming as it did within his text, limited his scope for action. Luke had to begin at the head of a new column and, given the material available, it had to be at the head of either column two or of column three of Q77F5R.

Choosing the former option would have allowed scribe D to write the last five columns of Mark, including one partial column, at a normal density of text, of around 625 characters per column. But the text of Luke in this bifolium over seven columns would then have been on average well below the norm, at 594 characters per column. Scribe D instead took the route provided by the latter option, either deliberately or through failing sufficiently to look ahead. He stretched out the text of Mark considerably and then had to compress the text of Luke, beginning at the head of column three of Q77F5R.

In the case of the third bifolium, comprising folios three and six of quire 85, scribe A probably got it about right in the space he allocated for the first folio but left too little space for the second.

In the case of the first folio, he decided to leave the whole folio for scribe D to finish 1 Thessalonians and continue himself with 2 Thessalonians on a new page and folio. He had left adequate space. Scribe D, however, began to compress text in the first three columns. There are three logical possibilities to explain this, acting alone or in combination. Either scribe D miscalculated and as a result began to compress text, leaving off when he realised his mistake. Or he found that he had marginal corrections, which were in the exemplar, to add. Or he added text from another source.

But there would have been a miscalculation by scribe D, even in the case of these latter eventualities. The text could still have been written at normal density, to run into the last column.

In the case of the second folio containing part of Hebrews, scribe A does appear to have been less than generous in the amount of space he left. Scribe D had in consequence to compress his text by 28 lines, as against the average number of characters in a column.

There is, interestingly, evidence that scribe D had to make adjustments at some of the points where he reached the end of a folio and encountered pages already written by scribe A. Given that one of his folios was located mid-quire, there were in all five re-entry points where scribe D stopped and scribe A took over.

One of the points was at the end of 1 Thessalonians and involved a partially filled column. So, no adjustment would have been needed there. In two of the remaining four, it appears that scribe D had over-compensated somewhat in compressing text. As a consequence, just before the end of the verso of his second folio in each case, he had to stretch out his copy to fill the space. There are thus two columns of 592 and 596 characters at the end of the Matthew bifolium and one of 582 characters at the end of the 1 Thessalonians–Hebrews bifolium.

In each case, there is a sudden switch from being well above average to being below average in terms of the number of characters per column.

This cooperation between the two scribes, albeit on a more limited scale, has parallels with what happened in the Old Testament, with the same sort of calculations and miscalculations taking place. The false assumption of massive errors and consequent corrections is no longer needed to explain the places where there is major compression of text. Of course, the scribes sometimes did make changes for various reasons, including harmonisation to other passages and the elimination of apparent mistakes in the exemplar. We can allow for this possibility.

We can also envisage the elimination or addition of text, as against the exemplar, on a big enough scale to have an impact on scribe D's writing within the confines of a bifolium. This certainly seems to have been the case with the ending of Mark, and may also have been a factor with the first part of 1 Thessalonians.

What we have now is an understanding of the mechanism by which the bifolia by scribe D were produced. The chief constraint was that scribe D was writing within the confines of a limited space, scribe A having at each point gone on ahead. Scribe D was affected by the amount of space allowed to him by scribe A's decisions as to which points to pick up the text.

Scribe A appears to have got it right or almost right some of the time. But he left scribe D with a very insufficient amount of space in Hebrews. He may also have failed to allow for a partial column break between Mark and Luke and thus allowed insufficient space here also. Scribe D appears to have added his own miscalculations. In addition to which, he may have incorporated marginal corrections or made alterations, either or both having an impact on the density of text.

There is, at least theoretically, another possibility. This is that scribe D wrote his three sheets from another exemplar that had considerably more copy. So, while scribe A in this scenario provided finishing points that were reasonably accurate in relation to his own exemplar, it meant that scribe D, in working from a (hypothetical) alternative exemplar, had to squeeze in more text. This should have entailed the scribes working at the same time. Otherwise, why would scribe D have gone to the extremity of using a variant alternative when he could instead have used the same exemplar as scribe A?

But, as we have noted, the overall pattern in the New Testament is indicative of the fact that scribe D was not immediately available. In which case, he could have borrowed scribe A's exemplar at some time when scribe A was not working. In addition to which, it is hard to see why the scribes might have allowed variations from another exemplar to creep in, simply as a matter of expediency. There is, moreover, no evidence of another exemplar that might have had such very large variations in the amount of text.

It would also be extraordinary that substantial additional amounts of text, as against the main exemplar, should have happened to occur in an alternative exemplar so as to affect all three sheets and, especially, both the folios of sheets of discontinuous text. This latter is just as improbable as the idea that such folios had required corrections for massive blunders that scribe A had coincidentally committed on each.

A similar drawback applies to the idea that the scribes might have been following the main exemplar for New Testament Sinaiticus, not only line by line, but according to the exact same layout. In such circumstances, there would have been no difficulty in scribe A leaving off for scribe D to take over and in scribe D knowing where to stop and start. This would have been dictated by the layout of the exemplar that both were following.

The major compressions in scribe D's text would now have to be explained as additions from another, hypothetical source. But this results again in the implausibility of huge added amounts of text concentrated in D's work, occurring against very strong odds in separated sheets and without any evidence for this either in the text or elsewhere. Since the compression in scribe D's sheets cannot be explained in this way, it is further evidence that the scribes were not in fact trying to make a page-by-page copy of their exemplar.

There is, as it happens, a check on the passage from Hebrews from 4, 16–8, 1 that forms the second folio of the third bifolium by scribe D. The mid second century papyrus manuscript **P46** contains all of this, except for the first verse. It happens to agree in great detail with the text of Codex Sinaiticus. So there is no support here for the idea of large amounts of text having been added from an alternative source. Smaller sections of text are also found in the early papyrus manuscripts, **P30**, **P45** and **P46**, similarly matching parts of 1 Thessalonians and Matthew that are in the bifolia by scribe D. Another check is provided by **P13**, from the third century that has verses 5, 1–5 from Hebrews, once again matching the text of Codex Sinaiticus in detail.

The logic of the situation, and the evidence, thus do not give any support to the idea that scribe D might have been using another exemplar with considerably more text.

The theory that we have offered by contrast, involving an alternation of work and miscalculation of space, is consistent with the pattern elsewhere in Codex Sinaiticus. It also provides one explanation to cover satisfactorily three very similar, though highly unusual, interventions. It is coherent. It accounts for circumstances that are otherwise difficult to explain and that are not, in fact, explained in alternative hypotheses. It does not depend on improbable coincidences or unlikely circumstances.

That is, however, as far as the theory goes. What we do have is a good explanation of the mechanism of cooperation between scribe A and scribe D. What we do not have yet is an explanation of the motivation for an unusual alternation of work involving three, widely separated single sheets.

To examine what may have happened, we shall start by looking at scribe A's work in copying Matthew, the first book of the New Testament. This is the first of the four gospels which together comprise the centrepiece of the Christian message. Reproducing these gospels was, and must have been regarded as, the most important part of the task of producing the new bible, one of the first ever produced and we have argued a master copy from which to make further copies. Scribe A had been entrusted with this, as indeed he had been with the greater part of the task of producing Codex Sinaiticus.

There are several key features indicating that scribe A's work in Matthew was written in an awareness of two sheets, together forming a single bifolium, produced or to be produced by scribe D.

Firstly, scribe A began increasingly to depart from his normal pattern of spelling, as he approached the first of the two folios that was to be written by scribe D.

Jongkind has shown that, in respect of deviations of iotacism, scribe D performed better overall than scribe A. But both were generally consistent throughout the whole of the Old and New Testaments. However, in the first two quires (74 and 75) of Matthew, scribe A's pattern differs markedly and significantly from that which he established elsewhere.[10] In particular, he far more often shortened the diphthongs AI to E and EI to I.

This could have reflected simple mistakes against the then established usage. But it could as likely have represented greater deviation from what had been agreed between the scribes in dealing with exemplars that had been written perhaps 150 years previously, when different styles and rules of orthography applied. The Greek language was evolving in a direction in which diphthongs were being replaced by single vowels. What scribe A may more often have been forgetting was to use the archaic form of the exemplar, as opposed to his own vernacular.[11] Either way, it appears that, for a considerable period at the outset of his task of copying out the New Testament, scribe A was for some reason less focused and more careless. This in turn is indicative that he may have been under some stress.

We cannot agree with the idea that this might have been the work of another scribe, as Jongkind suggested[12] because in other key respects, including the style of handwriting, this text can be identified as the work of scribe A.

The first two folios of quire 74 do not have a pattern of iotacisms significantly out of keeping with the pattern exhibited by the scribe elsewhere. But, beginning with folio three of quire 74 and continuing into the next quire, the frequency of spelling deviations increase, suggesting that something was beginning to distract scribe A's attention (see Fig. 8). The pages that have the greatest frequency of iotacism occur before the first folio written by scribe D, continue up until scribe D's next folio and persist for one more folio before reverting to scribe A's normal pattern. The aberrant pattern of iotacisms, indicative that scribe A was under stress at the time, is thus closely associated with

Synoptic gospels: iotacisms per folio

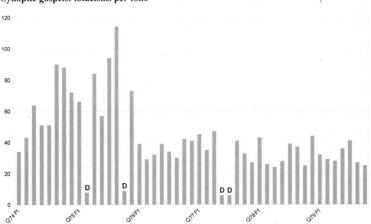

Adapted from a chart of data prepared by Dirk Jongkind, qv Scribal Habits of Codex Sinaiticus

Fig. 8. Errors of iotacism in synoptic gospels, Codex Sinaiticus

the intervention for just one bifolium by scribe D. If, as this suggests, scribe A were responding to what was happening, it reinforces the case that the allocation of this sheet to scribe D occurred at this time, rather than later to replace work by scribe A.

The folios by scribe D are easily identifiable from Jongkind's histogram, reproduced on the previous page, as two that generate very short columns, indicating a much lower frequency of iotacisms. The two folios are consistent in this respect with scribe D's performance elsewhere, and differ even from the normal pattern for scribe A. Scribe D conformed better to a template employing more diphthongs or he made fewer errors, or possibly a mixture of both.

The folios cover the text of Matthew 16, 9–18, 12 and Matthew 24, 35–26, 6. This was not the inner bifolium of the quire and so did not comprise continuous text (Fig. 9).

Fig. 9. Bifolium by scribe D in quire 75, Codex Sinaiticus

There is a second feature also indicating that, when scribe A was writing his copy just before each of the pages by scribe D in Matthew, it was with an awareness of the work that was to be written by another scribe.

The sheet by scribe D in Matthew is, very unusually, for each folio framed by two corrections to omissions.[13] In the first, the scriptorium corrector Ca has, in the third line from the end of the verso of folio one of quire 75, reinserted an omitted phrase 'Do you not remember' (OYΔE MNHMONEYETAI) into the passage, 'Do you not understand? Do you not remember the five loaves for the five thousand and how many baskets you gathered?' The correction could either have resulted from a simple oversight by the scribe or a skip error based on the final TE of NOIETE, if it were spelt OYΔE MNHMONEYETE in the exemplar for Sinaiticus, as it is in Codex Vaticanus. The phrase is less likely to have been absent in the exemplar and an addition by Ca, for example to harmonise with Mark 8, 18, because it is needed for the passage in Matthew to make sense.

The second such omission and correction occurs at the very end of the verso of folio six of quire 75, after the last character on the last line of the page penned by scribe A. The passage, amounting to 50 characters, is part of the 'little apocalypse' found in all three synoptic gospels. Since the author of Matthew otherwise faithfully reproduced Mark's copy in this section, it is fair to assume that the omitted passage was in the exemplar for Sinaiticus but then accidentally left out in copying.[14] The passage, reinserted by Ca, is verse 24, 35, 'Heaven and earth will pass away but my words will by no means pass away'. There is nothing in the text to indicate that this could have been a skip error. Whether a skip, or a simple oversight, such an error of omission is not likely at the very end of this page. At this point, as we have established, the scribes were cooperating by alternating the work. Scribe A's task here was *not* to write the next verse but to tell scribe D, either verbally or in a note, where he had to begin. And that is, at any time or in any language, notoriously open to confusion!

We suggest scribe A conveyed that he had got up to the verse beginning O OYNOC KAI H ΓH (heaven and earth). Did that mean he had reached that verse or just completed that verse? Scribe A could easily have failed to make this clear. Between them, the scribes managed to get it wrong, so that scribe D started the next folio in the wrong place, leaving out a whole verse. The mistake was identified and later remedied by the scriptorium corrector, Ca.

A third significant feature, indicating scribe A's awareness of the interpolation by scribe D in Matthew, is related to the fact that, consistently throughout the Old and New Testaments, the scribes signed off their work at the end of each chapter with a decorative flourish known as a coronis. These are distinctive and unique to each scribe, such that the scribe working on the immediately preceding pages can be identified by this decoration alone. Scribe A's design was thin and wavy, sometimes with leafy additions. Scribe B had a hatched pattern. Scribe D employed a combination of dotted lines and scrolls. Whenever two scribes worked together on a book, it may be observed that it was always the one writing the finishing section who added his own decorative signature.

In the case of the gospel of Matthew, there is a coronis at the end. But its twisted design is distinctive and quite different from scribe A's usual wavy decoration, or for that matter the signatures of the other two scribes. There is furthermore very exceptionally no written book title which the scribe would usually have added, together with his decorative flourish, to sign off the book. So, as well as not being the work of scribe A, the colophon was incomplete.

It would appear that someone else, possibly the scriptorium corrector, at this point added a decorative coronis to sign off scribe A's work. Scribe A must have finished Matthew and gone to work on Mark, leaving the previous book without a colophon, unsigned (Fig. 10).

Why would he have departed from the normal practice among the scribes, in such an unprecedented way? The usual reason for failing to sign off work would presumably have been a reservation about its quality or accuracy. But scribe A's own work was within his control and he could have gone back and corrected anything he felt was not up to standard. It is then a reasonable conclusion that scribe A

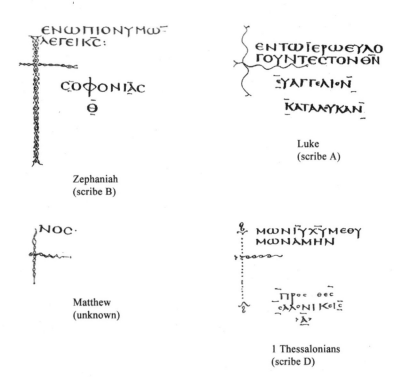

Zephaniah
(scribe B)

Luke
(scribe A)

Matthew
(unknown)

1 Thessalonians
(scribe D)

Fig. 10. Decorative signatures (coronides) typical of each scribe, Codex Sinaiticus

254

decided that he could not sign off the work allocated to scribe D. It may simply be because, as we have suggested is quite possible, when scribe A reached the end of Matthew, scribe D had not yet disengaged from whatever else he had been doing and written his two folios in Matthew. It could equally have been because of something that, either written or proposed, was within scribe D's bifolium.

What must have been a deliberate decision by scribe A, not to provide a colophon and coronis at the end of Matthew, is yet another indication of his awareness of a sheet allocated to another scribe. His behaviour in respect of iotacisms, errors and the spurned task of providing a coronis reinforces the conclusion reached that what was happening was an alternation of work between the scribes.

There is finally another unusual feature, which is hard to comprehend, of this first bifolium written by scribe D. It is that the marginal reference notes for the Eusebian tables are missing from this sheet, while present in the folios by scribe A on either side. On the assumption that it was a replacement sheet, Jongkind explained this on the basis that the references must have been put in before the replacement occurred.[15]

He appears to be following Skeat, who argued in his later article that scribe D was replacing a sheet by scribe A in Matthew, due to some extensive but unidentified and unspecified error. Skeat suggested that the reason that scribe D failed to put in the references, before his very eyes in scribe A's putative first attempt, was twofold: scribe D made the correction very late and it had just been decided to omit the canon tables from the codex and put in no more marginal references.[16]

This is a more than a little odd as an explanation, given that the canon table references are present in the other gospel sheet by scribe D, folios four and five of quire 77 covering the end of Mark and the beginning of Luke. If, as seems likely, scribe A wrote the gospels in sequence, this would require everyone at the time to have missed the supposed major blunder or blunders by scribe A in Matthew, scribe D to have been called in to replace the Mark–Luke bifolium, the exercise of putting in the canon tables to have been called off during this exercise, and then and only then for scribe D to have been called in to firefight the newly-discovered serious (though entirely hypothetical) solecism by scribe A in Matthew.

This is all very implausible. It is not surprising, given that we have in any case found that all three sheets by scribe D were written most probably in an alternation of work between the scribes, with the theory of replacement depending on improbable, unidentified blunders and extraordinary coincidences of significant errors in disconnected sheets. The Matthew bifolium is particularly indicative, with patterns of errors and omissions on several levels indicating scribe A's awareness of sheets that were going to be undertaken by another scribe.

However, we do already have in the observed non-availability of scribe D and the evidence of alternation, as opposed to replacement, a way of explaining how the gospel sheets by scribe D came to have the canon table references in one sheet and not the other. We have suggested that scribe A made a note of where scribe D had to start and finish for the single or double folios of each of the three sheets, and went on ahead. He left scribe D with three blank sheets to fill, the exemplar with which to do it and either separate notes to help or reference marks on the exemplar. In one instance, he conveyed the information incorrectly, or scribe D misunderstood, and a whole verse in Matthew was missed out.

When scribe D came to make his contributions, it was at the end or towards the end of the task of creating Codex Sinaiticus, and he had three sheets to do. He had no need to do the work in any particular order, and could well have undertaken the Mark–Luke bifolium before the Matthew bifolium.

Scribe A began to add the Eusebian canon table references to Matthew, but the bifolium consisting of folios two and seven quire 75 was still physically separated from the rest of the manuscript. It had been given to scribe D, along with notes for each folio of where to begin and end. But scribe D may not yet have written it, or possibly simply have not returned it.

So scribe A put in the references for the sheets he had, with the help of the canon tables and the exemplar. The scribes continued with this task, along with the insertion of other material including page numbers and running titles, to run into Mark and then Luke, covering also folios four and five of quire 75 that scribe D had by now done.

The Mark–Luke bifolium by scribe D therefore does contain Eusebian section number and canon table references. But this is only up to and including number 106 at the end of Chapter 9 in Luke, apart from one insertion later by a different hand. This suggests that the decision not to include the Eusebian canon tables in Sinaiticus and to discontinue inserting the section numbers and references (see pp 42–44) was probably taken at this point. Luke must have been last in line to have the apparatus added.

But the addition was done, most probably in a cooperative effort, in no particular order at or towards the end of the project. There are section numbers in John, which comes after Luke, and it would seem logical that these were inserted before the application was abandoned in Luke.

Jongkind's analysis of the application of the section numbers and references indicates that there was some confusion and quite a high degree of error. The procedure was abruptly abandoned. There were points at which it was not perfectly applied, including scribe D's bifolium in Matthew.

Our suggestion would fit in with what was evidently a somewhat chaotic way of working. Scribe D may have made the Mark–Luke bifolium a priority. Or it may have simply been handed back or retrieved before his Matthew bifolium. The sheets from the gospels thus came back out of order. Because the canon tables were applied only to the gospels, it is just these two sheets that are relevant. Scribe D may well have written his sheets very late. The canon table references were at this stage being added in. The scribe who put in the references for Matthew, quite possibly scribe A, managed without scribe D's sheet.

The scribes did, however, have the relevant sheet when it came to putting in the references for Mark and Luke. The section numbers and canon table references were added to Mark, up to and including scribe D's sheet before being abandoned some way into Luke. The work on the bulk of Matthew had already been done. It was no longer thought worth the trouble to put the references into scribe D's sheet in Matthew, when it was finally retrieved or handed in. This is because it had been decided, after all, not to include the canon tables in the codex and to stop putting in any further section numbers and table references.

Without the canon tables, it would not have been possible to decipher and apply the marginal references for the purposes of comparing passages in the gospels. Continuing with the exercise any further might therefore have been seen as futile. It may have been decided that these were not required for the role which we have suggested was intended for Codex Sinaiticus, to be a master copy.

The scribes had certainly made lots of mistakes, omitting all or part of some canon table references, putting others in the wrong place and getting some numbers wrong. They may not have fully appreciated the value, purpose or possibly even the mechanics of what was then a relatively new innovation. So the manuscript's commissioner could have decided to pull the plug on that part of the exercise, on the grounds that it had been too badly done.

This brings us to the third sheet written by scribe D, comprising folios three and six of quire 85, taking in the end of 1 Thessalonians in the first folio and part of Hebrews in the second. On the last column of the page prior to the first folio of this sheet, when there would have been just four lines to run to the point where scribe D took over, there is a very substantial repetition of 128 characters amounting to ten lines of text.

It seems on the face of it that it was a simple dittography, based on the key phrase TOY ΘY (of God) that occurs in verse 2, 13 of 1 Thessalonians and then again in verse 2, 14. On this reading of the situation, when scribe A got to the second occurrence, his eye lit on the first, possibly in the same position at the end of the line in his exemplar. He then continued writing what he had already written until he again reached the point where he had initiated the mistake.

Dittographies are fairly rare, if only because they depend on the scribe being unaware of repeating text that he had only just written. It is, therefore, odd that scribe A should have committed one on such a scale, just before scribe D was about to take over. The mistake could indicate that, at the time, scribe A was in some way distracted.[17]

Scribe A also made an apparent mistake in Matthew, just before the first of scribe D's interventions, though in that instance it was an error of omission, possibly a skip error (see p 252). Just before the second folio in Matthew, there is a whole verse missing, which we have suggested was the result of a simple failure of communication between the scribes. Scribe had A had failed to get across to scribe D where he had to start on the second folio of his sheet.

The substantial dittography just before the first folio of scribe D's third bifolium suggests, like the similarly placed errors in Matthew, scribe A's awareness of and reaction to the copy being provided by scribe D.

The increased frequency of iotacisms in the vicinity of scribe D's intervention in Matthew, taken together with the error just before the first of the two folios, indicates that scribe A was here under some stress. His failure to sign off this book could mean that this stress was connected with his assessment of the quality or accuracy of the work by scribe D. He might instead, or indeed as well, have been registering that scribe D, having had the sheet to work on, had not yet completed it.

Let us review the evidence for the three bifolia by scribe D in the New Testament. We started with an examination in Chapter 11 of the ending of Mark in one bifolium, the middle sheet of quire 77. We concluded that Milne and Skeat's explanation, that this eventuated as a correction sheet as a result of a presumed and unidentified massive dittography by scribe A, was both implausible and insufficient. We found the same for Jongkind's argument that it was to do with a presumed, similarly huge error of omission of text by scribe A.

The stretching and compression of text in the first part of the Mark–Luke bifolium can be explained by decisions first to substitute and then to eliminate an ending of Mark in the main exemplar. This explanation does not require the postulation of massive errors by scribe A nor the substitution of a hypothetical sheet originally written by scribe A. Neither of these ideas is based on evidence and neither explains the text as it appears.

We therefore concluded that the observed pattern, in which scribe D wrote a single bifolium incorporating the end of Mark and the beginning of Luke, was the product of an alternation of work between the scribes, though it remained to be explained why scribe D took on just one sheet and what caused compression of text in Luke. Our working hypothesis was and is that it is more likely that there would be one explanation covering the genesis of the three sheets by scribe D, as opposed say to three distinct explanations.

We found that the hypothesis of massive errors by scribe D was if anything even more unsustainable for the other two sheets by scribe D, covering parts of Matthew and of 1 Thessalonians and Hebrews. Presumed massive errors in the separated text of these two bifolia simply could not be explained in this way. Tindall's idea that compressed text was the result of material being systematically added also did not withstand examination. Nor could it be explained as the result of scribe D using a second exemplar with considerably more text.

However, there is a marked association of major compression, and in one case stretching, with scribe D's three bifolia in the New Testament, such that this could not be the product of chance. It has therefore to be explained.

We found that our alternative theory of an alternation of work, combined with the type of miscalculation of space that Jongkind found in the Old Testament when the scribes worked together, provided an overall explanation that is both coherent and sufficient. This covers all the elements of the mechanism of cooperation between scribe A and scribe D including, what had previously been mind-bendingly baffling, the existence of major compression of text in separated folios of two of the sheets by scribe D.

It is interesting that Jongkind's comparative analysis of individual features, mostly small mistakes giving rise to singular readings, of the two scribes in Paul and in Matthew are consistent with our conclusions. Scribe D did not write out scribe A's putative original text, with his own improvements, but instead wrote out the text from his exemplar to generate a pattern of singularities that is all his own.

Assuming that he had in front of him on three occasions an earlier attempt by scribe A, he might each time have remedied whatever was the serious fault while using the rest of scribe A's text. That might have saved some time, as against the option of ignoring what scribe A had done and working entirely from the exemplar.

Jongkind's analysis has shown that he did in fact adopt the latter course. The reason we suggest is that he did not have an earlier version by scribe A available. He thus had no option but to use the exemplar.[18]

What remains to be explained is why scribe D was called in to write three specific bifolia. What was the motivation? It would have been a cumbersome arrangement. Any gains from providing scribe A with a break would have been offset by the intricacies of calculating where text had to begin and end, the bother of passing sheets around and the nuisance of scribe D having to switch from whatever else he was doing. Why go to such trouble in each instance for precisely one sheet?

It seems possible, if not likely, that this may have had something to do with content. We know that the ending of Mark was changed and we suspect that there may have been some change introduced towards the beginning of 1 Thessalonians. At the same time, we found that much of the compression could be accounted for by the way in which the scribes cooperated.

If the introduction of changes to the text does provide the motivation, then it may be that what really mattered was the significance of what was proposed in each case, as opposed to the quantity of affected text. Some changes may, in terms of number of characters, have been quite minimal. Since the scribes routinely made small changes, for example to deal with errors in the exemplar or incorporate marginal corrections, the impact, as well as being minimal, may also have been masked. So counts of characters will have to be treated with caution and may not always help.

We have found evidence that scribe A was disturbed in some way, especially in relation to the first of the three sheets written by scribe D. Just before this sheet in Matthew, and continuing through it until just afterwards, scribe A made a higher frequency of deviations from the pattern that had been agreed for vowels and diphthongs. He more often reverted, we suggest, to his own vernacular, as opposed to keeping to the more archaic form of the exemplar.

On three occasions, including two in Matthew, scribe A made what may have been mistakes or unusual adjustments just before the folios written by scribe D. As the last scribe working on Matthew, Scribe A should have provided a colophon to sign off the book. But the written part of the colophon is missing and the decorative flourish or coronis at the end is completely different from the otherwise characteristic decorative signatures of scribe A.

So, scribe A did not sign off Matthew. Perhaps this was simply because scribe D had not, at that point, yet finished and returned his sheet. It could equally be that scribe A was dissatisfied with some aspect of it, not of his own work that he could have corrected but of the work done by scribe D that he could not.

If Matthew were, as seems highly probable, the first of the gospels written by scribe A, then it was also the first point at which the new arrangement between the two scribes was generated. There is more evidence of stress here, and then less later, because the arrangement itself may have done something to resolve or at least alleviate whatever was the problem. It was certainly an awkward and highly unusual arrangement. There must have been a powerful reason for it. In such circumstances, some weight needs to be given to the observed associations.

Piecing together the evidence that we do have, we find first of all that scribe A was disturbed at around the time he would have written the first folio of the bifolium consisting of folios two and seven of quire 75 in Matthew. His stress diminished but did not entirely disappear, once scribe D had stepped in, for the next folio and for the other two sheets.

He made more errors of iotacism, or failed more often to use the agreed spelling, before and after the first folio of Mathew. There are corrections to errors of omission, just before each of scribe D's folios in this gospel. Scribe A also failed to sign off Matthew. Something was clearly bothering him. There is also a feature, a major dittography, just before Scribe D took over in 1 Thessalonians.

Whether it was intentional, or coincidental, scribe A avoided having to write a sheet in which there was a substantial change to the ending of Mark. The possibility, which has to be entertained, is that all these circumstances are inter-related. It could be that scribe A was avoiding having to be involved in alterations for this sheet and also for the other two sheets written by scribe D. That would account for scribe A's apparent stress, his mistakes and his decision not to sign off Matthew in the usual way. It would be enough to explain an unusual arrangement by which another scribe stepped in to write just three sheets.

But was scribe A, in the Mark–Luke bifolium, reluctant to implement changes made to the end of Mark? If this is also the key to all of the sheets, what was it in the other sheets that might have given him cause for concern and then to make a stand?

We are now in turbulent waters. But that would be no excuse for failing, as others have, to look at the evidence or consider the issues. It is going to be interesting, even though the picture that emerges may well be provisional.

Our conclusions in this chapter are:

- **The pattern of cooperation between the scribes for the last three books of Sinaiticus is similar to that found in the Old Testament.**
- **Irregular features of quires 91 and 92, which could have been contained within a single quire, can be explained as a consequence of the need to replace a damaged or spoiled sheet.**
- **The theory, that scribe D's bifolia were replacements for errors made by scribe A, is not supported by evidence, depends on improbable circumstances and fails to explain key features of the sheets.**
- **The three bifolia by scribe D in the New Testament result instead from an alternation of work between the scribes.**
- **The three bifolia were separated and allocated to scribe D to complete, while scribe A went on ahead with the rest of the work.**
- **Substantial compression in all three bifolia by scribe D can be explained as a result of miscalculations by the scribes as to the available space.**
- **The patterns of behaviour by scribe A and scribe D in the New Testament indicate that each was aware of the other's work.**
- **There is as association between behaviour by scribe A and the interventions by scribe D suggesting that scribe A was at the time under stress.**

CHAPTER 13

Rome and Church

The working hypothesis, put forward at the end of the last chapter, was that scribe A had taken exception to some changes proposed for the text. As a consequence, he did not write the passages affected. Scribe D stepped in instead to write the folios that would be affected. This, we suggest, is a possible motivation for an unusual working arrangement between the scribes.

The mechanism by which this happened has already been accounted for and does not need at this point to be re-evaluated. Scribe D was not immediately available and, as a consequence, was left with work to do for three whole sheets while scribe A pressed on ahead. Scribe D worked within a fixed extent and, as result of miscalculation, some of his text was substantially compressed.

The changes that we have proposed were made in the three bifolia by scribe D, which scribe A avoided doing, must have been of real significance for scribe A to have taken a stand, possibly at some personal risk. However expert in his profession, the scribe would have been acting as an employee of the scriptorium and ultimately of the Church.

Creating Codex Sinaiticus was a major undertaking, both costly and time consuming. Even as a single example of a bible containing both the Old and New Testaments, it was one of the very first and would have been one of relatively few generated during the fourth century. But the codex had an additional significance. It was, as we have argued, intended as an exemplar or master copy from which to make and disseminate further copies. This purpose was a reason that it was retained for so long, giving it a better chance to survive until the present day.

As an exemplar or master copy, Sinaiticus was an important element in the propagation of the Christian message in the fourth century. It would have been supported by the Church authorities and, moreover, with the conversion of Constantine, it had the backing of Rome. This is why it might have been difficult and even hazardous for a scribe to have challenged changes to the text, ordered by the manuscript's commissioner, on grounds perhaps of inadequate provenance or indeed for any reason.

We suggest that it was for reasons of provenance[1] that scribe A, the reluctant scribe, stood his ground and opted not to write the sheets ultimately undertaken by scribe D. Scribe A was otherwise able to continue with his work, which suggests that this was an arrangement between the scribes designed to achieve two objectives. It allowed scribe A to satisfy his professional scruples or conscience and at the same time it disguised from the authorities the refusal of one scribe to accede to the brief. Because scribe D did write the sheets, it has to be taken that he was less concerned with changes from the main exemplar.

The close working relationship, particularly in dealing with sections of the Old Testament, is evidence that the scribes were colleagues and possibly friends. It may have been in such a spirit that scribe D helped his fellow scribe out.

As to what was concerning scribe A, we already have some clues from the detailed examination of the ending of Mark undertaken in Chapter 11. But let us look at the matter first of all from the perspective of the Church, which would have been involved in commissioning and controlling the production of new copies of the Christian texts.

This was a pivotal time, one of unprecedented opportunity. At the beginning of the fourth century, there had been a great persecution undertaken by Diocletian. But Galerius, who had actively promoted the persecution, came to admit towards the end of his reign in 311 CE that the strategy had not been a great success. So, there was a switch from then on to a policy of greater toleration. The Edict of Milan, published by Constantine and Licinius in 313 CE, allowed Christians the freedom to practise their religion.

Constantine exerted crucial influence over a period of 31 years from 306 CE to 337 CE, first as co-emperor and then as sole emperor after he had eliminated his rivals. Although he is described as having converted to Christianity, it can also be argued that what he was doing was attempting to combine different religions to serve the Empire. While adopting Christianity as a state religion, he still retained his position as head of the pagan priesthood. He took an active interest, encouraging Christians to reach agreement on what they believed. In 330 or 331 CE, he ordered copies of the scriptures from Eusebius, the Bishop of Caesarea, for churches in his new capital. This was based on the old city of Byzantium, rebuilt and then renamed after the Emperor as Constantinople.

It may have been hard at first, for the Church and its officials, to keep up with changing circumstances. Eusebius had been put under pressure to fulfil the Emperor's order for just 50 copies of the scriptures. But it would soon have become apparent to Eusebius and his successors what a great challenge and opportunity there was. Christian texts had often been held and copied under conditions of secrecy and fear, but now the message could be actively disseminated to all corners of the Empire with the backing or Rome. Under Diocletian, books had been actively sought out and destroyed, so that a significant proportion must have been lost. From this low point, the situation changed over a period to one in which there were many more Christian texts in circulation: individual books, copies of the gospels, whole New Testaments with epistles and gospels and even some bibles containing both the Old and New Testaments.

The opportunity was presented to get across a uniform message, as the Church wanted it. There were of course existing texts in circulation, not all of which could or would have been immediately recalled. With new books soon to form by far the greater part of the literature, however, it would have been possible to reframe orthodoxy in some ways, by for example careful choice among the available exemplars. The Church would have relied on the enhanced authority it had acquired to cause its chosen versions to predominate and ultimately supersede any earlier, variant texts.

The challenge was to make the decisions and get it right, because there would be no second chance. Once there were many hundreds of copies of the New Testament in circulation, once these were in every far corner of the Empire, there could be no going back to have another look and perhaps rewrite a part of Mark or rephrase a sentence or two in one of the epistles attributed to Paul. It would then have been too late. It was under this sort of pressure that we believe that Codex Sinaiticus was written. We consider that it could well have been produced in Caesarea, not only because of the clues contained in the text, but also because the great library there, with ancient texts assembled from all over the world, provided the sources the scribes would have needed.

It was, we have argued, generated as a robust master copy or exemplar from which to make further copies. It was very carefully checked by the scriptorium corrector. The many mistakes that were made, and had to be corrected, suggest that it was produced under some time pressure. As a master copy, however, its appearance might not have greatly mattered.

Copies made from it were used and reused daily in churches, eventually worn out and then replaced. Sinaiticus, however, would have been carefully kept and preserved, brought out when needed for the production of further copies or to check a reading. Soon, however, the Latin vulgate came into general use, supplanting many of the Greek bibles. There was no longer such a need for a Greek master copy. Centuries on, when the original purpose of Codex Sinaiticus had been forgotten, it was nevertheless still respected and retained as an ancient Christian text. It had been taken to a fortified monastery in Sinai and there it was relatively safe.

One of the other books produced at this time also survived. This was Codex Vaticanus, whose detailed correspondences with Sinaiticus indicate that it was, in the New Testament, copied from Sinaiticus or from the same exemplar. It may well have been written at the same place and about the same time, with the exemplar and Codex Sinaiticus available to check against. Codex Vaticanus also lacks marks of regular usage and so must have been kept primarily as a reference copy.

It could be that Codex Sinaiticus was created to serve as a master copy for the scriptures that Constantine ordered for churches in his new capital. This was, however, only a small part of the production of texts to serve the Christian Church within the Roman Empire. There is as good a case, possibly an even better case, that Sinaiticus was generated to serve such a role in a much more extensive operation conducted a few years later.

Despite the persecutions that had taken place and the consequent destruction of manuscripts, it is likely that the scribes producing Codex Sinaiticus at the scriptorium in Caesarea or elsewhere had a number of much earlier sources from which to draw. Towards the end of the second century, the four canonical gospels began to be collected together, sometimes with other material such as Acts and some of the letters attributed to Paul.

This was still a time of fluidity and change, with many new books being created and at the same time the first Christian texts being altered and amended. The Church was developing its doctrine and promoting the versions it favoured. But it was nonetheless a time when alternatives were jostling for favour and there was no definite, fixed text. It is likely that the Sinaiticus scribes had variant material among their sources.

The situation was very different 150 or so years later. Doctrine had become more clearly established through a series of debates and decrees and there was little room for latitude in interpretation. Moreover, Eusebius and his successors as commissioners wanted to use the unprecedented opportunity provided by Roman patronage to ensure that only an entirely approved message would henceforth be promoted.

It seems reasonable to suppose that the Sinaiticus scribes were at the outset instructed to use their earliest and most reliable sources. From the analysis of skip errors, it is apparent that scribe A was using one main exemplar for the greater part of the New Testament. While he may have used others for some of the books, this will not affect the thrust of our argument.

We have shown that the three bifolia in the New Testament written by scribe D represented not the substitution of copy for work already done, but an alternation of work between the scribes. There are strong indications that the two scribes were aware of and adjusted to each other's contributions. In particular, scribe D had to work within the framework of the space left by scribe A and that is why, as a result of his and scribe A's miscalculations, there is compression in the separated halves of two bifolia. It also why there is major compression in the second folio of an inner sheet that has, in its first folio, substantial stretching of the text.

We have generated a theory from an analysis of the ending of Mark, that the prime reason for scribe D coming in to write the inner bifolium Q77F4–5 was to replace text that had been in scribe A's exemplar. Scribe A, we suggest, was content with the material he had and that is why another scribe was called in to make the substitution.

There are some very detailed parallels between the circumstances of the three major interventions in the New Testament text. It was in each case one particular scribe coming in to write a section in the midst of work by the other. It was in each case, very exceptionally, just a single bifolium. Each bifolium has associated with it unusual major adjustments in terms of compression and, in one instance, stretching out of the text. It does seem likely therefore that there will be one explanation covering these three highly unusual interventions, as opposed to a quite separate explanation for each.

The analysis for the ending of Mark should therefore provide a guide to, and be consistent with, the circumstances of the other two interventions by scribe D in scribe A's work. We found that there was most probably a two-stage substitution. In the first instance, the plan was to replace the ending in scribe A's exemplar with the longer ending of Mark. This could have existed as early as the late second century, as indicated in apparent quotes by Irenaeus and its use by Tatian.

To accommodate the longer ending, text began to be compressed in the last column of the recto of Q77F4R. But then there was a switch to a strategy of eliminating the ending entirely and thereafter in Mark the text was stretched out. It may well be this was done because, as Eusebius himself recognised, the longer ending was not at all satisfactory.

It is extraordinarily difficult to add text later on to another writer's work without the disjunction between the original and the added material being immediately apparent. This is the case with the added, longer ending of Mark and it is also the case with much of the rewriting of Mark that the author of Matthew did in creating his gospel (see Chapter 7).

What we are dealing with here then is a choice between competing exemplars from a time, the mid to late second century, when there was just such competition and when the text of the New Testament had not been finalised in all its details.

What scribe A had in his exemplar was an alternative ending of Mark, not necessarily the lost ending, but one that did not provide what the Church needed in terms of doctrine: resurrection appearances followed by a miraculous ascension into heaven. What we suggest scribe A had was an all too naturalistic description of meetings between Jesus and his family and followers. There are indications in other sources, such as the gospel of the Hebrews and the gospel of Peter, that this is what an earlier version of Mark might have contained. Whatever it was, it was not what the Church, in the form of the manuscript's commissioner, wanted and so it was rejected.

The source that scribe A had must have been considered to be generally reliable, which is why scribe A was permitted to go on using it. And it would have been unnecessarily untidy, given that the problem was evidently anticipated, to have allowed scribe A to proceed with his version and then deal with it by means of wholesale alterations afterwards. In addition to which, it might well have been considered undesirable to retain evidence of an alterative version that sat uneasily with Church doctrine.

This is a consideration that, as will be seen, applied equally to the other interventions by scribe D. To put it bluntly, whatever was in scribe A's exemplar and for that matter other exemplars that did not conform was going to be suppressed.

The perceived problem with the Mark–Luke bifolium was to do with the ending of Mark and this was dealt with by a process of elimination and stretching of text. But there is no such stretching in the other two bifolia by scribe D. Although there is compression of text, this we have argued may be a product of miscalculations arising from the alternation of work between the scribes. If there is therefore a similar explanation for these other two sheets, it is likely to involve additions or alterations that may not involve a great deal of material. Is there anything in these sheets that now stands out as being unusual or out of place?

There is a crucial passage, towards the beginning of the first bifolium by scribe D in Matthew, that appears to be highly anomalous and could provide one of the answers. This is where the Church stakes a claim for succession back to the followers of Jesus, through Simon Peter:

> *And I tell you, you are Peter (Petros) and on this rock (petra) I will build my church, and the gates of Hades will not overcome it (?you).*
>
> *I will give you the keys of the kingdom of heaven. And whatever you bind on earth will be bound in heaven. And whatever you loose on earth will be loosed in the heaven.*

Matthew 16, 18–19

Now, this statement is not in Mark, from which the early author of Matthew extensively copied,[2] nor is it in Luke. The narrative in both these other synoptic gospels here follows Mark, except that Matthew has the additional copy represented by verses 16, 17–19, whereas Luke does not. This is an indication that these verses were added to Matthew at a later stage.

There is indeed no other reference to a church in connection with Jesus, in Matthew or elsewhere in the New Testament. The evidence is that Jesus was a practising Jew, attending the temple and observing the Jewish Law. As Acts indicates, his brother James and his followers continued to do this. There is no indication, apart from this one reference, that Jesus intended to set up an ecclesia or church that was separate from Judaism.

The development of such an organisation, with a hierarchy of bishops and deacons, came much later. The statement does not therefore read well as original to the late first century, about the time that the gospel of Matthew was written. It makes a claim for the authority, from Jesus through Simon Peter, which the Church was later beginning to assert. As such, it reads better as a second century or later insertion.

It may have been added in the second century, given that Tertullian and Origen made reference to this passage in Matthew around the beginning of the third century.[3] This would be consistent with the circumstances found for the ending of Mark: competing versions arising during the second century and then a move to an approved text in the fourth century, with the elimination of any versions that varied in key respects.

The authority given to Simon Peter, to 'bind' and 'loose' on earth as well as in heaven, appears to refer to rather more than purely spiritual power.[4] We suggest that the commissioner, in choosing which exemplar to follow, wished for textual support for the position the Church had adopted, of Peter as its first head. What better means could there have been than a direct statement bestowing the honour from Jesus himself?

If scribe A's exemplar had included an alternative ending of Mark, not in line with current doctrine, then it is plausible that it also lacked the statement in respect of Simon Peter, added at some stage to the text of Matthew.

Though relatively minor in terms of the amount of text, this added statement could account for some of the compression in the first folio of the Matthew bifolium. But it should be noted that compression in both folios is in any case a likely outcome of the mechanism by which the scribes alternated their work.

The second bifolium by scribe D, comprising the end of Mark and the beginning of Luke, has been considered at some length. It was concluded that the compression and stretching of text at the beginning was in response to a decision not to use an ending of Mark that was in the main exemplar used by scribe A.

Scribe A, we suggest, may have preferred an ending (now, no longer surviving) in his exemplar, on the grounds of better provenance. It could also be that some other elements towards the end of Mark were altered without, in scribe A's view, sufficient grounds. We earlier analysed the alterations to the passage, in Matthew 27, 56, describing key relatives of Jesus who were present at the cross (Chapter 10, pp

188–194). The wholesale nature of the alterations indicates that it was not a question of correcting an error, but of changing the meaning of an original passage. This, as it had been written, had what might have been regarded as controversial implications for the family of Jesus.

We suggested that the author of Matthew would have got this material from Mark, or an earlier common source. The verse describing the women at the cross, Mark 15, 40, is on the verso of folio four of quire 77 written by scribe D. But it appears in the same form, as Matthew 27, 56 does, *after* having been subject to the attentions of the scriptorium corrector, Ca. So it may be that Mark 15, 40 was also changed, from what was in the exemplar used by scribe A, when the sheet came to be written by scribe D. As such, it could have been another reason, if not the reason, for scribe A not wanting to write the passage.

The intervention of scribe D to write this second bifolium was thus, in one way or another, related to the Church's concerns to support its key doctrines. The version of the ending of Mark in scribe A's exemplar may have had unwelcome information on the family of Jesus or given a naturalistic description of Jesus' movements after leaving the tomb, indicating that he may have survived, or indeed could have done both.

As to the compression of the first six columns of Luke, on the second folio, our explanation is that this chiefly results from miscalculations by the scribes as to the space that scribe D had, within the confines of a single sheet. Some part could have arisen from the normal process of correcting the text. It is also feasible that the opportunity was taken to add something to the beginning of Luke.

We cannot rule these latter possibilities out, especially given that there are, as with many other key passages, no earlier surviving papyrus sources against which to check. But we have found a mechanism that for the most part satisfactorily explains the wholesale compression in scribe D's sheets, including both sheets of a folio where the text is separated. So we do not need to look for, or rely on, any really major additions to the text.

The third bifolium undertaken by scribe D, comprising sections of 1 Thessalonians in the first folio and of Hebrews in the second folio, is similar in many respects to the first bifolium by scribe D found in Matthew. The bifolium is the third sheet within a quire, so also comprising disconnected text. A substantial dittography, just before scribe D's bifolium, indicates possible distraction or, as will be seen, calculation by scribe A and also consciousness of the division of work with scribe D. As in the case of the Matthew bifolium, a sharp drop from above average to below average, in terms of numbers of characters per column, at the end by scribe D suggests an adjustment to make the copy fit within the confines of the bifolium, to finish neatly on the last line of the last column before the next bifolium by scribe A.

As to text to which scribe A might have objected, there is something that shouts out as being unusual and out of keeping. This is an outrageous accusation attributed to Paul that goes far beyond his hostility to Jews, in the person of James, and the general anti-Jewish sentiment that runs through the gospels. It comes right at the beginning of the bifolium, as now written, in 1 Thessalonians 2, 15. The passage begins with verse 2, 14, part of which, given in brackets, is on the previous page:

> *[For you brothers became imitators of the churches of God in Christ Jesus that are in Judea, because you suffered the same things from your own] fellow-countrymen as they did from the Jews who killed both the Lord Jesus and the prophets and persecuted us; they displease God and oppose everyone, hindering us from speaking to the Gentiles in order that they may be saved.*
>
> *Thus, they have constantly filled up the measure of their sins, but the wrath (of God) has come on them at last.*

1 Thessalonians 2, 14–16

Our suggestion is that Paul, as a competent propagandist, knew how far he could stretch his argument. He would not have included something so provocative that not only he knew to be false, but could easily have been countered.[5] Verse 2, 15, containing the accusation that Jews killed Jesus, is thus likely to have been inserted into the text later than the first century when it is believed 1 Thessalonians was written. It would have helped, in the developing relationship between Rome and Church, to have shifted the blame for the death of Jesus emphatically from the Romans to the Jews. We therefore believe that it was a later addition. While it may well have been available, among competing exemplars from the second century, we suggest that scribe A may have had to hand a version that lacked verse 2, 15 and believed that it was more authentic and original.

Verse 2, 16 is often seen as a puzzle since it is assumed that the 'wrath of God' refers to consequences of the failed Jewish uprising from 66 CE to 70 CE, whereas 1 Thessalonians is believed to have been written around 50 CE. It could not however have been written at this time, in respect of a disaster that was yet to happen. This is an argument for this verse also being a later interpolation.

However, there was unrest in Palestine during the early forties CE, in which the Nazorean Jews may have been involved, leading to reprisals by the Romans.[6] Paul could have been taking comfort from the plight of those he considered had hampered him from developing for non-Jews a form of Judaism, stripped of the requirement for strict adherence to the Jewish Law. It may be that the version of events alluded to in verse 2, 16 in scribe A's exemplar was considered a little too explicit, thus providing another possible reason for the commissioner's decision to use another exemplar at this point.

The 'Jews' who persecuted Paul and his followers are described as opposing 'everyone', meaning – something perhaps too delicate to be said directly – everyone, including the Romans.

We suggested several reasons, or a combination of reasons, why scribe D might have compressed text of 1 Thessalonians, in the first three columns of Q85F3R, when there was apparently no need. He may simply have initially miscalculated the amount of space. He may have added something. We suggest that it could have been verse 2, 15 or even 2, 15 and 2, 16. Again, as with the Mark–Luke bifolium, he would have miscalculated in not appreciating that there would be a partial column at the end to accommodate extra text.

It will be noted that scribe A did sign off Hebrews with his characteristic wavy coronis, even though the book contained the text that scribe D had written, in the second half of his bifolium. This is because, as we have suggested, the scribe's problem had been with something that was to be included in 1 Thessalonians. He had no particular issue with Hebrews and so was able to sign off this book with a clear conscience.

The crucial difference, as against the first of scribe D's three sheets in the New Testament, is that in the first sheet by scribe D both of his folios were within Matthew. So, wherever the offending text was located within the bifolium, it would still have entailed scribe A signing off something of which he may have disapproved.

As it happened, the end of Mark and the end of 1 Thessalonians in each case came within scribe D's bifolium. As the last scribe working on these books, scribe D signed them off. There would thus have been no issue here as far as scribe A was concerned.

The blunt accusation of deicide[7] against the Jews in 1 Thessalonians stands with the Jesus' confirmation of Simon Peter as Church founder in Matthew and the missing ending of Mark as major anomalies in the text. The three single sheets by scribe D share this in common, as well as the other features already noted. All three dealt with very sensitive matters and all three, we suggest, were produced from an alternative exemplar or exemplars. The purpose was to bring the text into line with Church policy and thinking at the time.

With the support of Rome, in the mid fourth century, the text of the gospels was going to reach a much wider audience. Codex Sinaiticus, we have argued, was one of the vehicles by which this would be achieved. We suggest that the text would have been reviewed in respect of aspects relating to politics, Church authority and doctrine. The three sheets by scribe D contain or relate to passages that are, arguably in the whole of the New Testament, the most crucial in these three key respects. We suggest that this scribe ended up implementing changes to the main exemplar, using another source, to achieve what the commissioner for Sinaiticus wanted.

As a major priority, the commissioner would have wanted a text that not only did not disturb, but positively fostered the relationship with Rome. That had been hard enough to achieve when it was a matter of necessity, when Christianity had to live with the reality of Roman power, at some times simply tolerated and at other times actively suppressed. The story of Jesus was modified from the time of Paul onwards, so that the Romans were seen in a more positive light. In various passages, the blame for Jesus' death was shifted towards the scheming Jewish authorities (chief priests and elders), an archetype betraying 'Judas' and an incited and inflamed mob of ordinary Jews. The Roman governor Pontius Pilate was at the same time portrayed as a man acting reluctantly and under pressure.

Now that the Romans were the hosts of Christianity, now that it was a Roman religion, it was if anything even more important that this perspective should be reinforced. The problem was, and is, that the propaganda was not much in accordance with an easily perceived historical reality. It was the Romans who captured, tortured and then executed a treasonable, messianic contender for the Jewish throne. Not the Jews.

But it was nevertheless important under Roman patronage to choose a text that still firmly shifted the blame. This would explain one of the sheets, Q85F3/6, comprising text from 1 Thessalonians and Hebrews, that scribe D was brought in to write, we have argued from another exemplar. We have suggested that the commissioner, in marking up his required changes to the main exemplar, may have been unaware of the consequence in terms of a change in the pattern of work between the scribes. That is, he may not have been made aware that one scribe was reluctant to do it and that another had been brought in.

Another consideration would have been the relationship between the Christian Church, which had grown up within the diaspora, and Jesus himself, his family and followers who were in fact Jews. The Church's schizophrenic attitude on this issue is reflective of the fact that, while it may have been convenient in one context to blame 'the Jews' for the death of Jesus, the accusation was not helpful for the claim it was making for the Jewish Jesus.

Portraying Jews as perpetrators, rather than victims, was in fact rather more than a convenient parking of blame to avoid pointing the finger at Romans. It sprang from a deep-seated and very long-running conflict between Christians and the followers of Jesus. This was a conflict that went right back to the time of Paul and his rift with James, the brother of Jesus, and the Jewish Nazorean movement. It was characterised by animosity, hostile verbal exchanges and possibly even actual violence, as recorded in Acts, Paul's letters and the *Pseudoclementine Recognitions*.[8]

The Church needed a means of getting round this chasm that would provide continuity with a Jesus, sanitised from aspects of Jewishness that might have threatened both the relationship with Rome, and the Christian doctrine that had since been developed.

It needed a plausible line of succession to justify its claimed authority. But a pedigree could not be provided by Paul who appeared on the scene later, at least in an active role, after the death of Jesus.[9] It could not be provided by James, with whom Paul and his followers had evidently been at odds.

So it needed instead to be provided by Simon (Peter), moulded into an intermediary in the Christian story, bridging the gap between the emerging Christians and the Nazorean Jews.[10] The recasting of Jesus' fiery commander as convert to, and fountainhead for, a Hellenised form of Judaism, shorn of strict adherence to the Jewish Law, was hard to make convincing. It was, however, incorporated into a version of Matthew and it was from an exemplar that included this that scribe D wrote his bifolium Q75F2/7 in Matthew.

There was, we suggest, a third area of concern, besides writing to appease the Romans and putting a case that established the Church's credentials. This was to reinforce the core elements of Christian doctrine, of which most crucial was the assertion of Jesus' divine status, as evidenced by the claim of his resurrection. While the four gospels all deal with this to a degree, there are now and were then from a Christian point of view some unsatisfactory and worrying aspects.

The longer ending of Mark was even then regarded as suspect. But, in the version with an abbreviated ending, there was no description of resurrection, no miraculous appearances and no miraculous ascension into heaven. The story ended up short, with a young man posted at the tomb telling the disciples that Jesus had gone on to Galilee. Matthew's version, as we can assess now, is uncharacteristically circumscribed and vague, possibly a result of the original author of Matthew working from a version of Mark that had only the abbreviated ending.

The commissioner of Codex Sinaiticus might well have wanted to ensure that the best presentation was given of a key Christian doctrine. His first option, we suggest, in circumventing a troublesome version in scribe A's exemplar was to substitute the longer ending from an alternative, second century exemplar. Scribe D was again called in to do the work. But then there was a change of plan, given the acknowledged defects of this material, and the ending of Mark was instead eliminated entirely.

The commissioner provided instructions for the use of text from alternative exemplars for certain, key passages. It may not, as we have surmised, have been apparent to him how precisely the scribes carried his wishes out. What would have been clear to the scribes, however, is that the commissioner did not want these passages, as they appeared in scribe A's main exemplar, to remain in the text. Not concordant with the Church's thinking at the time, these were to be expunged.

So the option of leaving scribe A to write from his exemplar and for the text then to be corrected later was not available. This would have left the evidence of the non-conforming version of events still there for all to see. And it might also have pointed up scribe A's dissension.

Only at three points was there a change to the text, seen as being of such crucial importance that it entailed the use of another exemplar, the suppression of what had been in the main exemplar and consequently a highly unusual alternation of work between the scribes. We have put forward what we believe, on the evidence, were the crucial changes. The evidence cannot, of course, be direct because the original exemplars are no longer available. If suppression of an alternative version has taken place, then to this extent it has been effective.

With at least two, and possibly more exemplars in use, it is likely that there will have been other alterations in the normal course of events to scribe A's text. Such changes could be expected as a result of re-evaluations of the relative merits of versions in different exemplars, while the work was in progress.

This we believe is what lies behind the deletion of three passages in scribe A's text in Luke (see p 113) by Ca, whom we have deduced was the scriptorium corrector. In contrast with the arrangement involving scribe D, this approach left the original passages available to be read though marked as deleted. We suggest that it may here have been just a question of preference. The corrector noticed that some verses in scribe A's exemplar for Luke were not in other versions and so decided to leave them out.

These verses were not ones that the manuscript's commissioner had anticipated should be eliminated as being at variance with doctrine. Though corrected, scribe A's original versions were left still visible. It was presumably felt that there was, in these instances, no issue at stake serious enough for this to matter.

Having established, not only how the arrangement between scribe A and scribe D worked, but now what its purpose was, let us look at the interventions again from scribe A's perspective, as he encountered them.

Besides the compression of text, associated with this working arrangement, what characterises all three sheets are adjustments, indicating that the scribes writing the sheets were aware of each other's contributions, and features of scribe A's work suggesting that he was at times under stress.

Scribe A's failure to sign off the book of Matthew, containing the bifolium written by scribe D, may also be significant. What could explain this, as well as the circumstance of an unusual intervention by a second scribe, is concern by scribe A over the provenance of changes implemented or intended in Matthew.

The New Testament, as it appears in Sinaiticus, was almost certainly copied out in sequence by scribe A. So, it would have been in Matthew that he encountered for the first time a problem of the kind we have described. Scribe A exhibits considerable stress here, making more mistakes and more often forgetting what had been agreed in terms of spelling. He was facing a threatening, new situation and the uncertainty of how it would be resolved. His stress could have reflected the fact that failing to do what he was told might, at the very least, have lost him his job.

The same level of stress, especially in terms of spelling deviations in the form of iotacisms, is not associated with the second and third sheets written by scribe D. This is because, by that stage, and arising from the experience of the first episode in Matthew, a means of dealing with the situation had been reached. When a variation from the main exemplar was proposed, or in fact imposed, to which scribe A had an objection in terms of provenance, the work would be passed to scribe D.

This scribe would write the folio containing the variation. Scribe A would in the meantime continue, having calculated ahead, with the main part of the text.

As a result of the practicalities of the arrangement, scribe D also ended up writing the second folio of the sheet within Matthew and also of two other sheets. There were thus three occasions when there was a switch of scribe as a result of a significant variation involving, we have suggested, another exemplar.

Because scribe D was not either generally or at the time available, we have argued that scribe A provided the sheets that he had to do, together with notes as to where to start and end each folio. Scribe D had in each instance to operate within the confines of a bifolium. As a result of miscalculations, scribe D ended up compressing several sections of his text.

We thus have an overall explanation that is plausible, explains the variations in the text, including most importantly apparent anomalies, and accords with what is known of the scribes' ways of working.

How convenient, it might be thought, that in each case a major change happened at or towards the beginning of a bifolium. Scribe A could thus anticipate what was coming up and pass the text on to another scribe who did not have similar reservations concerning provenance. What would have happened had scribe A been confronted with a proposed alteration, through a switch to an alternative, more doubtful exemplar, much further into a bifolium?

The answer is, first of all, that the points requiring modification *did* all happen in different places. In the first instance in Matthew, it was on the first page, the recto of the first folio of a bifolium. In the second instance, in the Mark–Luke bifolium, it was on the verso of the first folio, continuing on to the recto of the second folio. And, in the third instance, in 1 Thessalonians, it was in text from the exemplar that would actually have been on the verso of the *previous* folio, that is Q85F2V.

This was the page on which scribe A began 1 Thessalonians, having just completed Colossians in the last column of the previous page, the recto of the same folio. Had scribe A not committed a substantial dittography of 128 characters, amounting to 10 lines, at the very end, he would have had to write the offending text on that page himself. Or, he would have had to call attention to the delicate position in which he was placed by getting another scribe to finish his folio.

It was more plausible and practical to deal with the situation through the tested means of an alternation of work. This, we suggest, scribe A achieved by contriving a dittography that pushed the text (just) on to the next bifolium for scribe D to undertake.

So, he *was* caught out. Scribe A must have discovered too late, after he had finished or was well into the last page of Colossians, that the intention was to write a section of the beginning of 1 Thessalonians from a different exemplar.

This is certainly quite extraordinary. But it fits with the evidence. It provides an explanation of how and why scribe D undertook the third bifolium, in accordance with what was found for the other sheets, and also in accordance with a more general explanation of what was happening with interpolations into the main exemplar's text.

Looking at the sheets together, we have a situation where the main feature of a highly unusual, single bifolium intervention by a second scribe is a significant change, the elimination of an ending of Mark. It is logical to link this intervention and the resulting change, even without other supporting evidence.

There are two other such highly unusual interventions, with significant characteristics and some common aspects. The major repetition just before the beginning of scribe D's bifolium, with sections of 1 Thessalonians and Hebrews, had the effect of pushing a piece of very contentious text into scribe D's copy for him to deal with. In fact, just as he also dealt with other thorny issues in Mark and we suggest in Matthew.

So, what in isolation might have seemed far-fetched is, in context, not so extraordinary. It is even *likely* as an explanation, in view of all the other features of the alternation of work between scribe A and scribe D.

If the first page of 1 Thessalonians is examined, Q85F2V, it will be seen that scribe A did first make an effort to stretch the text out to push the deicide passage into the next page, without having to resort to more drastic measures. Stretching began in the first column that has a below-average amount of text, with 613 characters. The second column was stretched further still with only 607 characters. In the third column, the text amounted to just 589 characters. At which point, scribe A must have realised that it could not be done. He now needed a final column of no more than 510–520 characters, for the accusation of deicide against the Jews just to scrape on to the next page, to be written by scribe D. The column would have stood out as highly unusual, perhaps drawing attention to what scribe A had been doing.

For much the same reason, the option of simply abandoning the incomplete folio at this point, for scribe D to complete later, might also have not been feasible. We have deduced that scribe D was not immediately available and so the gap could then have remained visible for some time. Scribe A might have had to explain why it was there to anyone checking or vetting the text.

A missing bifolium could, on the other hand, have been represented as simply the product of a division of labour, as had operated in the Old Testament. Moreover, two such bifolia covering part of Matthew and the transition between Mark and Luke had already been allocated to scribe D. In this context, another such sheet would not have appeared so unusual.

Scribe A was, however, still left with the problem of how to get the text that offended him out of the folio that he was writing and into the folio that would be written by scribe D. He decided, we suggest, as a last resort to create an error of repetition in his last column.

There were plenty of points in the text where words were repeated. Scribe A found two instances of a nomen sacrum, ΘΥ for God, separated by about the right amount of text. By going back to the first and repeating himself, he was able to generate enough extra text to do what was required. In so doing, he created a very convincing dittography. Having found this way of pushing the text that he would otherwise have had to write on to the next page, he reverted to a more normal spacing. The last column, with the dittography, thus has 638 characters.[11]

It should be noted that this is an alternative explanation of the repetition of text. Rather than being another indication of scribe A's distraction and stress, just before an intervention by scribe D, it would by this reading of the situation have been something done with conscious intent.

As with the other sheets, scribe D was not immediately available, so scribe A went on writing, leaving gaps for the first folio and also for the second folio containing text from Hebrews. The compression in these folios can be accounted for by miscalculations by both scribes as to the space needed by scribe D. It is possible however that some part of it, in the first folio, arose from the insertion of the defamatory charge made against Jews.

Our proposal of a consciously created apparent error, if a little challenging, does at least cover all the evidence. It explains the unusual pattern of scribe A's work in the last page before the bifolium by scribe D. It explains the untypical and unlikely substantial dittography just before this bifolium. It offers an explanation for this bifolium, and the indications of the scribes' awareness of each other's work, that is consistent with the explanations for the other bifolia by scribe D.

It substitutes, for a stack of what would be coincidences, each in varying degrees unlikely and taken as a whole improbable, a description of what took place that makes sense. The coincidences for these sheets are otherwise many, from unusual compression happening to occur in both halves of each interpolated sheet to the association of each sheet with exceptionally charged passages. There is also the unusual pattern of one scribe taking over for a single sheet, the stress evidenced by scribe A at the outset, the association of his errors with the interpolations by scribe D and scribe A's disavowal in failing to sign off Matthew. There is the enormous coincidence of the late dittography that just happened to push a piece of contentious text into a following folio and sheet that could then be written by another scribe.

So we will, until another explanation comes along that even better explains the data, rest with our explanation also for the third sheet by scribe D. As with our suggestion of an overall reason for the interventions by scribe D, that scribe A was unhappy with the provenance of some intended changes, it is not proof. But it may be the best explanation so far available.

In the case of the third bifolium, we suggest that awareness of the switch to text that scribe A would find unacceptable came almost too late for it to be accommodated by an alternation between the scribes. It was to be incorporated in the main exemplar, within a bifolium on which scribe A was already well advanced. But he managed to eke out his material on the last page and in this way avoid the issue.

In the first of the three sheets, Q75F2/7 in Matthew, scribe A came upon the issue immediately, and so was able to pass the bifolium on to scribe D before becoming embarked upon it. In the case of the second sheet, Q77F4/5, the issue was to do with the ending of Mark, beginning on the verso of the first folio. As the ending of Mark was known to be a problem, this is something that the scribes might well have discussed in advance, so enabling them to come up with the arrangement of an alternation between scribe A and scribe D in good time.

Scribe A could have been unwilling to accept changes to the text on purely professional grounds. He may have believed that the main exemplar he used was the best and most accurate. It should not therefore have been cut with passages that were in his view of more doubtful provenance.

He may similarly have had religious reservations, objecting to what he saw as tampering with sacred scripture, the very word of God. This would, of course, have been on the basis of his judgement of what text was or was not more valid.

We have deduced that there was a main exemplar for the core of the New Testament and at least one other exemplar used by scribe D in the production and modification of his three bifolia. What we now have available, of course, is the product of the scribes' joint efforts and we can only deduce what may have been in the main exemplar for the passages that were spliced with another version.

We do not have direct evidence for several reasons. In the first place, if we are correct that one of the main objectives in creating Codex Sinaiticus and possibly also Codex Vaticanus was to generate an authorised version, then the original alternatives would not themselves have been disseminated. Indeed, the variant main exemplar is likely to have been subsequently destroyed because it showed differences from the newly created authorised version at crucial points.[12]

There are, it will be observed, no surviving versions besides patristic citations earlier than Codex Sinaiticus for any of the crucial passages: covering the end of Mark, the beginning of Luke, the 'rock' and 'keys of the kingdom' passages in Matthew and the 'who killed both the Lord Jesus and the prophets' and 'wrath' passages in 1 Thessalonians. This is undoubtedly at the very least partly the result of chance; the papyrus record is very patchy and individual books were particularly liable to suffer damage and loss of text at the beginning and at the end.

On the other hand if, from the mid fourth century onwards, variant texts were actively suppressed by being recalled and destroyed, this would reduce the chances of fragments for such texts from worn manuscripts being among those casually discarded.

But, let us suppose for the moment, that some fragments for the relevant passages do ultimately turn up among the desiccated spoil at somewhere like Oxyrhynchus in Egypt. Let us assume that these fragments were deposited at an earlier period and are from manuscripts written in the early second century. What might we expect to find?

As far as the ending of Mark is concerned, we have argued (Chapter 10) that this was eliminated very early on, such that the author of

Matthew did not have access to it. Even if there were an original, or an alternative version, the abbreviated version of Mark was what was most immediately available. So, even if some alternative had survived to be deposited in the library at Caesarea, we suggest that our early second century fragment will most likely be found still to follow Mark in the abbreviated version or, if the fragment were late enough, in the version with 12 added verses. Both of these might well read much as they do now.

But, we would expect that, if the appropriate fragment of Matthew turned up, the distinction accorded Simon Peter as founder of the Church would be missing. And so too might the descriptions of the Jews as the killers of Jesus in 1 Thessalonians. This is because these passages reflect matters that Christians later on were wanting to sort out in the gospels. So, we suggest, they were added later, probably during the late second century.

Much nearer to the time, and much nearer to the action, scribe A could see this. For whatever reason, he did not want to be part of it.

The production of the fourth century codex bibles was the culmination of a process that had been going on for a long time. But the process of conscious editing could not continue much longer, given the wide dissemination of texts thereafter under the auspices of the Roman Empire. It was the moment to fashion and fine-tune the message: if not now, then never.

It meant, if the message were to be changed, making some calculated decisions among the available exemplars. The evidence is that the commissioner of Codex Sinaiticus did just that, so bringing about the cause of scribe A's discomfiture. There may be some irony in that what we have deduced scribe A was defending had already been subject to a long period of editing and conscious adjustment. It was not, and had never had been, a pure scripture. Its provenance and authenticity were lost, centuries before, when a Jewish Nazorean story was converted into a Christian one.

We have found that the process of writing New Testament Sinaiticus was not a wholly neutral exercise. Using exemplars to fashion the scriptures involved more than just copying and interpretation. There was also selection, substitution and change.

The scribes were necessarily involved as agents of the commissioning authority and as active participants in the process.

There were, however, divisions that centred on considerations of political and religious expediency as against demands for accuracy and honesty in transmitting the text. It was not apparently a conflict that set scribe against scribe. Indeed, it appears that the scribes cooperated in disguising an imperfect obedience to the demands made of them. It was rather a clash between religious power and individual scruple.

The struggle in the scriptorium, in which the commissioner was bound to triumph, left its marks in the text which we, centuries later, have to some extent been able to decipher.

These are our conclusions in this chapter:

- The three bifolia by scribe D in Codex Sinaiticus were all written to incorporate changes to the main exemplar used for the core of the New Testament.
- The practical arrangement under which the bifolia were generated involved an alternation of work between scribe A and scribe D, with scribe A going ahead for each bifolium and separated folio, and ensuing miscalculations of space by each of the scribes.
- The mechanism of cooperation between the two scribes accounts for compression in all three bifolia.
- Some variations in the density of text, at the end of Mark and towards the beginning of 1 Thessalonians, may be a reflection of changes introduced.
- The reason for the arrangement of alternation between the scribes, which explains both scribe A's behaviour and the fact of the arrangement itself, was that scribe A was reluctant to implement changes ultimately undertaken by scribe D.
- The best explanation for scribe A's motivation is that he believed that the changes proposed to the text of Codex Sinaiticus lacked proper provenance.

CHAPTER 14

Inventing Jesus

Fool and knave, leave the old reading and do not change it!
(ἀμαθέστατε καὶ κακέ, ἄφες τὸν παλαιόν, μὴ μεταποίει)
Marginal note against Hebrews 1, 3 in Codex Vaticanus by a writer
who objected to an earlier corrector changing the original scribe's
ΦΑΝΕΡѠΝ (manifests) to ΦΕΡѠΝ (bears)

Our sympathy lies to an extent with the irritated scribe who, many centuries ago, added to Codex Vaticanus his own exasperated note in the margin on the tendency of previous readers to tinker with the text. We would, however, add a rider: if only it were that simple.

The marginal note is alongside a correction to the text. Without the correction, this reads:

ΦΑΝΕΡѠΝΤΕΤΑΠΑΝΤΑ
ΤѠΡΗΜΑΤΙΤΗCΔΥΝΑ
ΜΕѠCΑΥΤΟΥ
[Jesus] manifests all things by the word of his power.

The corrector had changed ΦΑΝΕΡѠΝ (manifests) to ΦΕΡѠΝ which means 'sustains' or 'bears', a very different reading. The switch is from Jesus revealing all things to Jesus keeping all things, that is, the entire universe, together. Neither of these propositions would seem to have much going for them from an entirely objective point of view. From a Christian point of view, however, one or other might have seemed more preferable at different points in time, according to developing Church doctrine.

The scribe who subsequently erased the first corrector's word 'bears' and rewrote the word 'manifests' evidently felt that the earlier reading was, from a doctrinal standpoint, more likely or more acceptable or both. Thus, he must have felt that it was also more accurate. But was it, in *any* sense, original?

Bart Ehrman quotes this example[1] as a demonstration that the bible is not inerrant but full of mistakes, corrections and contradictions. So, in this respect, he abandoned the Christian fundamentalism that he had been brought up with. But he still seems to believe that the originals of the texts, however much transmuted by change and however difficult to disentangle, are somehow out there.[2]

Implicit in his approach is a profoundly mistaken assumption, that the 'original' authors must have been Christians. The first narrative and the first verbal tradition would have originated from the followers of Jesus and James, then to be used and remoulded by Paul and his followers in the creation of their schismatic sect. These latter certainly *were* Christians or came to be known as Christians (Acts 11, 26). But the people from whom their information came were Jews.

Codex Vaticanus is a key manuscript. Along with Codex Sinaiticus, both dating from around the mid fourth century, it provides the earliest available evidence for much of the New Testament. We have shown that Codex Sinaiticus was probably created as a robust master copy from which to make further copies. We have also demonstrated that Codex Vaticanus was copied with reference to Sinaiticus itself and its main exemplar.

In this instance, Codex Sinaiticus has in the above passage from Hebrews, ΦΕΡѠΝ, meaning 'bears'. The clear implication is that the Vaticanus scribe, in copying from the common exemplar or Sinaiticus (either or both), made a mistake and wrote a similar-sounding and similar-looking word ΦΑΝΕΡѠΝ, 'manifests', which also in context happens to make sense. The first corrector checked against the exemplar or Codex Sinaiticus or both and restored what had been in the original.

So he was not, as the later scribe charged in his marginal comment, adding his own embellishment. He *was* in fact restoring what had been in the source! We can, in this case, potentially take the source further back in time. For once, there is an earlier papyrus manuscript that has the relevant passage. This is **P**46, dating from around the mid second century. Like Codex Sinaiticus, it has in Hebrews 1, 3, not 'manifests' but ΦΕΡѠΝ, 'bears'.

This all provides a very salutary lesson. Not only was the indignation of the later scribe and re-corrector of the passage most probably misplaced, but he had ended up doing precisely what he had criticised. That is, he was himself tinkering with the text without enough knowledge and without sufficient justification. Had Codex Vaticanus been copied, incorporating his change, and had all previous versions as well as Vaticanus then been lost, ΦΑΝΕΡωΝ would have stood as original, in the sense of being from source. But, on the evidence, which we fortunately still do have, it was not.

The question of what may, in some sense, have been 'original' here blends with other considerations to do with authenticity. Most experts agree, from considerations of language and style, that the anonymous letter to the Hebrews, though often attributed to Paul, was not in fact written by Paul. Or, rather, it was not by the same single author who appears to have written, 1 Thessalonians, 1 and 2 Corinthians, Galatians and Romans. It is a curious polemic, mostly directed towards demonstrating to Jews that they should accept Jesus as their High Priest, as appointed by God.[3]

The example from Hebrews shows how even well-intentioned alterations can and do modify a more original text. Other instances have come up, in the course of this book, where a scribe may have meant to improve the clarity of a passage, or deal with something that he believed had been omitted, and ended up making significant changes to a more original text. We have argued, for example, that this is what happened when the scriptorium corrector Ca was checking copy in Mark written by scribe D in Codex Sinaiticus. The passage in question related to women going to the rock tomb where Jesus had been taken (Mark 15, 47–16, 1).

The corrector was, we deduced, checking the copy against two parallel but different manuscripts. He noticed, from looking at one, that something appeared to have been missed out. So he reinstated an apparently missing piece of text. It appears that the wording in one version did provide a bit of extra information, that the women had observed Jesus being put in the tomb. But what Ca did, to try to remedy this, was insert a sentence that was already in scribe D's version, though in a different form. Hence the women who went to the tomb are listed twice in succession, generating a degree of redundancy, repetition and confusion.[4]

In our study, we have looked at changes that for the most part have been consciously made for reasons of policy or doctrine over a period of four centuries. It is not only that textual analysis shows that 'fundamentalism' is, in the words of Parker, inadmissible and ahistorical.[5] It opens up all of Christian belief, all of the theology based on biblical texts, to the light of reason.

Most biblical textual analysis has been done by, and continues to be done by, Christians. From our appraisal of the field, it could even be nearly all. That certainly does raise problems. On a simple level, it has meant that progress has been limited. Many practitioners have, perhaps understandably, not been able to see beyond their preconceptions. So they have not been able at times to make connections and reach conclusions justified by the evidence.

Starting from their beliefs, Christians naturally look at the textual evidence for support and interpret this evidence in the light of their beliefs. So their conclusions have, in very many contexts, come first. This is quite the opposite of what might be described as an objective or scientific (even, academic) approach where the evidence is examined first and conclusions drawn from it. Then, in the light of fresh evidence or analysis, these conclusions are reexamined and, where necessary, modified or substituted. The faith-based approach to textual analysis is in this way flawed. And that is as important as the fact that it often contrives false conclusions.

There is also no discontinuity between the fundamentalism that sees the bible as inerrant, perhaps what Parker means by the term, and an approach that starts from preconceptions and seeks to justify them. It is there in journals of biblical studies. It is there in everyday Christianity.

One preoccupation, from the very start, has been to seek to reconstruct from surviving examples some form of 'true' text, reflecting a presumed authentic and contemporaneous account of events early in the first century. This is what motivated Westcott and Hort, who spent almost three decades in the nineteenth century creating a text of the New Testament that depended heavily on the two early manuscripts, Codex Vaticanus and Codex Sinaiticus. The authors rightly believed that the two manuscripts were connected but made a wild leap in concluding that their two ancestries 'started from a common source not much later than their autographs'.[6]

Our own study indicates a possible exemplar for Codex Sinaiticus from about the end of the second century, incorporating all of the gospels as well as possibly Acts and many of the epistles. This was a proximate exemplar and both it and Codex Sinaiticus were available to, and used by, the writers of Codex Vaticanus. It cannot have been much earlier, when such compilations of the gospels and other works did not exist.

So, as far as any possible 'autographs' for the gospels are concerned, there is a time gap of about 100 years between these and the common source used for the two codices. During this period, there would have been a number of stages including oral transmission, the creation of Jewish texts, the moulding of an archetypal Christian narrative and then subsequent versions generated by editing including a 'Cross' narrative and Secret Mark. It is only at this point that we reach a possible exemplar for Codex Vaticanus and Codex Sinaiticus and, for that matter, get a surviving manuscript for part of the gospel of Mark. That is **P**45, dating from the early third century.

These manuscripts are vastly removed in time and in context from any original autograph. It is a misconceived presumption that the analysis of texts can arrive at something that is truly original. It is indeed the same pious presumption that prevents an understanding of what a welter of evidence indicates, that doctrine has been the major force in the evolution of the Christian texts.

Our critique is not alas limited to the antique writings of Victorian clerics but can be applied with as much force to contemporary works of textual analysis. Bruce Metzger's *The Text of the New Testament: its Transmission, Corruption, and Restoration* is regarded by many as a standard work and it has gone through several editions over a period of decades. It contains in the title its prospectus. This is the presumption of an original text that has been changed, or 'corrupted', but can by assiduous analysis at least partly be restored. The irony is that, if there is or were any original, it is not remotely what Metzger might have imagined it to be: a Christian story reflecting what he already believed.[7]

Even in the final edition of Metzger's book, in which Bart Ehrman was taken on board as co-author, there are only three pages out of 300 devoted to 'alterations made because of doctrinal considerations'. Even here, the authors have only considered a few examples that have little or no impact on the current critical text. This is admittedly at a slight remove from Westcott and Hort who asserted that 'there are no signs of deliberate falsification of the text for dogmatic purposes'! But it does nonetheless give a false impression of the processes that have been at work and of the many examples of deliberate change for doctrinal reasons, some unearthed by Ehrman himself, to biblical text that significantly alter an earlier meaning. What we have found is that doctrinally motivated editing, far from being the exception in the early centuries, was the means by which the text was generated.

So, in our book, the position is reversed. We are certainly interested in all the ways that biblical and, for that matter, other stories come to be changed. Accidental errors and well-intentioned but misguided 'corrections' do therefore feature. But the predominance of examples, where changes have been made to reflect evolving Church doctrine, simply and fairly reflects the material under investigation.

We have seen for example how a concept, alien to the messianic nationalists, came gradually to be absorbed into the texts. There is no Jesus as Lord in Mark. But Paul, in his accommodation with Rome, was at home with the ideas of masters and slaves, rulers and subjects, the lord and his servants. Jewish zealots were however, at the very same time, fighting and dying under the slogan of 'No Lord but God'.

We have shown how, the further back the trail is taken, the fewer references there are to Jesus as the son of God. A point is reached, in the earliest of Paul's letters that predate the gospels, when it can no longer reliably be found. Using the earliest sources, we have even been able to identify one of the points when the title was deliberately inserted. We have shown instead that the title consistently applied to or adopted by Jesus was if anything a messianic one, son of man, appropriate to an aspirant for the Jewish throne.

We have been able to understand how Paul was, on the evidence, seeking to create a form of Judaism for gentiles, shorn of irksome dietary rules and the requirement for circumcision. But he and his followers had unleashed something they could not entirely control, and were overwhelmed by events. Pagan converts brought with them their preexisting rituals and beliefs, into which Jesus was assimilated. He became their son of God and Paul responded with the idea of Jesus qualifying as such, by virtue of what was claimed to be his resurrection.

We have demonstrated how an attempt was made, from Matthew onwards, to defuse a highly-charged ascription. Jesus was one of the Nazoreans or Nazarenes, keepers of the Covenant, like his brother James. He was at the very least what Paul was accused of being, a 'ringleader' of the sect. It did not mean merely that Jesus came from Nazareth, as the author of Matthew sought to claim.

We have shown how the term Nazarene or Nazorean has been deliberately mistranslated. We have also analysed the early texts to show how the phrase 'of Nazareth', as applied to Jesus, was retrospectively inserted into the narrative in Mark.

We have considered how the family of Jesus, a normal and ordinary Jewish family, was in the texts progressively disguised. In Codex

Sinaiticus, we have even been able to identify the process in action, as the corrector manipulated copy which the scribe had reproduced.[8]

We could have gone back further still, analysing the text for tell-tale inconsistencies, which reveal traces of an earlier story. But we have already done this elsewhere, demonstrating how Christian writers adapted a Jewish tale of resistance and survival.[9]

Here, we have instead looked forward to the time when the Roman Empire adopted Christianity and the bible was copied and spread to all corners of the empire. There are two early manuscripts surviving from this period, given names describing their origins: Codex Sinaiticus and Codex Vaticanus.

We have examined these to see how and why they were made and how they relate to each other. In so doing, we have developed some useful tools of analysis and made some interesting discoveries.

The manuscripts are more closely related than had previously been thought. They share at least one common exemplar. They were made within a short time of each other, quite possibly in the same place.

One, Codex Vaticanus, might well in part have been copied from, or with reference to, the other. Far from being abandoned, as had been supposed, Codex Sinaiticus was effectively completed in order to fulfil a purpose as a master copy or exemplar. Our conclusion, that the main corrector for Codex Sinaiticus was actually the scriptorium corrector, makes it possible to see this manuscript in an entirely new light. It makes coherent what would otherwise appear to have been a highly extravagant, pointless and futile enterprise.

We have learned something about the exemplars for these manuscripts and more about the way in which they were constructed. Perhaps most exciting of all, we discovered the reason for a very unusual alternation of work in Codex Sinaiticus, by which a second scribe prepared three separate sheets. In two cases, these bifolia were so situated within a quire as to involve disconnected text.

The explanation that previous writers had developed for the one continuous inner sheet, by the second scribe, was found to be severely wanting. Moreover, it could not be applied to, and left unexplained, the other two sheets. Our theory of an alternation of work, by contrast provides a single explanation for three quite clearly related interventions. It covers satisfactorily all of the evidence.

It brings vividly to life, from the centuries-old parchment characters, some of the human story of the scribes: their anxieties, failings, struggle, protest and cooperation. It also brings out what was happening in the most crucial phase of the dissemination of the

New Testament, which offered a last chance to mould the message and the text. Our examination of the three aberrant sheets in Codex Sinaiticus shows that these had material taken from other sources or exemplars, introducing changes that were, at least in one scribe's view, of inferior provenance.

The reality is that the commissioners of these manuscripts had considerable scope, from a choice of available exemplars, to ensure that what they wanted went into the text. The original mandate for the scribes may have been to use whatever was most original and best. When it came to certain crucial points, however, the imperative to consolidate and sustain doctrine was an overriding consideration. One way or another, the scribes had to accommodate this. Changes were made for reasons of politics, to bolster the position of the Church and to protect its doctrine.

So it was that, over a period of four centuries, there was an accumulation of many adjustments and alterations, big and small, which progressively moulded the narrative and the persona of Jesus. Some, however perverse or misguided, may have been well-intentioned. Some clearly reflect the situations in which the authors found themselves. Some were made with the conscious intent of bringing past history, or rather past perceptions of history, in line with current belief.

Albeit imperfectly, we can trace this. We can, through the evidence, follow the process back in time. What we ultimately find is disconcertingly very little: a movement within Judaism in opposition to Roman occupation, a loose alliance of sons of David, some of whom were related and one of whom may have been called Yeshua.[10]

The Jesus of the New Testament, the culmination of a long process of editing and amendment, can now be seen to be almost entirely invented. We have looked at the source manuscripts for the last phase of this process when, with Roman authority, the Christian message would be widely disseminated. We have seen how there was a struggle in which the powerful within the Church enforced its will on its professionals.

Yet the scribes have had, in a real sense, the last word. We are able to discover from their writings much of what went on, in processes of production involving both cooperation and conflict.

Any dissent was, at the time, effectively suppressed and disguised. The scribes nevertheless left their message, with clues like blank columns that are eloquent, and perhaps even on occasion intentioned, in the text. We can read it, thanks to the survival of fourth century manuscripts that now provide an invaluable witness.

Examples of homeoteleuton/ homioarcton from Codex Sinaiticus

Note that words have been separated, for ease of reading, although the text reads continuously in the original. In some instances, slightly awkward original wording has been retained to show the origin of error within the text.

Old Testament

Numbers 19, 19 (32 characters, scribe A, correction by Cb1)

KAI EN TH HMEPA
TH EBΔOMH ˆ KAI ΠΛΥ
NI TA ÏMATIA AΥTOΥ
ˆK(AI) AΦAΓNICΘHCETAI TH HMEPA TH EBΔOMH
' ... and on the seventh day (and she shall cleanse him on the seventh day). And he shall wash his clothes ... '

Judges 6, 21–22 (49 characters, scribe A, correction by S1)

KAI O AΓΓEΛOC KΥ ˆ
ˆ OΥTOC ECTIN KAI
ˆ EΠOPEΥΘH AΠO OΦΘAΛMωN AΥTOΥ K(AI) ÏΔEN ΓEΔEωN OTI AΓΓEΛOC KΥ
'And the angel of the Lord (vanished from his sight. Then Gideon realised the angel of the Lord) this was. And ... '

Esther 2, 8 (23 characters, scribe A, correction by Ca)

        CΥNH
XΘHCAN ˆ THN ΠO
ΛIN. ŸΠO XEIPA . ΓAI
ˆ TA KOPACIΛ ΠOΛΛA EIC COΥCAN
' ... were gathered (many maidens in Susa) the capital, under the control of Gai'

Psalms 6, 9–10 (31 characters, scribe D, correction by Ca)

OTI EICHKOYCEN KC ˆ THC ΔEHCEωC MOY
ˆ THC ΦωNHC TOY KΛAYΘMOY MOY HKOYCEN KC
' ... that has listened the Lord (to the sound of my weeping. Has heard the Lord) my supplication'

Isaiah 42, 10 (21 characters, scribe B, correction by Ca)

ŸMNON KAINON
H APXH AYTOY ˆ AΠ A
KPOY THC ΓHC.OI KA ...
ˆΔOΞAζETAI TO ONOMA AYTOY
' ... a new song, the creation of him, (glorify the name of him) from the ends of the earth, you that go ... '

Jeremiah 4, 19 (39 characters, scribe B1, correction by Ca)

THPIA THC KAPΔI
AC MOY ˆ OY CIωΠH
ˆMEMACCI H ΨYXH MOY CΠAPACCETAI KAI H KAPΔIA MOY
' ... walls of the heart of me! (My soul rushes out and the heart of me) is torn'

Jeremiah 8, 9 (10 characters, scribe B1, initial correction by Ca)

KAI
EΠTOHΘHCAN ˆ OTI
TON ΛOΓON KY AΠE
ΔOKIMACAN
ˆKAI EAΛωCAN
' ... and shall be dishonoured (and shall be taken) because the word of the Lord they have rejected ... '

New Testament

Matthew 13, 39 (35 characters, scribe A, correction by S1 and Ca)

O CΠEIPAC AYTA ECTI
O ΔIABOΛOC OI ΔE ˆ
ΘEPICTAI AΓΓEΛOI

ˆ ΘΕΡΙϹΜΟϹ ϹΥΝΤΕΛΕΙΑ ΤΟΥ ΑΙωΝΟϹ ΕϹΤΙΝ ΟΙ ΔΕ
' ... the one who sowed them is the devil. And the (harvest is the end of the age. And the) reapers are angels ... '
(NB: first 'ΟΙ ΔΕ' overwritten by corrector S1 with 'Ο ΔΕ')

Luke 10, 32 (54 characters, scribe A, correction by Ca)

                      ΑΥ
ΤΟΝ ΑΝΤΙΠΑΡΗΛΘΕΝ ˆ
ϹΑΜΑΡΙΤΗϹ ΔΕ ΤΙϹ
ˆ ΟΜΟΙωϹ ΔΕ ΚΑΙ ΛΕΥΪΤΗϹ ΚΑΤΑ ΤΟΝ ΤΟΠΟΝ ΕΛΘωΝ ΚΑΙ ΪΔωΝ
ΑΝΤΙΠΑΡΗΛΘΕΝ
' ... him, he passed by on the other side. (So likewise a Levite, when he came to the place and saw him, he passed by on the other side). But a Samaritan ... '

John 3, 20 (22 characters, scribe A, correction by Ca)

ΤΟ ΦωϹ ˆ ΙΝΑ ΜΗ ΕΛΕΓ
ˆ Κ(ΑΙ) ΟΥΚ ΕΡΧΕΤΑΙ ΠΡΟϹ ΤΟ ΦωϹ
' ... the light (and does not come to the light) lest there be exposed ... '

Galatians 2, 8 (42 characters, scribe A, correction by S1)

ΤΗϹ ΠΕΡΙΤΟΜΗϹ ˆ Ε
ΝΗΡΓΗϹΕΝ ΚΑΙ ΕΜΟΙ
ˆ Ο ΓΑΡ ΕΝΕΡΓΗϹΑϹ ΠΕΤΡω ΕΙϹ ΑΠΟϹΤΟΛΗΝ ΤΗϹ ΠΕΡΙΤΟΜΗϹ
' ... to the circumcised. (For he who worked through Peter for the apostolate to the circumcised) worked also through me ... '

Revelation 4, 3–4 (41 characters, scribe A, correction by Ca)

                  ΚΑΙ
ΪΕΡΕΙϹ ΚΥΚΛΟΘΕΝ
ΤΟΥ ΘΡΟΝΟΥ ˆ ΘΡΟΝΟΥϹ
ΕΙΚΟϹΙ ΤΕϹϹΑΡΕϹ
ˆ ΟΜΟΙωϹ ΟΡΑϹΙ ϹΜΑΡΑΓΔΙΝΟ Κ(ΑΙ) ΚΥΚΛΟΘΕΝ ΤΟΥ ΘΡΟΝΟΥ
' ... and a rainbow around the throne (in the likeness of an emerald. And around the throne) twenty-four thrones ... '

Corrected omissions or added insertions in Codex Sinaiticus Matthew and Mark of eight characters or more

These omissions or added insertions are listed as they appear for the purposes of identification; the reader can thus find the omissions in Codex Sinaiticus online. Instances of skip error are designated with the letter H for Matthew and h for Mark, and numbered in sequence.

Errors that cannot be accounted for in this way, but which could in some instances still be skip errors, are designated with the letter M for Matthew and m for Mark. Corrections, meeting the 8 characters criterion, which are amendments to the text or harmonisations to other text by the scribe or corrector, are also identified with these letters.

For each instance, the following are listed: chapter and verse, quire number (Q), folio number (F), page side – recto (R) or verso (V), number of characters, scribe responsible for passage (A or D), identity of corrector as given in Codex Sinaiticus online. The omitted passage is then given, translated into English. If applicable, the key characters in Greek, repeated in the text, are also shown. Finally, the type of error or correction is given.

While the usual English word ordering is followed in translation, the Greek word ordering is sometimes retained so as to indicate how an error in copying has occurred.

There are 58 identified instances. Their occurrence and frequency are examined in Chapter 4.

At the end, there are two further instances identified of an apparent skip error that the correctors missed.

Matthew

H1　5, 19 Q74F2V 62 characters. A corrected by S1.
heaven OYNΩN (but he who does them and teaches them shall be called great in the kingdom of heaven OYPANΩN). Skip error, skipping from NΩN to NΩN, or from whole word OYPANΩN either in full, or as abbreviated nomen sacrum, in exemplar.

H2　5, 45 Q74F3R 29 characters. A corrected by A.
good AΓAΘOYC (and send rain on the just and on the unjust AΔIKOYC). Skip error, skipping from OYC to OYC.

H3　7, 27 Q74F4R 19 characters. A corrected by S1 and Ca.
and KAI (the winds blew and KAI). Skip error.

H4　9, 10 Q74F5R 12 characters added in replacing line. A corrected by Ca.
was reclining at the table ANAKEIMENω (it came about while he AYTOY).
The character ω is at the end of a line and has a bar over it, indicating that the word has been shortened. The spelling for 'was reclining at the table' that scribe A abbreviated would most likely have been ANAKEIMENOY. For this reason, the example has on balance been treated as a skip error.

H5　9, 15 Q74F5R 44 characters. A corrected by A
bridegroom NYMΦIOC (the day will come when will be taken away from them the bridegroom NYMΦEIOC). Skip error.

H6　10, 9 Q74F5V 10 characters. A corrected by S1.
nor MHΔE (silver nor MHΔE). Note that APΓYPO (silver) is abbreviated from APΓYPON. Skip error.

M1　10, 39 Q74F6R 31 characters. A corrected by D with help from Ca.
he O (who finds his life will lose it and he O). Categorised as a simple omission because the key is only one character. But it may well have been a skip error.
　The scribe skips from O to O. But the corrector makes the correction before the first O, so starting his correction with O.

M2 12, 46–47 Q74F7V 84 characters. A corrected by A.
stood outside (seeking to speak to him. One of his disciples said,
'Look, your mother and brothers are outside seeking you').

A passage has apparently at some point been omitted, possibly in
the original exemplar, so that the narrative no longer fully makes
sense. The insertion may be the scribe or corrector's effort to reconstruct what is missing.

H7 13, 39 Q74F8R 35 characters, allowing for overwrite of four with
three characters. A corrected by Ca.
and the OI ΔE (harvest is the end of the age and the OI ΔE). Skip
error. This could also have been a skip error based on the first letters
(ΘEPIC) of harvest and reapers.

M3 13, 44 Q74F8V 8 characters. A corrected by S1.
hidden (in the field). Categorised as a simple correction. But this may
have been a skip error, involving the same last character (ω) of 'hidden'
and 'field'

H8 14, 23 Q75F1R 21 characters. A corrected by D.
crowds OXΛOYC (and after he had dismissed the crowds OXΛOYC).
Skip error.
Having missed out text by skipping on to the second OXΛOYC, the
scribe appears to have added a linking 'KAI' for the next sentence,
which the corrector then marked as deleted.

H9 15, 18–19 Q75F1V 48 characters. A corrected by D.
heart KAPΔIAC (comes out, and this defiles a man. For out of the
heart KAPΔIAC). Skip error.

M4 16, 9 Q75F1V 16 characters. A corrected by Ca.
understand? (Do you not remember). Simple omission, though it
could possibly be a skip error based on final TE of NOIETE if Ca has
corrected MNHMONEYETE to MNHMONEYETAI.

M5 17, 21 Q75F2V 51 characters. D corrected by Cb2.
for you (but this kind does not come out except by prayer and fasting).
Addition by corrector to harmonise with Mark 9, 29 plus the elaboration 'and fasting'.

H10 19, 18 Q77F3V 20 characters. A corrected by S1
murder ΦONEYCIC (Do not commit adultery. Do not steal

ΚΛΕΨCΕΙC). Skip error, skipping from IC to IC.

M6   19, 20 Q75F3V 9 characters. A corrected by Cb2.
followed (from my youth) Addition by corrector to harmonise with
Mark 10, 20. Mark has just 'one' (or 'a man') in his story, such that
following the commandments 'from my youth' implies a longish time.
Matthew misses a trick by making his character a 'young man' so that
the qualification 'from my youth' loses some of its force. The subtlety
is apparently lost on Cb2.

H11   19, 26 Q75F3V 9 characters (possibly 13, as word for 'men'
abbreviated). A corrected by D.
to them ΑΥΤΟΙC (with men ΑΝΟΙC). Skip error, skipping from ΟΙC
to ΟΙC.
Note that ΑΝΟΙC is abbreviated from ΑΝΘΡΩΠΟΙC.

M7   21, 17 Q75F4V 12 characters. A corrected by D.
he went (out of the city). Simple omission.

M8   21, 30 Q75F4V 17 characters. A corrected by Ca.
the same (And answering him he said). Simple omission.

H12   23, 3 Q75F5V 10 characters. A corrected by D and Ca.
practise ΠΟΙΗCΑ(ΤΕ observe ΤΗΡΕΙ)ΤΕ. Skip error.
The scribe skips from ΤΕ to ΤΕ, but the corrector puts the text back
in before the first ΤΕ, so starting rather than ending his correction
with ΤΕ.

H13   23, 8 Q75F5V 22 characters. A corrected by S1.
rabbi ΡΑΒΒΕΙ (but you are not to be called rabbi ΡΑΒΒΕΙ). Skip error.

H14   23, 35 Q75F6R 12 characters. A corrected by Cb2.
of Zechariah ΖΑΧΑΡΙΟΥ (son of Barachiah ΒΑΡΑΧΙΟΥ). Skip error,
skipping from ΙΟΥ to ΙΟΥ. This also fits as a possible explanatory elaboration by Cb2. However, in a second century fragment (P77), the title
was also written in full.

M9   24, 35 Q75F6V 50 characters. A corrected by Ca.
take place. (Heaven and earth will pass away, but my words will not
pass away.) Omission of a whole verse, possibly the result of a miscom-
munication between one scribe and another, about to take over on the
next page.

H15   25, 43 Q75F7V 23 or 25 characters. D corrected by Ca.
me ME, (naked and you did not clothe [me ME]). Skip error. The corrector inserts the omitted text, but forgets to put in the final ME.

H16   26, 62. Q75F8V 71 characters. A corrected by Ca and possibly originally S1.
the high priest said to him AYTῳ, ('Have you no answer to make? What is it that these men testify against you?' But Jesus was silent. And the high priest said to him AYTῳ). Skip error.

H17   27, 33 Q76F1V 9 characters. A corrected by Ca.
place TOΠON (called ΛEΓOMENON). Skip error, from ON to ON.

H18   27, 52 Q76F1V 21 characters. A corrected by Ca.
were   split   ECXICΘHCAN   (And   the   tombs   were   opened ANEῳXHCAN). Skip error, from HCAN to HCAN.

M10   27, 56 Q76F1V 18 characters. A corrected by Ca.
was (Mary Magdalene and Mary). Complex amendment.
A complex correction which has to be seen in conjunction with the substitution of text which occurs later in the verse. This has the effect of harmonising the whole of the verse with the version of the same passage in Mark. See pp 188–192.

H19   28, 3 Q76F2R 15 characters. A corrected by S1.
him/it AYTOY (And the appearance of him AYTOY). Skip error.

M11   28, 5 Q76F2R 12 characters. A corrected by S1 and then Cb2.
said (to the women). Categorised as a simple correction (harmonising with Mark 16, 6). But this may have been a skip error, involving the same last character (N) of 'said' and 'women'.

M12   28, 12 Q76F2R 11 characters, allowing for abbreviation of KAI.
A corrected by S1, recorrected by Ca, and then SI's correction reinstated by Cb2.
they made (i.e. took) counsel (And having taken). Simple correction. S1 adds 'And having taken'. While accepting 'having taken', Ca removed 'they made and'. This deletion was then restored by Cb2.

Mark

h1 1, 28 Q76F2V 13 characters. A corrected by Ca.
of him AYTOY (immediately everywhere ΠΑΝΤΑΧΟΥ). Skip error.
The corrector has identified and made good the omission. But he has
used an H, rather than OY, for the ending of 'everywhere' in his correction. On balance, it seems that ΠΑΝΤΑΧΟΥ may be what appeared
in the exemplar.

h2 1, 32–34 Q76F2V 102 characters. A corrected by Ca.
all those who were sick (and KAI those who were possessed by
demons. And the whole city was gathered together about the door.
And he healed many who were sick with various diseases) and KAI.
Skip error.
As with H12, the corrector makes the insert before the key characters
or word.

h3 3, 8 Q76F3V 18 characters. A corrected by Ca.
from Jerusalem (and KAI from Idumea) and KAI. Skip error, with
insert before the key word.

m1 4, 19 Q76F4V 20 characters. A corrected by S1.
coming in (they choke the word) and. Simple omission.

h4 4, 28 Q76F4V 10 characters. A corrected by Ca.
grass (then EITA the ear of grain then) EIT' EN. Skip error. Ca makes
an omission mark to show that the scribe has omitted an A, reinserting the skipped text before the key word.

h5 4, 38 Q76F4V 25 characters. A corrected by S1.
boat ΠΛΟΙΟΝ (so that already was filling up the boat ΠΛΟΙΟΝ). Skip
error.

h6 6, 4 Q66F5V 19 characters. A corrected by S1.
and among KAI EV (relatives and in his KAI EV). Skip error.

h7 6, 7–8 Q76F5V 52 characters. A corrected by S1.
them AYTOIC (authority over the unclean spirits and he charged
them AYTOIC). Skip error.

m2 6, 34 Q76F6R 9 characters. A corrected by Ca.
they were (like sheep) without a shepherd. Amendment or correction
to harmonise with Matthew 9, 36.

h8 8, 7 Q76F7R 13 characters. A corrected by S1.
them AYTA, (he said that also these are TAYTA) to be served. Skip
error, skipping from AYTA to AYTA.
But, in the same correction, S1 (who is possibly the scribe) alters
'served' (past tense), which does not in context make sense, to 'to be
served' which does.

m3 9, 7 Q76F7V 11 characters. A corrected by S1.
my son, the beloved, (with whom I am well pleased) listen to him.
Addition by corrector/scribe to harmonise with Mark 1, 11.

m4 9, 29 Q768R 10 characters. A corrected by Cb2.
prayer (and fasting). Elaboration by corrector, as with Matthew 17, 21
(M3). It may be that Cb2 had access to an earlier, variant text, such as **P45**.

h9 9, 47 Q76F8R 8 characters. A corrected by Ca.
one-eyed to ent … EIC (… er EΛΘIN into EIC). Skip error.
The corrector simply inserts EICEΛΘIN in the text before EIC, but
the error is likely to have originated with the scribe's eye running
from EIC in this word, at the end of a line in the exemplar, to EIC at
the end of the next.

h10 10, 19 Q76F8V 11 characters. A corrected by A.
murder ΦONEYCHC; (do not commit adultery MOIXEYCHC). Skip
error, skipping from CHC to CHC.

h11 10, 29 Q76F8V 13 characters. A corrected by Ca.
or fields (for the sake ENEKEN of me and) for the sake ENEKEN. Skip
error, with insert before the key word.

m5 10, 30 Q76F8V 69 characters. A corrected by S1 and Ca.
this age (houses and brothers and sisters and mothers and fathers
and children and fields with persecutions). This looks like a deliberate omission by the scribe to try to make sense of an incoherent
passage. As it stood, it appeared to be saying that those who give up
the things listed will get them all back in this life (but 'with persecutions') and then also, in the next life, receive life eternal. Clearly
possessions and family ties, once given up, are not always retrievable.

And why receive them with persecutions? So scribe A cut it all out, leaving just a hundredfold reward in this life, plus eternal life in the next. SI restored the list of rewards, leaving out the oddity of persecutions and probably accidentally omitting fields and fathers. Ca then restored these omissions.

h12   10, 33 Q77F1R 19 characters. A corrected by Ca.
chief priests APXIEPEYCI(N) (and the scribes ΓPAMMATEYCIN). Skip error. This could have been a skip error based KAI, but it is more likely to have been based on a key of EYCIN, with the scribe omitting the final 'N' of APXIEPEYCIN. The corrector might alternatively have put in 'and the scribes' to harmonise with other references, eg Mark 14, 1.

h13   10, 35–37 Q77F1R 84 characters. A corrected by Ca.
we wish (that INA you do for us for us whatever we ask of you'. And he said to them, 'What do you want me to do for you?' And they said to him, 'Grant us) that INA ... ' Skip error. As in other instances, the corrector puts the correction in before the key word. The repetition and location of the key word identify this most probably as a skip error. On the other hand, the passage makes perfect sense without the circuitous approach to the question by the brothers James and John. So scribe A may simply have made a decision to cut this text out.

m6   11, 2 Q77F1R 15 characters. A corrected by Cb2.
village (opposite you). Omission, possibly deliberate, restored by corrector. Scribe A may have considered 'opposite you' superfluous.

h14   12, 25 Q77F2R 12 characters. A corrected by S1.
they rise ANACTωCIN (they do not marry ΓAMOYCIN). Skip error skipping from CIN to CIN.

h15   13, 8 Q77F2V 10 characters. A corrected by Ca.
king ... BAC(... dom IΛIA against king ... EΠI BAC) dom ... IΛEIAN. Skip error skipping from BAC to BAC.

h16   13, 8 Q77F2V 21 characters. A corrected by Cb2.
CICμOI earthquakes (in various places, there will be famines ΛIMOI). Skip error skipping from OI to OI or, possibly, from MOI to MOI (with scribe A choosing to use the lower case μ for M). Mark's text does not read well with just 'earthquakes' which suggests that the omitted material was there and accidentally omitted – as opposed to Cb2 harmonising a shorter version in Mark with Matthew 24, 7.

m7   13, 18 Q77F2V 9 characters. A corrected by Cb2.
Pray that it (your flight) may not happen in winter. Addition by corrector to harmonise with Matthew 24, 20.

m8   14, 7 Q77F3R 13 characters. A corrected by Ca.
' ... and whenever you will, you can (to them always) do good'. On the surface, it appears that the corrector has noticed that the scribe has missed out 'to them' (AYTOIC) and has thrown in another 'always' (ΠANTOTE) for good measure. But it could possibly be that Ca has misplaced his correction (there is no insert mark in this case). If the omitted phrase was originally before 'you can', then this would make the scribe's error a skip error, as follows:
you will ΘEΛHTE (to them always ΠANTOTE) you can do good. Skipping from TE to TE. This would, accepting the reconstruction, restore the literary power of a threefold repetition of 'always'. The text then reads:

> For you always have the poor with you and, whenever you
> will, you can always do good to them; but you will not always
> have me.

m9   14, 16 Q77F3R 8 characters. A corrected by Ca.
And the disciples set out (and went) to the city. Restoration of phrase omitted by scribe, who may have felt the 'and went' was unnecessary.

h17   15, 47–16, 1 Q77F4V 78 characters. D corrected by Ca.
the tomb. (Now Mary H ΔE MAPIAH Magdalene and Mary {the mother} of Joses saw where he was laid. And, when the Sabbath was past), Now* Mary MAPIAH). Skip error.
* Deleted by Ca
It is unusual that Ca, in apparently correcting the skip, placed the omitted/extra text before the word Now (ΔE) preceding the key word Mary (MAPIAH). Having begun his insert with H ΔE, he then had to delete Now (ΔE) from the following text for it to make sense. This is at the very least awkward; see pp 224–226. There is a case that the corrector was instead utilising a second version of Mark in order to add extra detail.

h18   16, 6 Q77F5R 12 characters. D corrected by S1.
seek (the TON Nazarene), the one TON who was crucified. Skip error, skipping from TON to TON, with insert before the key word.

Matthew (uncorrected)

15, 6 Q75F1R 12 or 15 characters, depending whether MHTEPA (mother) was abbreviated to MPA in the exemplar. 'Father' (ΠATEPA) is abbreviated to ΠPA in the preceding text so it appears that mother would have been similarly treated.
the father of him AYTOY (or the mother of him AYTOY).

Mark (uncorrected)

10, 7 Q76F8V 38 characters.
and the mother of him AYTOY (and be joined to the wife of him AYTOY).

Skip errors in the Sinaiticus New Testament with chapter and verse references and character length

Skip errors based on a key of two or more characters

Matthew: 5, 19 (62), 5, 45 (29), 7, 27 (19), 9, 10 (12), 9, 15 (44), 10, 9 (10), 13, 39 (35), 14, 23 (21), 15, 6 (12), 15, 18 (48), 19, 18 (20), 19, 26 (9), 23, 3 (10), 23, 8 (22), 23, 35 (12), 25, 43 (25), 26, 62 (71), 27, 33 (9), 27, 52 (21), 28, 3 (15)

Mark: 1, 28 (13), 1, 32 (102), 3, 8 (18), 4, 28 (10), 4, 38 (25), 6, 4 (19), 6, 7 (52), 8, 7 (13), 9, 47 (8), 10, 7 (38), 10, 19 (11), 10, 29 (13), 10, 33 (19), 10, 35 (84), 12, 25 (12), 13, 8 (10), 13, 8 (21), 15, 47 (78), 16, 6 (12)
Note: excluding 4, 19 (23) which would presume an omitted 'KAI' and 14, 7 (13) which would be based on a reconstruction, but including 10, 33 (19) which could arguably have been instead the outcome of the corrector's harmonisation.

Luke: 2, 12 (11), 4, 5 (13), 5, 29 (8), 6, 14 (15), 8, 55 (18), 9, 7 (10), 10, 32 (54), 12, 37 (27), 12, 39 (16), 12, 52 (48), 13, 14 (18), 13, 33 (9), 14, 15 (54), 16, 16 (22), 16, 21 (9), 17, 10 (44), 17, 35 (65), 19, 46 (8), 20, 10 (9), 20, 16 (12), 20, 28 (46), 22, 6 (15), 24, 31 (17), 24, 51 (23)

John: 3, 20 (22), 3, 21 (55), 4, 5 (29), 4, 45 (24), 5, 26 (34), 6, 11 (23), 6, 39 (34), 6, 42 (9), 6, 55 (29), 12, 31 (24), 13, 32 (19), 15, 10 (46), 16, 15 (74), 16, 17 (29), 17, 17 (19), 20, 5 (99)

Romans: 1, 31 (9), 3, 22 (12), 4, 12 (18), 10, 15 (24), 14, 9 (9), 15, 24 (17)

1 Corinthians: 2, 15 (53), 5, 7 (8), 7, 5 (11), 10, 19 (18), 13, 1 (109), 15, 13 (26), 15, 25 (33), 15, 28 (24), 15, 54 (33)

2 Corinthians: 4, 4 (10), 4, 17 (12), 7, 9 (15)

Galatians: 2, 8 (42), 4, 26 (9)

Ephesians: 1, 15 (9), 2, 7 (99), 5, 30 (35), 6, 10 (10)

Philippians: 2, 18 (11), 3, 16 (18)

Colossians: 4, 7 (12)

2 Thessalonians: 2, 4 (16)

Hebrews: 2, 8 (18), 8, 6 (37), 8, 12 (18)

2 Timothy: 4, 8 (14)

Acts: 2, 9 (11), 14, 20 (66), 17, 16 (9), 28, 27 (17)

James: 4, 4 (9)

2 Peter: 1, 12 (101), 3, 12 (13)

1 John: 4, 8 (24), 5, 15 (25)

Revelation: 2, 19 (15), 4, 3 (41), 4, 5 (44), 6, 15 (15), 9, 2 (24), 10, 6 (25), 10, 8 (17), 11, 8 (16), 12, 14 (9), 14, 8 (111), 16, 2 (49), 16, 13 (53), 18, 9 (16), 18, 16 (16), 19, 1 (8), 19, 9 (10), 20, 9 (84), 20, 12 (21), 22, 18 (13)

Barnabas: 12, 11 (9), 14, 9 (110), 19, 4 (20), 19, 10 (16)

Hermas: 2, 2 (8), 4, 1 (18), 8, 1 (35), 9, 9 (73), 10, 9 (32), 12, 3 (13), 24, 7 (21), 29, 11 (34), 67, 2 (40)
Note: large sections of the latter part of this book are missing.

Possible skip errors based on a key of a single character

Matthew: 10, 39 (31), 13, 44 (8), 28, 5 (12)

Luke: 7, 6 (9), 7, 11 (10), 11, 1 (10), 19, 38 (10), 20, 2 (9)

John: 4, 50 (11), 12, 25 (12), 17, 8 (10)

1 Thessalonians: 5, 8 (9)

Hebrews: 2, 18 (8)
Note: or 10 characters if corrector Ca has altered spelling from
ΠΕΙΡΑCΘΕΙC ΤΟ ΠΙΡΑCΘΙC.

1 Timothy: 6, 2 (15), 6, 11 (8)
Note: or 9 characters if Ca has altered spelling from EYCBEIAN to
EYCBIAN.

Acts: 1, 13 (9), 10, 4 (13), 13, 23 (15), 21, 15 (11), 23, 10 (12)

Revelation: 9, 13 (16)

Barnabas: 4, 11 (16), 19, 1 (15), 19, 10 (17)

Hermas: 5, 2 (17)

General notes

No skip errors were found in Titus, Philemon, 1 Peter, 2 John, 3 John and Jude.

In making additions to their text, scribes and correctors often abbreviated KAI to K but the word is not abbreviated in the text itself nor is it usually abbreviated in other earlier texts which might have been contemporaneous with an exemplar. It is therefore highly likely that the exemplar would have had KAI rather than K and this assumption has been made in counting the character length of the skipped text.

In a few cases, abbreviated sacred names (nomina sacra) are found within the skip error corrections (e.g. ΘC for ΘΕΟC (God), IC for IHCOYC (Jesus), KC for KYPIOC (Lord) and XC for XPICTOC (Christ). Such abbreviations are found in nearly all of the earliest source manuscripts for the Old and New Testaments, dating from the second to the fourth centuries.

Codex Sinaiticus dates from the early to mid fourth century. Its scribes would likely have copied from the earliest available authoritative exemplar or exemplars available to them. The pattern of skip errors indicates, however, that one main exemplar was used for the gospels and possibly a large part of the rest of the New Testament. Given that the gospels were not collated until about the end of the second century, this in turn suggests that the exemplar for Sinaiticus would have had abbreviated nomina sacra and that the scribes and correctors copied them from the exemplar, as opposed to making their own abbreviations. The characters of abbreviated nomina sacra are therefore taken as they are presented in counting corrected skip errors.

It may be that both scribes and correctors sometimes changed the spelling of their original, and this could of course happen within a skip error. For the purposes of counting, the spelling is assumed to be correct given that there is no longer an original to check against. See also Chapter 4, p 74.

Correctors sometimes made errors in reinstating omitted text, for example by missing out words. This makes the task of identifying skip errors more difficult.

APPENDIX IV

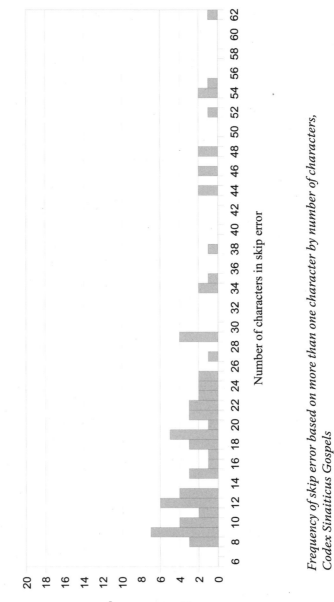

Frequency of skip error based on more than one character by number of characters, Codex Sinaiticus Gospels

Appendix V

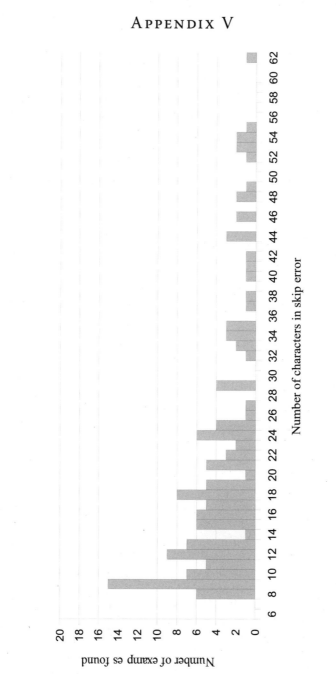

Frequency of skip error based on more than one character by number of characters, Codex Sinaiticus New Testament

Frequency of skip error based on one character by number of characters,
Codex Sinaiticus New Testament

APPENDIX VII

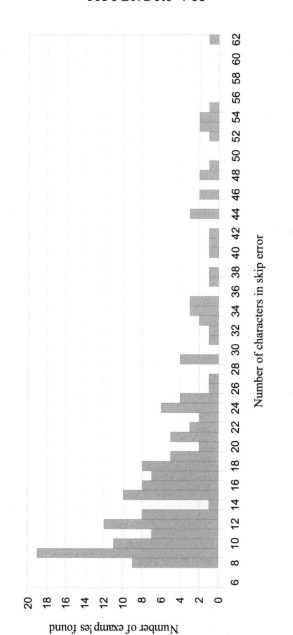

Frequency of skip error based on one or more characters by number of characters, Codex Sinaiticus New Testament

313

Skip errors in Codex Vaticanus

Note that words have been separated, for ease of reading, although the text reads continuously in the original.

New Testament

Matthew 10, 37–38 (46)

ΥΠΕΡ ΕΜΕ ΟΥΚ ΕCΤΙΝ ΜΟΥ
ΑξΙΟC ^ ΚΑΙ ΟC ΟΥ ΛΑΜΒΑ
ΝΕΙ ΤΟΝ CΤΑΥΡΟΝ ΑΥΤΟΥ
^ Κ(ΑΙ) Ο ΦΙΛωΝ ΥΙΟΝ Η ΘΥΓΑΤΕΡΑ ΥΠΕΡΙ ΕΜΙ ΟΥΚ ΕCΤΙΝ μΟΥ ΑξΙΟC
' … more than me is not of me worthy (and the one loving a son or a daughter more than me is not of me worthy). And [the one] who does not take up his cross … '
key characters: ΑξΙΟC.

Matthew 15, 6 (15)

ΜΗCΕΙ ΤΟΝ ΠΑΤΕΡΑ ΑΥ
ΤΟΥ ( ) ΚΑΙ ΗΚΥΡωCΑΤΕ
( ) uncorrected, text missing: Η ΤΗΝ ΜΗΤΕΡΑ ΑΥΤΟΥ

' … honour the father of him (or the mother of him) and you nullify … '
key characters: ΑΥΤΟΥ. Skip error, possibly transcribed from exemplar.

Matthew 25, 40 (13)

CΟΝ ΕΠΟΙΗCΑΤΕ ΕΝΙ ΤΟΥ
ΤωΝ ΤωΝ ^ ΕΛΑΧΙCΤωΝ
ΕΜΟΙ ΕΠΟΙΗCΑΤΕ
^ ΑΔΕΛΦωΝ (μΟΥ) ΤωΝ

' ... as you did it to one of these the (brothers of me the) least, you did it to me.'
key characters: TωN.

Matthew 26, 4 (15)

IN ΔΟΛω ΚΡΑΤΗCωCIN   ΚΑΙ ΑΠΟΚΤΕΙΝωCIN
ΕΛΕΓΟΝ ΔΕ ΜΗ ΕΝ ΤΗ ΕΟΡ
correction written at end of line
' ... Jesus by guile they might seize (and kill). But they said, "not at the feast ... '
key characters: ωCIN.

Mark 10, 7 (38)

ΛΙΨΕΙ ΑΝΘΡωΠΟΣ ΤΟΝ
ΠΑΤΕΡΑ ΑΥΤΟΥ ΚΑΙ ΤΗΝ
ΜΗΤΕΡΑ ( ) ΚΑΙ ΕCΟΝΤΑΙ ΟΙ
ΔΥΟ ΕΙC CΑΡΚΑ ΜΙΑΝ ωC
( ) uncorrected, text missing: ΚΑΙ ΠΡΟCΚΟΛΛΗΘCΕΤΑΙ ΠΡΟC ΤΗΝ ΓΥΝΑΙΚΑΙ ΑΥΤΟΥ
' ... a man will leave his father and mother (and he will be joined to his wife) and the two will become one flesh. So ... '
key characters: ΚΑΙ. The skip, possibly in a common exemplar for Codex Sinaiticus and Codex Vaticanus, could alternatively have been based on ΑΥΤΟΥ. This word is present after ΜΗΤΕΡΑ in Sinaiticus but is here omitted by the Vaticanus scribe. See p 305 above.

Mark 10, 19 (13)

ΧΕΥCΗC ΜΗ ΚΛΕΨΗC ΜΗ
ΨΕΥΔΟΜΑΡΤΥΡΗCΗC ^
ΤΕΙΜΑ ΤΟΝ ΠΑΤΕΡΑ COΥ
^ ΜΗ ΑΠΟCΤΕΡΗCΗC

' ... adultery. Do not steal. Do not bear false witness. (Do not defraud.) Honour the father of you ... '
key characters: ΡΗCΗC.

Mark 10, 46 (21)

ΤΗΝ ΨΥΧΗΝ ΑΥΤΟΥ ΛΥ
ΤΡΟΝ ΑΝΤΙ ΠΟΛΛΩΝ^
ΚΑΙ ΕΚΠΟΡΕΥΟΜΕΝΟΥ
ΑΥΤΟΥ ΑΠΟ ΙΕΡΕΙΧω Κ(ΑΙ)
ΤωΝ
^ Κ(ΑΙ) ΕΡΧΟΝΤΑΙ ΕΙΣ ΙΕΡΕΙΧω

' ... the life of him [as] a ransom on behalf of many. (And they came to Jericho.) And as he was going out from Jericho and the ... '
key characters: ΚΑΙ.

Luke 22, 40 (9)

ΕΙΣΕΛΘΕΙΝ
ΜΗ ΕΙΣ ΠΕΙΡΑΣΜΟΝ ΚΑΙ
ΑΥΤΟΣ ΑΠΕΣΠΑΣΘΗ Α
correction written above line

' ... not (to enter) into temptation and he was withdrawn from ... '
key characters: ΕΙΣ.

John 1, 13 (21)

ΘΕΛΗΜΑΤΟΣ ΣΑΡΚΟΣ^   ^ΟΥΔΕ ΕΚ ΘΕΛΗμΑΤΟΣ ΑΝΔΡΟΣ
ΑΛΛ ΕΚ ΘΥ ΕΓΕΝΝΗΘΗΣΑΝ

' ... the will of flesh (nor of the will of a husband) but of God were born.'
key characters: ΟΣ.

John 17, 15 (36 characters, initially)

ΜΟΥ ΟΥΚ ΕΡωΤω ΙΝΑ Α
ΡΗΣ ΑΥΤΟΥΣ ΕΚ ΤΟ Υ Κ οσμΟΥ ΑΛΛ ΙΝΑ ΤΗΡΗΣΗΣ ΑΥΤΟΥΣ
  . . . . .   Π ΝΗΡ
  ΝΗΡΟΥ ΕΚ ΤΟΥ ΚΟΣΜΟΥ   ΕΚ ΤΟΥ ΚΟΣμΟΥ
  ΟΥΣ ΕΙΣΙΝ ΚΑΘωΣ ΕΓω

Two-stage correction:
(1) Initial homeoteleuton, which the scribe embarks on:

> ... *world. I do not ask that you take them from the world. (But that you keep them from the evil one. Of the world) they are not, just as I ...*

(2) The scribe sees that this does not make sense, hesitates in writing, looks back at his exemplar and *thinks* he has skipped from ΕΚ ΤΟΥ (from the) just before ΠΟΝΗΡΟΥ (evil one), whereas he has in fact skipped forward from an earlier part of the text. So he changes course and writes (omitted text in brackets):

> ... *world. I do not ask that you take them from th e w(orld. But that you keep them from the) ( )vil one. Of the world, they are not, just as I ...*

This makes grammatical sense (and is still effectively a homeoteleuton!). But the sense is now disturbing – 'I do not ask that you keep them from the evil one'. *Very* uncharacteristically, he has left a space within the word ΤΟΥ in the course of hesitating. He has also started the first letter Κ of 'world'. He decides to leave it for when he will go back later to sort out and correct. He misses out the first letters ΠΟ of 'evil one' on the next line, perhaps initially intending to put these in place of the Κ left hanging loose on the previous line.
(3) The scribe/corrector subsequently sees the mistake that has really been made, marks the remaining letters of 'evil one' for deletion, changes 'world' to 'evil one' on the same line and inserts text, smaller and mostly upper case, in the margins of this line and the previous one to make the text conform with the exemplar.
key characters: initially ΚΟCΜΟΥ, subsequently ΕΚ ΤΟΥ

Acts 23, 28 (28 characters, making 33 with addition to correction of ΑΥΤΟΝ)

ΑΙΤΙΑΝ ΔΙ ΗΝ ΕΝΕΚΑΛΟΥΝ
ΑΥΤω^ ΟΝ ΕΥΡΟΝ ΕΓΚΑ
^ ΚΑΤΗΓΑΓΟΝ ΑΥΤΟΝ ΕΙC ΤΟ CΥΝΕΔΡΟΙΝ ΑΥΤωΝ

' ... cause for which they were accusing him. (I brought him down to the Council of them). Whom I found being accused ... '
key characters: AYTω/AYTωN.

1 Peter 1, 1 (11)

ΠΟΝΤΟΥ ΓΑΛΑΤΙΑC ΚΑΠ
ΠΑΔΟΚΙΑC ΑCΙΑC ΚΑΤΑ
correction in left-hand margin: ΚΑΙ ΒΙΘΥΝΙΑC

' ... of Pontos, of Galatia, of Cappadocia, of Asia (and of Bithynia) according ... '
key characters: ΙΑC.
Note that something, possibly in the exemplar, has caused the scribe to leave a gap in the sentence between 'Cappadocia' and 'Asia'.

1 John 4, 21 (13)

ΑΠ ΑΥΤΟΥ ΙΝΑ Ο ΑΓΑΠω   ΤΟΝ ΘΝ ΑΓΑ ΠΑ Κ(ΑΙ)
ΤΟΝ ΑΔΕΛΦΟΝ ΑΥΤΟΥ

' ... from him that the one loving (God should love also) the brother of him.'
key characters: ΤΟΝ.

Romans 9, 3 (13)

ΠΟ ΤΟΥ ΧC ΥΠΕΡ ΤωΝ ^
CΥΓΓΕΝωΝ ΜΟΥ ΚΑΤΑ
^ ΑΔΕLΦωΝ ΜΟΥ ΤωΝ

' ... (separated) from Christ on behalf of (the brothers of me) the kinsmen of me according ... '
key characters: ΤωΝ.

Old Testament

2 Esdras 12, 10 (22)

ΗΚΟΥCΕΝ CΑΝΑΒΑΛΛΑ
Τ ΑΡωΝΕΙ ^ΚΑΙ ΠΟΝΗΡΟ

ΑΥΤΟΙϹ ΕΓΕΝΕΤΟ ΟΤΙ

^ ΚΑΙ ΤωΒΙΑ Ο ΔΟΥΛΟϹ ΑΜΜωΝΕΙ

' ... heard it Sanaballat the Haroni (and Tobia the slave, the Ammoni) and it was very bad to them ... '
key characters: ΝΕΙ.

Esther 9, 19 (115)

ΠΛΗϹΙΟΝ ^ΕΓΡΑΨΕ

^ ΟΙ ΔΕ ΚΑΤΟΙΚΟΥΝΤΕϹ ΕΝ ΤΑΙϹ ΜΗΤΡΟΠΟΛΕϹΙΝ Κ(ΑΙ) ΤΗ
ΠΕΝΤΕΚΑΙΔΕΚΑΤΗ ΤΟΥ ΑΔΑ ΕΥΦΡΟϹΥΝΗϹ ΑΓΑΘΗΝ ΑΓΟΥϹΙΝ
ΕΞΑΠΟϹΤΕΛΛΟΝΤΕϹ ΜΕΡΙΔΑϹ ΤΟΙϹ ΠΛΗϹΙΟΝ

' ... nearby. (But those living in the large towns also celebrate on the fifteenth of Adar a joyful holiday. They send a gift of food to those nearby). Now ... '
key characters: ΠΛΗϹΙΟΝ.

Esther 10, 3g–h (90)

ΤΟΙϹ ΕΘΝΕϹΙΝ ^ ΚΑΙ ΕΜΝΗ
ϹΘΗ Ο ΘϹ ΤΟΥ ΛΑΟΥ ΑΥ
ΤΟΥ

^ Κ(ΑΙ) ΗΛΘΟΝ ΟΙ ΔΥΟ ΚΛΗΡΟΙ ΑΥΤΟΙ ΕΙϹ ωΡΑΝ Κ(ΑΙ) ΚΑΗΡΟΝ Κ(ΑΙ) ΕΙϹ
ΗΜΕΡΑΝ ΚΡΙϹΕωϹ ΕΝωΠΙΟΝ ΤΟΥ ΘΥ Κ(ΑΙ) ΠΑϹΙ ΤΟΙϹ ΕΘΝΕϹΕΙΝ

' ... the nations. (And these two lots will come into the hour and time and into the day of judgement before God and for all the nations.) And God remembered his people ...
key characters: ΤΟΙϹ ΕΘΝΕϹΙΝ.

Judith 8, 6 (12)

ΚΑΙ ϹΑΒΒΑΤωΝ ΚΑΙ ΠΡΟ ΝΟΥμΗΝΙωΝ ΚΑΙ
ΝΟΥΜΗΝΙωΝ ΚΑΙ ΕΟΡ

' ... and the Sabbaths, and the eves of the new moons (and the new moons) and ... '
key characters: ΝΟΥΜΗΝΙωΝ. The corrector has reinstated the skipped text before the key word.

Tobit 8, 15 (13)

ΠΑСΗ ΕΥΛΟΓΙΑ ^ ΚΑΙ ΕΥ
ΛΟΓΕΙΤωСΑΝ
^ ΚΑΘΑΡΑ Κ(ΑΙ) ΑΓΙΑ

' ... every blessing (pure and holy) and may you bless ... '
key characters: ΓΙΑ.

Nahum 1, 2 (9)

ΘСΖΗΛωΤΗСΚΑΙΕΚΔΙΚ ωΝ ΚС ΕΚΔΙ
ΚСΜΕΤΑΘΥΜΟΥΕΚΔΙ
ΚωΝΚСΤΟΥСΥΠΕΝΑΝ

'God is zealous and the Lord avenges. (The Lord avenges) with wrath.
The Lord avenges (against) his enemies ... '
key characters: ΚС.
Note that the scribe has omitted ωΝ from ΕΚΔΙΚωΝ (avenges) at the
end of the first line. The corrector restored this but then omitted ΚωΝ
from 'avenges' in his insertion.

Isaiah 12, 2 (18)

ΘωС ΕСΟΜΑΙ ΕΠ ΑΥΤω Κ(ΑΙ) СωΘΗСΟΜΑΙ ΕΝ ΑΥΤω
ΚΑΙ ΟΥΦΟΒΗΘСΟΜΑΙ
' ... I will trust in him and (I will be saved by him) and I will not be
afraid ... '
key characters: ΑΥΤω.

Isaiah 13, 3 (32)

ΕΓω СΥΝΤΑССω ΚΑΙ ΕΓω ^
^ ΑΓω ΑΥΤΟΥС ΗΓΙΑСμΕΝΟΙ ΕΙСΙ ΚΑΙ ΕΓω ΑΓω

' ... I command and I lead (them. They are sanctified and I lead) ... '
key characters: Γω.

Isaiah 29, 15 (38)

ΠΟΙΟΥΝΤΕС ^ ΚΑΙ ΕСΤΑΙ
^ Κ(ΑΙ) ΟΥ ΔΙΑ ΚΥ ΟΥΑΙ ΟΙ ΕΝ ΚΡΥΦΗ ΒΟΥΛΗΝ ΠΟΙΟΥΝΤΕС

' ... those deep counsel making (and not through the Lord. Woe to them secret counsel making). And it is ... '
key characters: ΠΟΙΟΥΝΤΕϹ.

Isaiah 35, 10 (21)

ΑΙωΝΙΟϹ ΥΠΕΡ ΚΕΦΑ ΛΗϹ ΑΥΤωΝ ΕΠΙ ΓΑΡ Τ(ΗϹ) ΚΕΦΑ
ΛΗϹ ΑΥΤωΝ

' ... everlasting over the head (of them for upon the head) of them
key characters: ΚΕΦΑ.

Isaiah 47, 9 (51)

ΦΝΗϹ ΕΠΙ ϹΕ ^ ΕΝ ΤΗ ΦΑΡ
^ ΤΑ ΔΥΟ ΤΑΥΤΑ ΕΝ ΗμΕΡΑ μΙΑ ΑΤΕΚΝΙΑ Κ(ΑΙ) ΧΗΡΙΑ ΗξΙ ΕΙξΑΙΦΝΗϹ ΕΠΙ ϹΕ

' ... suddenly upon you (these two things in one day, the loss of children and widowhood suddenly shall come upon you) for your sorcery ... '
key characters: ΕΠΙ ϹΕ.

APPENDIX IX

New Testament dittographies, Codex Sinaiticus and Codex Vaticanus

Codex Sinaiticus

Luke 17, 16 (71)

ΔΟΞΑΖⲰΝΤΟΝΘΝ
ΚΑΙΕΠΕCΕΝΕΠΙ
ΠΡΟCⲰΠΟΝΠΑ
ΡΑΤΟΥCΠΟΔΑCΑΥ
ΤΟΥΕΥΧΑΡΙCΤⲰΝ
ΑΥΤⲰΚΑΙΑΥΤΟCΗΝ
CΑΜΑΡΙΤΗC
ΚΑΙΕΠΕCΕΝΕΠΙΠΡΟ
CⲰΠΟΝΠΑΡΑΤΟΥC
ΠΟΔΑCΑΥΤΟΥΕΥ
ΧΑΡΙCΤⲰΝΑΥΤⲰ
ΚΑΙΑΥΤΟCΗΝCΑ
ΜΑΡΙΤΗC
ΑΠΟΚΡΙΘΕΙCΔΕΟ

' ... glorifying God. And he fell on (his) face at the feet of him thanking him. And he was a Samaritan. **And he fell on (his) face at the feet of him thanking him. And he was a Samaritan**. Answering ... '
key: no apparent key.

1 Corinthians 1, 8 (60)

ΠΟΚΑΛΥΨΙΝΤΟΥΚΥ
ΗΜⲰΝΙΥΧΥΟCΚΑΙ
ΒΕΒΑΙⲰCΕΙΥΜΑCΕ
ⲰCΤΕΛΟΥCΑΝΕΓ
ΚΛΗΤΟΥCΕΝΤΗΗ
ΜΕΡΑΤΟΥΚΥΗΜⲰ(Ν)
ΙΥΧΥΟCΚΑΙΒΕΒΑΙ

ωCEIΥΜΑϹΕωϹΤΕ
ΛΟΥϹΑΝΕΓΚΛΗΤΟΥϹ
ΕΝΤΗΗΜΕΡΑΤΟΥΚΥ
ΗΜωΝΙΥΧΥΠΙϹΤΟϹ

' ... revelation of our Lord Jesus Christ. He will also strengthen you to
the end, so that you are blameless on the day our Lord Jesus Christ.
**He will also strengthen you to the end, so that you are blameless
on the day of our Lord Jesus Christ.** Faithful ... '
key: ΤΟΥ ΚΥ ΗΜωΝ ΙΥ ΧΥ (of our Lord Jesus Christ).

Ephesians 6, 3 (42)

ΓΕΛΙΑΙΝΑΕΥϹΟΙΓΕ
ΝΗΤΑΙΚΑΙΕϹΗΜΑ
ΚΡΟΧΡΟΝΙΟϹΕΠΙ
ΤΗϹΓΗϹΙΝΑΕΥϹΟΙ
ΓΕΝΗΤΑΙΚΑΙΕϹΗ
ΜΑΚΡΟΧΡΟΝΙΟϹ
ΕΠΙΤΗϹΓΗϹ
ΚΑΙΟΙΠΑΤΕΡΕϹΜΗ

' ... promise: so that it may be well with you and you will live a long
time on the earth **so that it may be well with you and you will live a
long time on the earth.** And fathers, do not ... '
key: no apparent key.

1 Thessalonians 2, 13–14 (126)

ΤΟΥΘΥΕΔΕξΑϹΘΕΟΥ
ΛΟΓΟΝΑΝΘΡωΠωΝ
ΑΛΛΑΚΑΘωϹ*ΕϹΤΙΝ   *ΑΛΗΘωϹ (insertion by S1)
ΛΟΓΟΝΘΥΟϹΚΑΙΕ
ΝΕΡΓΕΙΤΑΙΕΝΗΜΙ
ΤΟΙϹΠΙϹΤΕΥΟΥϹΙΝ
ΥΜΙϹΓΑΡΜΙΜΗΤΑΙ
ΕΓΕΝΗΘΗΤΕΑΔΕΛ
ΦΟΙΤωΝΕΚΚΛΗϹΙ
ωΝΤΟΥΘΥΕΔΕξΑ
ϹΘΕΟΥΛΟΓΟΝΑΝ
ΘΡωΠωΝΑΛΛΑΚΑ

ΘωCECTINΛΟΓΟΝ
ΘΥΟCΚΑΙΕΝΕΡΓΙ
ΤΑΙΕΝΗΜΙΝΤΟΙC
ΠΙCΤΕΥΟΥCΙΝ
ΥΜΕΙCΓΑΡΜΙΜΗΘΗ
ΤΕΕΓΕΝΗΘΗΤΕΑΔΕΛ
ΦΟΙΤωΝΕΚΚΛΗCΙ
ΩΝΤΟΥΘΥΤωΝΟΥ

' ... of God. You received (it) not (as) the word of men but as it is (*truly), the word of God which also works in you, the ones who believe. For you became imitators, brothers, of the churches of God **you received (it) not (as) the word of men but as it is, the word of God which also works in you, the ones who believe. For you became imitators, brothers, of the churches of God** that are ... '
key: ΤΟΥ ΘΥ (of God).

Revelation 6, 10 (18)

ΘΥΚΑΙΔΙΑΤΗΝΜΑΡ
ΤΥΡΙΑΝ**ΚΑΙΔΙΑΤΗΝ
ΜΑΡΤΥΡΙΑΝ**ΗΝΕCΧΟΝ (Ca corrects to ΕΙΧΟΝ)

' ... of God and because of their testimony **and because of their testimony** which they had given.'
key: no apparent key.

Revelation 7, 13 (25)

ΚΑΙΑΠΕΚΡΙΘΗΕΙCΤωΝ
ΠΡΕCΒΥΤΕΡωΝΛΕΓωΝ
ΜΟΙ**ΕΙCΤωΝΠΡΕCΒΥ
ΤΕΡωΝΛΕΓωΝΜΟΙ**
ΟΥΤΟΙΟΙΠΕΡΙΒΕΒΛΗ

'Then answered one of the elders, saying to me, **one of the elders, saying to me,** "These ones clothed ... '
key: no apparent key.

Codex Vaticanus

Matthew 21, 4 (20)

ΙΝΑΠΛΗΡΩΘΗΤΟΡΗΘΕΝ
ΔΙΑΤΟΥΠΛΗΡΩΟΗΤΟ
ΡΗΘΕΝΔΙΑΤΟΥΠΡΟΦΗ
ΤΟΥΛΕΓΟΝΤΟΣ

'to fulfil what had been spoken through the **fulfil what had been spoken through the** prophet saying'
key: the scribe began with the Π of 'prophet' and possibly his eye skipped back to the beginning Π of 'fulfil'.

Matthew 26, 57 (26)

ΕΦΥΓΟΝΟΙΔΕΚΡΑΤΗCΑΝ
ΤΕCΤΟΝΙΝΕΦΥΓΟΝΟΙΔΕ
ΚΡΑΤΗCΑΝΤΕCΤΟΝΙΝ
ΑΠΗΓΑΓΟΝΠΡΟCΚΑΙΑΦΑ

' ... fled. And those who had arrested Jesus **fled. And those who had arrested Jesus** led him away to Caiaphas ... '
key: no key; it seems the scribe still had 'fled' in his mind from the previous sentence.

Luke 1, 37 (16)

CΤΕΙΡΑΟΤΙΟΥΚΑΔΥΝΑ
ΤΗCΕΙΟΤΙΟΥΚΑΔΥΝΑ
ΤΗCΕΙΠΑΡΑΤΟΥΘΥΠΑΝ
ΡΗΜΑ

' ... barren. For will be impossible **for will be impossible** with God nothing.'
key: no apparent key.

John 13, 14 (42)

ΚΑΙΚΑΛΩCΛΕΓΕΤΕΕΙμΙ
ΓΑΡΕΙΟΥΝΕΓωΕΝΙΨΑ
ΥΜωΝΤΟΥCΠΟΔΑCΟΚC
ΚΑΙΟΔΙΔΑCΚΑΛΟCΕΙΟΥ(Ν)

ΕΓѠΕΝΙΨΑΥΜѠΝΤΟΥС
ΠΟΔΑСΟΚСΚΑΙΟΔΙΔΑСΚΑ
ΛΟСΚΑΙΥΜΕΙСΟΦΕΙΛΕ

'And it is well that you say I am. If then I washed your feet (being) the Lord and teacher **if then I washed your feet (being) the Lord and teacher** you also ought ...'
key: no apparent key, although some repeated words in the text may have made the mistake more likely. Note that the scribe abbreviated OYN by means of a bar over the Y.

John 17, 18 (31)

ΚΟСΜΟΝΚΑΓѠΑΠΕСΤΕΙ
ΛΑΑΥΤΟΥСΕΙСΤΟΝΚΟС
ΜΟΝΚΑΓѠΑΠΕСΤΕΙΛΑ
ΑΥΤΟΥСΕΙСΤΟΝΚΟСμΟ(Ν)
ΚΑΙΥΠΕΡΑΥΤѠΕΤѠ

' ... world. (So) also I sent them into the world. **(So) also I sent them into the world**. And for them I ... '
key: ΚΟСΜΟΝ (world). Note that the scribe used a lower case 'μ' for 'M' in the third rendering of 'world' and abbreviated the ending by means of a bar over the 'O'.

Acts 19, 34 (21)

ΖΟΝΤѠΝΜΕΓΑΛΗΗΑΡΤΕ
ΜΙСΕΦΕСΙѠΝΜΕΓΑΛΗ
ΗΑΡΤΕΜΙСΕΦΕСΙѠΝ
ΚΑΤΑСΤΕΙΛΑСΔΕΤΟΝΟ

' ... crying out, "Great (is) Artemis of the Ephesians! **Great (is) Artemis of the Ephesians**!" Having restrained the crowd ... '
key: possibly the letters ѠΝ at the end of ΚΡΑΖΟΝΤѠΝ (crying out) and then ΕΦΕСΙѠΝ (Ephesians). However, it is also possible, as with the cry of 'Master! Master! We are perishing!' by the disciples (see p 80), that the Vaticanus scribe included the repetition for dramatic emphasis.

Romans 4, 4–5 (59)

ΤѠΔΕΕΡΓΑΖΟΜΕΝѠΟ
ΜΙСΘΟСΟΥΛΟΓΙΖΕΤΑΙ
ΚΑΤΑΧΑΡΙΝΑΛΛΑΚΑΤΑ
ΟΦΕΙΛΗΜΑΤѠΔΕΜΗ
ΕΡΓΑΖΟΜΕΝѠ**ΟΜΙСΘΟС**
ΟΥΛΟΓΙΖΕΤΑΙΚΑΤΧΑ
ΡΙΝΑΛΛΑΚΑΤΑΟΦΕΙΛΗ
ΜΑΤѠΔΕΜΗΕΡΓΑΖΟ
ΜΕΝѠΠΙСΤΕΥΟΝΤΙΔΕ

'Now, to the one working, the reward is not reckoned as a gift but as due recompense. But, to the one not working, **the reward is not reckoned as a gift but as due recompense. But, to the one not working** but believing ... '
key: ΕΡΓΑΖΟΜΕΝѠ (working)

Romans 9, 18 (14)

ΑΡΑΟΥΝΟΝΘΕΛΕΙΕΛΕ
ΕΙΟΝΔΕΘΕΛΕΙ**ΕΛΕΕΙ**
ΟΝΔΕΘΕΛΕΙСΚΛΗΡΥΝΕΙ

'So then on whom he wills he has mercy and on whom he wills **he has mercy and on whom he wills** he hardens.'
key: ΘΕΛΕΙ (he wills)

1 Corinthians 13, 7 (11)

ΤΗΑΛΗΘΕΙΑΠΑΝΤΑСΤΕ
ΓΕΙΠΑΝΤΑ**СΤΕΓΕΙΠΑΝ**
ΤΑΠΙСΤΕΥΕΙΠΑΝΤΑΕΛ

' ... the truth. All things it bears. All things **it bears. All things** it believes. All things ... '
key: ΠΑΝΤΑ (all things)

2 Corinthians 3, 15–16 (67)

ΚΑΛΥΜΜΑΕΠΙΤΗΝΚΑΡ
ΔΙΑΝΑΥΤѠΝΚΕΙΤΑΙΗΝΙ

ΚΑΔ(Ε)ΑΝΕΠΙΣΤΡΕΨΗΠΡΟΣ
ΚΝΠΕΡΙΕΡΕΙΤΑΙΤΟΚΑ
ΛΥΜΜΑ**ΕΠΙΤΗΝΚΑΡΔΙ**
ΑΝΑΥΤωΝΚΕΙΤΑΙΗΝΙ
ΚΑΔ(Ε)ΑΝΕΠΙΣΤΡΕΨΗΠΡΟΣ
ΚΝΠΕΡΙΕΡΕΙΤΑΙΤΟΚΑ
ΛΥΜΜΑΟΔΕΚΣΤΟΠΝΕΥ

' ... veil on their heart of them lies. But whenever one turns to the Lord is taken away the veil **on the heart of them lies But whenever one turns to the Lord is taken away the veil.** Now the Lord the spirit ... '
key: ΚΑΛΥΜΜΑ (veil). Note that a corrector has changed the second 'Ε' to 'ΑΙ' in ΠΕΡΙΕΡΕΙΤΑ (is taken away) in both lines.

Galatians 1, 11 (12)

ΡΙΖωΓΑΡΥΜΙΝΑΔΕΦΟΙ
ΤΟΕΥΑΓΓΕΛΙΟΝ**ΤΟΕΥ**
ΑΓΓΕΛΙΟΝΤΟΕΥΑΓΓΕ
ΛΙΟΝΤΟΕΥΑΓΓΕΛΙΣΘΕΝ

' ... make known to you brothers the gospel **the gospel the gospel** having been preached ... '
key: ΕΥΑΓΓΕΛΙ. This is a double dittography based on the fact that 'gospel' and 'preached' have the same root (roughly equates to, 'the good news goodnewsed'). The scribe reached the 'Ι' of 'ΕΥΑΓΓΕΛΙΣΘΕΝ' and twice in succession switched to 'ΕΥΑΓΓΕΛΙΟΝ'.

Colossians 4, 2 (8)

ΡΑΝωΤΗΠΡΟΣΕΥΧΗ
ΠΡΟΣ**ΕΥΧΗΠΡΟΣ**ΚΑΡΤΕ

' ... heaven, In prayer **prayer** persevere ... '
key: ΠΡΟΣ. 'Prayer' and 'persevere' have the same initial letters.

Appendix X

Gospel language

For a long time, it was assumed that the New Testament gospels were all originally written in Greek. But this assumption began to be challenged by critical examination of the language and form of the Greek gospels and also by comparison with two manuscripts in Old Syriac, a dialect of Aramaic. One of these, the Curetonianus, is named after William Cureton who found the ancient codex at the monastery of St Mary Deipara in Egypt in 1842. The second was discovered by two sisters, Agnes Lewis and Margaret Gibson, 50 years later at the monastery of St Catherine in Sinai. It was on parchment which had been reused, partially obscuring the original text; hence the name used to describe it, the Sinaiticus palimpsest.

Both documents appear to date from about the end of the fourth century CE and, like examples of the Greek New Testament from the fourth century onwards, would have been copies of earlier manuscripts. The study of the gospels and their origins is hampered by the fact that mostly fragments exist of these earlier records, in Greek or in Syriac.

Mistakes would have been introduced in copying and, indeed, some early Christians may have felt themselves free to amend text according to their own experience and inspiration. Familiarity may have led scribes to adapt the text of one gospel to another, so obscuring evidence of their early transmission and evolution. There are in fact many thousands of variations between surviving Greek texts.

We have found examples suggesting deliberate harmonisation and also (see Chapters 12 and 13) evidence of other deliberate change.

One broad conclusion, supported by the evidence, is that Mark has primacy over the other canonical gospels which were written later (see Chapter 7). Their authors quarried Mark and used other sources, including a body of sayings, attributed to Jesus, which would have been in Aramaic. Another clear distinction comes in the use of language. Jesus is addressed by Jews as rabbi/teacher in the stories in Mark, but in Matthew and Luke he is regularly addressed as 'Lord' which indicates a later and more strongly developed Christian perspective. Mark gives several quotations of words attributed to Jesus in Aramaic, while Luke retains none. Matthew has the Hebrew equivalent for Jesus' cry from the cross (itself a quotation from Psalm 22, 1) and the place name Golgotha, which probably also comes from Hebrew. One Aramaic word 'bariona', meaning outlaw, may have been retained in the Greek of Matthew, as a nickname given to Simon Peter, in the mistaken belief that it meant 'bar Jona', or son of Jona.

Many scholars believe that the Greek gospels of Matthew, Luke and possibly John show signs of being based on an Aramaic original. The following example serves to illustrate the case that has been made in respect of primacy for Old Syriac/Aramaic for Matthew.

Old Syriac will here be used to refer to the Curetonianus and the Sinaiticus palimpsest. Early Greek will refer to Codex Sinaiticus and Codex Vaticanus, supported by papyrus manuscripts that provide a witness to some passages.

Wrangle or clamour

There are a number of passages in the Old Syriac gospels of Matthew and Luke which differ from those in the early Greek in ways that can only have come through a misrepresentation of a Syriac original in Greek translation, and not vice versa. The evidence is strong because, as far as we have been able to discover, it is all one way. There is not even a small body of sayings in the Syriac that could only have come from a Greek original.

The example that follows is drawn from the introduction to Jan Wilson's *The Old Syriac Gospels*. It relates to a verse quoting the Old Testament prophet Isaiah as justification for Jesus asking those whom he had healed to keep quiet about it.

The relevant part of the quotation (Matthew 12, 19) is as follows in the Greek, 'He will not wrangle or cry aloud, nor will any one hear his voice in the streets.'

In the original Old Testament passage (Isaiah 42, 2), from which the quote is taken, there is a significant difference. It reads, 'He will not cry or lift up his voice, or make it heard in the street.' To wrangle or dispute is very different from to cry out. The Old Testament version is the original. So, where has the mistake in the Greek translation come from? It is not in the Old Syriac Sinaiticus or Curetonianus, which render the quotation from Isaiah as, 'He will not cry out nor clamour, nor shall any man hear his voice'.

However, as Wilson points out, the Syriac root for to make a noise or clamour is the same as the Hebrew root meaning to strive or contend – or, as it is rendered in the Greek, to 'wrangle'. The error must therefore have originated in a scribe translating into Greek from a Syriac original and probably derives from his greater familiarity with Hebrew than with the Old Syriac dialect of Aramaic. The scribe should have gone back to source, where the statement in Isaiah is in fact a classic threefold repetition of the same idea expressed in different ways (cry/lift up his voice/make it heard in the street) to give dramatic emphasis. In the context, wrangle is out of place.

This example does suggest that there was a translation from Old Syriac/Aramaic during the process by which the Greek version of Matthew came into being.

Robes or porches

There are very few points where it appears that the early Greek version of Mark may have been based on a Syriac original. But if the case is maintained that Mark, the earliest of the canonical gospels, was originally written in Greek, then any counter-evidence must be explained. Wilson gives one clear example. Mark 12, 38–39 offers in the words of Jesus a warning, 'Beware of the scribes, who like to walk about in long robes, and to be greeted in the market places and to have the chief seats in the synagogues and places of honour at feasts.'

The Old Syriac (Sinaiticus) has this variation, 'Beware of the scribes who like to walk about in the porches and who love greetings in the market places.' As Wilson notes, the porches of public places were well known at the time as gathering places. Parading in porches, moreover, fits better with the context than going about in long robes. The first part of the denigration of the scribes deals with strutting about in two types of public spaces, the porches of buildings and market places. The second part deals with getting the best seats, again in two types of public space, at the synagogues and at feasts. Wearing long robes sits less easily in this context.

The mistake could have come about because the Syriac words for 'robes' and porches' differ by only one letter. So a scribe could easily, in translating from Syriac to Greek, have mistaken a word where there was only one letter difference. It could equally have happened in making another copy of the Syriac text (ie going from Syriac to Syriac before translation into Greek). The Peshitta, the Aramaic version of the gospels used in the Eastern Church, follows the New Testament Greek in using 'robes'. This and other examples indicate that the Peshitta is a later translation of the gospels from the Greek back into Aramaic.

The situation is complicated because there is the same discrepancy between the corresponding verse in Luke (20, 46) and the Old Syriac versions. It does appear unlikely that a scribe would have happened to make the same error twice.

Wilson suggests that a scribe in copying or translating the gospels as a whole might have made a conscious decision that the original should have been 'robes' rather than 'porches' and made a systematic correction, this despite the fact that porches fits in better, as has been seen.

There is however a pointer as to how this might have come about, in that that the version in the Old Syriac Luke (both Sinaiticus and Curetonianus) varies from the Old Syriac Mark by having the scribes love greetings 'in the street' rather than 'market places'. Instead of following this, the early Greek Luke has 'greetings in the market places' which is identical with the early Greek Mark. It is possible that there is another lost version of the Old Syriac for Luke which is identical for this verse with Old Syriac Mark. But it may also be that the scribe who generated the Greek (as it is now) was cross-checking against other sources, no longer had access to an Aramaic/Syriac original, and decided, in making a copy from his Greek text of Luke, to conform with Mark. So he changed the text as a whole, losing both 'porches' and 'street' in the process. His Greek source manuscript, which may well have reflected the Aramaic/Syriac, eventually disappeared. His copy in Greek did however survive in providing text which has become part of the New Testament Luke which we now have.

The gospel of Mark may then have had input from the Old Syriac but the processes by which the gospels evolved is, as this example shows, complicated.

There is unfortunately a long period of more than two centuries from about 75 CE to 300 CE, for which there is limited evidence in terms of original manuscripts, during which time many changes will have occurred. A working hypothesis of how the gospels evolved, rather than a complete explanation, is probably the best that can ever be achieved.

Mother or daughter

The evidence is that the four canonical gospels writers were all seeking to place at the scene of the crucifixion the three most signifi-cant women in Jesus' life (see Chapter 10). These were, in order of precedence, his partner Mary/Mary Magdalene, his mother Mary and his aunt (mother's sister) Salome. It is also apparent that the first of these was not merely Jesus' partner but his wife. One pivotal piece of evidence is that the relevant passage in John's gospel was incorrectly read in the Greek and so was mistranslated into other languages. It reads properly as a description which has these same three women present. It then also makes sense against the other gospel descriptions of the same scene together with statements in the gospels and other sources about Jesus' brothers.

John describes the women present as 'his mother, Mary the wife of Clopas, his mother's sister and Mary Magdalene' (Chapter 10, pp 182–185). This relates to three women: his mother Mary who was the wife of Clopas, his mother's sister (unnamed) and Mary Magdalene. John departs here from Mark and Matthew in placing the partner of Jesus last instead of first (John 19, 25). These gospel writers list Mary Magdalene first at this point and in several other references, as also does Luke. They place second, in the list of women near to the cross, Mary the mother of James and Joseph, and thus also of Jesus (Mark 15, 40 and Matthew 27, 55–56). Third placed is Salome in Mark and the mother of the sons of Zebedee in Matthew. The third woman in John is his (Jesus') mother's sister. These, we have argued, refer to attributes of the same person: by name Salome, married to Zebedee, mother of James and John ('sons of thunder') and sister of Mary. Luke gives no names for the women present at the scene of the crucifixion (Luke 23, 49).

There is a very striking difference between the early Greek versions of Mark and Matthew and the Old Syriac, in that the former describe one of the three women present at the cross as 'the mother of James (the less) and of Joseph/Joses' while the Old Syriac Sinaiticus refers to 'the daughter of James (the less) and mother of Joseph'. In the Greek, the word 'mother' is displaced, so that the text literally reads 'Mary the ( ) of James the less and of Joses mother'. Words defining a relationship are sometime left out in the Greek, or put later in the sequence, so that 'mother' here qualifies both James and Joses.

333

However, some commentators have maintained that the Old Syriac is both original and correct, so that the Mary described here really was James' daughter. There are several good reasons for believing that this view is erroneous. In the first place, if Mary were being described as the daughter of James, this would have meant that a fourth unnamed woman was also present, the mother of Joses. This would be at odds with the other gospels descriptions of the women present at the cross.

Not only that, but we know from other textual references that James and Joseph/Joses were brothers. This is spelt out in Mark 6, 3. Jesus is, with no omissions, described as 'the son of Mary and brother of James and Joses and Judas and Simon'. The same arguments apply to the parallel passages in Matthew (27, 55–56 and 13, 55).

If Mary were Joses' mother, then she was also James' mother, rather than his daughter.

A third substantial piece of supportive evidence comes in this earlier passage in the Old Syriac versions. The passage in Mark is missing from these manuscripts. But the passage in Matthew has been preserved. It reports the mother of Jesus as Mary and his brothers as 'James and Joseph and Simon and Judas', precisely as in the Greek New Testament! It hardly needs pointing out that this stands in direct contradiction to the statements later in the Old Syriac texts that Mary, though indeed the mother of Joseph, was *daughter* of James.

It does need to be repeated that, fourthly, the gospels writers had a sense of contemporary, cultural precedents and would have placed at the cross women who were significant in Jesus' life and this would have included his mother. So Mary had therefore to be the mother rather than daughter of James, who was also one of Jesus' brothers. It takes enormous mental gymnastics (which some have indeed engaged in), involving the invention of other characters present, who just happened also to be called Mary and James, to distract from the fact that Jesus was part of a normal biological family with brothers and sisters – and a mother who was the mother of these brothers and sisters as well. It is worth noting here that Luke, who does not name the women present, nevertheless describes them as 'relatives'. This is at least supportive of the conclusions that one Mary was the mother of Jesus, another was his wife and a third character was his aunt. It does not support the thesis that one Mary, being daughter of some person called James, was not his mother, the second Mary being merely a female supporter was not his wife and the third character, being the sister of someone who was not his mother, was not his aunt!

The fifth and final argument depends on the observation that there is no coherent means by which 'daughter of James and mother of Joseph' would have become in translation from Syriac where the words are spelled out, 'mother of James and Joseph' in the Greek. Nor is there a rational explanation how the earlier text in the Old Syriac concerning the brothers of Jesus, if this had happened, could have come to differ from the later text relating to the women at the cross. But there is a complete explanation deriving from the Greek usage, assuming that the translation in this instance took place the other way, from Greek to Syriac.

It is now quite simple. Where the relationships are spelled out in the Greek, as in 'son of Mary and brother of James and Joses and Simon', and there is no scope for ambiguity, the passage is rendered the same way in the Old Syriac. Wherever there is an omission, assuming in Greek knowledge from context of the relationship between Mary and James, it has at some point been wrongly decided in translation to Old Syriac that Mary was the daughter rather than the mother of James. This applies to all such passages in the synoptic gospels, including one reading for 'Mary the ( ) of Joseph' (Mark 15, 47) which is also translated in Old Syriac as 'daughter of James'! This latter does rather suggest a scribe blindly following a general prescription.

The text for the women at the cross in John in the Greek uses the word 'mother' and so there is no reason for thinking that the Old Syriac would here be different. But that cannot be decided because this portion of the text, as well as most of the rest of the passion sequence in the gospel of John, is missing from the Syriac manuscripts. It is possible that the Old Syriac derived from an early Greek version that had a lot in common with what we have deduced was the source, before being amended, of Matthew's version of the women at the cross in Codex Sinaiticus (see pp 188–192).

We have argued that the Greek version that Mary was the mother of James is accurate, or at least is the more original presentation. We have further contended that the Syriac is based on a misunderstanding or misrepresentation in translation, facilitated by the way the Greek was constructed.

This does now leave a problem. In the previous sections, we presented the case, based on the analysis of sayings, that two if not three of the Greek New Testament gospels derive from the Old Syriac. Here, however, we have a demonstration of mistranslation of Greek text in Old Syriac.

It is hard to reconcile the two positions since the examples presented for both types of transmission, from Syriac to Greek and from Greek to Syriac, are spread between the gospels and through the text. Some further insight, at least on the early stages of transmission, comes from considering quotes of Aramaic in the Greek text.

Son of Timaeus

Mark is the only gospel which quotes a number of words or sayings in Aramaic attributed to Jesus. One example, (Mark 7, 34) describes how he restores the hearing and speech of a man who was both deaf and had a speech impediment:

He took him aside in private, away from the crowd, and put his fingers into his ears, and he spat and touched his tongue. Then, looking up to heaven, he sighed, and said to him, 'Ephphatha,' which means, 'Be opened.'

There are several other examples where Aramaic words reportedly spoken by Jesus are given and translated: cry from the cross (Mark 15, 34), raising the 'sleeping' child (Mark 5, 41), respect due to parents (Mark 7, 11), naming of James and John (Mark 3, 17) and prayer at Gethsemane (Mark 14, 36). There is also a name 'Bartimaeus' translated as 'son of Timaeus' (Mark 10, 46). Where in these instances the other gospels have equivalent passages, the original Aramaic sayings are left out. This indeed supports the idea that Mark was the earliest Christian gospel and was written in Greek for a Greek audience, utilising sometimes directly quoted Aramaic source material. Among this material, we have suggested, was a Jewish Nazorean account of the crucifixion intimating that Jesus had survived. The author also used a Greek source, Paul's account (1 Corinthians 11, 23–26) of a eucharist meal, and this was also followed by the other synoptic gospel writers. John, however, incorporated the reference as a saying by Jesus.

In the Old Syriac version of Mark, the quotations in Aramaic are, except in one instance, left out. Because Old Syriac is just a dialect of Aramaic, the wording of the Greek rendered into Old Syriac and the Aramaic quoted word or phrase would have been the same or very nearly the same. Saying the same thing in the same language twice, one apparently as a translation of the other, would have appeared nonsensical. So this does not happen; the words attributed to Jesus are simply given in Syriac. Here, for example is the Old Syriac Sinaiticus version of the healing of the deaf man:

And he held him back from the crowd and put his fingers and spat into his ears and touched his tongue. And he gazed into the heavens and sighed and said to him, 'Be opened!'

There are two ways that the difference between the Greek and the Old Syriac for these particular passages in Mark could have originated. Either these sayings came from an early Greek text, quoting Aramaic, and the quotes attributed to Jesus were then eliminated in translating back to Syriac. Or the quotes in Aramaic were inserted, to add authenticity and dramatic emphasis, in going from Aramaic to Greek. However, the Aramaic quotes only appear in Mark, the earliest of the gospels. This argues for an original version of Mark in Greek, using Aramaic, possibly Nazorean, sources for the passion and other narrative. Following that, the gospels of Matthew and Luke may have been composed in Aramaic, chiefly because they were taking large amounts of text from a collection or collections of sayings (Q from Quelle for source) attributed to Jesus and written in Aramaic. But these gospels also used Mark as a source. They lost the quotations, in going from Greek to Aramaic, for the very same reason that the Old Syriac versions of Mark did the same.

The original Aramaic gospels of Matthew and Luke would have been required, very soon after their composition, for gentile Christians in Greece and Rome. So these were swiftly translated as a whole into Greek.

It is interesting that one significant saying attributed to Jesus in Matthew used an Aramaic word which was faithfully reproduced in Greek, but has subsequently been mistranslated or misunderstood. In the sentence, 'Blessed are you, Simon Bariona (Matthew 16, 17), Simon's surname is treated as 'son of Jona'. This is unlikely and the more straightforward explanation is that this comes from 'bariona' meaning 'outlaw' in Aramaic. Hence, the nickname, 'Simon the outlaw'.

The assumption might subsequently have been easy to make, given that 'bar' does mean 'son of' in Aramaic. But Iona or Jona is not comprehensible in Aramaic. Furthermore, if this part is Greek in origin, it is hardly appropriate for the name of a father. It has a feminine ending.

It seems that 'bariona' was translated either by someone with limited understanding of Aramaic, or by someone who did realise what the word probably meant but wished to disguise its meaning.

We suggest that, in some of the Greek versions, Jona was given a given a consonant ending, to eliminate the feminine form. This was then reproduced as 'Simon bar Jonah' (John 1, 42) and 'Simon bar Yonan' (John 21, 15, ff) in the Syriac. At some point, a Greek interpreter decided that 'Yonan' must have come from the Hebrew 'Yohanan', so that the same references in John are rendered in the Greek New Testament as 'Simon son of John'.

As this indicates, there was considerable interplay in going from one language to another. Aramaic speakers gained a translation from the original Greek gospel of Mark at around the same time that the sayings gospels of Matthew and Luke were translated into Greek. It was at this point that the quotations in Mark were lost in text that would become the basis of the Old Syriac gospels.

The one exception to the absence of the quotations in the Old Syriac versions of Mark is the reference to the blind beggar who was the son of Timaeus. This exception does in fact provide powerful support for the idea of transmission from Greek to Old Syriac, in the case of Mark. The version in the Old Syriac Sinaiticus exemplifies the type of nonsense that can occur, in translating a whole passage with a quotation, which is not clearly signposted, back into the original language in which the quotation was made.

The text in the Greek reads, 'the son of Timaeus, Bartimaeus, a blind beggar was sitting by the roadside' (Mark 10, 46). The writer of Mark is clearly giving for his readers a translation in Greek of what he perceives to be an Aramaic name. But, in this instance, he gives no alert that he is offering a translation by saying, as in other cases, 'which means' or 'that is'. To be both clear and consistent, he should have written, 'A blind beggar Bartimaeus, that is the son of Timaeus, was sitting by the roadside. He defines the beggar, though without actually mentioning his name, through his relationship to his father Timaeus.

The translator of this passage, aware that sons often took their fore-names from their fathers and missing a prompt, subsequently failed to read the passage properly and rendered it in Syriac as 'Timaeus, the son of Timeus (sic), was blind and sitting by the way and begging.' It is understandable how this could have happened, in going from Greek to Syriac. It is hard to generate a sensible theory for a mistake occurring in going the other way, from Syriac to Greek, particularly as the passage in Greek is consistent with other usages of quotations in Mark where the Aramaic word is given together with a translation into Greek.

Some progress has been made. There is now an explanation for the gospels existing in parallel versions in Greek and Aramaic, reading the same in considerable detail but with some mistakes in the Greek in rendering Aramaic source material and omissions or errors in generating a Syriac version of Mark. The gospel of John may have followed a similar course to the gospels of Matthew and Luke, though a little later and with some independent source material.

The Greek versions were subsequently collated into a Greek New Testament which became the official text for the Church of the Roman Empire. The Aramaic gospels were transmitted into a parallel Old Syriac New Testament. For a number of connected reasons, few copies of the latter have survived. Greek was first of all the language of Empire and thus the language of the early Church. It could have been expected that groups of followers, wherever they were located, would understand and use Greek texts.

Another contributory factor was a period of persecution initiated under the Emperor Diocletian from 296 CE, involving the destruction of churches and the burning of Christian books. This was carried out more thoroughly and persisted longer in the eastern part of the Empire, where Syriac texts might have been used. Christianity was subsequently tolerated and then elevated to an official religion. Under Constantine, Bishop Eusebius was commissioned in 331 CE to produce 50 new copies of the scriptures for the Emperor's new capital, according to a letter from the Emperor that Eusebius quotes.

If the 'scriptures' required were complete bibles, this would seem rather a large number for one city. But, even if the scale has in this case been exaggerated or imperfectly conveyed, this order and others subsequently like it would have helped to make up for books previously destroyed. Production on a substantial scale, and with central control, would have helped to ensure that the bibles were consistent and conveyed the then current orthodoxy. The Old Syriac gospels did, of course differ, and in some ways which might have been regarded as an affront to the developing view of Jesus' family. So their promulgation may not at the time have been encouraged, and the Greek versions may have been promoted instead.

Some elements from a very early Aramaic text may have survived into the Old Syriac and some other manuscripts (see 'Wine and bread', p 341).

The Peshitta by contrast closely follows the Greek, and appears therefore to have been a translation made in response to later demands by the Eastern Church for a copy of the official scriptures in Syriac, the language of many of its people.

While Greek and Aramaic/Syriac were the main mediums of transmission, there are some words which may be Hebrew in origin.

Skull or stone press

We have suggested that the gospel of Mark was first written in Greek for an audience of Paul's followers, using Nazorean source material, and that Matthew and Luke were written in Aramaic/Syriac, perhaps primarily because there was substantial input from a large body of sayings attributed to Jesus. At this time, in the first century CE, it is believed that Aramaic was the common language of Palestine and many other parts of the Middle East. Hebrew, the language of the Torah, was a religious medium used by and for Jews. It was not widely spoken or understood, so that even Jews in the Mediterranean diaspora had been provided with a translation of the Torah, the Septuagint, from Hebrew into Greek.

There are a few words which appear to have a Hebrew origin in the gospels. One of the twelve appointed by Jesus is described in Mark (3, 18) as 'Simon the Cananean' while Luke (6, 16) describes the same character as 'Simon who was called the zealot'. It appears that the description originated from the Hebrew word 'cana', meaning zealot, which the author of Mark either failed to understand or deliberately misrepresented, either way based on the knowledge that there was a place called Cana in Galilee. In these instances, the Old Syriac versions of the gospels follow the usages in Mark and Matthew.

Another significant word that may have a Hebrew origin is Golgotha, the site of the crucifixion. John describes this as a Hebrew name ('which is called in Hebrew Golgotha'), meaning 'the place of a skull'. Mark and Matthew provide the same description, 'Golgotha' and the same meaning in Greek, 'the place of a skull'. Luke just gives the place name, 'Golgotha'.

However, the nearest written Hebrew equivalent (remembering there are no vowels) would be 'glglth' which means 'skull', not 'place of a skull'. Golgotha (glgth) in Hebrew would mean 'stone press', more convincing for the name of a garden (see Chapter 8) in or near to which Jesus was crucified.

It could be argued that the author or editor of John got it wrong and should have indicated that Golgotha was an Aramaic rather than a Hebrew word. But Golgotha also relates imperfectly to the Aramaic, Gulgalta, which means 'skull' and not 'place of a skull'.

The Old Syriac version of Mark departs from its practice of eliminating repetitions for quotations evidently in Aramaic, and follows the Greek format 'which translated is, the skull'. So clearly here 'Golgotha' was not recognised as the Aramaic for 'skull'.

Wine and bread

As has been shown, investigating the path along which the gospels evolved is complicated by the practice of compilers in making alterations in the light of comparisons between different gospels and different versions of the same gospel. Such a process may explain evidence which apparently contradicts the case that Matthew and Luke had an Aramaic origin, while Mark was first written in Greek.

The creation of the 'last supper' in the gospels illustrates elements of comparison and copying.

This, in outline, was first generated as a description by Paul of a ritual that he and his Christian sect had adopted, amalgamating Mithraic ritual with Jewish customs of breaking bread and drinking wine with blessings during a meal. Mark, writing later, projected the words attributed to Jesus (in a vision to Paul) into a Passover meal eaten by Jesus and his disciples. Mark closely follows the sequence and the wording given by Paul. The bread is blessed, broken and offered round with the words 'this is my body'. Then a cup of wine is blessed and passed round with the statement that it is 'my blood' representing a 'new covenant'. The same applies to Matthew, whose text follows Mark.

Luke departs from the other two synoptic authors in recognising one difference between practice for a normal Jewish meal and the seder, the celebratory Passover meal (Luke 22 17–20). At the seder, the wine is blessed first, and the first cup drunk before the bread is broken. He has Mark as a source for the narrative incorporating the ritual, including the vow or affirmation not to drink wine. But he reverses the sequence of bread and wine:

> *Then he took a cup and, having given thanks, he said, 'Take this and share it among yourselves. For I say to you that, from now on, I may not drink of the fruit of the vine until the kingdom of God comes.' Then he took bread and, having given thanks, he broke it and gave it to them, saying, 'This is my body, which is given for you. Do this in my memory.'*
>
> *And, after they had eaten, he did the same with the cup, saying, 'This cup is the new covenant in my blood being shed for you.'*

What is odd about this version, in the early Greek including **P**75 from the late second or early third century, is that the wine appears to have been offered twice. However, it may be that the second offering of wine was not originally in Luke but added later.

This is supported by the fact that the fifth century Codex Bezae, which is thought to have had some Syriac/Aramaic input, ends this passage with the words, 'this is my body'. A number of Latin manuscripts also follow Codex Bezae in this respect.

The Old Syriac follows the Greek, avoiding a repetition by removing the element of offering and the reference to a cup. So, Jesus is given to say after the meal, 'This, my blood is the new covenant.'

We suggest that there may have been an Aramaic/Old Syriac original for Luke that, because the author was familiar with Jewish practice at Passover, had the offerings in the order of wine and then bread. Mark, originally in Greek, and Matthew followed the order that developed in Christian ritual. Luke in its early version could have ended with 'this is my body', omitting the reference to a new covenant.

This was, however, remedied very early on, reflecting a widening split between the Nazorean Jews[1] and early Christians. The references to sacrifice and to a new covenant were inserted by the simple expedient of running on text, directly from 1 Corinthians 11, 23–25, to conclude the passage in Luke. A side effect is that, in the amended text, the cup is now offered twice.

On this view, Codex Bezae and some other manuscripts have, in the eucharist sequence in Luke, reproduced an element of an Aramaic/Old Syriac text from very early times.

History and text

As we have seen, the process of trying to make the gospels conform does also provide an explanation for the counter-indications of a

Syriac original for Mark and a Greek original for Matthew and Luke.

The mistake of using 'robes' instead of 'porches' in Mark may have originated when the gospel was originally compiled in Greek from Aramaic sources. Mark was written with Aramaic quotes and translations but largely lost them when the gospel was translated back into Aramaic. The Aramaic version was ultimately incorporated into the Syriac version of the gospels. But a Syriac writer, who possibly had access to original Aramaic sayings (since lost), recognised in making a comparison that the Greek author of Mark had made a mistake. So he corrected, in creating the copy of Mark which has survived in the Old Syriac (Sinaiticus palimpsest), reinstating 'porches' instead of 'robes'.

It was argued earlier that the references in the Greek gospels to Mary ( ) of James, Mary ( ) of Joseph and Mary ( ) of James and Joseph/ Joses had to be to the mother of these brothers, and therefore of Jesus, to be consistent with other gospel references, including one (Matthew 13, 55) in the Old Syriac. It is also possible to see how an error or falsification could easily have originated in going from the Greek text to the Old Syriac, though not the other way round. But this conflicts with the evidence indicating that Matthew and Luke originated in Aramaic/Old Syriac.

The discrepancy arose, we suggest, at a point where the cult of Mary was being developed. It was recognised that it might be interpreted that Jesus' mother was present at the scene of the crucifixion, but this could not be contemplated if it entailed her also being mother of James and Joseph. That would conflict with the doctrine of her 'perpetual' virginity.

The solution was to interpret all the passages in the Greek, where the relationship was not specified, as 'daughter of' rather then 'mother of', notwithstanding the inconsistency this then created with other text. When an Old Syriac version of the gospels came to notice that spelled out 'mother of James', it was decided that this had to be in error, a misreading of the Greek, and 'mother of James' was systematically changed to 'daughter of James' throughout. There was a problem of course with the one reference to 'mother of Joseph' in Mark, since Mary could not be the daughter of both James and of Joseph. So the amender was forced, as an alternative to recognising the fallacy in what he was doing, to alter this in the Syriac to 'daughter of James' as well!

The original words may have been scratched out and the changes written in, or the changes made in copying the manuscript as a whole. The original was however destroyed or lost.

Surviving Old Syriac texts from the fourth century cannot be taken as fully representing an Old Syriac/Aramaic original, of say Matthew from perhaps the early second century, any more than it could be argued that Codex Sinaiticus represents the first Greek version of Mark. In both instances, considerable change is possible and indicated in an intervening period of some two and a half centuries.

It is nevertheless possible to offer a working model of how the gospels may have originated and evolved. Mark was first written in Greek for followers of Paul who had abandoned his efforts to ingratiate himself with the Nazoreans. He set up a rival sect instead, gaining ground among gentiles and some of the 'god fearers' among diasporan Jews. His movement adapted the rituals and ideas of Mithraism, in gaining followers from among this sect.

Mark used as a source a Nazorean account of the crucifixion and some Aramaic sayings, as well as Paul's account of the eucharist. When the Jewish messianic movement was crushed in the first Jewish revolt, the Nazorean block to the sect's progress among Aramaic speakers was removed. New versions of the gospel (Matthew and Luke) were created in Aramaic, using a body of sayings in Aramaic attributed to Jesus and the original Greek version of Mark. In the case of John, there may also have been a separate Aramaic source for the passion sequence. These gospels were translated into Greek and the original Mark was likewise translated into Aramaic. Errors, elaboration and interpretation led to variations and there were also efforts to make the texts conform. The various versions were attributed to different authors and so gained their current names.

Two bodies of four gospels, in Greek and Old Syriac (a dialect of Aramaic), were collated and existed alongside each other. Roman persecution at the beginning of the fourth century led to many of the Greek copies of the gospels being destroyed and almost all the Old Syriac versions used in the East.

New copies were prepared in Greek under Eusebius a few years later and an effort was made to make surviving Old Syriac gospels consistent with Church doctrine. But it may have been evident that this was not entirely a success. So, instead a translation was made of the new Greek text into Syriac. This became the Peshitta, the version still used by the Eastern Church. Though the earlier Old Syriac was proscribed, some incomplete copies (the Sinaiticus palimpsest and the Curetonianus) have survived.

The Greek gospels came to dominate, as far as the Christian Church was concerned. The original followers of Jesus and James were not able to contest changes to their version of Judaism, broadly within the mainstream, which had Jesus as fully human, though endowed with prophetic powers by God (Epiphanius writing on the Ebionites). Their ability to do this was greatly reduced as a result of the destruction of the temple in Jerusalem, widespread social disruption and loss of life that were a consequence of the failed Jewish revolt in 70 CE.

But this form of Judaism did not disappear immediately. Communities of Nazoreans and later Ebionites ('poor' ones) have been identified as persisting for centuries in places like Perea in Palestine. According to Irenaeus, writing in the second century, the Ebionites used only the gospel of Matthew. This accords with what was written later by Epiphanius in the fourth century in his *Panarion* on heresies. Epiphanius gives a number of quotes from this gospel 'according to Matthew' that the Ebionites used.

Epiphanius saw it as 'false and mutilated', this latter partly because it began with the introduction of John the baptiser, missing out at the beginning the genealogy of Jesus, the nativity story, flight to Egypt and the argument that 'Nazarene' (used later in the text and in Mark) really meant 'someone from Nazareth' (see Chapter 8) . It is also very possible, given that the use of a form of Matthew is attested early for the Ebionites, that the version without all this material is more original.

Eusebius, writing in the fourth century, stated that the Ebionites used only a gospel 'according to the Hebrews', by which it would seem he meant a gospel by or for Jews. All the early patristic sources agree that the Ebionites relied on only one gospel. There is the implication, for all these observations to be consistent, that this one gospel was a version of Matthew (in fact a forerunner of Matthew), used by Jews.

This use of 'Hebrew' to mean 'Jew' or 'Jewish' is also what appears to be at root of the earliest witness, Papias in the early second century, who wrote that 'Matthew composed the sayings in the Hebrew dialect and each one interpreted them as he was able'. The commonly used 'Hebrew', that is Jewish, dialect was of course Aramaic. And this is the language in which it has been argued (see above) that the gospel of Matthew was first written. Irenaeus made the point in this way, that 'Matthew also issued a written Gospel among the Hebrews (that is, Jews) in their own dialect'.

Furthermore, Jerome (fourth century) adds the information that the writing in the gospel of the Hebrews was in Hebrew script but the language used was Chaldee and Syriac, both variants of Aramaic.

There is a degree of convergence between this historical evidence and the analysis made on the basis of the text. The gospel of Matthew, we have suggested, used a very early version of Mark, written in Greek but itself using an Aramaic source, for much of its narrative including the passion sequence. It was written in Aramaic using a collection of sayings, which were also in Aramaic, as a second source.

In its prototype form, Matthew may not have had the nativity story and other material at the beginning. It may also, like Mark without 16, 9–20, have had no account of a miraculous raising from the dead or ascension into heaven.

There is one passage however, quoted by Jerome from the gospel according to the Hebrews, that does suggest supernatural resurrection rather than physical survival. This is when Jesus, after giving up his burial cloth, went to James and shared food with him. Jesus is quoted as saying, 'My brother, eat your bread, for the son of man is risen from them that sleep.' This oddly echoes the non-canonical gospel of Peter when Jesus is asked by a voice from the heavens if he has 'preached to them that sleep'. This is just after he has been helped from the tomb by two men supporting him (which suggests, alternatively, rescue and survival).

These accounts, as they have come down to us, do have some very prosaic elements mixed in with the supernatural. If, notwithstanding the burial cloth passage quoted by Jerome, the prototype Matthew did cast Jesus as a great prophet but not a divine being (how, according to Epiphanius, the Ebionites regarded him), then this could have provided common ground for the Nazorean Jews and Paul's first followers. The central disagreement between the two groups would then have been over the question of how much of Jewish Law and custom gentiles should have to follow; in fact, just as it is described in Acts and Paul's letter to the Galatians.

The gentile movement expanded, taking on not just the former adherents of Mithraism, but also in some instances their buildings and ritual practices. Jesus was absorbed into the central role that had been taken by Mithras. At this stage, a number of supernatural elements were added to the story, possibly in the first translation of Matthew from Aramaic to Greek.

In the meantime, the Nazoreans and the later Ebionite followers of James retained a gospel that lacked these elements and had Jesus as a special prophet, appointed by God. Deemed by Christians and then by Jews as heretical, these groups were squeezed out of existence and their writings prohibited, to survive only through quotations.

References

Bellinzoni A J, *The Two-Source Hypothesis: a Critical Appraisal*, Mercer University Press, 1985

British Library, National Library of Russia, St Catherine's Monastery, Leipzig University Library, *Codex Sinaiticus*, published online, 2009

Canart P, Bogaert P M and Pisano S (contributors), *Bibliorum Sacrorum Graecorum Codex Vaticanus B*, vol I facsimile text, vol 2 Prolegomena: essays and index, Istituto Poligrafico e Zecca delo Strato, 1999

Colwell E C, *Method in Evaluating Scribal Habits: a Study of P45, P66 and P75*, Eerdmans, 1969

Comfort P W and Barrett D P, *The Text of the Earliest New Testament Greek Manuscripts*, Tyndale House, 2001

Cresswell P A, *Censored Messiah*, O Books, 2004

Cresswell P A, *Jesus the Terrorist*, O Books, 2010

Cresswell P A, *The Women who Went to the Tomb*, The Heretic, vol 3, 2013

Crossan J D, *The Historical Jesus*, T and T Clark, 1991

Dain, A, *Les Manuscrits*, Les Belles Lettres, 1975

Ehrman B D, *Misquoting Jesus*, HarperCollins, 2007

Eisenman R, *Paul as Herodian*, Institute for Jewish-Christian Origins, 1996

Eisenman R, *The Dead Sea Scrolls and the First Christians*, Element Books, 1996

Eisenman R, *James, the Brother of Jesus*, Faber and Faber, 1997

Eisenman R, *The New Testament Code*, Watkins, 2006

Howard G, *Hebrew Gospel of Matthew*, Mercer University Press, 1995

Jongkind D, *Scribal Habits of Codex Sinaiticus*, Gorgias Press, 2007

Kiraz G A, *Comparative Edition of the Syriac Gospels*, E J Brill, 1996

Kirby P, *Early Christian Writings*, published online, 2001–2011

Maccoby H, *The Myth Maker*, Weidenfeld and Nicolson, 1986

Metzger B M, *Manuscripts of the Greek Bible: an Introduction to Palaeography*, Oxford University Press, 1981

Metzger B M, *The Text of the New Testament: its Transmission, Corruption, and Restoration*, Oxford University Press, 1992

Metzger B M and Ehrman B D, *The Text of the New Testament: its Transmission, Corruption, and Restoration*, Oxford University Press, 2005

Milne H J M and Skeat T C, *Scribes and Correctors of the Codex Sinaiticus*, British Museum, 1938

Morton Smith, *The Secret Gospel*, Harper and Row, 1973, Dawn Horse Press, 2005

Nestle E, Aland B, Aland K, *Novum Testamentum Graece*, 27th edition, Hendrickson, 1993

Parker D C, *Codex Bezae: an Early Christian Manuscript and its Text*, Cambridge University Press, 1992

Parker D C, *An Introduction to the New Testament Manuscripts and their Texts*, Cambridge University Press, 2008

Parker D C, *Codex Sinaiticus: the Story of the World's Oldest Bible*, British Library, 2010

Payne P B and Canart P, *The Originality of Text-Critical Symbols in Codex Vaticanus*, Novum Testamentum, vol 42, 2000, pp 105–113

Reed R, *Ancient Skins, Parchments and Leathers*, Academic Press, 1973

Skeat T C, *The Use of Dictation in Ancient Book Production*, Proceedings of the British Academy, 1956

Skeat T C, *The Codex Vaticanus in the Fifteenth Century*, Journal of Theological Studies, vol 35 (2), 1984, pp 454–465

Skeat T C, *The Oldest Manuscript of the Four Gospels?* New Testament Studies, vol 43, 1997, pp 1–34

Skeat T C, *The Codex Sinaiticus, the Codex Vaticanus and Constantine*, Journal of Theological Studies, vol 50 (2), 1999, pp 583–625

Snapp J E, *The Authenticity of Mark 16: 9–20*, published online, 2007

Streeter B H, *The Four Gospels: a Study of Origins*, Macmillan, 1924

Tindall C, *Contributions to the Statistical Study of the Codex Sinaiticus*, Oliver and Boyd, 1961

Tischendorf A F C, *Novum Testamentum Sinaiticus*, Brockhaus, 1863

Tischendorf A F C, *Novum Testamentum Graece*, 1865

Tregelles S P, *A Lecture on the Historical Evidence of the Authorship and Transmission of the Books of the New Testament*, 1852

Tregelles S P, *An Introduction to the Textual Criticism of the New Testament*, 1856

Westcott B F and Hort F J A, *An Introduction to the Study of the Gospels*, 1860

Westcott B F and Hort F J A, *Introduction to the New Testament in the Original Greek*, Harper Brothers, 1882, reprinted by Hendrickson, 1988

Wilson E J and Kiraz GA, *The Old Syriac Gospels*, Gorgias Press, 2003

Notes

Introduction

1   This question is touched on at a number of points in Robert Eisenman's *James the Brother of Jesus* and dealt with more directly in his article *Paul as Herodian*. See also *Jesus the Terrorist*, pp 140–154.
2   See *Jesus the Terrorist*, pp 221–232.
3   See *Jesus the Terrorist*, pp 26–53, 232–242.

Chapter 1

1   See *Jesus the Terrorist*, pp 338–340, 395–401.
2   See *Jesus the Terrorist*, pp 355–361.

Chapter 2

1   Note that, for the convenience of the non-Greek reader, we are using basic English translations, while conscious of the continuing debate over semantic ranges and equivalence.
2   Column width is, strictly speaking, a physical measurement. But the column width puts a limit on the number of characters, of a particular size and style, that can be included in a line. It does thus relate to the average number of characters per line.
3   We use the term 'exemplar', rather than 'original' to refer to the text from which a scribe made his copy. This is because the biblical text written by an original author is rarely, if ever, available. What usually survive are copies of copies, at many removes from any presumed, original source.
4   Or homioarctons. See following text.

Chapter 3

1   See *Codex Sinaiticus* by D C Parker, p 50. Our view, following Jongkind's analysis of the cooperation between the scribes in the Old Testament (see pp 47–49), is that the scribes operated more as colleagues. The idea that scribe D was more senior loses some

force against the conclusion that his interventions in the New Testament reflected an alternation of work between the scribes (see Chapters 11 and 12).

2 This is the how the bibles were produced according to Eusebius' own account. But see also note 1 to Chapter 6.

3 Stephen does not appear to have been a historical character, given that there is no reference to him outside of Acts. Eisenman suggests that he may have been stand-in for James, whose death was a subject too hot for the early Church to handle. See *James the Brother of Jesus*.

4 See *Ancient Skins, Parchments and Leathers* by Ronald Reed, p 120.

Chapter 4

1 See *Jesus the Terrorist*, pp 35–36.

2 Codex Vaticanus has the text in full and EIT EN in both places.

3 Although the scribes wrote text in blocks, there did appear to be some working rules in going from one line to the next. For example, consonants usually went with a following vowel to begin the next line and compound words were usually divided into their component parts. See *Manuscripts of the Greek Bible* by Bruce Metzger. Our own analysis suggests that there was also a tendency to complete words on a line, where this would not have added greatly to the number of characters in the line, as against the average. The impact of these factors on the frequency with which skip errors might come at the end of a line in the copy by chance is difficult to calculate.

4 These errors, repeated in Codex Vaticanus, are discussed further on pp 105–108.

We decided in advance what criteria to use in defining, identifying and counting skip errors. Having established that an exemplar for Sinaiticus may also have had the same average line length, it is interesting to look back at individual instances in this light. For example, in Matthew 19, 26 (H11) the word for 'men' is abbreviated in the correction of the skip error. While there is no earlier papyrus source for this passage, in Codex Vaticanus the word is written out in full as ΑΝΘΡWΠΟΙC. If this were also the case in the exemplar for Sinaiticus, then the skip error could be assigned as 13 characters instead of 9 characters. Selective interpretation, such as this, would not however add to the weight of proof.

5   There is further support for the case that Ca was the scriptorium corrector from the fact that the scribe for Codex Vaticanus, a document closely related in time, appears at points to recognise and make use of Ca's corrections. See Chapter 5, p 113.

Ca will crop up frequently in our analysis as a profuse corrector of the text. We could (but will not) couple this each time with a qualification that, on the evidence and as the best explanation, he (or she) must have been the scriptorium corrector. We shall simply describe him as the scriptorium corrector and take this as read.

Chapter 5

1   While scribe A wrote most in Mark in Sinaiticus, the last page was written by scribe D. It was the custom for the last scribe working on a particular chapter to sign it off. See Chapters 11 and 12 for the transition from Mark to Luke.

2   Constantin Tischendorf was the first to propose the idea of a scribe common to the two codices. But we agree with Milne and Skeat that Tischendorf's identification of scribe D with hand B was incorrect.

3   Our conclusion that Isaiah must have been copied from a separate exemplar, with an average line length more in line with Codex Vaticanus itself, is in line with Bruce Metzger's observation concerning the varying content of this book. See *Manuscripts of the Greek Bible: An Introduction to Palaeography*, p 74.

4   This passage is also omitted in Codex Bezae which suggests that this codex may have used Codex Vaticanus or a copy derived from Vaticanus as a source.

5   This is a contentious point in the text in that Jesus, in successive sentences, is described as arriving in Jericho and then leaving Jericho. As there is nothing describing what happened there, this may indicate that something has been omitted from an earlier exemplar. There is in fact text describing events in Jericho, quoted in a letter attributed to Clement (Secret Mark), the authenticity of which is subject to dispute.

It could be that the Vaticanus scribe saw the lack of sense in the text, and decided to deal with it by eliminating 'And they came to Jericho'. The Vaticanus corrector observed that the phrase was in the exemplar and so put it back.

6   It may be that Ca correctly saw the passage as a harmonisation with John 19, 20. On the other hand, the passage may have been in scribe A's exemplar with as good a claim that it was ultimately the source for the version in John.

7   See Ernst Colwell's, *Method in Evaluating Scribal Habits: a Study of P45, P66 and P75.*

Chapter 6

1   There is some doubt concerning the meaning of what Eusebius says he did. It has even been suggested that the 'threes and fours' sent to Constantine meant bibles in either three columns like Codex Vaticanus or four columns like Codex Sinaiticus. Skeat's interpretation of batches of three and four copies remains the best hypothesis.

Chapter 7

1   What may be nearer to historical reality is that the followers of Jesus and James were in opposition to the High Priest's faction among the Sadducees; see *Jesus the Terrorist*, pp 338–340.

2   Many of these arguments can be found in *The Two-Source Hypothesis: a Critical Appraisal* edited by Arthur Bellinzoni and are also set out in Peter Kirby's online resource, *Early Christian Writings.*

3   This is not to say that Mark describes a custom that ever existed or that his description clearly conveys who the prisoner was; see for example *Jesus the Terrorist*, pp 235–236.

4   This example is taken from *Misquoting Jesus* by Bart Ehrman, pp 133–139.

5   See *Jesus the Terrorist*, pp 341–348.

6   Eusebius in his *Ecclesiastical History* quotes an early, first century source Papias, on the origins of these two gospels. As Papias is quoted, it could be taken to mean that either Matthew collected sayings (oracles) or that he organised sayings 'in the Hebrew language'. It may be that, rather than Hebrew, what was meant here was the language of the 'Hebrews' which for everyday purposes was Aramaic. Irenaeus (second century) reports that

Matthew's gospel for the Jews was written in 'their language'. The reported statement by Papias could be taken to indicate that Matthew collected sayings separately or that he edited sayings in Mark or both.

7   Translators thus have to make a sensible adjustment. For example, Victor Hugo in writing on William Shakespeare quotes from Robert Greene's pamphlet attacking the playwright (as a 'crow' and then as a 'tiger') for plagiarism and for being a mere actor with the temerity to write plays. 'Shakespeare est promu tigre. Voice le texte: *tyger's heart wrapt in a player's hide.* Coeur de tigre caché sous la peau d'un comédien.' (*A Groatsworth of Wit,* 1592.) Translated into English this should be, 'Shakespeare is promoted to a tiger. Here is the text: tyger's heart wrapt in a player's hide. Tyger's heart wrapt in a player's hide.' Of course, in the English editions the repetition is eliminated. Just as it would have been for quotes in Aramaic in a Greek Mark, used as a source for an (initially) Aramaic Matthew.

8   Just such confusion did creep in with Bartimaeus in the Old Syriac, a variation of Aramaic; see Appendix X, p 337.

9   A summary of the evidence in respect of the early use of Aramaic in these gospels is set out in Appendix X.

10   According to Mark, John the Baptist criticised Herod Antipas for marrying his brother's wife, Herodias, who had divorced her husband Herod (Philip, in the gospels). Another objection could have been that Herodias was their niece. Jewish fundamentalist groups like the Essenes objected to the Herodian practice of uncle–niece marriage, in their eyes a category of 'fornication'.

Chapter 8

1   See *Censored Messiah,* pp 69–70.

2   For a discussion of the role of Paul, see chapter 5 of *Jesus the Terrorist,* pp 97–155 and also pp 84–86, 92–95 and 190–192.

3   The Old Testament prophecy (Micah 5, 2) was that a future ruler of Israel would come from Bethlehem, traditionally the birthplace of King David. So, the author of Luke created a fiction whereby people were required to return to their ancestral homes for the purposes of a Roman census. This was to get Joseph and Mary from where they were in the north in Galilee to the south in Bethlehem so that Jesus could be born there. No matter that

the census in question took place some 12 years after Jesus' birth, or that such a disruptive and preposterously ill-defined arrangement would ever have been contemplated by the Romans. See *Censored Messiah*, pp 81–82.

4 See, for example, *Jesus the Terrorist*, pp 376–82.

5 Zealous groups were at this time advocating strict adherence to the Law but, according to Eisenman, were phrasing this in terms of creating a new and stricter covenant. The idea was borrowed by Paul but its meaning and context were changed. See *The New Testament Code*, pp 975–990, et al.

6 See *James the Brother of Jesus* by Robert Eisenman, pp 310–408 and *Jesus the Terrorist*, pp 73–95.

7 Hyam Maccoby in *The Myth Maker* p 125 and Peter Cresswell in *Jesus the Terrorist*, pp 231–232 provide explanations of what the Nazoreans claimed or believed; in neither case does this involve a Christian conception of Jesus as divine.

8 See, for example, *Jesus the Terrorist*, pp 185–186.

9 See *James the Brother of Jesus* by Robert Eisenman, pp 310–312.

10 To illustrate the extent to which these words were used interchangeably, in Mark 14, 67 (the story of Peter's denial), the word that is used is 'Nazarene' (NAZAPHNOY). In Matthew 26, 71, which tells the same story, the word is 'Nazorean' (NAZωPAIOY) (source: Codex Sinaiticus). The current critical text, however, renders both of these as if the scribe had written 'from Nazareth' (AΠO NAZAPET)!

11 These two genealogies going back to King David and beyond establish messianic credentials for – in the original context – a contender for the throne of Israel. But, while the one in Luke relates to Jesus, the one in Matthew on closer analysis appears to have related to Mary. The wife of a king of Israel might, not unreasonably, have been expected to have the right credentials. See *Jesus the Terrorist*, pp 399–400.

12 There are some strong parallels between the organisation of the Essenes as described by Josephus and that of the Nazoreans under James (see *Jesus the Terrorist*, pp 74–78). This would suggest that the two groups were related, if not identical, and it would account for Epiphanius using both terms in describing the antecedents of Christians. The labels applied to different groups may at times have had something to do with the standpoint of the observer. If Essenes and Nazoreans/Nazarenes were entirely distinct groups existing at the same time, then it might be expected that major

contemporaneous sources would have had had had something to say about both. Yet the gospels and Acts refer to Nazarenes/ Nazoreans but fail to mention the Essenes, while Josephus goes into considerable detail on the Essenes but says nothing about the Nazarenes. This is excepting the reference in *Antiquities* to 'Nazirites' whose ritual observances Herod Agrippa funded on coming to power.

There is thus a case that the two groups were one and the same.

13   The fourth century Church apologist Jerome sought to portray the brothers of Jesus, mentioned in Mark and Matthew, as really cousins. See *Jesus the Terrorist*, p 16 and pp 42–48.

14   See *Jesus the Terrorist*, pp 25–53, 306–309, 388–393.

15   The term 'zealot' goes back to the declaration of Mattathias, who took his followers into the desert to fight a guerrilla war against the Persian King Antiochus, 'Let everyone who supports the covenants and is zealous for the Law come out with me!' See *Censored Messiah*, p 70 and *Jesus the Terrorist*, p 37.

16   For example, in Matthew 5, 17–20.

17   'Holy ones' most accurately describes the Greek term Paul used for the Nazarenes (ΑΓΙΟΥC). It is unfortunately translated by 'saints' in the critical text, as derived from the Vulgate Latin 'sancti' for holy or sacred ones. The Latin term has since acquired overtones derived from Christian practices, including bestowing the title on dead persons, that do not have much to do with what was going on in first century Palestine.

18   At an early stage (Acts 4, 4), the number of followers was estimated at five thousand and growing (Acts 6, 1). James is reported as having referred to a very large number of followers in his confrontations with Paul/Saul (Acts 15, 21 and 21, 20–22). When Paul was accused of belonging to the group, it was described as a 'sect' (Acts 24, 5). The Ebionite *Pseudoclementine Recognitions* (chapter 43) describes how 'we who have been very few became, in the course of a few days, more than they.'

19   And perhaps can deduce who specifically she was; see *Jesus the Terrorist*, pp 388–393.

20   The exception to this is where a person's place of origin is used as a stereotype. In the story in Luke 10, 29–37, this is used to good effect where someone from a group maligned by Jews, a Samaritan, is nevertheless the only person to help a man who had been robbed, wounded and abandoned by the roadside.

21 For example: *Simon the Cananean* as in Mark and Matthew, rendered 'called a zealot' in the equivalent apostles list in Luke, from the Aramaic 'cana' which means zealot and is quite possibly also the root of the place name Cana in Galilee; *Mary Magdalene*, from Aramaic 'magdala' meaning 'tower', 'elevated' or 'magnificent', possibly a messianic title for the consort of Jesus, possibly also the root of the place name Migdal in Galilee); *Joseph of Arimathea* in all four gospels, possibly from 'ab Mariah' (Hebrew) or 'ab Mariam' (Aramaic), thus father of Mary (Magdalene); *Simon the leper*, possibly scrambled from Aramaic 'gabara' meaning 'responsible male', in context, in relation to Martha who served at table at Simon's house; *Judas Iscariot*, left in the gospels as an unrelated title, likely to have come from 'sicarius' (Latin), one of the sicarii assassins, and ultimately from the Greek with a sigma and iota simply transposed, and treated by later Christian commentators as meaning from Kerioth. Joseph of Arimathea, innocent of the blood of Jesus (Luke 23, 50), could have been described in this way, resulting in a second, non-existent character *Nicodemus* (from Aramaic or Hebrew for 'innocent' and 'blood'), not present in the synoptics, being misidentified in translation by the author of John.

22 John, in his version, has the same deficiency as Mark with its Nazareth insert: nothing to explain the transition from Nazareth to Capernaum. Luke, possibly with access to Matthew as well as the revised Mark, cut out all references to Capernaum being home to Jesus and his family and pushed forward the action in Capernaum to later in the narrative. He has Jesus coming back from the desert to Nazareth where, to emphasise the distinction, people ask Jesus why he cannot do the miracles he had done in Capernaum 'here also in your own country'. This rather shows up the marks of Luke's cut and patch since it is only later, in Luke's narrative, that Jesus even gets to Capernaum to do any miracles!

23 What the prophecy by Isaiah (9, 1) actually stated was that, just as God had brought affliction in the past on the lands of Zebulun and Naphtali (west of the Sea of Galilee), so he would in the future favour three territories: the east Mediterranean coast (around Caesarea), the land east of the Jordan and Galilee as a whole. Nazareth and Capernaum were close to each other within Galilee and within Zebulun. So, even if Jesus had gone from Nazareth to Capernaum, this move could not be construed as anything other than irrelevant in the context of Isaiah's prophecy.

24 There is an intriguing possibility, though not at all essential to the argument, that Nazareth did not even exist at the time. It has no mention in the Old Testament. There is no record of it outside of the gospels and just a single reference in Acts. The one reference in Mark, the earliest of the gospels, we have argued was retrospectively inserted. Josephus lists all the towns and villages that were defended or fortified, when he was Governor of Galilee and Nazareth is not among them. He also makes no reference to Nazareth anywhere else in his writings.

25 In *Jesus the Terrorist*, the gospels are examined in historical context, for consistency and coherence and in relation to other documentary evidence.

Chapter 9

1 See *Jesus the Terrorist*, pp 161–164.
2 See *Jesus the Terrorist*, pp 173–177.
3 And quite apart from any consideration whether or not it is a rational belief.
4 See *Codex Sinaiticus* by D C Parker, pp 108–109.
5 See *Misquoting Jesus* by Bart Ehrman, pp 158–60.
6 Ehrman is reduced to arguing that the search for an original 'true' text, though difficult, is not insurmountable on the grounds that 'the chain of transmission has to end *somewhere*, ultimately at a manuscript produced either by an author or by a secretarial scribe ... ' (op cit with original italics, pp 210–211).

We cannot reconstruct the originals of the first texts for a period of decades, in some instances even centuries, because the evidence has disappeared. But, if we could, it is likely that we would find text written (or Jewish tales rewritten) in the context of a polemical struggle between a breakaway sect and a broader movement within Judaism in which scoring points, expanding the membership and keeping on the right side of the Romans, rather than historical accuracy, were the prime considerations. We might even find texts written hastily and retrospectively to accommodate the reality 'on the ground', as pagan converts took the initiative and adopted the legend of a Jewish rebel leader into their narrative of the divine Mithras. The *somewhere* that might be arrived is perhaps *something* that cannot be contemplated by those looking at the texts to find support for what they already believe.

7   See *Jesus the Terrorist*, pp 35–36.
8   See note 7 to Chapter 8.

Chapter 10

1   Isaiah 7, 14. See *Censored Messiah*, p 41.
2   There was another son, Levi, it may be of the same Alphaeus. In the story in Mark, he was called from the tax office by Jesus (Mark 2, 14). However, when this story was retold (Matthew 9, 9), this character was simply referred to as Matthew.
3   A similar issue is raised by the references in John to Judas (of) Simon Iscariot (John 6, 71 and 13, 3). This could be taken to indicate that Judas, whose only slightly misrendered sobriquet indicates that he was a member of the sicarii, was the son of someone called Simon whom the gospel authors nowhere else care to mention. Or it could, as suggested in *Jesus the Terrorist*, pp 302–303, be evidence of an alternative scenario in which there was just one character Judas, brother of Jesus and thus as in these references also brother of Simon.
4   See *Jesus the Terrorist*, pp 25–38.
5   Luke 23, 32 provides another example where a text is made to fit in translation. The Greek reads, 'Two other criminals were led away with him to be executed.' Christian translators could not have Jesus represented as a criminal, even if this is what the text said. So this has usually become in translation, 'Two others, who were criminals, were led away ...' Rather than mistranslate, it would be better to add a footnote indicating that the author of Luke was here using terminology that reflected the Roman point of view: Jesus was a criminal agitator in their eyes.
6   But it is possible that modified references to Jesus survive, if the names Joses and Joseph were in their original form references to Jesus himself as opposed to one his brothers. See p 194.
7   Surviving papyrus fragments are missing the endings of Mark and Matthew so that, for these passages, Codex Sinaiticus is the earliest witness.
8   We favour the argument that scribe D introduced a version of the women at the cross in Mark 15, 40, consistent with Ca's changes to Matthew 27, 56, from a source other than the main exemplar used by scribe A. This stems from, and is consistent with, the conclusion that the three sheets written by scribe D in

the New Testament represented an alternation of work between the scribes, as opposed to the correction of one scribe's work by another (see Chapters 11 and 12).

It is also possible that Mark 15, 40 was already changed in the main exemplar. Ca's alteration of Matthew 27, 56, effectively to harmonise with this, would then have amounted to a second stage in the introduction of a modified version of the women at the cross.

9   But something that we believe we have in this book achieved.

10   See also *Jesus the Terrorist*, pp 173-177.

11   See *Jesus the Terrorist*, Appendix I, pp 395–401.

Chapter 11

1   See *Misquoting Jesus* by Bart Ehrman, pp 133–139, and *Jesus the Terrorist*, pp 341–348.

2   See *Jesus the Terrorist*, pp 222–232.

3   James Snapp in *The Authenticity of Mark 16, 9–20* and other commentary online.

4   There is a continuing debate over the authenticity of passages allegedly from an early version of Mark (Secret Mark) contained as references in a letter attributed to Clement, now only existing in photographs with the original believed to be lost.

5   See p 429 of *The Historical Jesus* by Dominic Crossan.

6   Pagan converts may also have brought elements of ritual, including a meal involving wine and bread marked with a cross (see Chapter 6, p 121).

7   There is some evidence for this that will be considered in a subsequent paper.

8   We should be wary of projecting from what we now have to what Eusebius once wrote. He had access to many more copies of Mark than have survived a further seventeen centuries. One or more in the library at Caesarea, among a minority that he saw as less 'accurate', could have had verses beyond 16, 8 that differed from the longer ending that has survived.

9   The variation in column density and its association in some instances with efforts by the scribes either to add more text, or to stretch out text, are discussed further in Chapter 12.

10   Scribe A did certainly repeat a block of text from 1 Chronicles that appears to have got mixed up with 2 Esdras in the manuscript

from which he was copying. This was after an interval of over 60 pages, possibly long enough for the familiarity of the text not to register. The weakness of the postulated dittography however is that, as well as being a rare type of error without a precedent on such a scale, there is actually no direct evidence of it.

11 The 10-line dittography at 1 Thessalonians 2, 13–14 was, for example, dealt with in just this way. This text, preceding the third of scribe D's three sheets and of some interest, is discussed in Chapter 12.

12 How alternation between the scribes explains characteristics of their work is explored for this sheet and the other sheets by scribe D in Chapter 12. Possible reasons for such an arrangement are discussed in Chapter 13.

13 Or even another scribe at some earlier point. See discussion of example h17, Mark 15, 47–16, 1, in Appendix II, p 304.

14 This is just how the author of Matthew, who closely followed Mark, has it. He introduced an interpolation indicating that the tomb was guarded to counter the argument that followers of Jesus must have stolen the body. After the digression, the names of the women, 'Mary Magdalene and the other Mary', had then for clarity to be repeated. But this is essentially the version that it can be argued was superimposed by Ca, possibly more original than the uncorrected version used by scribe D.

15 We cannot at present test this theory further as there are no earlier papyrus texts available for Mark 15, 46–16, 2 and the text from Codex Sinaiticus is, we have argued, the earliest Greek witness.

16 There is no earlier surviving witness than Codex Sinaiticus for these verses, and so nothing to disprove the contention that some of the present text of Luke 1, 1–56 may have been added in at this point. However, it is not necessary for this to have happened, in the theory we develop. See Chapter 12.

17 There is a similar issue of logistics with the first folio of scribe D's sheet in 1 Thessalonians, where the verso has a partially filled column due to the chapter end. Scribe D could have used this space to deal with some of the compression he needed to fit in extra text on the recto, had he looked that far ahead. See Chapter 12, p 247.

18 The evidence indicates that the two codices had a common exemplar, were produced within a short time of each other and could have come from the same scriptorium. The distinctive decorative

signatures at the end of chapters, coronides, suggest that scribe D
may have worked on both. See Chapter 5.

Chapter 12

1   We have used the counts of characters provided in *Contributions
     to the Statistical Study of the Codex Sinaiticus* by Christian Tindall.
     While we have found this to be reasonably accurate, Tindall
     did make occasional small mistakes. Some bigger discrepancies
     may be the result of printer's errors. Thus the full column one of
     Q77F6V has 634 as opposed to 534 characters. We count the last,
     partial column of John as 452 as opposed to 614 characters.

2   There is a likely skip error in Acts 23, 28 in Codex Vaticanus,
     discussed on page 101, corresponding with two lines, each of 13
     characters, in Codex Sinaiticus. This indicates that the common
     exemplar with the same average line length, which we suggest
     the Sinaiticus scribes were following, extended at least to include
     the second part of Acts.

3   The adjustment of text to quires, where it occurs, is indicative
     of a different layout for the copy. The lack of major compression,
     outside of a few locations, indicates that the scribes were for the
     most part able to run on to the next page when text had to be
     added, for example in incorporating marginal corrections and
     notes. Also, the strong association of compression with scribe D's
     sheets argues against a single examplar with precisely the same
     page layout as the copy.

4   In the Old Testament, there is evidence of stretching to fit text
     within a defined space in Judith and, in 4 Maccabees, extra lines
     have been added so that the book occupies a whole quire. See
     Scribal Habits of Codex Sinaiticus by Dirk Jongkind, pp 42–43.

5   The feeding of the four thousand (Mark 8, 9 and 20), **P**45;
     Conversation during the transfiguration (Luke 9, 31–37), **P**45;
     The angels of God (Luke 15, 10), **P**75; Lazarus and the angels
     (Luke 16, 22), **P**75.

6   In Tindall's defence, it has to be said that the book attributed to
     him was published posthumously on the basis of notes that he
     had made and quite possibly never intended for publication. Had
     he been alive to do so, it may be that he would have revised his
     argument.

7   *Scribal Habits of Codex Sinaiticus* by Dirk Jongkind, p 26.

8   Jongkind offered the explanation (op cit pp 48–51; that scribe A
     originally wrote the second folio with three blank columns after
     Revelation on the recto and Barnabas beginning on the verso.
     He suggested that the scribe then realised that this would not
     leave enough space for the whole of Barnabas within the four
     sheets originally allocated to the quire. So, it is suggested, scribe
     A discarded his first attempt and rewrote the folio without a
     blank column after Revelation. Leaving a blank space of three
     columns between books would, however, have been unprec-
     edented in Sinaiticus and it is without any obvious motivation.
     So, it is unlikely and our own explanation seems more probable.
     In addition to which, Jongkind's account offers no reason why the
     scribe might not have simply added another blank sheet and so
     have completed a regular quire.
9   Jongkind, op cit, p 44.
10   The frequency of errors of iotacism for scribe A follows a
     consistent pattern throughout the Old and New Testaments,
     apart from a section between quires 74 and 75. Jongkind's bar
     chart for the Old Testament (not shown) can be found on p 260
     of *Scribal Habits of Codex Sinaiticus.*
11   In *Scribal Habits of Codex Sinaiticus*, Dirk Jongkind arrived
     at his frequency of iotacisms by comparing Sinaiticus with
     the critical text which is heavily dependent on both Codex
     Vaticanus and Codex Sinaiticus. So, this may in effect here be
     a comparison of scribe A's work in Codex Sinaiticus with the
     same work by hand B in Codex Vaticanus. Having examined
     the data, it is our view that what is chiefly being highlighted is
     the degree to which the different scribes either replicated the
     more archaic forms of their exemplars or substituted their own
     topical spellings.
12   Jongkind op cit, p 127.
13   Just how unusually is indicated by the fact that Matthew is
     written over 35 pages, four by scribe D and 31 by scribe A. Of
     the 31 corrections or alterations of eight characters or more
     in this book, there are three instances where a correction
     occurs at the very end of the last column of the verso of a folio.
     There are 15 places where this could occur in Matthew, at
     the very end of a folio, or 17 if scribe D's pages are included.
     The odds that two of the three should have occurred in the
     two positions just before scribe D's work, purely by chance,
     are low.

14 There is no earlier surviving papyrus manuscript for either of the errors framing scribe D's bifolium in Matthew, against which to check.

15 *Scribal Habits of Codex Sinaiticus* by Dirk Jongkind, pp 41 and 110.

16 *The Codex Sinaiticus, the Codex Vaticanus and Constantine* by Theodore Skeat, p 610.

17 The dittography, especially on such a scale is however an unusual feature. It is, like some other features of scribe A's work, located just before one of the folios by scribe D – at the bottom of the last column of the recto of the preceding folio. The possibility should therefore not be discounted that it is in some way associated with the switch of scribe. See Chapter 13.

18 See Jongkind, op cit, pp 202–246.

Chapter 13

1 We use the term provenance in the sense of whether a particular document is considered to be closer to an original often, though not always, by virtue of being earlier in time. In making a judgement, place of origin if known can be a consideration but need not be of vital importance.

2 The argument that this is the case can be found in Chapter 7.

3 As with the gospels and Paul letters, there are issues to do with dating and authenticity with patristic sources. There are rarely if ever copies still available from around the time that the works are estimated as having been written. Here we are taking it, without evidence to the contrary, that Tertullian's comments were directed to the passage relating to Simon Peter in Matthew and were written circa 200 CE.

4 See *Jesus the Terrorist*, pp 27–31.

5 Scribe A would also have been aware that the statement could only harm relations between Jews and Christians. Both groups were well established in Caesarea where, some evidence indicates, Codex Sinaiticus may have been written.

6 See *Jesus the Terrorist*, pp 108 and 321.

7 We have argued (p 172) that the description of Jesus as son of God earlier in 1 Thessalonions may also be an interpolation.

8 See *Jesus the Terrorist*, chapter 5.

9   And who was, on the evidence, neither a Jew, nor even accepted by the followers of Jesus. See *Jesus the Terrorist*, pp 109–151.
10   See also *Jesus the Terrorist*, pp 85, 117–120 and 374–375.
11   In fact, if scribe A had continued to stretch text in the fourth column of Q85F2V, the dittography would have run on to scribe D's page. Assuming the dittography was contrived, his solution, involving a more usual density of text in the last column, was thus the optimum one. He managed to shunt the offending passage into pages that scribe D would have to write and he did it without involving the other scribe.
12   No great value appears, in any case, to have been placed on originals. Jerome records that papyrus manuscripts in the library at Caesarea, having been worn by use, were replaced by parchment codices.

Chapter 14

1   Ehrman, *Misquoting Jesus*, p 56.
2   Ehrman, *Misquoting Jesus*, p 210.
3   Given the opportunity, one of the first actions of first century messianic nationalists was to slaughter the Sadducee appointees of Romans and Herodian client kings and install their own High Priests.

Jesus was described as King of the Jews. Pilate is even represented as recognising this (John 19, 19–22). His treason could simply have been to be a passive focus for nationalist aspiration or, as traces in the text suggest, to have taken direct action.

Jesus' brother James did, according to early authorities, act as an opposition High Priest. Responsibilities were in this way divided up, much as they had been among the Maccabeans who did for a time gain real power.

It is doubtful whether the promotion in Hebrews of a Christian version of Jesus as spiritual High Priest would have had much success among Jews.
4   This example is discussed in more detail in Chapter 11, pp 224–226. See also Cresswell P A, *The Women who Went to the Tomb*, The Heretic, vol 3, 2013.
5   Parker, D C, *An Introduction to the New Testament Manuscripts and their Texts*, pp 185–90.

6   See facsimile edition of Westcott and Hort's *Introduction to the New Testament in the Original Greek*, p 247.

7   For an idea of what a first century contemporary account by one of the messianic followers of the Jewish leaders Jesus or James might have looked like, see the Commentary on Habakkuk or the Commentary on Psalm 37, in *The Dead Sea Scrolls in English* by Vermes, pp 235–245 and see also *Jesus the Terrorist*, pp 179–202.

8   See Chapter 10, pp 188–192.

9   See *Jesus the Terrorist*, chapter 8.

10   Yeshua became Iesous in Greek, then Iesus in Latin and more recently Jesus, with the addition of the letter J to the Latin alphabet. See *Jesus the Terrorist*, p 13.

Appendix X

1   It is worth noting that it was Jewish zealot practice to take a vow to abstain until something was accomplished or an offence expiated. Thus, zealots took an oath neither to eat nor drink until they had killed Paul (Acts 23, 12–14). James is reported as similarly swearing that he would not eat until he had met Jesus, after the crucifixion (gospel of the Hebrews). Jesus vowed not to drink wine until the coming of the kingdom of God. If, 'on earth', this might reflect an original Nazorean story that was more to do with the overthrow of the Romans. The uprising in the original was a failure, and cut out in the Christian version.

Index